Babylonian Magic and Sorcery

Being the Prayers of the Lifting of the Hand
Babylonian and Assyrian Incantations and Magical Formulae

by Leonard William King

with an introduction by Dahlia V. Nightly

This work contains material that was originally published in 1896.

COVER CREDITS

PLEASE NOTE :

As with all reprinted books of this age that are intended to perfectly reproduce the original edition, considerable pains and effort had to be undertaken to correct fading and sometimes outright damage to existing proofs of this title. At times, this task can be quite monumental, requiring an almost total rebuilding of some pages from digital proofs of multiple copies. Despite this, imperfections still sometimes exist in the final proof and may detract slightly from the visual appearance of the text.

DISCLAIMER :

Due to the age of this book, some methods or practices may have been deemed unsafe or unacceptable in the interim years. In utilizing the information herein, you do so at your own risk. We republish antiquarian books without judgment or revisionism, solely for their historical and cultural importance, and for educational purposes.

Introduction

We at *Black Books* are so excited to bring to you this extremely rare find – an incredible antiquarian text on ancient Sorcery and Magic.

This special edition of ***Babylonian Magic and Sorcery*** was written by Leonard William King, and first published in 1896, making it over 120 years old.

This strange and knowledgeable old text is filled with information on Magic and Sorcery, and concentrates on the areas of ancient Babylon and Assyria.

The book is transcriptions into cuneiform of the ancient stone tablets from the *Kuyunjik Collections* that reside at the *British Museum*. The translations include prayers, incantations and magic formulae.

This rare old find is an absolute essential addition to the libraries of all enthusiastic readers and researchers on the *Dark Arts*.

Strangely yours...

~ Dahlia V. Nightly

State of Jefferson, June 2018

I DEDICATE THIS BOOK

TO

THE REV. A. F. KIRKPATRICK, D.D.,

REGIUS PROFESSOR OF HEBREW AND FELLOW OF TRINITY COLLEGE
CAMBRIDGE;
CANON OF ELY CATHEDRAL,
ETC., ETC., ETC.,

AS A TOKEN OF REGARD AND ESTEEM.

PREFACE.

The object of the present work is to give the cuneiform text of a complete group of tablets inscribed with prayers and religious compositions of a devotional and somewhat magical character, from the Kuyunjik collections preserved in the British Museum. To these texts a transliteration into Latin characters has been added, and, in the case of well preserved or unbroken documents, a running translation has been given. A vocabulary with the necessary indexes, *etc.* is also appended. The cuneiform texts, which fill seventy-five plates, are about sixty in number, and of these only one has hitherto been published in full; the extracts or passages previously given in the works of the late Sir Henry Rawlinson, Dr. Strassmaier, and Prof. Bezold will be found cited in the Introduction.

It will be seen that the greater number of the texts formed parts of several large groups of magical tablets, and that certain sections were employed in more than one group. As they appear here they are the result of the editing of the scribes of Ashurbanipal, king of Assyria about B. C. 669—625, who had them copied and arranged for his royal library at Nineveh. There is little doubt however that the sources from which they were compiled were Babylonian. The prayers and formulae inscribed on the tablets, which bore the title of "Prayers of the Lifting of the

"Hand", were drawn up for use in the private worship, either of the king himself, or of certain of his subjects. Some of the tablets are inscribed with single prayers, and these appear to have been copied from the larger compositions for the use of special individuals on special occasions. As examples of this class of text K 223, K 2808, and K 2836 may be mentioned, which contain Ashurbanipal's personal petitions for the deliverance of Assyria from the evils which had fallen upon the land in consequence of an eclipse of the moon.

Unlike the prayers of many Semitic nations the compositions here given are accompanied by an interesting series of directions for the making of offerings and the performance of religious ceremonies, and they show a remarkable mixture of lofty spiritual conceptions and belief in the efficacy of incantations and magical practices, which cannot always be understood. In language closely resembling that of the penitential psalms we find the conscience-stricken suppliant crying to his god for relief from his sin, while in the same breath he entreats to be delivered from the spells and charms of the sorcerer, and from the hobgoblins, phantoms, spectres and devils with which his imagination had peopled the unseen world.

The scientific study of the Babylonian and Assyrian religion dates from the publication of the Kosmologie der Babylonier by Prof. JENSEN in 1890. In this work the author grouped and classified all the facts connected with the subject which could be derived from published texts, and it was evident that no farther advance could be made until after the publication of new material. It then became clear that the science could be best forwarded by a systematic study of the magical and religious series, class by class, rather than by the issue of miscellaneous texts however complete and important. Following this idea in the present year Dr. Tallqvist produced a scholarly monograph on the important series called by the Assyrians Maklû, and it is understood that Prof. Zimmern is engaged on the preparation of an edition of the equally important series called Shurpu. Since this little book has been prepared on similar lines and deals with a connected group of religious texts, it is hoped that it may be of use to those whose studies lead them to the careful consideration of the ancient Semitic religions of Western Asia.

My thanks are due to Prof. Bezold both for friendly advice and for help in the revision of the proofs; I am also indebted to Prof. Zimmern and a few private friends for suggestions which I have adopted.

LEONARD W. KING.

November 13th, 1895.

CONTENTS.

	PAGE
Preface	V—VII
Introduction	XI—XXX
List of Tablets	XXXI
Transliteration, Translations and Notes	1—129
Vocabulary	131—181
Appendixes —	
I. Proper names	182—188
II. Numerals	186
III. Words and ideographs of uncertain reading	187—194
Indexes —	
I. Tablets and duplicates	195—197
II. Registration-numbers	198—199
Cuneiform texts	PLATES 1—75

INTRODUCTION.

The clay tablets, from which the texts here published have been copied, are preserved in the British Museum and belong to the various collections from Kuyunjik. The majority are of the K. Collection, but some have been included from the Sm., D.T., Rm., 81—2—4, 82—3—23, 83—1—18 and Bu. 91—5—9 collections. The tablets, to judge from those that are complete, are not all of the same size but vary from about $4\frac{7}{8}$ in. $\times$ $2\frac{3}{4}$ in. to $9\frac{1}{2}$ in. $\times$ $3\frac{3}{4}$ in. All contain one column of writing on obverse and reverse, and, with one exception, are inscribed in the Assyrian character of the VIIth century B.C., the longest complete inscription consisting of one hundred and twenty-one lines, the shortest of twenty-nine lines. They were originally copied for Ashurbanipal, king of Assyria from about 669 to 625 B.C., and were stored in the royal library at Nineveh; many of them contain his name and the colophon which it was customary to inscribe on works copied or composed for his collection. The tablets are formed of fine clay and have been carefully baked, and those that escaped injury at the destruction of Nineveh, and have not suffered from the action of water during their subsequent interment, are still in good preservation.

The principal contents of the tablets consist of prayers and incantations to various deities, which were termed by the Assyrians themselves "Prayers of the Lifting of the Hand". It is not difficult to grasp the signification of this title, for the act of raising the hand is universally regarded as symbolical of invocation of a deity, whether in attestation of an oath, or in offering up prayer and supplication. With the Babylonians and Assyrians the expression "to raise the hand" was frequently used by itself in the sense of offering a prayer, and so by a natural transition it came to be employed as a synonym of "to pray", *i. e.* "to utter a prayer". Sometimes the petition which the suppliant offers is added indirectly, when it is usually introduced by *aššu*[1], though this is not invariably the case[2]. In other passages the phrase introduces the actual words of the prayer, as at the beginning of the prayer of Nebuchadnezzar to *Marduk* towards the end of the *East India House Inscription*[3]. In accordance with this extension of meaning the phrase *niš ḳâti*, "the lifting of the hand", is often found in apposition to, or balancing, *ikribu*, *supû*, *etc.*, and in many instances it can merely retain the general meaning of "prayer", or "supplication"[4]. In the title of the prayers collected in this volume, however, there is no need to divorce the expression from its original meaning; while the phrase was employed to indicate the general character of the composition, we may probably see in it a reference to the actual gesture of raising the hand during the recital of the prayer[5].

The title was appended to each prayer as a colophon-line together with the name of the deity to whom the prayer was addressed; it is always found following the composition, and is enclosed within two lines ruled on the clay by the scribe:—

[1] *Cf.*, *e. g.*, Annals of Sargon, l. 55 f. (WINCKLER, *Die Keilschrifttexte Sargons*, I, p. 12): *ana Aššur bîliya aššu turri gimilli Mannai ana iṣir Aššur turri ḳâti aššima*; and Cyl. B of Esarhaddon, ll. 3 ff. (III R, 15): *aššu ipiš šarrûti bît abiya . . . . . ana Aššur Sin Šamaš Bîl Nabû u Nirgal Ištar ša Ninua Ištar ša Arba'ilu ḳâti aššima.*

[2] *Cf.*, *e. g.*, Sargon Cyl., l. 54.

[3] Col. IX, ll. 45 ff.: *ana Marduk bîliya utnin ḳâtiašši Marduk bîlu mûdû ilâni etc.*

[4] In some colophon-lines it is employed in the sense of "prayer", or "incantation", *cf.* IV R, pl. 18, no. 2, l. 15, and pl. 53 [60], Col. IV, l. 29; *see* also IV R, pl. 55 [92], no. 2, Rev., l. 6, where the phrase *INIM.INIM.MA ŠU IL.LA* is combined with the usual title of a penitential psalm.

[5] *See* below, p. 13. On cylinder-seals a suppliant is frequently represented with one or both hands raised.

The five dots mark the space where the name of the god or goddess is inserted. In the case of prayers to astral deities the name of the deity is preceded by the determinative [cuneiform], while occasionally the suffix [cuneiform] takes the place of the more usual [cuneiform]. With these exceptions, however, the form of this colophon-line is invariably the same[1] and furnishes one of the most distinctive characteristics of the present collection of texts[2]. It may perhaps not unfairly be compared to the title [cuneiform][3], which generally accompanies the "Penitential Psalms" together with a note as to whether the tablet is to be confined to the worship of a particular deity or is suitable for general use.

A further resemblance to the "Penitential Psalms" may be seen in the fact that the "Prayers of the Lifting of the Hand" do not form a series of tablets labelled and numbered by the Assyrians themselves, such as the *Maḳlû*-Series, or the *Šurpu*-Series, or the series [cuneiform]. Strictly speaking they do not form a series but merely a class of tablets, which can, however, be readily distinguished from other religious texts not only by their writing and arrangement but also by their style and the recurrence of certain fixed colophon-lines and formulae. A somewhat similar "class" of texts which is not a "series" may be seen in the "Hymns in paragraphs"[4], the greater part of which have been published by Brünnow in the *Zeitschrift für Assyriologie*[5]. The Assyrian prayers to the Sun-god published by Knudtzon[6], which also form a class but not a series, can hardly be cited in this connection in view of their special scope and character.

One of the principal guides in the selection of tablets of

---

1 In No. 51, l. 9 the title is not essentially different, but merely did duty for two incantations addressed to the same astral deity.

2 The colophon-line is very rarely found in texts belonging to other classes; but *see* K 2538 *etc.* (*cf. infra*, p. 15); Sm. 290, obv., l. 4; Sm. 1025, l. 9; Sm. 1250, l. 3, *etc.*

3 *See* Zimmern, *Babylonische Busspsalmen*, pp. 1, 53, 66, 81.

4 *Cf.* Bezold, *Catalogue*, *passim.*

5 *See* *ZA* IV, pp. 1 ff., 225 ff., and *ZA* V, pp. 55 ff.

6 *Assyrische Gebete an den Sonnengott*, Leipzig, 1893.

this class is to be found in the distinctive colophon-line or title already referred to, and the fact that BEZOLD in his Catalogue of the K. Collection has given where possible the colophon-lines and titles, which occur on religious texts, has proved of material assistance. This title taken in conjunction with certain resemblances in the style of the compositions, the shape and quality of the tablets and the character of the writing renders the recognition of the class comparatively simple. It is true that in such a process of selection resemblances in style and writing are of no slight importance[1], but taken by themselves they prove unsafe guides; and, although the collection might have been largely increased if a resemblance in these two particulars had been deemed sufficient to warrant the inclusion of a tablet, yet an element of uncertainty would by this plan have been necessarily introduced[2]. In the first five Sections therefore only those tablets are included in which the distinctive colophon-line occurs. Such has been the method of selection, and by its adoption it was found necessary to include a few tablets which had been already partly published or referred to. Of four of the texts here published in full extracts are to be found in STRASSMAIER's *Alphabetisches Verzeichniss*[3]; the nearly

[1] A practical illustration of this statement may be seen in the fact that my selection of tablets on these principals has resulted in over forty "joins", and the recognition of several duplicates.

[2] Among the fragments thus rejected are some with additional recommendations, *e. g.* K 3310, l. 2 of which, the first line of an incantation, agrees, so far as it goes, with the catch-line of No. 11; K 13231, l. 4 of which corresponds to the catch-line of No. 16; and K 9252, the first line of which corresponds to l. 5 of K 2832 *etc.*, the catalogue of incantations published below. Since printing off I have come across a prayer on K 10695 which is probably of the class of "Prayers of the Lifting of the Hand", as ll. 13 and 14 contain traces of the distinctive colophon-line and rubric; only a few signs of the prayer have been preserved, from which it would appear to have been directed against various forms of sickness; the tablet, the surface of which has suffered considerably from the action of water, must, when complete, have resembled No. 33 in size. The fragment Rm. 446 may possibly have belonged to a "Prayer of the Lifting of the Hand to *Ištar*", though too little of the tablet has been preserved to admit of a certain decision; its colophon of five lines, in which Ashurbanipal names himself the son of Esarhaddon, and the grandson of Sennacherib does not occur elsewhere in prayers of this class; the fragment K 10757 probably belonged to a similar tablet.

[3] Of K 140, which forms part of the text here published as No. 22, ll. 1—22

complete tablet K 163 + K 218 (No. 12) has been published in IV R^1 64 and repeated in IV R^2 57, while the reverse of K 2379, part of its duplicate which is cited as *C*, is to be found on p. 11 of the *Additions* to IV R^2; finally Bezold in *ZA* III, p. 250 has published K 9490, which contains the conclusion of the text of No. 50[1].

Although the "Prayers of the Lifting of the Hand" do not consist of a series of tablets numbered by the Assyrians themselves, there are not lacking indications that groups of them were arranged in some definite order or sequence. What modifications and changes their original arrangement has undergone will be apparent after a brief examination of the data. The most obvious indications of arrangement are the catch-lines which are found on all the tablets the ends of which have not been broken off. As these repeat at the end of one tablet the first line of the next, they point to some definite arrangement of the texts. The following is a list of those catch-lines which have been preserved: —

1, 53 *šiptu bîlu muš-ti-šir kiš-šat nišî*^{pl} *gi-mir nab-ni-ti*
6, 132 *šiptu ilu šú - pu - ú* [. . . . . .ˀ. . . .]
11, 46 [*šiptu* . . . .] *ṣi-i-ru git-ma-lu ši-tar-ḫu*
12, 121 *înuma amîlu ḳaḳḳad-su ikkal-šu lišânu-šu ú-zaḳ-ḳat-su*
16, 12 [*šiptu* . . . .] *šamî u irṣiti*
18, 20 *šiptu ga - aš - ru šú - pu - u i - dil* ^{ilu}*Igigi*
19, 34 *šiptu ru - ba - tú rabîtu(tu) i - lat ši - ma - a - ti*
21, 93 *ilu bîlu šú-pu-u git-ma-lum ilâni*^{pl} *ra-šub-bu*
22, 70 *šiptu* ^{ilu}[*Na-bi-um a-ša-ri-du bu-kur*] ^{ilu}*Marduk*
29, 3 [*šiptu* . . . .] *ti-iz-ḳa-ru bu-kur* ^{ilu}[. . . . .]
30, 30 *šiptu îl - ti* ^{ilu}*Igigi bu - uk - rat* [. . . . .]

---

and 62—66 are cited in AV, nos. 8247, 8297, 8510 and 9071; of K 155 (No. 1), ll. 1—10, 23—25 and 43—45 are given in AV, nos. 6700, 7845, 8063 and 8297; of K 2396, which contains part of the text of No. 8, ll. 22—24 are quoted in AV, no. 6043; and of K 3283, a duplicate of No. 11, ll. 6—10 are given in AV, nos. 7586 and 8483.

1 For the quotations made by Sayce, Delitzsch and Schrader from K 2836 (a dupl. of No. 27) and K 3358 (No. 32), *see* Bezold, *Catalogue*, pp. 480, 526. Moreover Delitzsch, in the first two parts of his *Handwörterbuch* which have at present appeared, quotes from K 155 (No. 1), and Tallqvist in *Die assyrische Beschwörungsserie Maqlû* cites passages from K 235 (No. 11).

33, 47 *[šiptu . . . .] šar-rat kib-ra-a-ti idit bi-li-i-ti*
35, 15 *[šiptu . . . .] saḫ(?) ki-bit ana A.BA L DA.RA*
36, 10 *[šiptu . . . .* ^{ilu}*]Igigi butuktu ḫa-si-[. . . . .]*
38, 5 *šiptu šur - [. . . . .]*
41, 3 *[šiptu . . . .] šarru ni-mi-ki ba-nu-u ta-šim-ti*
42, 26 *šiptu* ^{ilu}*Marduk bîlu rabû [. . . . .]*
47, 8 *[šiptu . . . .] gaš - ru - ú - ti*
48, 17 *šiptu bîlu šur-bu-u ša ina šamî-i šú-luḫ-ḫu-šu illu*
50, 29 *šiptu at-ta* ^{kakkabu}*KAK.SI.DI* ^{ilu}*NINIB a-šą-rid ilâni*^{pl} *rabûti*^{pl}
52, 5 *šiptu šarru ilâni*^{pl} *gaš-ru-ú-ti ša nap-ḫar ma-a-ti šú-pu-ú* ^{ilu}*IMINA.BI at-tu-nu-ma*

Even fewer beginnings of tablets have been preserved. In the following list, however, the first line of any incantation, without regard to its position on the tablet, is included for comparison with the catch-lines given above: —

1, 1 *šiptu* ^{ilu}*Sin* ^{ilu}*Nannaru ru-šú-bu ú - [. . . . .]*
1, 29 *šiptu ḳá - rid - tú* ^{ilu}*Iš - tar ka - nu - ut i - [lá - a - ti]*
2, 11 *šiptu ap - lu gaš - ru bu - kur* ^{ilu}*Bîl*
2, 43 *[šiptu . . . .] kib - ra - a - ti i - lat bi - li - i - ti*
3, 10 *[šiptu ap-lu gaš-ru] bu-kur* ^{ilu}*Bîl* ⯎ *šur-bu-ú git-ma-lu i-lit-ti I.ŠAR.RA*
4, 9 *šiptu* ^{ilu}*Dam - ki - na šar - rat kal ilâni*^{pl} *lá - tú*
4, 24 *[šiptu* ^{ilu}*Ba'u] bîltu šur-bu-tú a-ši-bat šamî-i [illûti*^{pl}*]*
5, 11 *[šiptu] ḳá - rid - tum* ^{ilu}*Iš - tar ka - nu - ut i - [lá] - a - [ti]*
6, 1 *šiptu bîlu šur - bu - [ú . . . .]*
6, 18 *šiptu* ^{ilu}*Nusku šur - [bu - ú i - lit - ti Dûr - ilu*^{KI}*]*
6, 36 *šiptu* ^{ilu}*Sin na - [. . . . .]*
6, 71 *šiptu* ^{ilu}*Ba'u bîltu šur-bu-tum ummu ri-mi-[ni-tum a]-ši-bat šamî-i illûti*^{pl}
6, 97 *šiptu šur-bu-ú git-ma-[lu a-bi-rum* ^{ilu}*Marduk . . . .]*
7, 9 *šiptu* ^{ilu}*Bi-lit ili bîltu šur-[bu-tum ummu ri-mi-ni-tum a-ši-bat šamî-i illûti*^{pl}*]*
7, 34 *šiptu* ^{kakkabu}*Išḫara [. . . . .]*
8, 22 *šiptu at-tu-nu kakkabâni šar-ḫu-tum ša mu-[. . . . .]*
9, 1 *[šiptu ga - áš - ru šú - pú - ú i - dil* ^{alu}*Aššur]*
9, 28 *[šiptu . . . .] ṣir-tum ŠA.TAR i-[. . . . .]*
10, 7 *šiptu šur-bu-ú git-ma-lu a-bi-rum* ^{ilu}*Marduk [. . . . .]*

11, 1	*[šiptu] ḳarradu ^{ilu}Marduk ša i - zis - su a - bu - bu*
12, 1	*înuma lumun murṣi DI.PAL.A ZI.TAR.RU.DA KA.LU.BI.DA dubbubu ana amîlu úl itiḫi*
12, 17	*šiptu ^{ilu}Marduk bîl mâtâti šal-[ba-bu . . . .]-ru-bu*
12, 105	*šiptu at-ta AN.ḪUL ma-ṣar šulmi(mi) ša ^{ilu}I-a u ^{ilu}Marduk*
13, 15	*[šiptu] bi-lum ^{ilu}Marduk mu-di-i [. . . . .]*
14, 14	*[šiptu . . . .] - ḫu*
20, 8	*šiptu šur - bu - ú git - ma - lu [. . . . .]*
21, 34	*[šiptu] šur - bu - ú [. . . . .]*
21, 76	*[šiptu] ^{ilu}Rammânu [. . . . .]-ta-az-nu šú-pu-u ilu gaš-ru*
22, 1	*šiptu rubû ašaridu , bu - kur ^{ilu}Marduk*
22, 35	*šiptu bît nu - ru ab - kal [. . . . .] - ú*
27, 1	*šiptu bi-lum gaš-ru ti-iz-ḳa-[ru bu-kur ^{ilu}NU.NAM.NIR]*
28, 7	*[šiptu . . . .] - ú ilu ri - mi - nu - ú*
31, 11	*[šiptu . . . .]GI.GI bu-uk-rat ^{ilu}Sin ti-li-tú*
32, 6	*[šiptu . . . .] - na ^{ilu}Ištar ḳá-rid-ti i-lá-a-[ti]*
33, 1	*[šiptu . . . .]-zu-zu i-lat mu-na-[. . . . .]*
37, 7	*[šiptu . . . . bîltu] šur-bu-tum ummu ri-mi-ni-tum a-[ši-bat šamî-i illûti^{pl}]*
39, 6	*[šiptu . . . .] kakkabâni^{pl} i-lat šar-[. . . . .]*
46, 11	*šiptu ^{ilu}Nirgal bîl [. . . . .] ^{kakkabu}Piṣû ti-iḫ šamî-i u irṣitim(tim)*
50, 1	*[šiptu ^{kakkabu}SIB.ZI.AN.NA . . . .]*

A glance will show that not many lines in the two lists correspond. In fact, of the twenty-one catch-lines that have been preserved only one corresponds to the first line of any of the tablets, it being probable that No. 29, l. 3 should be restored from No. 27, l. 1[1]; the catch-line of No. 48 may indeed refer to No. 6, l. 1, though this is far from certain as only two words of the latter have been preserved. A comparison of the catch-lines therefore with the beginnings of the tablets does not throw much light on the question of their original order. Some few of the catch-lines, however, may possibly be referred to incantations which do not occur at the beginnings of tablets; the catch-line of No. 11, for instance, may possibly correspond to

---

[1] *Cf. infra*, p. 92.

No. 14, l. 14, or that of No. 16[1] to No. 46, l. 11, or that of No. 30 to No. 31, l. 11. The catch-line of No. 33 may perhaps represent a variant form of No. 2, l. 43, while the catch-line of No. 38, of which only the first sign has been preserved, might equally well be referred to No. 6, l. 97, No. 10, l. 7, No. 20, l. 8, or No. 21, l. 34. But, even if these instances of correspondence were certain, they would not assist us in our inquiry, as in the case of each the context of the catch-line does not correspond to that of the incantation to which it is assumed to refer; in other words, the incantation or ceremonial section, which the catch-line in question follows, is not the same as that preceding the incantation, to the first line of which the catch-line corresponds. The only inference therefore that can be drawn from these facts is that the texts have undergone various changes and rearrangements at the hands of editors or redactors before they were copied by the scribes of Ashurbanipal.

In this connection it may be of interest to refer to an Assyrian catalogue of incantations that has been preserved on K 2832 + K 6680[2], as some of the first lines of compositions cited in Col. I of that tablet correspond to certain of the catch-lines and first lines of the present collection of texts. Col. II contains the beginnings of seven incantations which are addressed in the main to the Sun-god and probably have no reference to the "Prayers of the Lifting of the Hand"; the end of the last column, which is all that has been preserved of the reverse of the tablet is uninscribed. In Col. I, the text of which is given on the opposite page, it will be seen that l. 7 corresponds to the catch-line of No. 18, and l. 12 to the remains of the catch-line of No. 42, while l. 11 is identical with the first line of No. 9; the first line of the tablet, moreover, contains the name of the series to which No. 1, according to its colophon, belongs. It is, of course, possible that all the incantations enumerated in this column of the tablet belong to the class of texts here collected,

---

[1] It is possible that No. 16 and No. 42 are parts of the same tablet, as is suggested by BEZOLD, *Catalogue*, p. 1186; in that case the catch-line so formed would not correspond to No. 46, l. 11.

[2] *See* below, p. 15. Catalogues of tablets containing forecasts, mythological legends, *etc.* testify to the activity of the Assyrian scribes in the collection and classification of other classes of texts.

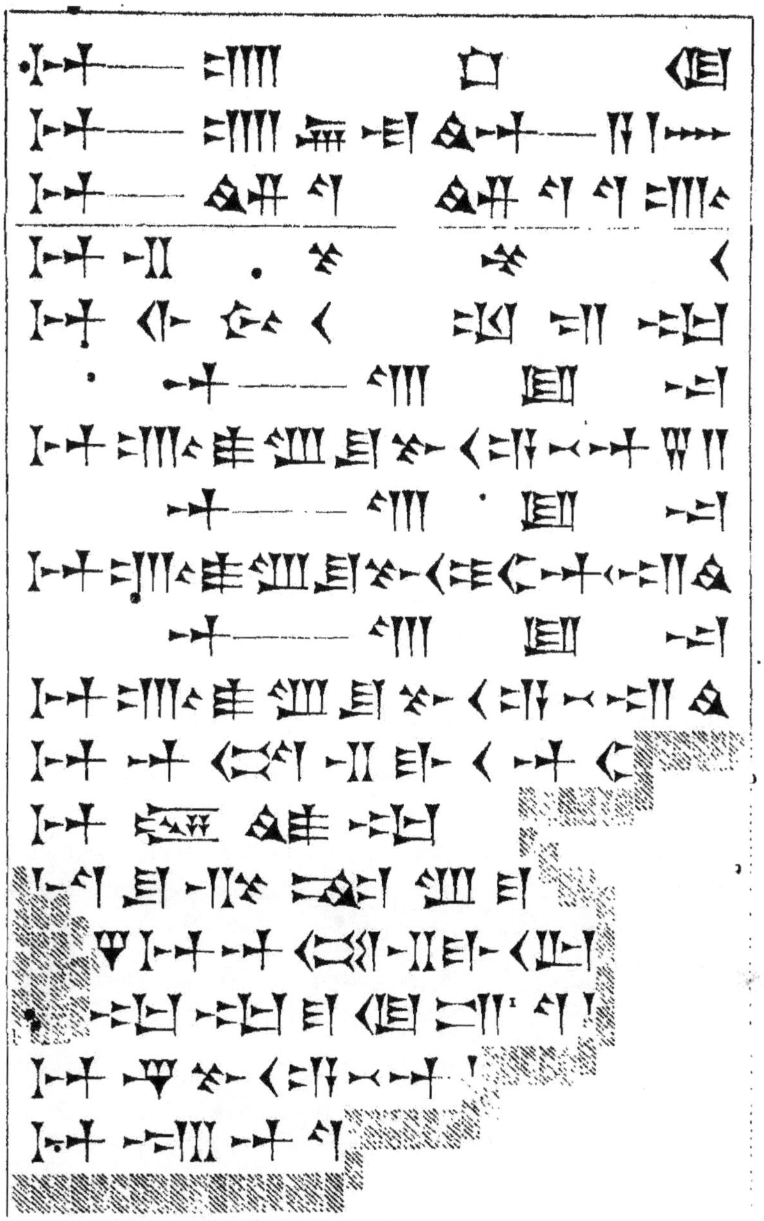

though, in that case, they have not yet been recognised, and are perhaps not preserved in the collections from Kuyunjik. It is equally possible that the incantations, apart from those already identified, have no connection with the "Prayers of the Lifting of the Hand". In the latter case the tablet affords striking proof of the manner in which scribes, either before or at the

---

[1] This character is partly effaced.

time of Ashurbanipal, re-edited the older collections and classes of tablets to which they had access.

The evidence afforded by an examination of their catch-lines and first lines leads therefore to the conclusion that the tablets, which have come down to us, have been subjected to several processes of editing, the incantations having been from time to time collected, selected and rearranged. A noteworthy instance of the way in which a favourite incantation was re-copied and employed in various connections is presented by the address to a goddess which begins: *šiptu* . . . . *bîltu šur-bûtu ummu rîminîtum âšibat šamî illûti*. In No. 6, ll. 71 ff., where it is addressed to the goddess *Ba'u*, it is preceded by a prayer to *Sin* and followed by one probably to *Šamaš*, in the duplicate *D* it is preceded by some directions for ceremonies, while it forms the first prayer on the tablet which is cited as the duplicate *E*; in No. 7, ll. 9 ff. we find the title *Bîlit ili* in the place of the name of the goddess *Ba'u*, the incantation is followed by one to the astral deity *Išḫara*, and it is set aside for use only during an eclipse of the moon; in No. 4 the version presents so many differences that it practically forms a fresh incantation. This is the history, so far as it can be ascertained, of one incantation, and the evidence afforded by the duplicates of other tablets is very similar.

Other evidence of this process of editing is to be found in the fact that some tablets are labelled as belonging to certain series. No. 1, for instance, is stated to be a tablet of the series [1], though the scribe has omitted to fill in the number of the tablet; No. 30 is the 134th tablet of the series  the rest of its title being broken; and No. 48 forms the eighth part of the composition 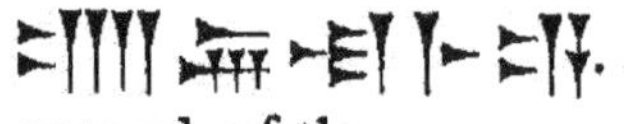. Possibly in the first, and certainly in the second of these cases, the series was a composite one made up of various classes of texts, for it is not necessary to conclude from the evidence of No. 30 that the other 133 or more tablets missing from that series were all "Prayers of the Lifting of the Hand"; more probable is the supposition that this class of tablets was merely

[1] *See* below, pp. 14 ff.

one of several classes laid under contribution by the compilers of the series.

A still further indication of editing may be seen in the colophons with which the tablets conclude. It is true the majority of them end with the formula which is commonly found on tablets from Ashurbanipal's library, and which may be translated as follows: "The palace of Ashurbanipal, king of the world, king of Assyria, who in *Aššur* and *Bîlit* puts his trust, on whom *Nabû* and *Tašmîtu* have bestowed broad ears, who has acquired clear eyes. The valued products of the scribe's art, such as no one among the kings who have gone before me had acquired, the wisdom of *Nabû*, ..., as much as exists, I have inscribed on tablets, I have arranged in groups[1], I have revised, and for the sight of my reading have set in my palace, I, the ruler, who knoweth the light of *Aššur*, the king of the gods. Whosoever carries off (this tablet), or with my name inscribes his own name, may *Aššur* and *Bîlit* in wrath and anger cast him down, and destroy his name and seed in the land!" This colophon is by no means universal however, for we find shorter ones on Nos. 11 and 33, while Nos. 18, 35, 38 and 41 present various differences to the normal conclusion, and No. 10 merely contains the note that the tablet was copied from an older original. The reason that no colophons occur on Nos. 19, 29 and 50, the ends of which are left blank, is to be sought in the fact that these tablets contain single prayers extracted from the larger tablets for some temporary purpose[2]. The evidence of catch-lines, duplicates, series and colophons therefore all leads to the same conclusion, that the tablets are not arranged on one plan but have undergone several redactions, and it is obvious that any attempt to restore the original order would be fruitless.

It was necessary therefore to arrange them for publication on some other principle, and the plan adopted has been to classify them according to the deities to whom the prayers and incantations are addressed. The fact that while some of

[1] *See* DELITZSCH, *Handwörterbuch*, p. 182.

[2] K 3332 (the dupl. *A* of No. 1), and K 2836 + K 6593 (the dupl. *A* of No. 27), which are also without colophons, contain similar extracts. These extracts from the longer texts are inscribed on small tablets in rather large characters.

the tablets contain prayers and incantations addressed only to one god, while the contents of others refer to several different deities in succession furnished a basis for classification, and the texts fell naturally into five divisions or sections. In the first are those tablets which contain prayers *etc.* addressed successively to each of a group of deities; in the second are tablets the contents of which refer only to one god; in the third the suppliant on each tablet addresses himself throughout to one goddess; the fourth section consists of fragmentary tablets from which the names of the deities addressed are missing, while in the fifth are collected prayers *etc.* addressed to astral deities. This method of arrangement, though convenient, is open to objection on one point. The tablets are classified according to their contents at the present moment; from many of them, however, large parts are missing, and it is possible that when complete they might have fallen under different sections to those they now occupy. This objection, however, is not confined to the present arrangement but might be urged against any alternative method; it is, in fact, a disadvantage which is inseparable from a collection of tablets comprising some that have not been preserved intact.

The uses to which the "Prayers of the Lifting of the Hand" could be put are somewhat varied, corresponding to the scope of the petitions and incantations they contain. With the exception of the tablets set aside for use after a lunar eclipse, they appear to have been intended for somewhat general use. It is true that from the accompanying ceremonies we can sometimes gather further details as to the time and occasion suitable for their employment, but in the majority of cases we are dependent on internal evidence to ascertain the circumstances which attended their recital. In form and structure they present a general resemblance to each other, each prayer or incantation consisting of three principal divisions, which vary considerably in their comparative length and importance. The beginning of a prayer as a rule consists of an introduction in which the deity addressed is called upon by name, his power or mercy praised, and his special functions or attributes referred to or described. The suppliant then turns to his own condition of distress, and his petitions for help and deliverance form the second main section of the prayer; the conclusion is generally in the form of a short doxology. In the invocation of a deity the most extravagant praise could be employed, the suppliant in his utterances not confining himself to strict theology; any deity, whose help he sought, however unimportant, was for him at that moment one of the greatest of the gods. It is true that the greater gods are praised for their special powers and characteristics, but the lesser deities share with them the most exalted titles — a practice which may have been the result of anxiety to secure by any means the favour of the deity addressed.

All the prayers are for the use of individuals, and in many of them a formula occurs in which the suppliant states his own name and adds those of his god and goddess. The importance to a man of the protection of his patron deities is obvious from the frequently recurring petitions for restoration to their favour, when in consequence of some act of sin they have withdrawn from him their guidance and support, and he, not relying on his own efforts to appease their anger, calls in some more powerful god or goddess to act as mediator. This fact is not sufficient, however, to explain the addition of their names to that of the suppliant, for the formula sometimes occurs in prayers, in which no other mention is made of the suppliant's god and goddess. As the prayers in most cases have not been expressly copied for any individual, the actual names are not inserted in the formula; an interesting exception, however, occurs in K 223, the duplicate of No. 2 which is cited as *D*. No. 2 is part of a large tablet containing prayers to *Tašmîtu, Ninib, etc.*, and K 223 is a small one inscribed with the prayer to *Ninib*, which has been extracted from the larger tablet for the private use of Ashurbanipal. In place of the formula which occurs in No. 2, l. 26 the duplicate *D* reads: "I, thy servant, Ashurbanipal, the son of his god, whose god is *Aššur*, whose goddess is *Aššurîtu*" *etc.* It is probable that no one but the Assyrian king could refer to *Aššur* as his god and to *Aššurîtu* as his goddess; this divine couple were the peculiar patrons of royalty, and, although they looked after the people and land of Assyria as a whole, the king was the only individual selected for their special protection. The data however is insufficient to determine what gods the private Assyrians and Babylonians were privileged to regard as their patron deities. It is possible a solution of the question might be obtained from a study of the cylinder-seals, on which the owner, after stating his own name and that of his father frequently adds the name of the god of whom he is the servant[1]; meanwhile it may be permissible to speculate whether each class or trade had not its own patron deity, who was also regarded as peculiarly the god of each member of that class.

We know that each city had its local god, who in prayers sometimes takes the place of the suppliant's patron deity[2], and it may be that a similar localization of deities existed with regard to the different trades and classes of society. Possibly this suggestion may serve to explain in some degree the various pairs and groups of deities whose blessings are invoked by the senders of letters on behalf of their correspondents. It is improbable that these gods were selected merely at the fancy of the writer, and it is easier to suppose that his choice was restricted either by law or custom to the deities who were connected with his own class or profession. A striking instance in point may be seen in the letters K 501, K 538, 83—1—18, 35 and 80—7—19, 23 written by *Arad-Nabû* to the king[3]; as the letters deal with religious matters it may be assumed that *Arad-Nabû* was a priest, and the fact that he invokes such a long list of important deities would on the above assumption be an

[1] The assumption that the god mentioned on a cylinder-seal is always the owner's patron deity is not quite certain. That amulets could be worn which were dedicated to other than patron deities is proved by the Assyrian amulet 95—4—8, 1. On this little cylinder of clay the owner *Šamaškillâni* addresses an incantation to the astral deity Kak-si-di in the course of which he states he is the son of his god, with whom it is evident the deity Kak-si-di is not to be identified.

[2] *Cf.* K 2493, l. 17 *[ana-ku pulânu apil] pulâni ša ilu ali-šu* ^{ilu}*Marduk* ^{ilu}*ištar ali-šu* . . . . .

[3] The introductory phrases on 83—1—18, 35 read as follows: *a-na šarri bîli-ya arad-ka* ^{m}*Arad-*^{ilu}*Nabû lu šulmu(mu) a-na šarri bîli-ya Aššur* ^{ilu}*Sin* ^{ilu}*Šamaš* ^{ilu}*Marduk* ^{ilu}*Zar-pa-ni-tum* ^{ilu}*Nabû* ^{ilu}*Taš-mi-tum* ^{ilu}*Ištar šá* ^{alu}*Ninua* ^{ilu}*Ištar šá* ^{alu}*Arba-ilu ilâni*^{pl} *an-nu-ti rabûti*^{pl} *ra-'-mu-ti šarru-ti-ka* C *šanâti*^{pl} *a-na šarri bîli-ya lu-bal-liṭ-ṭu ši-bu-tu lit-tu-tu a-na šarri bîli-ya lu-šab-bi-ú ma-ṣar šul-mi u ba-la-ṭi [ina] libbi šarri bîli-ya lip-ḳi-du.* K 501 has a similar introduction, while in K 538 and 80—7—19, 23 Sin is the only god omitted from the list.

indication of his high rank and position. It may be urged against this theory that the same writer does not invariably invoke the same gods; many explanations might be offered of this fact, it being conceivable that the letters in question were written at different periods of a man's career, or that certain higher positions included the privileges and rights of those beneath them, or that a man of higher rank in addressing a subordinate would not refer to his own gods but invoke those of the latter. However this may be, it is perhaps not impossible that in prayers and incantations the naming of a suppliant's god and goddess was to his contemporaries equivalent to a declaration of his rank and position in the state.

Following the formula in which the suppliant states his own name and those of his patron deities we frequently find in "Prayers of the Lifting of the Hand" a statement that the occasion on which the prayer is delivered is after an eclipse of the moon, the formula usually running as follows:—

> *ina lumun* ^{ilu}*atalî* ^{ilu}*Sin ša ina arḫi pulâni ûmi pulâni išakna(na)* | *lumun idâti*^{pl} *ittâti*^{pl} *limnûti*^{pl} *lâ ṭâbâti*^{pl} | *ša ina ikalli-ya u mâti-ya ibašâ-a*[1]

The tablets on which the formula occurs can only have been intended for the use of the king, for no private individual could address a god "in the evil of an eclipse of the moon which in such and such a month on such and such a day has taken place, in the evil of the powers, of the portents, evil and not good which are in my palace and my land". It is probable, however, that only the formula, and not the prayer or incantation itself, was composed for the eclipse. A great body of religious texts and incantations, containing general petitions for deliverance from evil influences and magical powers, would be quite suitable for use after such a calamity, and all that was needed in addition was a formula which could be inserted with

[1] *See* pp. 7 ff. On p. 10 it is suggested that the ideogram *ITI*, in the sense of "portent", should be rendered by *ittu* but this rendering was not adopted in the transliteration as I was unaware on what grounds DELITZSCH based his rendering *takiltu*. When the early sheets of the transliteration had been printed off the first part of the *Handwörterbuch* appeared in which *ittu* takes the place of his former rendering of the ideogram.

the necessary details of the month and day on which the eclipse had taken place. Such a formula is the one cited above, and the fact that it is found in some copies of the same prayer but omitted in others proves that it could be added or removed at pleasure. Thus in the copy of the prayer to Ninib which was made from No. 2 for the use of Ashurbanipal (*cf. supra*) the eclipse-formula has been inserted between the sixteenth and seventeenth lines of the prayer, and the same insertion has been made in K 2836 the duplicate of No. 27 which is cited as *A*. The prayer to *Ba'u* on No. 6 does not contain the formula, neither does it occur in the duplicate *D*; we find it, however, in the same prayer on No. 7, and in the duplicate *E* it occurs together with a statement of the suppliant's name *etc.* It is absent from the last prayer on No. 6, but it has been inserted in the duplicate *F* where it is also preceded by the suppliant's name and those of his god and goddess. The eclipse-formula may therefore be regarded as forming no essential part of any prayer or incantation; in fact, some of the passages in which it occurs would be improved by its omission as it interrupts the rythm or metre of the lines on either side of it.

A word must be said on the metre in which the "Prayers of the Lifting of the Hand" are composed. It has long been known that the poetical compositions of the Babylonians were cast in general in a rough form of verse and half-verse; GUNKEL and ZIMMERN, however, were the first to trace in detail the existence of a regular metre[1], pointing out that each verse contained a definite number of accented syllables or rythmical beats by which it was divided, each division or foot of the verse consisting of single words, or of two or three short connected words, *e. g.* particles with the words that follow them, words joined by the construct state, *etc.* ZIMMERN further drew attention to the fact that the metre was frequently indicated by the grouping of signs on the tablet, and that in publishing a text it was consequently of great importance to reproduce the exact position and form of the characters. In the plates, therefore, I have endeavoured to give as far as possible a facsimile of the original tablets. It will be

[1] *See* ZIMMERN, *Ein vorläufiges Wort über babylonische Metrik*, *ZA* VIII pp. 121 ff.

seen, however, that only in a comparatively few instances is the metre indicated in this manner, and the evidence of duplicates goes to show that different scribes attached different degrees of importance to the symmetrical arrangement of their lines. For instance, the carefully marked arrangement of No. 1, ll. 1—8, containing the invocation of *Sin*, is not reproduced in the duplicates K 3332 and Sm. 1382, nor is the form of the lines on No. 18 retained by the duplicate K 6804.

If, however, we apply to the prayers and incantations the rules which ZIMMERN has adduced from a study of Sp. II, 265*a*[1], we find that great sections of the various tablets fall naturally into the four-divisioned metre. This regular metre is, however, frequently interrupted by a line of only three feet or divisions; for instance four fifths of the prayer to *Ninib* on No. 2 consist of four feet, the remaining fifth of three feet. In many cases, moreover, the lines, though possessing a certain rythm cannot be regarded as composed in metre. The conclusion to which we are led, therefore, is that the "Prayers of the Lifting of the Hand", though occasionally running into regular metre, are not subject to the strict rules which apply to the poetry of the Babylonians. It is perhaps not improbable that this irregularity was intentional on the part of their composers. In the recital of a prayer or incantation the irregular lines would form a striking contrast or foil to those in metre, and the combination would serve to mark the suppliant's varying degrees of exaltation.

The "Prayers of the Lifting of the Hand" are frequently accompanied by directions for the performance of ceremonies and the observance of certain rites. The paragraphs containing these directions are separated from the incantations by lines ruled on the clay by the scribe and they generally commence with the words *ipuš annam* "Do the following"[2]. Their length varies considerably, ranging from rubrics of one line to sections of fifteen lines. The rubric of one line which is characteristic of the "Prayers of the Lifting of the Hand" is generally found closely following the title of the prayer, from which it is divided by a line on the clay:—

---

1 *Cf.* ZIMMERN, *Weiteres zur babylonischen Metrik*, *ZA* X, pp. 1 ff.

2 *Cf. infra*, p. 19.

It will be seen that after the introductory phrase the rubric refers to two alternative rites which are to be performed in connection with the recital of the prayer[1]. On one occasion[2] we find this rubric directly following the incantation, and it is there expanded into two lines by the additional injunction that the incantation is to be recited before *Sibziana*, an addition rendered necessary by the omission of the title.

Ceremonial sections of two lines are not uncommon. They are sometimes combined with the title which they follow without a break[3], containing two or three directions to the effect that incense is to be set before the god or goddess, a libation to be offered, and the incantation to be recited so many times; or they may follow the title from which they are divided by a division-line[4]; or finally they may follow a longer section of ceremonies when they contain additional rites to be performed in connection with those that precede them[5]. Sections of three lines, which are also common, generally follow the title[6], though they are sometimes found in combination with longer ceremonial sections[7]. Not so common are sections of four lines, which follow the title and are not found in connection with other sections[8]. The longer sections of five[9], six[10], seven[11], ten[12], fourteen[13], and fifteen[14] lines give directions for offerings in

---

[1] *See* below p. 71 f., where the rubric is more fully discussed and a list of the passages given where it occurs.

[2] No. 52, l. 3 f.

[3] Nos. 2, l. 9 f.; 6, l. 95 f.; 8, l. 20 f.

[4] Nos. 13, l. 13 f.; 14, l. 12 f.

[5] No. 12, ll. 101 f., 103 f.

[6] Nos. 21, ll. 73 ff.; 31, ll. 8 ff.; 32, ll. 3 ff.; 36, ll. 7 ff.; 44, ll. 3 ff.

[7] Nos. 21, ll. 25 ff.; 33, ll. 44 ff.

[8] Nos. 11, ll. 42 ff.; 22, ll. 31 ff.

[9] Nos. 12, ll. 96 ff.; 33, ll. 39 ff.

[10] Nos. 12, ll. 115 ff.; 15, ll. 18 ff.; 21, ll. 28 ff.

[11] Nos. 26, ll. 4 ff.; 51, ll. 10 ff.

[12] No. 30, ll. 20 ff.

[13] No. 40, ll. 3 ff.

[14] No. 12, ll. 2 ff.

greater detail, while some[1] cannot be classified as in each case only the beginning has been preserved.

By far the commonest injunction in these ceremonial sections is one to the effect that the recital of the incantation is to be accompanied by the burning of incense. The formula usually reads "a censer of incense before the god ..... shalt thou set", though sometimes the kind of incense to be employed is specified, and at other times the wood is mentioned, from which, when lighted, the censers are to be kindled. Certain drink-offerings and libations are also of common occurrence. It is from the longer sections, however, that we learn in greater detail the objects suitable for offering to a god. Water, honey, and butter are frequently mentioned together in the lists of offerings; directions occur for laying before the god dates, garlic, corn and grain, while various flowers, plants and herbs play a conspicuous part both in the offerings and the ritual. Offerings of various kinds of flesh are sometimes specified, while fragments of gold, lapis-lazuli, alabaster *etc.* might be presented by the suppliant. Pure water and oil are constantly mentioned in the ceremonial sections; the former might be simply offered in a vessel before the god, or used for sprinkling a green bough in his presence; the latter might also form the subject of an offering, or be used for anointing, or be placed in an open vessel into which various objects were thrown. In No. 11, for example, the seed of the *maštakal*-plant is ordered to be cast into oil, while in No. 12 the priest is to place oil in a vessel of *urkarinnu*-wood and then cast into it fragments of plaster, gold, the *bînu*-plant, the *maštakal*-plant, and other plants and herbs. When the rite of casting things into oil is to be performed, the amount of oil to be used is generally mentioned, and sometimes the kind of oil to be employed. The rite of the knotted cord[2] frequently accompanies the "Prayers of the Lifting of the Hand", and on one occasion the rite is followed by a magical formula; in No. 12, a tablet intended for the use of a sick man, when the priest loosens the knot he is to utter the words *ša uma'iranni*, after which the sick man is to return

---

[1] Nos. 15, ll. 24 ff.; 17, ll. 6 ff.; 23, ll. 7 ff.; 24, ll. 5 ff.; 25, ll. 6 ff.

[2] *See* below, p. 71 f.

to his house without looking backward. The occasions on which the tablets might be used are sometimes specified in the ceremonial sections; Nos. 12 and 31, for instance, are to be used at night, No. 30 on a favourable day, No. 24 during a certain phase of the moon, and No. 21 at night when the wind is in a certain quarter. The use of the majority of the tablets, however, appears to have been unrestricted.

It will be seen, therefore, that the ceremonies which accompany the "Prayers of the Lifting of the Hand" in general character resemble those which occur on other classes of ceremonial and religious texts. They were not merely symbols, but were regarded as potent in themselves, and, as the efficacy of an incantation depended on its correct recital, so their power resulted from a scrupulous performance of each detail. They are, with one exception, written after the prayer or incantation they accompany, but in most cases they describe rites which are to be performed before the recitation of the prayer. The god or goddess must be propitiated by the necessary gifts before the suppliant is in a position to make his appeal in the divine presence; the altar must be loaded with offerings and the censers lighted before the words of the incantation can take effect.

LIST OF TABLETS.

	No.
I. PRAYERS ADDRESSED TO GROUPS OF DEITIES:—	
1. Sin, Ištar and Tašmîtu	1
2. Ninib, Tašmîtu and another goddess	2
3. Ninib and Damkina	3
4. Ia, Damkina and Ba'u	4
5. Di-kud and Ištar	5
6. Anu, Nusku, Sin, Ba'u and Šamaš	6
7. Bîlit ili, Išḫara and a god	7
8. Ištar and certain stars	8
9. Marduk and Bîlit ili	9
10. Marduk and Šamaš	10
II. PRAYERS ADDRESSED TO GODS:—	
1. Marduk	11—18
2. Bîl	19
3. Rammân	20—21
4. Nabû	22
5. Sin	23—26
6. Nirgal	27—28
III. PRAYERS ADDRESSED TO GODDESSES:—	
1. Ša-la	29
2. Ištar	30—32
3. Tašmîtu	33
4. Mi-mi	34
5. Bîlit	35
IV. PRAYERS ADDRESSED TO DEITIES WHOSE NAMES HAVE NOT BEEN PRESERVED	36—45
V. PRAYERS ADDRESSED TO ASTRAL DEITIES:—	
1. Muštabarrû-mûtânu	46
2. Mul-mul	47—48
3. Kak-si-di	49
4. Sibziana	50—52
VI. PRAYERS AGAINST THE EVILS ATTENDING AN ECLIPSE OF THE MOON	53—62

Transliteration Translations and Notes.

Section I.

Prayers addressed to Groups of Deities.

The plan on which the following pages have been arranged requires perhaps a word of explanation. The tablets are numbered and are here treated in the same order as they occur in the plates at the end of the volume. I have not divided the Transliteration, Translations and Notes into three separate Sections, as I believe the theoretical simplicity of such an arrangement is purchased at a great practical disadvantage, the constant reference from one part of the book to another tending rather to weary than assist the reader. To reduce this inconvenience as far as possible I have collected together all the matter referring to each tablet. A full transliteration of the text is first given which is followed by a description and translation of the prayers, incantations and ceremonies that it contains. The notes follow the translation, the numbers at the head of each paragraph referring to the line of the text with which the note in question deals.

In the Transliteration those portions of the text that have been restored are placed within square brackets, while the signs within round brackets always denote phonetic complements. Variant readings are given at the foot of the page, the duplicate tablets being cited by the capitals A, B, C etc., the registration numbers of which are in each case given in the first

30. *DI.BAR*[1] *šamî-i u irṣiti(ti)*[2] *ša-ru-ru kibrâti*[^{pl}][3]
31. . . . . . .*-in-nin-na*[4] *bu-uk-[rat]* ^{ilu}*Sin i-lit-ti* ^{ilu}*NIN.[GAL]*
32. . . . . . .*-mat*[5] *dar-ri [šú-mì-í] ḳu-ra-di*[6] ^{ilu}*Šamaš* . . . . . .
33. [^{ilu}*Iš-tar] a-nu-[ti-ma*[7] *šamî-í] ti-bi-il-[li]*[8]
34. [. . . . . . ^{ilu}*Bîl [ma-li-ki ta-di-]im-mi da-* . . . .
35. [. . . . .*-mu] ba-an-[tú?* . . . . . *u* . . . . .*-tu dan-* . . . . . .

Rev.
36. [. . . . . .^{pl} *ru-ḳu-tu tu-šak]-na pânu-[ki* . . . .]
37. [^{ilu}]*Taš-mi-tum ilat(at)*[9] *su-pi u da-di bi-lit* . . . .
38. *[ana]-ku pulânu apil pulâni ša ilu-šu pulânu* ^{ilu}*ištar-šu pulânitum[(tum)]*
39. *ina lumun* ^{ilu}*atalî* ^{ilu}*Sin ša ina arḫi pulâni ûmi pulâni išakna[(na)]*
40. *lumun idâti*^{pl} *ITI.MIŠ limnîti*^{pl} *lâ ṭâbâti*^{pl} *ša ina ikalli-yà u mâti-a ibašâ-[a]*
41. *asḫur-ki imid-ki ši-mi-i a-ra-ti*[10]
42. *a-na* ^{ilu}*Nabû ḫa-'-i-ri-ki*[11] *bîlu ašaridu mâri riš-ti-i ša I.SAG.ILA a-bu-ti ṣab-[ti-ma]*
43. *liš-mi zik-ri ina ki-bit pi-ki* ⯎ *lil-ki un-ni-ni-ya lil-ma-da su-pi-ya*
44. *ina zik-ri-šu kabti(ti) ilu u* ^{ilu}*ištar lislimu(mu) itti-ya*
45. *li-in-ni-is-si murṣu ša zumri-ya* ⯎ *li-tá-kil ta-ni-ḫu ša šîri*^{pl}*-[ya]*
46. *lit-ta-bil ašakku ša bu'âni*^{pl}*-[ya]*
47. *lip-pa-aš-ru imti*^{pl} *imti*^{pl} *imti*^{pl} *šá ibašû-ú ili-yà*
48. *li-in-ni-is-si ma-mit*[12] *li-tá-kil*[13] *ni-* . . . . . .
49. *lit-lu-ud* ^{ilu}*NAM.TAR*[14] *li-ṣal-' irat-su* ⯎ *ina pî-ki*[15] *liš-ša-kin ba-ni-ti*
50. *ilu u*[16] *šarru liḳ-bu-u damiḳti(ti) ina ki-bit-ki ṣir-ti ša úl uttakkarum(rum)*[17]
51. *u an-ni-ki ki-nim ša úl inû-u* ^{ilu}*Taš-mi-tum bîltu*[18]

---

52. *INIM.INIM.MA ŠU IL.LA* ^{ilu}*Taš-mi-tum.KAN*

---

53. *šiptu bîlu muš-ti-šir kiš-šat niši*^{pl} *gi-mir nab-ni-ti*
54. *duppu* ...^{KAN} *bît rim-ki ikal* $^{m\,ilu}$*Aššur-bân-apli etc.*

---

[1] *B* . . . . .*-tú.* [2] *B irṣitim(tim).* [3] *B ša-ru-ur kib-ra-a-ti.* [4] *B* . . . . .*-in-nin-ni.* [5] *B* . . . . .*-am-ti.* [6] *B ḳu-ra-du.* [7] *B a-na-ti-ma.* [8] *B ta-bi-il-li.* [9] *C i-lat.* [10] *C as-ḫur-ki bîlti-yà ši-mi-i su-[pi-ya].* [11] *C ḫa-i-ri-ki.* [12] *C ma-mi-tu.* [13] *C lit-*. . . . . [14] *C* . . . . . *gallû.* [15] *C [ana] niši*^{pl} *a-pa-a-ti.* [16] *C ù.* [17] *C uttakkaru(ru).* [18] *C bi-il-tum.*

No. 1 (K 155) consists of the upper part of a large tablet of which fully half has been broken away. The text in its present condition falls into three main sections: (*a*) ll. 1—27, a prayer to *Sin* on the occasion of an eclipse of the moon, (*b*) ll. 29–35, the opening lines of a prayer to *Ištar*, and (*c*) ll. 36—51, the conclusion of a prayer to *Tašmîtu* which like (*a*) is directed against the evils resulting from a lunar eclipse. The prayer to Sin (*a*) commences with an address to the god describing his power and attributes. Ll. 12 and 13 state the occasion of the prayer: an eclipse of the moon has taken place bringing evil on the land of Assyria and the palace of the king who therefore appeals to the god of heaven and to the Moon-god himself, whose prerogative it is to give an oracle of the great gods when they so desire.

Translation.

1. O *Sin*! O *Nannar*! mighty one . . . . . .
2. O *Sin*, who art unique, thou that brightenest . . . . . .
3. That givest light unto the nations . . . . . .
4. That unto the black-headed race art favourable . . . .
5. Bright is thy light, in heaven . . . . . .
6. Brilliant is thy torch, like the Fire-god . . . . . .
7. Thy brightness fills the broad earth!
8. The brightness of the nation he gathers, in thy sight . . .
9. O *Anu* of the sky, whose purpose no man learns!
10. Overwhelming is thy light like the Sun-god [thy?] first-born!
11. Before thy face the great gods bow down, the fate of the world is set before thee!
12. In the evil of an eclipse of the Moon which in such and such a month on such and such a day has taken place,
13. In the evil of the powers, of the portents, evil and not good, which are in my palace and my land,
14. The great gods beseech thee and thou givest counsel!
15. They take their stand all of them, they petition at thy feet!
16. O *Sin*, glorious one of *Ikur*! they beseech thee and thou givest the oracle of the gods!
17. The end of the month is the day of thy oracle, the decision of the great gods;

18. The thirtieth day is thy festival, a day of prayer to thy divinity!
19. O God of the New Moon, in might unrivalled, whose purpose no man learns,
20. I have poured thee a libation of the night (with) wailing, I have offered thee (with) shouts of joy a drink offering of . .
21. I am bowed down! I have taken my stand! I have sought for thee!
22. Do thou set favour and righteousness upon me!
23. May my god and my goddess, who for long have been angry with me,
24. In righteousness and justice deal graciously with me! Let my way be propitious, with joy . . . . . .
25. And ZA.GAR, the god of dreams hath sent,
26. In the night season . . . . . . my sin may I hear my iniquity may . . . . . .
27. For ever may I bow myself in humility before thee!

Of (*b*) the prayer to *Ištar* only a few lines have been preserved containing the invocation of the goddess. She is addressed as: "*Ištar* the heroine, strong among goddesses! Lady(?) of heaven and earth, the splendour of the four quarters! . . . . . the first-born of *Sin*, offspring of *Ningal*! . . . . O *Ištar*, over these heavens dost thou rule." The reverse of the tablet (*c*) consists of the last fifteen lines of a prayer to *Tašmîtu*, in which the goddess is petitioned to intercede with her husband the god *Nabû* and to induce him to remove the sickness and enchantments caused by the Moon's eclipse. After addressing the goddess by name her suppliant continues: —

38. I so and so, son of so and so, whose god is so and so, whose goddess is so and so,
39. In the evil of an eclipse of the Moon, which in such and such a month on such and such a day has taken place
40. In the evil of the powers, of the portents, evil and not good, which are in my palace and my land,
41. Have turned towards thee! I have established thee! Listen to the incantation!
42. Before *Nabû* thy spouse, the lord, the prince, the first-born son of *Isagila*, intercede for me!

43. May he hearken to my cry at the word of thy mouth; may he remove my sighing, may he learn my supplication!
44. At his mighty word may god and goddess deal graciously with me!
45. May the sickness of my body be torn away; may the groaning of my flesh be consumed!
46. May the consumption of my muscles be removed!
47. May the poisons that are upon me be loosened!
48. May the ban be torn away, may the . . . . . be consumed!
49. May . . . .; at thy command may mercy be established!
50. May god and king ordain favour at thy mighty command that is not altered
51. And thy true mercy that changes not, O lady *Tašmîtu*!

The catch-line reads: "O lord, that directest the multitude of the peoples, the whole of creation!"

1. The word *ru-šu-bu* (= *rušûbu*), if my reading is correct, is an adj. of the form فُعُول, the usual forms of the word being *rašbu* and *rašûbu*. The character, however, which I read as 𒋗 is almost obliterated and might possibly be read 𒋢.

6. *šarâḫu* is proved by JENSEN to have the meaning "to shine, be bright"; *cf. Kosmologie* p. 105 f., where the present passage is quoted from STRASSMAIER, *A.V.*, no. 8063. For the meaning of *dipâru* "torch", *cf.* JENSEN, *ZK*, II, p. 53, and ZIMMERN, *BPS*, p. 47.

9. *ma-[am-ma-an]* is the probable restoration of the end of this line and of l. 19. From the end of l. 10 only one character appears to be missing; *bu-uk-ri-[ka]* would therefore be a possible restoration.

11. *ina* does not occur in the text with the first *pâni-ka* as we might be led to expect from the latter half of the line: for a similar use of *pânu* without the preposition *cf.* IV R 59 [66], no. 2, rev. l. 18, *pâni-ka lu-ḳir*, "in thy sight may I be precious".

12 f. The formula contained in these two lines, stating the occasion of the prayer, is of frequent occurrence in these texts (*cf. Introduction*). The first half of the second line, which in several tablets forms a line by itself, is in apposition to *ina*

lumun ^{ilu}*atalî* ^{ilu}*Sin*, as indicated in my translation, and the whole formula, which does not represent a complete sentence in itself, acts merely as an introduction to the sentence that follows it. The only difficulty in the two lines is in connection with the phrase  These two ideograms occur together not only in the formula under discussion but are occasionally to be met with in prayers incantatious etc., and whenever they so occur they are never joined by a copula but always stand in apposition to one another as in the present passage, *cf.* No. 12, l. 64 *ai idiḫâ-a lumun šunâti*^{pl} *ID.MIŠ ITI.MIŠ ša šamî-i u irṣitim(tim)*, Haupt's *ASKT*, No. 7, Rev. l. 4 f. *ina lumun ID.MIN.MIŠ ITI.MIŠ ši-kin uṣurti*^{pl}, l. 7 f. *aš-šum lumun ID.MIŠ ITI.MIŠ limnûti*^{pl} *ša ina bîti-yà bašâ*^{pl}*-ma pal-ḫa-ku*, and l. 9 f. *ina lumun ID.MIŠ ITI.MIŠ šú-ti-ka-an-ni-ma*, K 6343, l. 6 *ID.MIŠ ITI.MIŠ limnûti*^{pl} *lâ ṭabâti*, K 8005 + K 8845 + K 8941, a very fragmentary prayer of Aššurbânipal formed from three pieces I have lately joined, in l. 3 of which the phrase *ID.MIŠ ITI.MIŠ* occurs, IV R 17, Rev. l. 15 f. *mu-pa-aš-šir NAM.BUL.BI.I ID.MIŠ ITI.MIŠ limnûti*^{pl}, probably IV R 60 [67], Rev. l. 34 *[ID].MIŠ ITI.MIŠ BAR.MIŠ ana šarri u mâti-šu bašâ*^{pl}*-a*, *etc.* More commonly however the ideogram 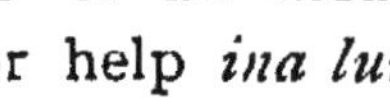 is found by itself, *cf.* No. 12, l. 65 *lumun ITI ali u mâti ai ikšudanni(ni) yá-ši*, the passages quoted from bilingual incantations in Brünnow's *List*, no. 9429, IV R 56 [63], Col. II, 11*b* ^{ilu}*Sin* . . . . *mu-kal-lim ITI.MIŠ*, K 9006, l. 5 *ITI limuttu ša ina su-pu-ri-ya*, K 9594, l. 2 (published and transliterated by Brünnow, *ZA* IV, pp. 233, 249), 79—7—8, 52 a corner of an incantation in ll. 3—6 of which the suppliant prays for help *ina lumun ITI* . . . . . . *ina lumun di-ḫu* . . . . . . *ina lumun ašakku* . . . . . . *ina lumun ḫu-uṣ-[ṣu?]*, the fragmentary prayer 82—3—23, 57 Rev. l. 4, K 6187, a Babylonian ceremonial text for obtaining magical results from stones (*cf.* Bezold, *Catalogue*, p. 769), in Col. III of which the *ITI limuttu(tú)* is constantly mentioned, K 3460, Col. I (*cf. op. cit.* p. 535), 79—7—8, 115, l. 16, Bu. 91—5—9, 14, l. 10 an astrological report from *Ištaršumîrîš*, K 21 (*cf.* R. F. Harper, *Assyrian and Babylonian Letters*, Pt. I, p. 49) a letter from *Nabû-nâdinšum* to the king which concludes (l. 12 ff.): *û inâ ili it-ti an-ni-ti šarru bi-ili* . . . . *-šu lu-* . . . . . *id-da-ab-bu-ub*

^{ilu}Bîl û ^{ilu}Nabû am-mar ITI ši-tu-uk-ki ma-ṣu a-na šarru bîli-yá ú-ši-tu-uk-ku šarru bi-ili lu la i-pa-laḫ, K 168, Obv. l. 16 f. (a letter, published by WINKLER, *Keilschriftt.* II, Leipzig, 1893, p. 28), *etc.* Though the interpretation of the ideogram *ITI* is entirely dependent on the context of the passages where it occurs, there is not much doubt as to its meaning. The word is generally rendered by some synonym of "sign" or "omen" (*cf.* LENORMANT, *Études accadiennes*, Vol. III, p. 136 f., DELITZSCH, *WB*, p. 169, SAYCE, *Hibbert Lectures*, pp. 449, 459, 512, 516, 538, JENSEN in SCHRADER'S *Keilinš. Bibl.*, Vol. II, pp. 249, 253, *etc.*), though in *ZK* I, p. 303 JENSEN assigned to it the active meaning "power, might *(ops)*". That the former is the more correct rendering of the two is I think put beyond a doubt by a passage occurring in a letter (K 112), the text of which has recently been published by R. F. HARPER, *Assyrian and Babylonian Letters*, Pt. II, p. 228, London 1894. The first fifteen lines of this letter read: *a-na ^{am}ik-karu bîli-ya arad-ka $^{m\ ilu}$Nabû-zîr-îšir lu šulmu(mu) a-na bîli-ya ^{ilu}Nabû u ^{ilu}Marduk a-na bîli-ya* (5) *šanâti^{pl} ma-'-da-ti lik-ru-bu ITI.MIŠ lu-u ša šamî-i lu ša irṣitim(tim) lu-u šá* 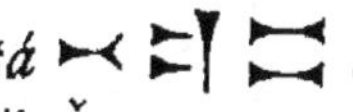 *am-mar lim-na-ni a-sa-tar ina ba-at-ta-ta-ai ma-ḫar ^{ilu}Šamas u-sa-ad-bi-ib-šu-nu* (10) *ina karân šutû-u ina mî^{pl} rimki ina šamni^{pl} piššâti^{pl}-šu amîlûti^{pl}* (?) *am-mu-tí ú-sa-ab-ši-il u-sa-kil-šu-nu šar pu-u-ḫi ša ^{mât}Akkadû^{ki} ITI.MIŠ uš-taḫ-ra-an-ni i-si-si* (15) *ma-a mi-nu-u ITI* . . . . . Though the interpretation of this text is in places exceedingly obscure the general drift of the letter is clear enough. In consequence of enquiries concerning the *ITI* Nabû-zîrîšir takes the necessary observations and returns his report to an official styled the *ikkaru*. After the usual salutations he states that he has observed "the *ITI*, whether of the sky, or of the earth, or of the " (possibly an exhaustive formula), and that they are unfavourable; and probably in consequence of this he has performed certain rites and ceremonies which he proceeds to narrate. It is obvious that the only possible meaning for *ITI* in this passage is "sign" or "portent", a rendering that suits all other passages in which I have met the word including the one already referred to as having been somewhat differently translated by JENSEN.[1] That

[1] Prof. BEZOLD has called my attention to the use of *ITI* in the colophon

the word is in itself colourless taking a favourable or unfavourable meaning from its context is suggested by the qualifying phrase *limnîti^pl lâ ṭâbâti^pl* inserted in the formula under discussion, and this is put beyond a doubt by Rm. 136, a fragment of an omen tablet, in ll. 13 and 16 of which we find the phrase *ITI damiḳtim[(tim?)]* as well as *ITI limuttim(tim)*. It is natural however that in prayers for help or deliverance *ITI* should generally occur in an unfavourable sense.

But while we can assign a meaning to the ideogram with something like certainty, we do not meet with the same success when we look for its Semitic equivalent. DELITZSCH indeed in *AL*³, p. 30, no. 256 suggests a rendering *takiltu*(?) and he is followed by LEHMANN in his explanation of K 168, ll. 14 and 16 (*cf. Šamaššumukîn*, p. 76 f.), in which he transliterates *ITI* with the plural-sign as *taklâti*, *tak-li-ta-šu-nu* occurring in close connection two lines above. But against this rendering is to be urged the fact that wherever the sign occurs in bilingual incantations it is, as for as I know, rendered not by *takiltu* but by *ittu*. As however I do not know on what grounds DELITZSCH bases his identification of the ideogram with *takiltu*, I have throughout my transliteration rendered the word by *ITI*, thus leaving the question in abeyance.

The explanation of *ID* is also conjectural. Though *ID.MIŠ* and *ITI.MIŠ* are in apposition it does not follow that they are synonymous, as they are taken by LENORMANT, *La Magie*, p. 164 and by SAYCE, *Hibbert Lectures*, pp. 173 and 538. It appears to me that DELITZSCH has given the true explanation of the word in his translation of the sentence *aš-šum lumun ID.MI ITI.MIŠ limnîti^pl ša ina bîti-ya bašâ^pl-ma*, to which reference has already been made and which he renders: "von wegen *(aššum)* der bösen Mächte, der bösen Zeichen, die in meinem Hause sind" (*cf. WB*, p. 169). Here apparently he renders *ID* by its most common equivallent *idu*, the plural of which constantly occurs in the sense of "forces, powers", and this view is supported by the

of K 8713, where the word apparently refers to and should be rendered by "astrological forecasts". I think however that the more general rendering "portent", which would of course include the special meaning attaching to the word in this tablet, is better suited to many of the other passages in which *ITI* is to be found; *see* especially IV R 3, Col. I, l. 29 f.

fact that in the same hymn (*cf. supra* p. 8) *ID* occurs with the dual as well as the plural-sign.[1] Morever in No. 6, l. 114 f. *i-da-tu-u-a* occurs in parallelism with *šunât^{pl}-u-a* and must therefore have a somewhat similar meaning to that of *ID* in the present passage. The meaning of the formula may therefore be regarded as practically settled though the Semitic equivalent of *ITI* is still a matter of some uncertainty.

15. That  is equivalent to *nazâzu* is clear from Brünnow, *List*, no. 4893. If on the other hand we read the group phonetically, the form *du-bu* must be explained as Perm. II 1 from *dabâbu*, for *dubbubû**, *dubb-bû**; the former explanation however appears to me the more probable of the two. The verb *uš-ta-mu-ú* in the second half of the line I take to be III 2 from √אמר, "to speak", with a causative signification, "to cause to speak", *i. e.* "petition".

16. *tâmîtu* in the technical sense of "an oracle" occurs in the regular formulae of the so-called "Downfall" tablets, in which "*Izib* 7" commonly consists of the phrase *izib ša i-na pî mâr ^{am}bâri ardi-ka ta-mit up-tar-ri-du*, "Grant that in the mouth of the magician's son thy servant a word (i. e. the oracle for which we ask) may hasten", or in the 1st pers. *ta-mit ina pî-ya up*(or *ip*)*-tar-ri-du*, *cf.* Knudtzon, *Assyrische Gebete an den Sonnengott*, Vol. II, p. 42, Leipzig 1893.

17. For the explanation of *bubbulum* as "the day of (the Moon's) disappearance" *cf.* Jensen, *Kosmologie*, pp. 91, 106.

19.  I have taken as an abbreviation of . It might be possible to read the group *ilu ina išid ûmi* "o god! in the foundation of (that) day is a power unrivalled *etc.*", referring to the thirtieth day of

[1] The sign of the dual is also to be found with *ID* in the name of the plant , which occurs in Col. V, l. 4 of Rm. 328, a tablet in which the names of plants are enumerated in short sections probably for use as prescriptions. This plant may have been so named from its employment in warding off the evils of the *ID.MIŠ ITI.MIŠ*. That certain prescriptions were used against such evils is clear from K. 6432, a tablet containing prescriptions, one section of which commences (rev., l. 4) *inuma ina arah Nisânu ûmi IKAN amilu ID.MIŠ-šu ITI.MIŠ-šu limuttu-[šu?]* . . . . . . (*cf.* Bezold, *Catalogue*, p. 787).

the month mentioned in the preceding line. But this explanation appears rather forced, and the parallelism of l. 9 seems to indicate that the group is the name of a god. That *namraṣit* = the New-Moon has been shown by Jensen, *Kosmologie*, p. 104 f., and the invocation of the Moon-god as the New-Moon, following immediately on the mention of the end of the month, is singularly appropriate.

20. *as-ruk-ka si-rik*; *cf.* No. 35, l. 9, *as-ruk-ki si-rik* addressed to *Išḫara*. The suffixes *-ka* and *-ki* are probably to be regarded as having the force of *ana ka-a-tu, ana ka-a-ti*. For a similar use of the suffix *cf.* K 5418a, Col. IV, l. 7, quoted by Bezold, *Catalogue*, p. 715: *biti-ši-na* (or *bît-si-na*) *i-pu-uš-ka na-rú-a aš-tur-ka*, "their house have I made for thee, my tablet have I inscribed for thee". A somewhat analogous instance occurs in an Old-Babylonian letter (V.A.Th. 575), published by Meissner, *Beitr. z. Assyr.*, Vol. II, pp. 561 f., 577, in l. 10 of which the verb *i-zi-ba-ak-ku-šu* occurs, governing two suffixes however and not a suffix and a substantive as in the present passage.  may be read *il-lu* in agreement with *mûši*, "an incantation of the bright night". But *lallartu* (*cf.* Brünnow, *List*, No. 11181) appears to me the preferable reading, as it balances *ri-iš-ta-a* in the second half of the line. For a similar use of the word *cf.* Sm. 954, Obv. l. 33, quoted by Zimmern, *BPS*, p. 95.

25. The title *ilu ša šunâti*^{pl} occurs in IV R 66, No. 2, Rev. l. 24, where it is applied to 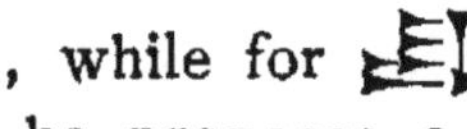, which Zimmern (*op. cit.* p. 105) explains as meaning "dream-god". 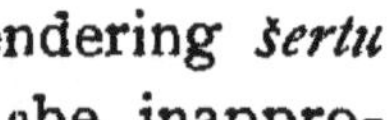 in l. 11a of the list of gods published in II R 54 is possibly to be regarded as a synonym of *Bîl*, as suggested by Brünnow, *List*, No. 11771.

26. The group *-tu* in V R 20, 3*e* is read as *sartu* "sin" by Zimmern, *op. cit.*, p. 12, while for *-ta*, *-ti* in IV R 61, no. 1, ll. 29 and 31 he proposes a rendering *šertu* "anger, wrath", where the meaning "sin" would be inappropriate (*cf. op. cit.*, p. 85). That "sin" is the meaning of the word in the present passage is clear from the corresponding *arniya* in the first half of the line. For my reading *širtu* and not *šartu* or *sartu cf.* Delitzsch in Zimmern's *BPS*, p. 115.

28. This colophon line, which is characteristic of the present collection of texts (*cf. Introduction*), is with one exception written throughout in Sumero-Akkadian, thus: *INIM.INIM.MA ŠU IL.LA* ^ilu^ (or ^kakkab^) . . . . *KAN* (or *KID*). The exception occurs in l. 14 of No. 35, which reads: . . . . *ni-iš ḳa-a-ti šá* ^ilu^*Bîlit.* The beginning of the line is unfortunately broken off and we are consequently left in doubt as to the Assyrian equivalent of *INIM.INIM.MA*. Our choice however appears to be restricted to *amâtu* and *šiptu* (*cf.* Brünnow, *List*, nos. 588 f.), and of these the former is to be preferred as it distinguishes the ideogram from  occurring at the commencement of almost all these incantations. In Assyrian the line should therefore in all probability run: *amât nîš ḳâti ša* ^ilu^ (or ^kakkab^) . . . . . . The expression *nîš ḳâti*, "hand-raising", has in many passages almost lost its original meaning and been transferred to the utterance that generally accompained the act. It is thus possible that the colophon-line in question is simply equivalent to: "The words of the prayer to such and such a god". My own opinion however is that *INIM.INIM.MA*, whether considered the equivalent of *amâtu* or not, has acquired in the colophons where it occurs the definite meaning of "prayer".[1] On this assumption *nîš ḳâti* must be regarded as retaining its original significance and we must see in the title an allusion to some act or ceremony accompanying the recitation of the prayer that precedes it. It may possibly be urged against this view that in No. 8, l. 21 *ŠU IL.LA* III *šanîtu îpuš(uš)* takes the place of the more usual *mînûtu(tú) an-ni-tu* III *šanîtu munu(nu)*[2], and should therefore be treated as its equivalent in meaning and translated: "the prayer three times perform". But such an inference is far from certain and it appears to me more probable that in the case of No. 8 the act of raising the hand three times is substituted for the threefold repetition of the prayer.

30. My translation of the ideogram *DI.BAR* is conjectural, for the fact that the sign-group 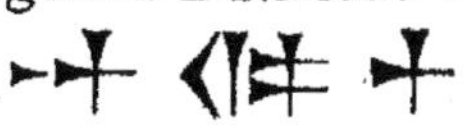 occurs in a

[1] It is possible that the group should be transliterated by some word with the definite meaning of prayer, such as *tiṣlîtu* or *ikribu*.

[2] For a discussion of this phrase *cf. infra, sub* No. 2, l. 10.

list of gods in II R 54 as an equivalent of *Bîl* (*cf.* Brünnow, *List*, no. 9544) does not throw much light upon its meaning. Of the reading of the duplicate B, which probably gave the phonetic equivalent of the ideogram unfortunately only the ending . . . . .-*tú* has been preserved.

35. In the duplicate B the sign following  is written very clearly thus . This may have been a slip on the part of the scribe for , or possibly for , in which latter case the first part of the line should be transliterated: . . . . . *MU] BA.AN.UD.DA* . . . . .

41. *a-ra-ti*, for *arrati*, is clearly used here in the sense of "incantation" or "invocation", as shown by the duplicate C, which reads *ši-mi-i su-[pi-ya]*. The end of l. 42 is restored from the somewhat similar line in Haupt's *ASKT*, No. 19, Rev. l. 5, which reads: — *ana ḳar-ra-di id-lum* *ilu**Šamaš* *ḫa-ʾ-i-ri na-ra-mi-ki a-bu-ti ṣab-ti-ma*. I have adopted Zimmern's explanation of the phrase in *BPS*, p. 59; *abbuttu* he derives from √עבט "to twist", explaining the word as meaning "chain, fetter", and to the phrase *abbuttu sabâṭu* he gives the meaning "to go bail, give security for someone, to intercede for him" (esp. of intercession to a deity). *Cf.* also Delitzsch in Zimmern's *BPS*, p. 117 f. and *WB*, p. 75 f., where he derives the word from √עבת.

48. *li-tá-kil* I take to be = *littakil*, IV 2 from *akâlu*. If the word be read *li-da-gil*, I 1 from *dagâlu*, then *li-in-ni-is-si* must be regarded as I 2, not IV 1 from *nisû*, and the line would run: "May he tear away the sickness of my body; may he behold the sighing of my flesh". But the more common form of the Pres. of *dagâlu* is *idagal*, and the reading of the duplicate C seems rather to support the former view.

49. *ba-ni-ti*, a subs. from *bânu* "to shine". From the meaning "brightness" the word comes to signify "mercy", *cf.* Zimmern, *op. cit.*, p. 60.

54. The scribe has left a space after *duppu* evidently with the intention of subsequently filling in the number of the tablet. Two other tablets of the Series *Bît rimki* are known to us, namely K 3245 *etc.* and K 3392, which are labelled respectively

the 1st. and 3rd. tablets of the series (*cf.* BEZOLD, *Catalogue*, p. 528 and Vol. III, p. VIII). The fragment K 6028 is a duplicate of K 3392 (*cf. op. cit.* p. 757) but it is broken off before the first line of the colophon, and of the catch-line the beginning only is preserved: *šiptu ga-aš-ru šú-* . . . . Now K 2538 etc. Col. VI, l. 1 reads *šiptu gaš-ru šu-pú-u i-ziz* ^{alu}*Aššur*. Therefore on p. 5 of the *Additions* to IV R, the tablet K 6028 has been published as "probably part of the same text" as K 2538 etc. But K 3392, which preserves the beginning of the colophon shows that this is not the case. The catch-line does indeed refer to the first line of the incantation contained in Col. VI, ll. 1—21 of K 2538 etc. but this incantation, which is a duplicate of No. 9, ll. 1—26, has evidently been taken from the present class of texts and inserted in the composite and partly bilingual tablet published in IV R, pl. 21*. K 3392 and its duplicate on the other hand would appear to belong to the present class of texts, for their style and colophon-line point in this direction. From the shape of the tablet however it is certain that it originally contained four columns, two on either side, an arrangement that is never met with in the texts collected in this volume. The most probable explanation therefore seems to be that the Series *Bît rimki* was a composite collection of texts including among others texts of the present class.[1] It has been already pointed out that K 2832 + K 6680 contains "a list of the first lines of various incantations" (*cf.* BEZOLD, *Catalogue*, Vol. II, p. XXII), and it is possible that in Col. I we possess a fragmentary catalogue of the first lines of some of the incantations of this series. The tablet in question commences , while l. 11 runs *šiptu ga-aš-ru šú-pu-ú i-ziz* ^{alu}*Aššur*, a commencement which is identical with the catch-line of K 3392 and the first line of the Obv. of No. 9 and of its duplicate K 2538, Col. VI, ll. 1—21, and which must therefore refer to that incantation. The *Bît rimki* itself, from which the series takes its name, may possibly have been a certain temple or more probably a special chamber or division

[1] K 3392 adds but little to its duplicate K 6028 already published; apart from the beginning of the colophon its most important addition is that to l. 10, the end of which it restores thus: 

of every large temple. That it actually existed in one or other of these capacities is clear from the passages where it is mentioned throughout the hymn to the Sun-god published in V R, pl. 50 f.; in Col. III, l. 20 occurs the phrase *ina bît rim-ki ina i-ri-bi-ka*, "when thou enterest the house of libation", and in l. 55 *ana bît rim-ki ina ṭi-ḫi-ka*, "when thou approachest the house of libation"; *cf.* also Col. III, ll. 55, 70 and Col. IV, ll. 21, 28 of the same text.

No. 2.

Transliteration.

Obv.

1. . . . . *da-* . . . .
2. . . . . *ina ilâni*^{pl} . . . .
3. . . . . *bîlti-yà aṣ-ṣa-ḫar* . . . .
4. . . . . *-ki i-ši-'* *bi-lut-ki*
5. . . . . *-man-ni-ma ki-bi-i damiḳtim(tim)*
6. . . . . *-ḳa ḫul-li-ki limuttim(tim)*
7. . . . . *ya - a - ti pa - liḫ - ki*
8. *[lib-bi-ki] lu-ša-pi dá-li-li-ki lud-lul*
9. *[INIM].INIM.MA ŠU IL.LA* ^{ilu}*Taš-mi-tum.KAN DU.DU BI ŠA-NA burași*
10. *[ana] pân* ^{ilu}*Taš-mi-tum tašakan(an) KAS.SAG tanaḳi(ki)-ma mînûtu(tú) an-ni-tú imunu(nu)*

---

11. *šiptu ap-lu gaš-ru bu-kur* ^{ilu}*Bîl*
12. *šur-bu-u*[1] *git-ma-lu i-lit-ti I.ŠAR.RA*
13. *šá pu-luḫ-tú [lit]-bu-šú*[2] *ma-lu-u*[3] *ḫar-ba-[šu]*
14. ^{ilu}*UT.GAL.LU [ša la im]-maḫ-ḫa-ru ḳa-bal-šu*
15. *šú-bu-u man-[za-za] ina ilâni*^{pl} *rabûti*^{pl}
16. *ina I.KUR bît ta-[ši]-la-a-ti ša-ḳa-a*[4] *ri-ša-a-ka*
17. *id-din-ka-ma* ^{ilu}*Bîl abu-ka*
18. *ti-rit kul-lat ilâni*^{pl} *ḳa-tuk-ka tam-ḫat*
19. *ta-dan di-in ti-ni-ši-i-ti*[5]
20. *tuš-ti-šir la šú-šú-ru i-ka-a i-ku-ti*[6]

[1] *A šur-bu-ú.* [2] *A lit-bu-šu.* [3] *A ma-lu-ú; B [ma]-lu-ú.* [4] *B . . . . . -lá-a* [5] *B di-in ti-ni-ši-i-ti.* [6] *B i-ku-tum.*

21. *ta-ṣab-bat ḳât [in-ši] la li-ʾ-a tu-ša-aš-ḳa*[1]
22. *ša a-na a-ra-al-[li]-i šú-ru-du pa-gar-šu*[2] *tutîra(ra)*
23. *ša ár-nu i-šú-ú ta-paṭ-ṭár*[3] *ár-nu*[4]

Rev.

24. *ša ilu-šu itti-šu*[5] *zi-nu-ú*[6] *tu-sal-lam*[7] *ár-ḫiš*
25. ^{ilu}*NIN.IB a-ša-rid ilâni*^{pl} *ḳu-ra-du at-ta*
26. *ana-ku pulânu apil pulâni ša ilu-šu pulânu* ^{ilu}*ištar-šu pu-lânîtum(tum)*[8]
27. *ar-kus-ka rik-sa KU.A.TIR áš-ruk-ka*
28. *áš-ruk-ka tar-[rin]-nu*[9] *i-ri-šu*[10] *ṭâbu*[11]
29. *aḳḳi-ka du-uš-[šú]-bu ši-kar áš-na-an*[12]
30. *itti-ka li-iz-[zi]-zu*[13] *ilâni*^{pl} *šú-ut* ^{ilu}*Bîl*
31. *itti-ka li-iz-[zi]-zu*[13] *ilâni*^{pl} *šú-ut I.KUR*
32. *ki-niš nap-lis-an-ni-[ma*[14] *ši-mi*[15]*] ḳa-ba-ai*
33. *un-ni-ni-ya [li-ki-ma*[16] *mu-ḫur] taṣ-lit*
34. *zik-ri [li-ṭib] ili-ka*
35. *si-lim itti ya-a-tu-u pa-liḫ-ka*
36. *[pa]-ni-ka a-ta-mar lu-ši-ra ana-ku*
37. *[mu]-up-pal-sa-ta*[17] *ki-niš nap-lis-an-ni*[18]
38. *[an]-ni pu-ṭur šĭr-ti*[19] *pu-šur*
39. *[ti?]-ti-iḳ ḳil-la-ti-ma ḫi-ṭi-ti ru-um-[mi?]*
40. *[ili]-yà u* ^{ilu}*ištari-yà li-ša-ki-ru-in-ni-ma liḳ-bu-u damiḳtim(tim)*
41. *[lìb]-bi-ka lu-ša-pi dá-lí-lí-ka lud-lul*

---

42. *[INIM.INIM].MA ŠU IL.LA* ^{ilu}*NIN.IB.KAN*

---

43. . . . . *kib-ra-a-ti i-lat bí-li-í-ti*
44. . . . . ^{ilu}*Da-gan ra-bit* ^{ilu}*I-gí-gí*
45. . . . . *ḫ-ti ilâni*^{pl} *ka-nu-tú ai ak-ki*
46. . . . . *tukulti(ti) I.ZID.DA*
47. . . . . *mu-kin um-mat ilâni*^{pl} *a-pil* ^{ilu}*Marduk*
48. . . . . *-šú* . . . . *nab-ni-ti*
49. . . . . *-ḫa-zi*
50. . . . . *-ra*

1 *B tu-šaḳ-ḳa-ri.* 2 *B* ^{am}*pagar-šu.* 3 *B tu-paṭ-ṭár; D ta-pa-*. . . . . 4 *B ár-na.* 5 *D* ^{ilu}*ištar-šu.* 6 *D zi-nu-u.* 7 *B [tu]-sál-lam.* 8 *D ana-ku arad-ka* ${}^{m\,ilu}$*Aššur-bân-apli mâr ili-šu | ša ilu-šu Aššur* ^{ilu}*ištar-šu* ^{ilu}*Aš-šú-ri-tum.* 9 *CD tar-rin-na.* 10 *CD i-ri-ša.* 11 *D ṭa-a-ba.* 12 *D aš-na-an.* 13 *D li-ziz-zu.* 14 *D naplisa-ni-ma.* 15 *E ši-ma-a.* 16 *D liḳi-ma.* 17 *D [mu-up]-pal-sa-at.* 18 *D naplis-an-ni.* 19 *DE šĭr-tim.*

The first eight lines of No. 2 (K 2487 + K 2502 + K 2591) contain the end of a prayer to *Tašmîtu*, in which the suppliant, after beseeching the goddess to confer favour and to destroy iniquity, concludes with the desire that he may extol her heart and bow in humility before her. Ll. 9 and 10 form a colophon containing directions for ceremonies, for a full discussion of which *cf.* p. 19 ff. These are followed by a complete prayer of thirty-one lines addressed to *Ninib* (ll. 11—41) commencing with fourteen lines in description and praise of the god; the suppliant then states the offerings that he has duly made, relying on which he concludes with the request to be cleansed from sin, comforted in sorrow, and restored to the favour of god and goddess. Ll. 20—23 are remarkable as they attribute a gentle character to *Ninib*, describing him as the guide of the wandering and the sustainer of the weak, the restorer of the dead and the cleanser of sins. It is probable that in this description the god is regarded in his solar character as the friend of mankind, a function that is not however inconsistent with his character as the god of battle.[1] The eight fragmentary lines, with which the tablet concludes, contain the beginning of a prayer to a goddess, which in its damaged condition does not admit of a connected translation.

Translation.

11. O mighty son, first-born of *Bîl*!
12. Powerful, perfect, offspring of *Išara*,
13. Who art clothed with terror, who art full of fury!
14. O *Utgallu* (?), whose onslaught is unopposed!
15. Mighty is (thy) place among the great gods!
16. In *Ikur*, the house of decisions, exalted are thy heads,
17. And *Bîl* thy father has granted thee
18. That the law of all the gods thy hand should hold!
19. Thou judgest the judgement of mankind!
20. Thou leadest him that is without a leader, the man that is in need!
21. Thou holdest the hand of the weak, thou exaltest him that is not strong!

---

[1] *Cf.* Jensen, *Kosmologie*, p. 475.

22. The body of the man that to the Lower World has been brought down thou dost restore!
23. From him who sin possesses, the sin thou dost remove!
24. Thou art quick to favour the man with whom his god is angry!
25. O *Ninib*, prince of the gods, a hero art thou!
26. I so and so, son of so and so, whose god is so and so, whose goddess is so and so,
27. Have bound for thee a cord, ... have I offered thee;
28. I have offered thee *tarrinnu*, a pleasant odour;
29. I have poured out for thee mead, a drink from corn.
30. With thee may there stand the gods of *Bîl*!
31. With thee may there stand the gods of *Îkur*!
32. Truly pity me and hearken to my cries!
33. My sighing remove and accept my supplication!
34. Let my cry find acceptance before thee!
35. Deal favourably with me who fear thee!
36. Thy face have I beheld, let me have prosperity!
37. Thou art pitiful! Truly pity me!
38. Take away my sin, my iniquity remove!
39. Tear away my disgrace and my offence do thou loosen!
40. May my god and my goddess command me and may they ordain good fortune!
41. May I praise thy heart, may I bow in humility before thee!

The first clause of the colophon contained in l. 9 f. has been already discussed, *cf.* p. 13 f., and in future I shall not again refer to this phrase which occurs on each of the texts published under Sections I—V. The expression  is to be found at the commencement of most directions for ceremonies interchanging with  and with   and evidently forming a sort of set introduction to the ceremonies that follow. Each of these three groups of signs is probably equivalent to *ipuš annam*, "do the following", as Bezold has pointed out in *ZA*, V, p. 111. The three directions however that follow this introductory phrase in the present text require some explanation. The first is to the following effect: — "a *ŠA.NA* of incense before *Tašmîtu* shalt thou set", and the question at once arises, what is a *ŠA.NA*? The phrase *ŠA.NA burâši* is of very common occurrence both in these texts and in regulations for ceremonies generally, and wherever it occurs there are only two alternatives possible as to its meaning. It must either be some measure of weight or capacity stating the exact amount of incense to be used, or else it must refer to the vessel in which the incense is contained. Which of these two meanings should be adopted is made clear from the use of *ŠA.NA* in K 3245, Col. II, l. 14*b*,[1] which reads, VII *ŠA.NA tašakan(an)*, and in a colophon-line that is characteristic of the present class of texts, *lû ina ŠAR lû ina ŠA.NA ipuš(uš)*, *cf.* Nos. 16, 11; 18, 19; 21, 92 *etc.* As in both these expressions *ŠA.NA* is used absolutely, it cannot be the name of any measure or weight. We are reduced therefore to the second of the two alternatives and must conclude that the *ŠA.NA* was a kind of vessel capable of containing incense and of being set before a god; it may have taken the form of a small brazier or tripod.[2]

The second injunction, *KAS.SAG tanaki(ki)-ma*, is also frequently to be met with in the ritual texts. The two signs  are not to be read phonetically as an adv. *bi-riš*, but are rather to be regarded as the name of some libation, for otherwise the verb *tanaḳi* would be left without an object. The *KAS.SAG* may have been the name of some drink or liquid, but it appears to me to be more probable that it was the name of the drink-offering itself. For in IV R 60 [67], 20*a* there occurs the injunction *KAS.SAG karâni tanaki[(ki)]*, definitely stating that the *KAS.SAG* is to be of wine. This

[1] The first eighteen lines of this column are published by BEZOLD, *Catalogue*, p. 516.

[2] In texts containing directions for ceremonies and rites we meet with the phrase *ŠA.NA GI.BIL.LA* (= *dipâru*) *cf.* No. 12, l. 86, K 6052, l. 5, IV R 55 [62], No. 2, Obv. l. 23, *etc.* If we here assign to *dipâru* its usual meaning of "torch" (*cf.* p. 6) it is not easy to see what meaning attaches to *ŠA.NA*. In fact the phrase appears inexplicable to me, unless we assume that *dipâru* has also the more indefinite meaning "flame" or "fire". It was apparently on such an assumption that STRONG (*Journal asiatique*, 1893, p. 382) suggests for the expression the meaning "un encensoir". In that case *ŠA.NA burâši* and *ŠA.NA dipâri* would be practically synonymous.

view is further supported by the fact that in Sm. 810, Obv. l. 8 (Bezold) there occurs the expression  , *KAS.SAG tumalli-ma tukân(an)* "the *KAS.SAG* thou shalt fill up and offer". To "fill up a liquid" would be extremely colloquial English and in Assyrian the phrase would be meaningless; there would be nothing strange however in speaking of filling up such and such a drink-offering. The expression *KAS.SAG*  (= *šatû*), "the *KAS.SAG* of drinking", *i. e.* that is drunk, which occurs in the same tablet, Obv. l. 17 and in Sm. 937, l. 4 (Bezold) would also seem to support this explanation. In No. 8, l. 21 *mi-iḫ-ḫa tanaki(ki)-ma* occurs in the place of the more usual *KAS.SAG tanaki(ki)-ma*. It is not possible however to argue from this passage alone that *mi-iḫ-ḫa* = *KAS.SAG*, for we have already seen (*cf.* p. 14) that the latter half of the same line contains a variation from the usual formula.

The colophon concludes with the direction 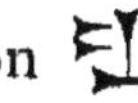-*tú an-ni-tu* -*nu*, my transliteration of which as *mînûtu(tú) an-ni-tú mu-nu(nu)* requires justification. If the phrase always occurred precisely in the form in which we find it in the present text, it might with plausibility be urged that the signs should be read phonetically: *šit-tú an-ni-tú šit-nu*, *šitnû* being regarded as Imperative I 2 from *šanû* "to repeat", and *šittu* a substantive of the form فِعْلَة derived from the same verb. This rendering however is upset by the fact that the verb does not always occur as -*nu*. For instance in IV R 55 [62], no. 2, Obv. l. 19 f. we find the direction *šiptu an-ni-tú* III *šanîtu ina pân* *ilu**Ištar* -*ma*, and  without -*nu* is also to be found in Nos. 6, 96; 11, 45; 12, 16 and 103; 30, 27; K 3292, l. 7 *etc.* Moreover in l. 29 of K 6679 + K 8083, two fragments of a large tablet containing ceremonies and prayers to the goddess *Ištar* which I have recently joined, we find the form -*ú*. These facts together prove conclusively that  is an ideogram, -*nu* and -*ú* being merely phonetic complements. The phonetic complement -*nu* indicates that  = *manû* in the present phrase, and this is put beyond a doubt by the fact that *ŠA.MI.NI.*𒈬 occurring in V R 50, Col. II, l. 63 in the sense of repeating an incantation is rendered in the Semitic translation by *mu-nu* (*cf.* Brünnow, *List*, no. 5972). But if 𒈬-*nu* = *munu(nu)* the substantive 𒈬-*tú* must be regarded as *mînûtu(tú)*, the whole phrase being equivalent to "This repetition (*i. e.* subject of repetition = incantation) repeat". The direction refers to the prayer or incantation that precedes, not to that which follows the colophon in which it occurs.

14. For a discussion of *ilu UT.GAL.LU* as a synonym of *ilu NIN.IB cf.* Jensen, *Kosmologie*, p. 461 f.

16. *ta-ši-la-a-ti* prob. = plur. of *tašiltu*, "decree, decision(?)", a subs. of the form تَفْعِلَةٌ (or possibly تَفْعَلَةٌ) from √שאל. Compare *tanittu* from √נאר.

20. The indiscriminate use of *i* and *í* in the phrase *i-ka-a í-ku-ti* is striking. For the meaning of the words *cf.* Delitzsch, *WB*, p. 370.

Ll. 27—29 recount the ceremonies and offerings which the suppliant states he has made to the god *Ninib.* After the formal statement of his name in l. 26, he continues: "I have bound for thee a cord". It is probable that this rite of binding a cord before the god belongs to the great body of sympathetic magic that plays so important a part in Babylonian sorcery. The spell was in all probability regarded as binding only so long as the cord remained knotted, its significance being somewhat similar to that of twisting the black and white threads mentioned as a spell in the sixth *šurpu* tablet, Col. III, ll. 28—31, *cf.* Jensen, *ZK* II, p. 42 ff. The offering mentioned in the second half of the line is somewhat obscure; *KU.A.TIR* is indeed translated by Sayce (*Hibbert Lectures*, p. 529) as "cones(?)" and in a footnote he gives the following three reasons for his translation: in K 4345, Col. III, l. 18 the signs *A.TIR* occur in the name of the plant *šam A-TIR-ti-a-ru*, *Tiyaru* is "the cedar" (II R 23, 23), and the determinative *KU* denotes the husk of a seed. Now *A.TIR* preceded by the derminative 𒌆 has in all probability an entirely different signification from *A.TIR* in combination with *ti-a-ru* and preceded by the determinative , and in the second place the determinative  (= *ḳîmu*) denotes not "the husk of a seed", but "field produce, grain", *cf.* JENSEN, *ZK* II, p. 31 and *ZA* III, p. 235. The *KU.A.TIR* is therefore probably an edible herb or serial. It is mentioned in the present passage as being offered to *Ninib* along with the sweet-smelling *tarrinnu*, and a drink-offering of mead, and forms a very common offering both in the ceremonies that accompany some of the present class of texts and in regulations for offerings generally, *cf.* Nos. 12, 3; 15, 20; 30, 21; 58, 26; IV R 23, no. 1, Rev. Col. III, l. 27; K 3245, Col. II, l. 12 (*cf.* BEZOLD, *Catalogue*, p. 576), K 6060, l. 6, K 6068, Col. II, l. 3 (*cf. op. cit.*, p. 760), K 6207 + K 6225, l. 7, K 6679 + K 8083, l. 4, K 8932, l. 5, *etc.*

No. 3.

Transliteration.

1\. . . . . *bi-lit* . . . .

2\. . . . . *liḳî-i* . . . .

3\. . . . . *ilu-šu u* ^{ilu}*ištar-šu* . . . .

4\. . . . . *a-ta-mar* . . . .

5\. . . . . 𒑱 *šamû-ú ḫidûtu-ki apsû* . . . .

6\. *[ilâni*^{pl} *ša kiš-ša-ti lik-ru-bu]-ki* 𒑱 *ilâni*^{pl} *rabûti*^{pl} *libbu-ki li-šú-[ru-u?]*

7\. . . . . *[*^{ilu}*]Î-a li-šar-bu-u bîlu-ut-[ki]*

8\. . . . . *[*^{ilu}*]Dam-ki-na bi-lit šamî-i u irṣitim[(tim?)]*

9\. *[INIM.INIM.MA] ŠU IL.LA* ^{ilu}*Dam-ki-na.[KAN]*

10\. *[šiptu ap-lu gaš-ru] bu-kur* ^{ilu}*Bîl* 𒑱 *šur-pu-ú*[1] *git-ma-lu i-lit-ti I.ŠAR.RA*

11\. *[šá pu-luḫ]-tú lit-bu-šu*[2] *ma-lu-ú*[3] *ḫar-ba-šu*

12\. *[*^{ilu}*UT.GAL.LU] ša la im-maḫ-ḫa-ru ḳa-bal-šu*

13\. *[šú-pu-u] man-za-za ina ilâni*^{pl} *rabûti*^{pl}

14\. *[ina I.KUR bît ta]-ši-la-a-ti ša-ḳa-a ri-ša-a-ka*

1 *A šur-pu-u.* 2 *A [lit]-bu-šú.* 3 *A ma-lu-u.*

15. *[id-din-ka-ma* *ilu Bil abu-ka] ti-rit kul-lat ilâni^{pl} ḳa-tuk-ka tam-[ḫat]*

16. *[ta-dan di-in ti-ni-ši-i-ti] tuš-ti-šir la šú-šú-ra*[1] *i-ka-a [i-ku-ti]*

No. 3 (K 8122) is a portion of what was probably a large tablet similar to No. 6. The sixteen lines that have been preserved consist of the conclusion of a prayer to the goddess *Damkina* (ll. 1—8) and the commencement of one to the god *Ninib* (ll. 10—16). The first four lines are fragmentary and give no connected text, but from the fifth line enwards the prayer reads: — "May Heaven be thy joy, may the Abyss . . . . 6. May the gods of the world be favourable to thee: may the great gods bless thy heart! 7. (May . . . .) *Ia* increase thy dominion! 8. . . . . O *Damkina*, lady of heaven and earth!" This conclusion, which has been restored from that of the prayer to the goddess *Ištar* in No. 8, is not an uncommon one; for somewhat similar endings *cf.* No. 6, ll. 127—129, No. 9, ll. 19—21, *etc.* In the latter of these two tablets the gods *Anu* and *Ia* are substituted for "the Heaven" and "the Abyss" invoked in l. 5 of the present text. The prayer to *Ninib* is duplicate of No. 2, ll. 11—20, for the translation of which *see* p. 18.

No. 4.

Transliteration.

1. . . . .

2. . . . . -*šu* . . . .

3. . . . . *u* *šîpu(?)*-. . . . .

4. *li-piš* *a-mi-ri*-. . . . .

5. *ina pî nišî^{pl}* *liš-ša-kin* . . . .

6. . . . . .-*ni* *taš-mi-i u sa-li-mu* . . . . .-*šut*-. . . . .

7. *[ilu]I-a* *ina lib-bi-ka* *damiḳti(ti)* *ši*-. . . . .

---

8. *INIM.INIM.MA* *ŠU IL.LA* *ilu Ia^{c}.KAN*

---

9. *šiptu* *ilu Dam-ki-na šar-rat kâl ilâni^{pl} lá-tú*

---

[1] *A šú-šú-ru.*

10. *al-ti* ^{ilu}*Î-a* *ka-rid-tú* *at-ti*
11. ^{ilu}*IR.NI.NA šar-rat kâl ilâni*^{pl} *lá-tú* ‹ *al-ti* ^{ilu}*Î-a ka-rid-tú at-ti*
12. *šur-ba-ti ina ilâni*^{pl} *lá-ú par-ṣu-[ki?]*
13. . . . . .*-mi-at* ^{ilu}*Anunnaki mu-da-at* ^{ilu}*Igigi*
14. *[bí]-lit I.TUR.RA ka-nu-ut I.A* . . . . . .
15. . . . . *-ti* . . . . . *-pi-* . . . . . ^{ilu}*Î-a a-ši-bat apsû*
bí-lit šamî u [irṣiti]
16. *[ana-ku pulânu] apil pulâni an-ḫu šú-ut-lu-* . . . .
17. *[ina lumun* ^{ilu}*atalî]* ^{ilu}*Sin ša ina arḫi pulâni ûmi [pulâni*
išakna(na)]
18. *[lumun idâti*^{pl}*] ITI.MIŠ limnîti[*^{pl} *lâ ṭâbâti*^{pl}*]*
19. *[ša ina ikalli-yà u mâti]-yà ibašâ-a murṣu dan-nu* . . . . . .
20. . . . . *lišâni-* . . . .
21. . . . . *im-* . . . .
22. . . . .

Rev.

23. *[INIM.INIM.MA] ŠU IL.LA* . . . .

---

24. *[šiptu* ^{ilu}*Ba'u] bîltu šur-bu-tú a-ši-bat šamî-i [illûti*^{pl}*]*
25. . . . . *rim-ni-tum ka-i-šat* . . . .
26. *[nap?]-lu-us-sa taš-mu-ú ki-bit-sa šul-[mu?]*
27. *[al]-si-ki bîltu i-ziz-zi-ma ši-mi-i ka-ba-[ai]*
28. . . . . . *di-ni da-ni purus parâsi(si) dug-gun di-* . . . . .
29. *[asḫur]-ki a-ší-'-ki ulinnu-ki aṣ-bat kîma ulinnu ili-yà u*
^{ilu}*[ištari-yà]*
30. *[di]-ni di-ni purussa-ai purusi(si) a-lak-ti ši-* . . . . .
31. *[áš-šum] í-ṭi-ra ga-ma-la šú-zu-ba ti-di-[í]*
32. *[áš-šum] bul-lu-ṭu šul-lu-mu ba-šú-ú it-ti-[ki]*
33. *[bîltu]* . . . . *bikîtu(?) ad-dan-ki šumu-ki aš-* . . . . .
34. *[ip-ša]-ki uzna*^{du}*-ai iṭ-ri-nì-in-ni-ma ilu-ut-ki lul-* . . . . .
35. *[nîš] kâti-yà muḫ-ri-ma likî-i un-ni-ni-[yà]*
36. *[lu-uš]-pur-ki ana ili-yà zi-ni-i* ^{ilu}*ištari-yà zi-ni-[ti]*
37. *[ana ilu] ali-yà ša šab-su gàm-lu libbu-šu it-ti-[yà]*
38. *[ina] šutti u bi-ri ša ša-* . . . . .
39. *[ina] lumun* ^{ilu}*atalî* ^{ilu}*Sin ša ina arḫi pulâni ûmi pulâni*
išakna[(na)]
40. *[lumun] idâti*^{pl} *ITI.MIŠ limnîti*^{pl} *lâ ṭâbâti[*^{pl}*]*
41. *[ša ina] ikalli-yà u mâti-yà ibašâ-[a]*
42. *pal-ḫa-ku ad-ra-ku u šú-ta-du-ra-[ku]*

43. *ina a-mat ki-bi-ti-ki ṣir-ti ša ina I.KUR* . . . .
44. *u an-ni-ki ki-nim ša úl inû-[ú]*
45. *ili šab-su litûra(ra) [ilu]ištari-yà zi-ni-tú* . . . .
46. *ilu ali-yà [ilu]Marduk ša i-gu-ga* . . . .
47. . . . . . *-zi-zu* . . . . *[ilu]Bau bîltu šur-bu-tú ummu*

48. . . . . . *[ilu]Marduk* . . . . *mâri riš-ti-í ša* . . . . .
49. . . . . *ki-bi-i* . . . .
50. . . . .

The Obverse of No. 4 (K 8105) commences with a few broken lines from a prayer to the god *Ía*, which is followed by the beginning of an address to the goddess *Damkina*, the wife of *Ía* and queen of the Abyss. The first line of the Reverse consists of a colophon-line referring to a preceding incantation, of which however no trace remains, and the name of the god or goddess to whom the incantation was addressed, which originally stood in the second half of the line, has also perished. The rest of the Reverse contains a prayer to the goddess *Ba'u*, from which in all probability not very much is missing. Like the prayers to *Sin* and *Tašmîtu* in No. 1 these two addresses to *Damkina* and *Ba'u* are intended for recitation on the occasion of an eclipse of the Moon (*cf.* ll. 17—19 and 39—41). To judge from its shape it would appear probable that the tablet when complete contained five or six incantations, of which the remains of these three only have been preserved. Of the prayer to *Ía* too little remains for translation, and that to *Damkina*, though better preserved, is somewhat fragmentary. After invoking the goddess in the first seven lines, her suppliant is apparently going on to entreat the removal of a great disease that has resulted from the eclipse, when the tablet ends abruptly.

Translation.

9. O *Damkina*, mighty queen of all the gods.
10. O wife of *Ía*, valiant art thou!
11. O *IR.NI.NA*, mighty queen of all the gods; O wife of *Ía* valiant art thou!
12. Thou art great among the gods, mighty is thy command!

13. O thou that . . . . . the *Anunnaki*, that knowest the *Igigi*,
14. O lady of the Abyss, strong one of . . . . ,
15. Thou that . . . . *Ía*, thou that dwellest in the Abyss, O lady of heaven and earth!
16. I so and so, son of so and so, am weak . . . . ,
17. In the evil of an eclipse of the Moon, which in such and such a month on such and such a day has taken place,
18. In the evil of the powers, of the portents, evil and not good,
19. Which are in my palace and my land, a terrible disease . . . .

In his petition to the goddess *Ba'u* the suppliant implores help in his extremity: he has had a vision at the time of an eclipse of the Moon, in consequence of which he feels that his god and goddess and Marduk the god of his city are angry and have deserted him; let *Ba'u* therefore in mercy use her influence to ensure their return and a renewal of their favour. The following is a translation of the prayer: —

24. O *Ba'u*, mighty lady that dwellest in the bright heavens,
25. O merciful goddess, the bestower of . . . . . . ,
26. Whose regard is prosperity, whose word is peace!
27. I beseech thee, O lady, stand and hearken to my cries!
28. . . . . . give judgement, make a decision . . . . !
29. I have turned to thee, I have sought thee, thy *ulinnu* have I grasped like the *ulinnu* of my god and my goddess!
30. Give my judgement, make my decisions, ... my path,
31. Since thou knowest to protect, to benefit, to save,
32. Since to raise to life, to give prosperity rests with thee!
33. O lady . . . . . tears have I given thee, thy name have I . . . . .
34. . . . . my ears, do thou protect me and let me . . . . . thy divinity!
35. The raising of my hand accept and take away my sighing!
36. Let me send thee unto my angry god, unto my goddess who is angry,
37. Unto *Marduk*, the god of my city who is incensed, whose heart is enraged (?) with me!
38. In the dream and the vision which . . . . . . ,
39. In the evil of an eclipse of the Moon which in such and such a month on such and such a day has taken place,

40. In the evil of the powers, of the portents, evil and not good,
41. Which are in my palace and my land,
42. I am afraid, I tremble and I am cast down in fear!
43. At the word of thy exalted command which . . . . . in *Ikur*,
44. And thy sure mercy which changeth not,
45. Let my wrathful god return, let my angry goddess . . . . .,
46. Let *Marduk* the god of my city who is enraged . . . . .,
47. . . . . O *Ba'u*, mighty lady, ... mother!

9. 𒇲-*tú*, which occurs in ll. 9 and 11, and 𒇲-*ú* in l. 12 I have transliterated *lá-tú* and *lá-ú* respectively. The adj. is probably a فُعْل formation of the √לאה, "to be strong", though the more usual form of the word is *li'u*.

25. The beginning of this line is probably to be restored *[il-tum] rim-ni-tum*, *cf.* No. 7, l. 35, *etc.*

26. For *tašmû*, "prosperity" *cf.* 82—9—18, 3737, l. 34 (Budge, *PSBA*, Vol. X, p. 86 ff.) *ú-ru-úḫ šú-ul-mu u taš-mi-i*, Jensen, *Kosmologie*, pp. 280, 332, *etc.*

28. One sign only appears to be missing from the beginning of this line, which may possibly be restored: *[ana] di-ni da-ni purus parâsi(si) etc.* In this case the sentence forms an introduction to the one that follows it, giving the suppliant's motive in seeking out the goddess. The end of the line contains a phrase similar to *di-ni da-ni* and *purus parâsi(si)*, the subs. *dug-gun* standing in parallelism with *di-ni* and *purus*, while *di-* forms the first syllable of the corresponding verb.

29. Besides the corresponding passages in the parallel text No. 6, ll. 71 ff. and its duplicates, phrases similar to those in ll. 29–32 are to be found in K 2587, Obv. ll. 34–38 (IV R 60 [67]). The *ulinnu* mentioned in l. 29 was probably a woven scarf or garment in which the figure of the god was draped, for, from IV R 21, no. 1 (B), Obv. l. 3 f. it is clear that the *ulinnu* was capable of being dyed and could be swathed around the hands, while the present passage shows that a god or goddess might possess one, which a suppliant could hold when making his appeal. *Cf.* also K 6034, l. 5 f. *iluŠamaš imid-ka iluŠamaš ulinnu-ka aṣ-bat [ulinnu-ka kîma ulinnu] ili-ya' iluištari-ya aṣ-bat*, No. 6, l. 73, No. 7, l. 11, *etc.*

30. For the restoration of the beginning of this line *cf.* K 2612, l. 5, etc.

37. *-lu* also occurs in the somewhat parallel text No. 7, l. 19, while in No. 6, l. 82 we find the word written *-lu*. There is no doubt therefore that the word should be transliterated *gam-lu* or *kam-lu* from √גמל (? כמל). The verb is used in parallelism with *šabâru* and is followed by the prep. *itti* (*see* especially No. 6, l. 82 *ša šab-su-ma gám-lu itti-ya*), so that in meaning it must be very similar to, if not synonymous with, *šabâsu*.

No. 5.

Transliteration.

1. . . . . *ina ilâni^{pl} ri-ša-a ri-i-* . . . . .
2. . . . . *ulinnu-ka ti-ki-* . . . . .
3. . . . . . *-bi šú-mi šu-ri-ka ûmî^{pl}-ya*
4. . . . . . *-bu-ri ru-up-piš li-im-id lil-li-ki*
5. . . . . *-ur murṣi-yà ki-bi ba-lá-ṭi*
6. . . . . . *-ni lip-pa-ṭir lit-ta-bil a-di-* . . . . .
7. . . . . . *-ma-ši ḳil-la-ti su-pu-uḫ ta-ni-[ḫi?]*
8. *[lu]-ša-pi lib-bi-ka lut-ta-id zi-kir-ka*
9. . . . . *DA GAN la pa-da-a ḳu-ru-ud-ka lud-lul*

10. *INIM.INIM.MA ŠU IL.LA ^{ilu}DI.KUD.[KAN]*

11. *[šiptu] ḳá-rid-tum*[1] *^{ilu}Iš-tar ka-nu-ut i-lá-a-[ti]*
12. . . . . . *-tú*[2] *šamî-i u irṣitim(tim)*[3] *ša-ru-ur kib-ra-a-ti*[4]
13. . . . . . *-in-nin-ni*[5] *bu-uk-rat ^{ilu}Sin i-lit-ti ^{ilu}NIN.GAL*
14. . . . . . *-am-ti*[6] *dar-ri šú-mì-i ḳu-ra-du*[7] *^{ilu}Šamaš* . . . .
15. *[^{ilu}]Iš-tar a-na-ti-ma*[8] *šamî-i ta-bi-il-li*[9]
16. . . . . . *^{ilu}Bîl ma-li-ki ta-di-im-mi da-* . . . .
17. . . . . *-mu ba-an-tú?* . . . . . *u* . . . .
18. . . . . *-tum ^{ilu}I-a ina apsî* . . . .
19. . . . . *-pur?-ru-ú* . . . .

---

[1] *A ḳá-rid-tú.* [2] *A DI.BAR.* [3] *A irṣiti(ti).* [4] *A ša-ru-ru kibrâti[^{pl}].* [5] *A . . . . . -in-nin-na.* [6] *A . . . . . -mat.* [7] *A ḳu-ra-di.* [8] *A a-nu-[ti-ma].* [9] *A ti-bi-il-[li].*

The upper portion of No. 5 (K 6019) contains the conclusion of a prayer to the god *DI.KUD.* Though most of the lines are imperfect the general sense of the various petitions is clear. After asking for the increase of his name and for length of days, the suppliant prays for life and the removal of his sickness: let his sin and his sighing be taken away that he may praise the heart of the god and glorify his name. Ll. 11—19 give the beginning of a prayer to *Ištar,* which is duplicate of No. 1, ll. 29 ff., for a translation of which *cf.* p. 5.

No. 6.

Transliteration.

1. *šiptu bîlu šur-bu-[ú]* . . . . 2. *^{ilu}A-nim šur-bu-[ú]* . . . . 3. *ilu šamî-í* . . . . 4. *^{ilu}A-nim ilu šamî-[í]* . . . . 5. *pa-šir ŭ-mi* . . . . 6. *^{ilu}A-nim pa-[šir ŭ-mi]* . . . . 7. *pa-šir šunâti[^{pl}?]* . . . . 8. *ši-it-ti* . . . . 9. *áš-ti-í* . . . . 10. *šal-mu* . . . . 11. *libbu ili-* . . . . 12. *ag-gu* . . . . 13. *lip-pa-aš-* . . . . 14. *lu-ṭaḫ-ḫi* . . . . 15. *da-lil* . . . . 16. *nir-bi ilu-* . . . .

---

17. *INIM.INIM.MA [ŠU IL.LA]* . . . .

---

18. *šiptu ^{ilu}Nuzku šur-[bu-ú il-lit-ti Dûr-ilu^{KI}]* 19. *na-ram ^{ilu}Bîl [ma-li-ki mu-šim* . . . .*]* 20. *suk-kal-lu*[1] *ṣi-[i-ru mu-ut-ta-'-ir]* . . . . 21. *ina šamî-í illûti[^{pl} ki-bit-ka]* . . . . 22. *ina I.ŠAR.RA [šur-ru-ḫat]* . . . . 23. *a-na a-[ṣi-ka*[2] *ú-pak-ku]-* . . . . 24. *ina ba-li-ka [^{ilu}A-nim a-bi]-* . . . . 25. *û ^{ilu}Bîl ma-[li-ku IŠ]* . . . . 26. *ina ba-li-ka*[3] *ul [uš-ti]-* . . . . 27. *ana-ku pulânu apil pulâni ša [ilu-šu pulânu ^{ilu}ištar-šu pulânîtum(tum)]* 28. *as-ḫur-ka iš-i-[ka]* . . . . 29. *[ri]-ša-a*[4] *ri-i-ak-[kil?]* . . . . 30. . . . . *-ḫar ^{ilu}Bîl* . . . . . *-kid-* . . . . 31. . . . . *-ya* . . . . *-ṭir* . . . . 32. *^{ilu}* . . . . *u ^{ilu}šîdu* . . . . 33. *pu-ú u li-ša-[nu?]* . . . . 34. *ana pâni-ka al-* . . . .

---

[1] *A sukkallu.* [2] *A ana aṣî-ka.* [3] *A ina bali-ka.* [4] *A ša-* . . . .

35. *INIM.INIM.MA* [*ŠU IL.LA*] . . . .

36. *šiptu* ^{ilu}*Sin na-*. . . . . 37. *ga-šir ina* . . . .
38. *šar kib-ra-[a-ti]* . . . . 39. *a-ša-rid ilâni*[^{pl} ?]
. . . . 40. *ša nap-ḫar gi-* . . . . 41. *ina*
ba-li-ka . . . . 42. *ba-ra-a-*. . . . . 43. *a-šir*
at-ta . . . . 44. *ma-ak-tum ša* . . . . 45. *di-*
in kit-ti . . . . 46. *ša-ap-la* . . . . 47. *la*
a-lit-tum ina . . . . 48. *šá iš-ti-ni-'* . . . .
49. *ša ka-a-ša'* . . . . 50. . . . . 51. . . . . .
-li-'[1]*-* . . . . *-ti* 52. *ša is-saḫ-ru* . . . .*-i-ma*
53. *ša sa-ap-ḫi* . . . .*-nun-šu* 54. *ša ár-na tuk-*. . . .
. . . . . .*-nam* 55. *ša ilu-šu iz-*. . . . . *itti-*. . . . .
-sal-lam 56. *i-nu-ma* . . . .*-mu* . . . .*-ya*
57. ^{ilu}*ištar* . . . .*-sa* . . . . *pî-ya* 58. *ul-tu*
. . . .*-at ni-ir-tú* . . . . *ili-ya* 59. *ṣi-ṣi-ti ḫu-*
. . . .*-ú bu-tuḳ-[ḳu ?]* . . . .*-ša-nu-nim-ma*
60. *i-ta-šu-uš-*. . . . .*-bi* . . . . *napištim(tim)* 61. *al-*
si-ka bi-lum . . . .^{pl} 62. *ki-niš nap-lis-an-ni-ma* . . .
. . . . 63. *ta-ai-ra-ta* ^{ilu}*Sin* . . . . 64. *i-ṭi-ra-ta*
^{ilu}*Sin* . . . . 65. *gam-ma-la-ta* ^{ilu}*Sin ina ilâni*^{pl} . . .
. . . . 66. *ša la ma-ši-i* ^{ilu}*Sin la* . . . . 67. *ili*
u iš-ta-ri zi-nu-ti . . . . 68. *i-lut-ka rabîta(ta) ki-i-*. . .
. . . .*-ma-am-ma* 69. *lib-bi-ka lu-ša-pi [dá-lí-lí]-ka lud-lul*

70. *INIM.INIM.MA* *ŠU IL.LA* ^{ilu}*Sin.KAN*

71. *šiptu* ^{ilu}*Ba'u*[2] *bîltu šur-bu-tum ummu ri-mi-[ni-tum*[3] *a]-ši-bat šamî-i illûti*^{pl}
72. *al-si-ki bîlti-yà i-ziz-zi-[im-ma ši-mí]-i*[4] *ya-a-ti*
73. *iš-i-ki as-ḫur-ki*[5] *kîma ulinnu [ili-yà u* ^{ilu}*ištari]-yà ulinnu-ki aṣ-bat*
74. *áš-šum di-in*[6] *da-a-[ni]* *purus* *parâsi(si)*[7]
75. *áš-šum bul-lu-ṭu u šul-[lu-mu] ba-šú-ú*[8] *itti-ki*
76. *áš-šum i-ṭi-ra ga-ma-[la u] šú-zu-ba ti-di-i*[9]

[1] Possibly *im*. [2] *BE* ^{ilu}*Bi-lit ili*. [3] *CE ri-mi-ni-tum*. [4] *CE ši-mi-i*. [5] *B asḫur-ki*. [6] *B di-ni*. [7] *D [pa]-ra-su*. [8] *CE bašû-u*. [9] For l. 76 *B* reads *aš-šum itîrâ gamâla* . . . ., *C* . . . . *[gamâla] ti-*. . . . ., *E* . . . . *[gamâla] ti-di-i*.

77. ^{ilu}*Bau*[1] *bîltu šur-[bu-tum]*[2] *ummu ri-mi-ni-tum*[3]

Rev.

78. *[ina ma-'-du]-ti kakkabâni*^{pl}[4] *šá-[ma-mi]*[5]
79. [6]. . . . . *as-ḫur-ki*[7] *ip-ša-ki [uzna*^{du}*-ai]*
80. *upuntu muḫ]-ri-in-ni-ma li-ki-í*[8] *un-[ni-ni-ya]*
81. *[lu-uš-pur-ki] ana ili-yà zi-ni-i* ^{ilu}*[ištari-yà zi-ni-ti]*
82. *[ana ilu ali-yà ša] šab-su-ma gám-lu*[9] *[itti-ya]*[10]
83. [11]. . . . . *da-ta-*. . . . .
84. . . . . *a-ta-*. . . . .
85. ^{ilu}*Bau*[12] *bîltu šur-bu-tum*[13] *ina a-mat ki-bi-ti-ki [ṣir-ti ša ina I.KUR* . . . .*]*
86. *û an-ni-ki ki-nim*[14] *ša [úl inû-ú]*
87. *ili-yà šab-su li-tu-ra* ^{ilu}*ištari-yà zi-ni-tum* . . . .
88. *ilu ali-yà ša šab-su-ma gám-lu [libbu-šu itti-ya]*
89. *ša i-zi-za li-nu-ḫa ša i-gu-ga* . . . .
90. ^{ilu}*Bau*[12] *bîltu šur-bu-tum ṣa-bi-ta-at a-*. . . . .
91. *ana*[15] ^{ilu}*Marduk šar ilâni*^{pl} *bîlu ri-mi-ni-ya pu-*. . . . .
92. *ṣu-lul-ki rap-šú*[16] *ta-ai-ra-tu-ki kab-[ta?]* . . . .
93. *gi-mil dum-ki u*[17] *ba-lá-ṭi íli-*. . . . .
94. *lib-bi-ki lu-ša-pi dá-li-[li-ki lud-lul]*

---

95. *INIM.INIM.MA ŠU IL.LA* ^{ilu}*Bau.KAN DU.DU [BI]* . . . . .
96. *KAS.SAG tanáki(ki) šiptu* III *šanîtu munu-ma* . . . .

---

97. *šiptu šur-bu-ú git-ma-[lu a-bi-rum* ^{ilu}*Marduk]*[18] . . . .
98. . . . . . *id-diš-šú-ú pi-tu-*. . . . .
99. . . . . . *muš-ti-šir* ^{am}*[mîtu u* ^{am}*balṭu]* . . . .
100. . . . . *nu-úr šamî-í [u irṣitim(tim?)]* . . . .
101. . . . .*-tú-ki* . . . .
102. . . . . ^{ilu}*Marduk [bîlu]* . . . .
103. . . . .*-ka* . . . .

---

[1] *B* ^{ilu}*bi-lit ili.* [2] *B ša-ku-[tum], D [ša]-ku-tum, E ša-[ku-tum].* [3] *D um-mu ri-mi-ni-tum.* [4] *B kakkab.* [5] *BDE ša-ma-mi.* [6] For the commencement of this line *B* reads: *bîltu ka-*. . . . . [7] *E* . . . . .*-kid?-ki.* [8] *E liki-i.* [9] *B gàm-[lu], E gàm-lu.* [10] *E itti-yà.* [11] L. 83 f. are omitted by *DE* and probably by *B*; in their place *D* reads *[ina? bi]-ri u šutti it-ta-na-aš-*. . . . ., *E* . . . . *šutti it-ta-na-aš-ka-nam-ma*; before l. 85 *B* inserts the eclipse-formula *ina lumun* ^{ilu}*atalî etc.* in three lines, which *E* introduces with the line *[ana-ku pulânu apil pulâni ša] ilu-šu pulânu* ^{ilu}*ištar-šu pulânîtum(tum).* [12] *B* ^{ilu}*bi-lit ili.* [13] *D šur-bu-tú.* [14] *D ki-ni.* [15] *B a-na.* [16] *B rap-šu.* [17] *B û.* [18] The bracketed portions of ll. 97—102 have been restored from No. 10, ll. 7—10.

104. . . . . *-bi-ti* . . . .
105. . . . .
106. . . . . *[balâṭu . . . . .-li]*
107. . . . . *[šamî-í tu-pat-ti]*
108. . . . . *-na-di-[. . . . . ta-šak-kan nu-ú-ru]*
109. . . . . . *-ar-ma . . . . .[. . . . . -ta-a ta-ša-as-si]*
110. . . . . . *-líp immiru ta-[ša-ṭar šîru]*
111. *daiân ilâni*^{pl} *bîl [* ^{ilu}*Igigi]*
112. ^{ilu}*Šamaš bîl ši-mat mâti*[1] *[. . . . .* ^{išu}*uṣurâti*^{pl} *at-ta-ma]*
113. [2]*šim-ti ši-im a-lak-[ti du-um-mi-iḳ]*
114. *li-ši-ra i-da-[tu-ú-a]*
115. *lid-mí-ḳa šunât*^{pl}*-[ú-a]*
116. *šuttu aṭ-ṭu-la ana damiḳti(ti) [šuk-na]*
117. *i-ša-riš lul-lik tap-pi-í [. . . . . .šú-tú]*
118. *ša ŭ-mi-yà lu-u [damiḳti(ti)*[3]*]*
119. *šú-ut-li-ma-am-ma ka-* . . . .
120. *ina ṣil-lu u ma-gir* . . . .
121. [4]*[ilu ul-ṣi] u ri-ša-a-ti lu-* . . . .
122. *[ilu ša la sâlimu li-iz]-ziz ina imni-yà* ^{ilu}*atalû* . . . .
123. *lit-tal-* . . . . . *ili-yà sal-li-* . . . .
124. *ai ip-[par-ki] râbiṣu šul-[mu]* . . . .
125. *li-ta-mi-ka* ^{ilu}*BU* . . . .
126. ^{ilu}*Ai ḫi-ir-tu na-[ram]-* . . . .
127. ^{ilu}*Šamaš a-ša-rid ilâni*^{pl} . . . .
128. *šamû-ú ḫidûtu-ka [irṣitim(tim) li-]* . . . .
129. *ilâni*^{pl} *ša kiš-ša-ti [lik-ru-bu-ka]*
130. *ilâni*^{pl} *rabûti*^{pl} *lib-[ba-ka li-ṭib-bu]*

---

131. *INIM.INIM.MA ŠU IL.[LA]* . . . .
132. *šiptu ilu sú-pu-ú* . . . .
133. *ikal* $^{m\,ilu}$*Aššur-bân-apli etc.*

It will be seen from the registration number (K 2106 + K 2384 + K 3605 + K 3393 + K 6340 + K 8983 + K 9576

[1] *F bîl šimâti*^{pl}. [2] After l. 112 *F* inserts *ana-ku pulânu apil pulâni ša ilu-šu pulânu* ^{ilu}*ištar-šu pulânîtum(tum)*, which is followed by the eclipse-formula *ina lumun* ^{ilu}*atalî etc.* in three lines. [3] The word *damiḳti* has been restored from No. 10, l. 19. [4] The bracketed portions of ll. 121f, 124, 126, 128 have been restored from No. 10, ll. 20–24.

+ K 9688 + K 11589 + K 12911 + K 13792 + K 13800) that No. 6 is built up of twelve comparatively small fragments of the K. Collection. Guided by the style of the composition and the character of the writing I have gradually collected and joined together these fragments to form the present text. Restorations also have been made from duplicates, so that even in its present somewhat imperfect state, the text furnishes a good idea of the original size of most of the tablets that are here published (*cf. Introduction*). The tablet contains five prayers addressed respectively to *Anu*, *Nuzku*, *Sin*, *Ba'u* and probably *Šamaš*, though in the first, second and fifth prayer the name of the god is missing from the colophon-line with which each concludes. Of the prayer to *Anu* (*a*) only the beginnings of the lines remain, from ll. 1—7 of which we gather that the god was invoked as: "Mighty lord . . . . ., O *Anu*, mighty lord . . . . ., God of the sky . . . . ., O *Anu*, god of the sky . . . . ., Loosener of the day . . . . ., O *Anu*, loosener of the day . . . . ., Interpreter of dreams . . . . .!" The second prayer (*b*) to the god *Nuzku* commences: "O *Nuzku*, mighty one, offspring of *Dûrilu*, The darling of *Bîl* the prince, the director of . . . . ., The exalted messenger, who ruleth . . . . ., In the bright heavens is thy command . . . . ., In *Išara* thou makest bright . . . . .!" The remainder of this prayer and the greater part of that to *Sin*, the Moon-god (*c*) which follows it, are too broken for translation; in the latter however ll. 61—65 read: "I have called upon thee, O lord . . . . ., Truly pity me and . . . . ., Thou art pitiful, O *Sin* . . . . ., Thou art a protector, O *Sin* . . . . ., Thou art a benefactor, O *Sin*, among the gods . . . . .!" The prayer to *Ba'u* (*d*), which stands fourth on the tablet and is to some extent complete, is a parallel text, though not a duplicate, to the prayer addressed to the same goddess on the Reverse of No. 4, as will be seen from the following translation.

Translation.

71. O *Ba'u*, mighty lady, merciful mother, that dwellest in the bright heavens,
72. I beseech thee, O lady, stand and hearken unto me!
73. I have sought thee, I have turned to thee, like the *ulinnu* of my god and of my goddess thy *ulinnu* have I grasped,

74. Since to give judgement, to make a decision,
75. To raise to life and to give prosperity rests with thee,
76. Since thou knowest to protect, to benefit and save!
77. O *Ba'u*, mighty lady, merciful mother,
78. Among the multitude of the stars of heaven,
79. [O lady,] I have turned to thee, ...
80. The *upuntu*-plant accept and take away my sighing!
81. Let me send thee unto my angry god, unto my goddess who is angry,
82. Unto the god of my city who is wroth and is enraged with me!
83. . . . . 84. . . . .
85. O *Ba'u*, mighty lady at the word of thy exalted command which . . . . . in *Ikur*,
86. And thy sure mercy which changeth not,
87. Let my wrathful god return, let my angry goddess . . . . .,
88. Let the god of my city (return) who is wroth and whose heart is enraged with me!
89. Let him that is incensed be pacified, let him that is enraged . . . . .!
90. O *Ba'u*, mighty lady, that dost hold . . . . .,
91. Unto *Marduk*, king of the gods, my merciful lord . . . . .,
92. Broad is thy protection, mighty is thy compassion . . . . .!
93. The gift of favour and life upon [me bestow],
94. That I may praise thy greatness, that I may bow in humility before thee!

After a colophon of two lines in which the *KAS.SAG* (*cf. supra*, p. 20 f.) is appointed to be offered and the incantation to be recited three times, there follows (*e*) the last prayer on the tablet. This is in all probability addressed to the Sun-god, though the prayer appears to commence with an invocation to *Marduk* beginning: "O mighty, perfect, powerful *Marduk* . . . . .! Who art unique, who openest . . . . ., The ruler of the dead and of the living . . . . ., ... the Light of heaven and earth!" The next ten lines are very broken, after which the tablet continues:—

111. O judge of the gods, lord of the *Igigi*,
112. O *Šamaš*, lord of the land's destiny, the . . . . . of charms art thou!

113. Decree my destiny, make pleasant my path!
114. Let my powers be propitious!
115. Let my dreams be favourable!
116. The dream I have beheld do thou establish favourably!

In these lines the occasion of the prayer is stated to have been a dream, the significance of which was evidently ambiguous, for the suppliant prays that its result may be favourable. The conclusion of the prayer, which has been already referred to (*cf. supra*, p. 24) as one that is not uncommon, runs: "O *Šamaš*, prince of the gods! . . . . . May heaven be thy joy, may the earth . . . . .! May the gods of the world bless thee! May the mighty gods benefit thy heart!" The catch-line commences: "O mighty god!"

18. For the city *Dûrilu cf.* Delitzsch, *Paradies*, p. 230. The sign-group *DUR.AN.KI* is, however, also explained by Jensen (*Kosmologie*, p. 485, n. 1) as a cosmic locality, "the place of the junction of heaven and earth".

23. The restoration *a-na a-[ṣi-ka]* may be regarded as almost certain, supported as it is both by the traces on the tablet and by the variant reading *ana* *-ka* of the duplicate A.

71. Before the incantation commencing with this line the duplicate D appears to have contained some directions for ceremonies, of which however only traces of three characters remain. *Cf.* pl. 12, n. 1.

73. In line 74 we should have expected some expression similar to *bašû ittiki* or *tîdî* for the two infinitives to depend on. Taking the text as it stands we must assume that the second *aššum* does not commence a fresh clause, but is merely a repetition of the first, the infinitives in l. 74 depending, like those in the following line, on *bašû ittika*. These three lines, describing the judicial but at the same time compassionate character of the goddess, give the reason for the appeal made in l. 73.

79. On the probable restoration of the beginning of this line *cf. infra sub* No. 7, l. 16. For *as-ḫur-ki* the duplicate E evidently reads some other verb, the traces of which may be taken to represent either . . . . . *-ḳid-ki*, or possibly . . . . *-dan-ki*; the reading of D, so far as it goes, agrees with that of E.

80. Though the meaning is clear the construction of *upuntu muḫ-ri-in-ni-ma* is unusual. While the suffix forms the direct object, *upuntu* must also be regarded as governed by the verb: "Accept me in respect of the *upuntu*", *i. e.* "accept my offering of the *upuntu*-plant". For a discussion of the meaning of *upuntu cf.* Jensen, *ZK.* II, p. 31 f., where he shows that it is a plant capable of being used for food, that it is not very tall, that it is often employed in religious ceremonies and that its seeds are planted and not merely sown. Halévy's comparison of the word with the Talmudic אפון "pea" he thinks not unlikely.

97. The bracketed portions of ll. 97—102, 121 f., 124, 126, 128 and of the word *[damikti](ti)* in l. 118 have been restored from No. 10, ll. 7—24. I have not throughout attempted a restoration of each of these incantations from the other, as they are too broken to admit of such a course, but in plates 13, 14 and 21 I have given each text as it occurs on the tablet and in my transliteration have restored those passages only about which there appears to be no doubt.

No. 7.

Transliteration.

1\. . . . . 2. *nar-bi-ka* . . . . 3. *I.SAG.ILA*
ḫidûtu-. . . . . 4. *I.ZID.DA* . . . . 5. *ilâni*^{pl}
ša šamî-i . . . . 6. *ilâni*^{pl} *rabûti*^{pl} . . . .
7\. ^{ilu}*A-nim* ^{ilu}*Bîl* . . . .

8\. *INIM.INIM.MA* *ŠU [IL.LA]* . . . .

9\. *šiptu* ^{ilu}*Bi-lit ili*[1] *bîltu šur-[bu-tum ummu ri-mi-ni-tum*[2] *a-ši-bat šamî-i illûti*^{pl}*]*
10\. *al-si-ki bîlti-yà i-ziz-zi-[im-ma* *ši-mi-i*[3] *ya-a-ti]*
11\. *is-i-ki asḫur-ki*[4] *kîma ulinnu [ili-yà u* ^{ilu}*ištari-yà ulinnu-ki aṣ-bat]*
12\. *às-šum di-ni*[5] *da-a-ni* *[purus parâsi(si)*[6]*]*

---

[1] *A* ^{ilu}*Ba'u.* [2] *A ri-mi-[ni-tum].* [3] *A [ši-mi]-i.* [4] *A as-ḫur-ki.* [5] *A di-in.* [6] *B [pa]-ra-su.*

13. *áš-šum bul-lu-ṭu*[1] *šul-lu-[mu bašû-u*[2] *itti-ki]*
14. *áš-šum iṭîra gamâla [ti-di-i]*
15. *^{ilu}Bí-lit ili*[4] *bîltu ša-ḳu-[tum*[5] *ummu ri-mi-ni-tum]*[6]
16. *ina ma-'-du-ti kakkab*[7] *ša-ma-mi*[8] *bîltu ka-. . . . .*
-ḳid?-ki[9] *ip-ša-ki uznâ^{du}-ai*
17. *upuntu muḫ-ri-in-ni-ma [liḳî-i*[10] *un-ni-ni-ya]*
18. *lu-uš-pur-ki ana ili-yà zi-ni-[i ^{ilu}ištari-yà zi-ni-ti]*
19. *ana ilu ali-yà ša šab-su-ma gàm-[lu*[11] *itti-yà*[12] [13] *ina? bi-ri u šutti it-ta-na-aš-ka-nam-ma]*
20. [14]*ina lumun ^{ilu}atalî ^{ilu}Sin ša [ina arḫi pulâni ûmi pulâni išakna(na)]*
21. *lumun idâti[^{pl} ITI.MIŠ limnîti^{pl} lâ ṭâbâti^{pl}]*
22. *ša ina ikalli-[yà u mâti-yà ibašâ-a]*
23. *^{ilu}Bí-lit ili*[15] *bîltu šur-[bu-tum*[16] *ina a-mat ki-bi-ti-ki ṣir-ti ša ina I.KUR . . . .]*
24. *û an-ni-ki [ki-nim*[17] *ša úl inû-ú]*
25. *[ili]-yà šab-su li-[tu-ra ^{ilu}ištari-yà zi-ni-tum] . . . .*
26. *ilu ali-yà ša šab-su-[ma gám-lu libbu-šu itti-ya]*
27. *ša i-zi-za li-nu-[ḫa ša i-gu-ga] . . . .*
28. *^{ilu}Bí-lit ili*[18] *bîltu šur-[bu-tum ṣa-bi-ta-at a]- . . . .*
29. *a-na*[19] *^{ilu}Marduk šar ilâni^{pl} bîlu [ri-mi-ni-ya pu]- . . . . .*
30. *ṣu-lul-ki rap-šu*[20] *ta-[ai-ra-tu-ki kab-ta?] . . . .*
31. *gi-mil dum-ki û*[21] *[ba-lá-ṭi ili]- . . . .*
32. *nar-bi-ki lu-ša-[pi dá-li-li-ki lud-lul]*

---

33. *INIM.INIM.MA [ŠU IL.LA] . . . .*

Rev.

34. *šiptu ^{kakkab}Išḫara . . . .*
35. *il-tum rim-ni-[tum] . . . .*
36. *ší-mat ik-ri-bi . . . .*

[1] *A* here inserts the copula *u*. [2] *AD ba-šú-ú*. [3] For l. 14 *A* reads *áš-šum i-ṭi-ra ga-ma- . . . . šú-zu-ba ti-di-i, D . . . . -ma-la u šú-zu-ba ti-di-i*. [4] *A ^{ilu}Ba'u*. [5] *A šur-[bu-tum]*. [6] *D um-mu ri-mi-ni-tum*. [7] *AE kakkabâni^{pl}*. [8] *A šá-[ma-mi]*. [9] *A as-ḫur-ki*. [10] *A li-ki-i; D [li]-ki-[i]*. [11] *A gám-lu*. [12] *D [itti]-ya*. [13] The latter half of the line from this point is omitted by *A*, and ll. 20—22 by *AD*; in their place *A* contains the two lines . . . . *da-ta- . . . .*, and . . . . *a-ta- . . . .* [14] Before l. 20 *E* inserts the line *[ana-ku pulânu apil pulâni ša] ilu-šu pulânu ^{ilu}ištar-šu pulânitum(tum)*. [15] *AD [^{ilu}]Ba'u*. [16] *D šur-bu-tú*. [17] *D ki-ni*. [18] *A ^{ilu}Ba'u*. [19] *A ana*. [20] *A rap-šú*. [21] *A u*.

37. *ḳa-i-šat napišti[(ti)]* . . . .
38. *ina ú-mi an-ni-i* . . . .
39. *ilu I.ŠUM* . . . .
40. *mu-ḳil-lu ad-mi-ki* . . . .
41. *i-zi-za-ma da-* . . . .
42. *li-iz-zi-zu* . . . .
43. *ilu ištarâti pl* . . . .
44. *ina ki-bit-ti-* . . . .
45. *ši-mu-ú ik-ri-bi* . . . .
46. *ú at-tu-nu ki-niš naplisû-nin-ni* . . . .
47. *ma-'-du ar-nu ya* . . . .
48. *ma-ḫar-ku-nu ar-ni lip-pa-ṭir* . . . .
49. *di-ni di-na purussa-ai [purusi(ši)]*
50. *šá a-na ya-ši kiš-pi* . . . .
51. *up-ša-ši-i limutti(ti) ša amîlûti pl ša* . . . .
52. *ú mimma šum-šu šá a-na ma-ka-li-i* . . . .
53. *ša murṣu lâ ṭâbtu(tú) DI.PAL.A KA.LU.BI.[DA* . . . . .
54. *ZI.TAR.RU.DA kâlu ša is-ḫu-ra* . . . .
55. *šá mimma šumšu u-ši-* . . . .
56. *ina ki-bit-[ku?-nu] kit-ti ša* . . . .
57. *up-ša-šú* . . . . *[ai] iṭiḫû-ni ai ik-ru-bu-ni*
58. *ana ili i-[pi-ši?] i-piš-ti li-* . . . .
59. *ilu Iš-ḫa-ra ummu rim-ni-tum šá nišî pl* . . . .
60. *ina lumun ilu atalî ilu Sin ša ina arḫi pulâni ûmi pulâni [išakna(na)]*
61. *lumun idâti pl ITI.MIŠ limnîti pl lâ ṭâbâti pl ša ina ikalli-yà u [mâti-yà ibašâ-a]*
62. *[a]-na šú-[a]-ti asḫur-ki al-si-ki* . . . .
63. . . . . *-ša?* . . . .

Parts of three incantations have been preserved by No. 7 (K 3330 + Sm. 394 + 81—2—4, 244). Of the first incantation only the beginning of the last few lines remain. The second has been restored from duplicates, so that it presents a text from which very little is now missing. It is addressed to a goddess whom it hails under the title of *Bîlit ili*, and is intended not for general recitation but for use only after a lunar eclipse, the usual eclipse-formula being introduced before l. 23. With these two exceptions the composition closely follows the hymn to the goddess *Ba'u*, in No. 6, for a translation of which *cf. supra*, p. 35 f. On the Reverse is a prayer to the astral deity *Išḫara* (in l. 34 she is addressed by her title of *kakkab Akrabu*, *cf.* JENSEN, *Kosmologie* p. 71), which like the second prayer on the tablet, contains the eclipse-formula (*cf.* l. 60 f.). The incantation commences: "O *Akrabu* . . . . ., Merciful goddess . . . . ., Who heareth supplication . . . . ., Who bestoweth life . . . . .!" The god *Išum* is next invoked, and he also is described as "the hearer of supplication". In ll. 46—48 both deities are addressed in a petition for mercy and the removal of sin ("Truly pity me . . . . .! Great is my sin . . . . .! Before you let my sin be loosened!") From l. 49 onwards the suppliant addresses himself solely to the goddess. After petitioning for judgement he comes to the main object of his prayer, which is to seek deliverance from sorcery and the spells which men may weave against him.

14. In both the duplicates C and E before *tidî*, the last word in the line, there is a blank space preceded by traces of the character . The third sign in the line is also , which = *iṭîra* (*cf.* the dupl. A, and BRÜNNOW, *List*, no. 7739). Since it is improbable that  would be used by itself twice in the same line as an ideogram for different words, the two following signs  must be regarded as a compound ideogram; and, unless the text of C and E is wholly different from that of A (an unlikely supposition in view of their close resemblance in the preceding lines), we must conclude that  = the inf. *gamâla* of A, while the inf. *šûzubu* is omitted altogether. It is already known that  (= *ŠU.GAR*) = *gamâlu* (*cf.* BRÜNNOW, *List*, no. 7250), so that  (= *ŠU.KAR*) would represent a difference in writing the same word.

16. The second half of this line, commencing *bîltu ka-*. . . . ., is probably to be restored *bîltu ka-[a-ši]* . . . . . The verb that follows in A is *as-ḫur-ki*, so that the line in that duplicate runs: "O lady! to thee have I turned etc." The text however is probably to be restored according to E, which it follows in many places in preference to the text of A (*cf.* ll. 9, 15 f., 19—22). For the reading of E *cf. supra* p. 36.

19. *[ina? bi]-ri u šutti it-ta-na-aš-ka-nam-ma* may possibly have been expanded to form l. 83 f. of A.

26. *gám-lu* has been restored from A, the only duplicate that covers that portion of the text. It is possible that the tablet read *gàm-lu* as in l. 19.

53 f. For a discussion of the phrases occurring in these two lines, *cf. infra sub* No. 12, l. 1.

62. This line has been restored from K 9909, a fragment of a prayer, which is also addressed to the goddess *Išḫara* and from l. 59 onwards forms a closely parallel text (*see* below).

No. 8.

Transliteration.

1. . . . . . . *ta-a-bu su-up-pu-ú-ki ki-i ki-ru-ub niš šumi-ki*
2. *[nap]-lu-us-ki taš-mu-ú ki-bit-ki nu-ú-ra*
3. *rîmi-nin-ni-ma* *ilu* *Iš-tar ki-bi-i na-ḫa-ši*
4. *ki-niš nap-li-si-in-ni-ma li-ki-i un-ni-ni-ya*
5. *ir-di UZ-ki iš-di-ḫu li-*. . . . .
6. *šar?-ṭa-a-ki a-ḫu-zu lu-bi-il ṭu-ub libbi-*. . . . .
7. *ú-bil ap-ša-na-ki pa-ša-ḫa šuk-*. . . . .
8. *ú-ki-ʾ kakkadu-ki li-ši-ra sa-li-mu*
9. *aṣ-ṣur ša-ru-ra-ki lu-ú taš-mu-ú ù ma-ga-ru*
10. *iš-ti-ʾ-ú nam-[ri]-ir-ri-ki lim-mi-ru zi-mu-ú-a*
11. *as-ḫur bi-lut-ki [lu]-ú balâṭu ù šul-mu*
12. *lu tas-lim* *ilu* *šêdu damiktu ša pa-ni-ki* ✢ *ša ár-ki-ki a-li-kăt* *ilu* *lamassu lu tas-lim*
13. *ša im-nu-uk-ki miš-ra-a lu-uṣ-ṣip dum-ka lu-uk-šú-da ša šú-mi-lu-[uk-ki]*
14. *ki - bi - ma liš - ši - mi zik - ri*
15. *a-mat a-kab-bu-ú ki-ma a-kab-bu-ú lu-ú ma-ag-rat*
16. *ina ṭu-ub šîri u ḫu-ud lìb-bi i-tar-ri-in-ni ŭ-mi-šam*
17. *ûmî**pl**-ya ur-ri-ki ba-la-ṭa šur-ki* ✢ *lu-úb-lut lu-uš-lim-ma lu-uš-tam-mar ilu-[ut-ki]*
18. *i-ma ú-ṣa-am-ma-ru lu-uk-šú-ud* ✢ *šamû-ú ḫidûtu-ki apsû li-riš-[ki]*

19. *ilâni^{pl} ša kiš-ša-ti lik-ru-bu-ki* ⁎ *ilâni^{pl} rabûti^{pl} lib-ba-ki li-ṭib[-bu]*

---

20. *INIM.INIM.MA ŠU IL.LA ^{ilu}Ištar.KAN ana pân ^{ilu}Ištar ŠA.NA burâši [tašakan(an)]*
21. *mi-iḫ-ḫa tanaki(ki)-ma* ŠU IL.LA III *šanîtu [ipuš(uš)]*

---

22. *šiptu at-tu-nu kakkabâni šar-ḫu-tum ša mu-* . . . .
23. *nam-ru-ti ša ilâni^{pl} rabûti^{pl}* . . . . :
24. *a-na ḫul-lu-ḳu lim-nu-ti ib-nu-ku-nu-ši ^{ilu}A-nim* ⁎ *ina ša-ma-mi* . . . .
25. . . . . *-ki li-ṭib ^{abnu}ṢIR.GAR.RA-ki su-* . . . .
26. . . . . *-su-ti ša bi-li-i MU-ú* . . . .
27. . . . . *-ḫu ṣîru da-li-ḫu* . . . .
28. . . . .

No. 8 is formed from two fragments of the K. Collection (K 2396 + K 3893) which I have joined. Only one side of the tablet has been preserved, and this is evidently the Reverse, as its beginning is too abrupt to form the commencement of an incantation. The first nineteen lines are addressed to the goddess *Ištar*, and only the beginning of the incantation is missing, in which the goddess is addressed by name, and which apparently concluded the Obverse of the tablet. Ll. 6—11 are regularly divided, the first half of each stating some attention or observance on the part of the suppliant towards his goddess, which balances and justifies the petitions contained in the second half of the line. The *colossi* whose favour is invoked in ll. 12 and 13 evidently surround the goddess on all sides and possibly flanked the entrances to her shrine. Then follow various petitions couched in general terms for prosperity, life and length of days, and the prayer concludes with a formula of benediction.

Translation.

1. . . . . . good is thy supplication when the spirit(?) of thy name is propitious!
2. Thy regard is prosperity, thy command is light!
3. Have mercy on me, O *Ištar*! Command abundance!
4. Truly pity me and take away my sighing! 5. . . . .
6. Thy . . . . . have I held: let me bring joy of heart!

7. I have borne thy yoke: do thou give consolation!
8. I have . . . . . thy head: let me enjoy success and favour!
9. I have protected thy splendour: let there be good fortune and prosperity!
10. I have sought thy light: let my brightness shine!
11. I have turned towards thy power: let there be life and peace!
12. Propitious be the favourable *šêdu* who is before thee: may the *lamassu* that goeth behind thee be propitious!
13. That which is on thy right hand increase good fortune: that which is on thy left hand attain favour!
14. Speak and let the word be heard!
15. Let the word I speak, when I speak, be propitious!
16. Let health of body and joy of heart be my daily portion!
17. My days prolong, life bestow: let me live, let me be perfect, let me behold thy divinity!
18. When I plan, let me attain (my purpose): Heaven be thy joy, may the Abyss hail thee!
19. May the gods of the world be favourable to thee: may the great gods delight thy heart!

After the colophon in l. 20 f., prescribing an offering of incense and a drink-offering to be set before *Ištar* and the ceremony of raising the hand to be three times performed (*cf. supra* p. 13 f.), there follows the commencement of a hymn to certain stars, beginning: "Ye brilliant stars, who . . . . .! 2. Ye bright ones, whom the great gods . . . . .! 3. To destroy evil did *Anu* create you!"

17 f. The ends of these lines have been restored according to No. 9, ll. 11, 24, *etc.*

21. In this line *mi-iḫ-ḫa* takes the place of the common ideogram *KAŠ.SAG* (*cf. supra* p. 21). The *miḫḫu* itself is not of uncommon occurrence in directions for ceremonies, *cf.* K 6209, l. 9 where an offering of the *mi-iḫ-ḫa* is prescribed, the phrase *[KAŠ].SAG tanaki(ki)-ma* occurring four lines above, K 6230 Col. IV, l. 3 *[mi]-iḫ-ḫa illa*, l. 7 *mi-iḫ-ḫi kun-ni*, etc.

No. 9.

Transliteration.

Obv.

1. *[siptu ga - dš - ru šú - pú - ú í - ziz ^{ilu}Aššur]*
2. *[rubû ti-iz-ḳá-ru bu-kur ^{ilu}NU.DIM.MUD]*
3. *[^{ilu}Marduk šal - ba - bu mu - riš I.ṬUR.RA]*
4. *[bîl I.SAG.ILA tukulti(ti) Bâbili^{KI} ra - im I.ZID.DA]*
5. *[mu-šal-lim napišti(ti) a-ša-rid I.MAḪ.TIL.LA mu-diš-šu-u balâṭu]*
6. *ṣu - [lul[1] ma - a - ti ga - mil ni - ši rap - ša - a - ti]*
7. *ušumgal [ka - liš parakkâni^{pl}]*
8. *šumu - ka ka - [liš ina pî niši^{pl} ṭa - a - ab]*
9. *[2] ^{ilu}Marduk bîlu rabû-ú . . . .*
10. *ina ki - bi - ti - ka ṣir - ti [lu - úb - luṭ lu - uš - lim - ma]*
11. *lu - uš - tam - mar [ilu - ut - ka]*
12. *í - ma ú - ṣa - am - ma - ru [lu - uk - šú - ud]*
13. *šú - uš - kin kit - tu [ina pî - yà][3]*
14. *šup - ši - ka damiḳtim(tim) [ina libbi - yà][4]*
15. *ti - i - ru[5] u na - an - za - zu lik - bu - [u damiḳtim(tim)[6]]*
16. *ili - yà li - iz - ziz ina imni - [yà][7]*
17. *^{ilu}ištari - yà li - iz - ziz ina šumîli - [yà][8]*
18. *ili - yà šal - li - mu ina idi - yà[9] lu - u - ka - [ai - an]*
19. *šur - gám - ma[10] ḳa - ba - a ší - ma - a u ma - ga - [ra]*
20. *a-mat a-ḳab-bu-ú ki-ma[11] a-ḳab-bu-ú lu-u ma-ag-[rat]*
21. *^{ilu}Marduk bîlu rabû-ú napištim(tim) ki-[bi][12]*
22. *ba - laṭ napišti(tim) - ya[13] ki - [bi]*
23. *ma - ḫar - ka nam - riš a - dál - lu - ka[14] lu - uš - [bi]*
24. *^{ilu}Bîl urru-ka ^{ilu}I-a li-riš-[ka]*
25. *[ilâni]^{pl} ša kiš - ša - ti lik - ru - bu - [ka]*
26. *[ilâni]^{pl} rabûti^{pl} lib - ba - ka[15] li - ṭib - [bu]*

---

27. *[INIM.INIM].MA ŠU IL.LA ^{ilu}[Marduk.KAN]*

---

[1] *B zu-lul.* [2] *B ^{ilu}Marduk bîlu rabû-ú ina ḳibît-ka ka-bit-ti lu-úb-lut.* [3] *B kit-tú ina pi-ya.* [4] *B damiḳti(ti) ina libbi-ya.* [5] *B ti-ru.* [6] *B damiḳti(ti).* [7] *B ina im-ni-ya.* [8] *B ina šú-mí-li-ya.* [9] *B i-da-ai.* [10] *B šur-gàm-ma.* [11] *B i-ma.* [12] *B rabû napišti(ti) [lu]-u.* [13] *B napišti-ya.* [14] *B a-dal-lu-ka.* [15] *B libba-ka.*

Rev.

28\. . . . . *ṣir-tum ŠA.TAR i-*. . . . .

29\. . . . . *[^{ilu}ištarâti]^{pl} ra-bît ilâni[^{pl}?]*

30\. . . . . *-tum i-til-lit ilâni^{pl} ka-nu-ut I*. . . . .

31\. *[šar]-rat ^{ilu}TUR.DUL.KU šal-ba-bu a-pil ^{ilu}NIN*. . . . . .

32\. *šar-rat I.SAG.ILA ikal ilâni^{pl} ša-du-[ú* . . . .*]*

33\. *bî-lit Bâbili^{KI} ṣu-lul ma-[ta-a-ti]*

34\. *^{ilu}Bî-lit ili šá búl-lu-ṭa*[1] *i-[ram-mu]*

35\. *iṭ-ṭi-rat ina puški u [dannati]*

36\. . . . . . *-ma-li-tu ṣa-bi-ta kâtâ^{du}*[2] *na-[aš-ki]*

37\. *[î]-pi-rat în-šî ša-pi-kăt [zîru]*

38\. *na-ṣi-rat napišti(ti) nadnat(at) [aplu u zîru]*

39\. *[ka]-i-šat balâṭu li-ḳat un-ni-ni ma-[ḫi-rat taṣ-lit]*

40\. *[ba?]-na-at nišî^{pl} gi-mir [nab-ni-ta]*

41\. . . . . . . *ṣi-ta-aš u ši-la-an ba-i-[lat*[3] *^{ilu}Bîl]*

42\. . . . . *ḫi?-iṭ-ṭi UD.DA.GAN ta-bar-ri-[i sa-an-dak?]*

43\. . . . . . . *-pal-ki kit-mu-sa [mûši u im-ma]*

44\. . . . . *-ki iš-tú ma-[*. . . . . *-ut-ki dal-la]*

45\. . . . . *[-at a-bu-ti în-šî]*

46\. . . . . *[ki-bi-i damiḳti(ti)]*

47\. . . . . *-[kir da-ba-bi]*

48\. . . . . *[lu-uk-šú-ud]*

49\. . . . . *-[bil pi-ya]*

50\. . . . . *[damḳûti^{pl}]*

51\. . . . . *[^{pl} ba-ni-ti]*

52\. . . . . *[tî-ni-ši-ti]*

53\. . . . . *[damiḳti(ti)]*

54\. . . . . *[ḳil-la-a-ti]*

55\. . . . . *[-ki šuk-*. . . . .*]*

56\. . . . . *[-tum-*. . . . .*]*

The two fragments K 2558 + K 9152, which I have joined and which form the basis of the text of No. 9, contain portions of two incantations, the first of which has been completed from Col. III, ll. 1—21 of K 2538 *etc.*, part of a composite and chiefly bilingual text (*cf.* IV R², pl. 21*). Ll. 1—12 have been restored from this tablet, which is cited as B, without alteration, but in ll. 13—17 several restorations have been made in accordance

[1] *A ša bul-lu-ṭu.* [2] *A ṣa-bi-ta-at kât.* [3] *B ba-'-lat.*

with other portions of the text (*cf.* also No. 22, ll. 14 ff.) in preference to the corresponding readings of B. The incantation is addressed to *Marduk* and reads as follows.

Translation.

1. O mighty, powerful, strong one of *Aššur*!
2. O noble, exalted, first-born of *Ía*!
3. O *Marduk*, the mighty, who causeth *Ítura* to rejoice!
4. Lord of *Ísagila*, Help of Babylon, Lover of *Ízida*!
5. Preserver of life, Prince of *I.MAḪ.TIL.LA*, Renewer of life!
6. Shadow of the land, Protector of distant peoples!
7. For ever the Sovereign of shrines!
8. For ever is thy name good in the mouth of the peoples!
9. O *Marduk*, mighty lord, ... , .
10. At thy exalted command let me live, let me be perfect and
11. let me behold thy divinity!
12. When I plan, let me attain (my purpose)!
13. Cause righteousness to dwell in my mouth!
14. . . . . . mercy in my heart!
15. Return and be established! May they command mercy!
16. May my god stand at my right hand!
17. May my goddess stand at my left hand!
18. May my god, who is favourable, stand firmly at my side,
19. To give utterance, to command, to hearken and show favour!
20. Let the word I speak, when I speak, be propitious!
21. O *Marduk*, mighty lord, command life!
22. The life of my life do thou command!
23. Before thee brightly have I bowed (?) myself, let me be satisfied!
24. May *Bîl* be thy light, may *Ía* shout with joy unto thee!
25. May the gods of the world be favourable to thee!
26. May the great gods delight thy heart!

The second incantation commences the Reverse of the tablet, and is addressed to a goddess to whom the following titles are ascribed:—

32. Queen of *Isagila* the palace of the gods, the . . . . . mountain!
33. Lady of Babylon, the Shadow of lands!
34. Lady of the gods, who loveth to give life,
35. Who giveth succour in sorrow and distress!

36. The . . . . . one, who holdeth the hands of . . . . .,
37. Who supporteth the weak, who poureth out seed,
38. Who protecteth life, who giveth offspring and seed,
39. Who bestoweth life, who taketh away sighing, who accepteth prayer,
40. Who hath made the peoples, the whole of creation!
41. [Lady?] of the rising and the setting, the mistress of *Bîl*!

1. This prayer is included in the list of incantations K 2832 + K 6680, Col. I, l. 11 (*cf. supra* p. 15).

3. *šal-ba-bu* is explained by Brünnow, *ZA*, IV, p. 242 as = "anger", since in V R, 29, 23 *h* the word is followed by *ni-ʾ-u* which occurs again in V R, 21, 43 *d* apparently as a synonym of *a-ga-gu* (ibid. l. 40 *d*). This explanation does not suit the word in the present passage. But *a-ga-gu*, besides meaning "to be angry", also = "to be strong", while *ni-ʾ-u* in the text cited by Brünnow stands between the words *ti-bu-ú* "to advance, press on" and *ṣal-tum* "battle"; *šal-ba-bu* would therefore appear to be an epithet, or possibly a substantive, denoting the attribute of strength.

9. *B* omits the latter half of the line, reading without break: "O *Marduk*, mighty lord, at thy weighty command let me live!"

15. In *B*, published in IV R², pl. 21*, for *na-an*-[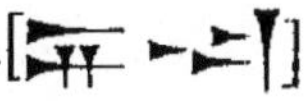] read *na-an*- according to the traces on the tablet.

23. In form *a-tal-lu-ka* might be II 2 from *ilû* "to be high" with the same meaning as II 1; but the prep. *ma-ḫar-ka* would then be out of place. I have therefore taken *adalluka* for *adallaluka*, the prep. merely repeating the suffix of the verb.

24. *li-riš-ka*, *cf.* K 7592 *etc.* Obv. l. 21 (Brünnow, *ZA*, V, p. 77) *li-riš-ka Bâbilu*[KI].

26. In *B* (IV R², pl. 21*) for  read  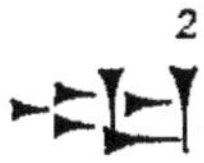. The  is carelessly written on the tablet.

41. This passage proves that *ṣi-i*- is to be read *ṣîtaš*, not *ṣi-i-TAŠ* (= *tan*) = *ṣîtan*, as is suggested by Jensen, *Kosmologie*, p. 14, probably on the authority of Delitzsch, *AL*³, p. 35, no. 311. The forms *ṣîtaš* and *ṣîtan* evidently existed side by side. Jensen (*loc. cit.*) explains the word as meaning "the culmination-point of the Sun".

No. 10.

Transliteration.

Obv.
1. . . . . 2. . . . . ù . . . .
3. . . . . -ri-šu-nu lim-nu-tú li-pat-tir rubû ilâni^{pl} ^{ilu}Marduk . . . . 4. miš-ri-tu-ú-a ili-ya li-ṭi-ba šamû-ú ḫidûtu-ka . . . . 5. ilâni^{pl} rabûti^{pl} . . . . -li-ša(?) li-ṭib-ka . . . .

6. INIM.INIM.MA ŠU IL.LA ^{ilu}Marduk.[KAN?]

7. šiptu šur-bu-ú git-ma-lu a-bi-rum ^{ilu}Marduk . . . . 8. . . . . . muš-ti-šir ^{am}mîtu u ^{am}balṭu . . . . 9. . . . . šamî-i u irṣitim[(tim?)] . . . . 10. . . . . ^{ilu}Marduk bîlu . . . . 11. . . . . rapšâti^{pl} ni- . . . . 12. . . . . -riš a-tu- . . . . 13. . . . . -tu šik-nat . . . . 14. . . . . 15. [daiân][1] ilâni^{pl} bîl [^{ilu}Igigi ^{ilu}Šamaš bîl ši-mat mâti . . . . . ^{iṣu}uṣurâti^{pl} at-ta-ma] 16. [šim]-ti ši-i-mi [a-lak-ti du-um-mi-iḳ] 17. [lid]-mi-ḳa [šunât^{pl}-ú-a li-ši-ra i-da-tu-ú-a] 18. . . . . . MI.MÌ aṭ-ṭu-la [ana damiḳti(ti) šuk-na i-ša-riš lul-lik tap-pi-i . . . . šú-tú] 19. ša ú-mi-yà lu-u damiḳti[(ti) šu-ut-li-ma-am-ma ka- . . . .] 20. ilu ul-ṣi ù ri-ša-a-[ti lu- . . . .] 21. ilu ša la sâlimu li-iz-ziz ina [imni-yà ^{ilu}atalû . . . . lit-tal- . . . . . ili-yà sal-li . . . .] 22. ai ip-par-ki râbiṣu šulmu(mu) [. . . . . li-ta-mi-ka ^{ilu}BU . . . .] 23. ^{ilu}Malik ḫir-tú na-ram [. . . . . ^{ilu}Šamaš a-ša-rid ilâni^{pl} . . . .]
24. šamû-ú ḫidûtu-ka irṣitim(tim) li- . . . .
25. ^{ilu}A-nim ^{ilu}Bîl u ^{ilu}Î-a li- . . . .

26. INIM.INIM.MA ŠU IL.LA ^{ilu}Šamaš.[KAN?]

27. [šiptu?] ilu nam-ri(?) ši-mu u ka-la-ma . . . .

Rev.
28. . . . . -ka . . . . 29. . . . . ṣi-bit-ti-ka . . . . 30. ^{ilu}Šamaš šá(?) ib-ba-nu u nap-ti- . . . . 31. pulânu apil pulâni . . . . -ṭu

---

[1] The bracketed portions of ll. 15—23 have been restored from No. 6, ll. 111—127.

lim-ḫu-ri . . . . 32. . . . . *-la i-di-a šá ilu-šu*

. . . . 33. *ana pânu-ka RA ZIB.BA MI* . . . .

34. *INIM.INIM.MA* . . . . . *A* . . . .

35. *ki-i pî* ^{isu}*[li-ʾ-um ša* . . . . *]*

No. 10 (K 5980 + K 8746) is, according to l. 35, a copy of an older tablet. Unlike the other texts in this volume it is written in the Babylonian character, and, though in ll. 6 and 26 it contains the distinctive colophon-line, in l. 34 it presents a different one to that usually found in this class of texts. It contains parts of three incantations, the first being addressed to *Marduk*, the second to *Šamaš*, and the third to a god whose name has not been preserved. The second of these three incantations is a duplicate of No. 6, ll. 97 ff. and has been partly restored from that text; in many places however the tablets are too broken to admit of restoration from one another (*cf.* p. 37).

7. It is possible that the horizontal wedge which follows  (*cf.* plate 21) is merely a slip made in writing the sign ; in this case read *a-pil* ^{ilu}*Marduk*.

17. The phrases in this line appear to have stood in the reverse order to that in which they occur in No. 6, for it is improbable that *li-ši-ra i-da-tu-ú-a* was included in l. 16, leaving *lid-mi-ḳa šunât*^{pl}*-ú-a* as a line by itself.

18. The traces of the character before 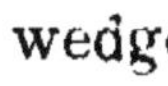 suggest the Bab. form of 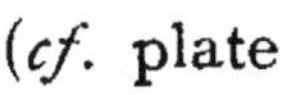, in which case the line would read: *šunâti*^{pl} *aṭ-ṭu-la etc.*

20. This line possibly contained l. 120 f. of No. 6 in the reverse order.

27. Only one sign is missing from the beginning of l. 27. In the transliteration I have restored this as 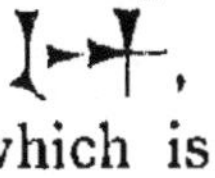, regarding the line as the beginning of the incantation which is continued on the Reverse. If however the line contained directions for ceremonies,  should be restored, giving as the commencement of the line the common ceremonial formula *ipuš an-nam*. The signs  should possibly be read as one character .

31. Possibly for 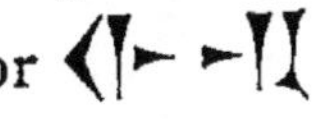 read , *ar-ri* . . . .

Section II.

Prayers addressed to Gods.

This Section, as its title indicates, is composed of tablets containing prayers addressed only to one god. They may indeed take the form of large tablets, each including several incantations interspersed with ceremonies, and resembling in arrangement those published under Section I; they differ from these, however, in that, instead of being addressed to various gods and goddesses, the prayers and ceremonies on each tablet are all addressed to the same god. Nos. 12, 21 and 22 are good examples of this class of text. A second subdivision might be made of smaller tablets such as Nos. 11, 18 and 19, which contain but one prayer in some cases accompanied by a few directions for ceremonies. In addition to their difference in size they are further distinguished from the former class by being inscribed on a somewhat coarser clay. They are moreover written in a slightly larger character and a few have the appearance of being extracts from the larger tablets made possibly for some temporary purpose.

Some of the Nos. included in this Section are merely fragments, of which so little has been preserved that it is impossible to say with certainty to what form of text they originally belonged. It is indeed probable that No. 13 was originally a large tablet similar to No. 12, and that No. 29 is a fragment of one of the smaller extracts, but in many cases there is insufficient data for a final classification. As however each contains a prayer to one god, and there is no definite indication that they included prayers to other deities, they have been classified under the present Section. The tablets containing prayers to the same deity have been placed together; the order in which the groups occur, however, has not been dictated by the relative importance of the deities addressed, but is that which was found most convenient for the arrangement of the plates.

No. 11.

Transliteration.

1. *[šiptu] ḳarrâdu*[1] *ilu Marduk ša i-zis-su*[2] *a-bu-bu*
2. *[nap]-šur-šú a-bu ri-mi-nu-ú*[3]
3. *[ḳa]-bu-ú u la ši-mu-ú it-tal-pan-ni*[4]
4. *[šá]-su-ú u la a-pa-lu*[5] *id-da-ṣa-an-ni*
5. *[am]-ma-ti-ya*[6] *ina líb-bi-ya*[7] *uš-ti-ṣi-[ma]*
6. *[kîma] ši-bi*[8] *uḳ-ta-ad-di-da-an-ni*[9]
7. *[bîlu]*[10] *rabû-ú ilu Marduk ilu ri-mi-nu-ú*[11]
8. *[a-mì-lu]-tum*[12] *ma-la šú-ma na-bat*[13]
9. *[a-na ra]-ma-ni-ša*[14] *man-nu i-lam-mad*
10. *[man-nu la i-ši-it ya]-ú la ú-kál-lil*
11. *[a-lak-ti ilu [man-nu?] i-lam-mad*
12. *[lu-ut-ta-id-ma] [za?]-lip-tú la a-ra-aš-ši*[15]
13. *[áš-rat ba-la]-ṭi lu-uš-ti-ʾ-ma*[16]
14. *[. . . . . ar-ra]-. . . . pu-šú ina ilâni^pl ḳa-bat*
15. . . . . *ilu ana amîlu ba-ba-lu*
16. [17]. . . . . *-ka ana-ku šit-tu-tú lu i-pu-uš*[18]
17. . . . . *-a ša ilu lu i-ti-iḳ*
18. . . . . *miš-šár-riš mudû u lâ mudû u mi-lim-ma*[19]
19. . . . . *-ka ai ik-tar an-ni pu-ṭur-ma*[20] *šír-ti pu-šur*
20. [21]*[i]-ša-ti-ya nu-um-mí-ir*[22]

[1] *A šiptu bît nu-ru ḳar-ra-du.* [2] *A i-zi-su.* [3] *A ri-mi-nu-ú-um.* [4] *A it-tal-pu-nin-ni.* [5] *A a-pa-lum.* [6] *A am-ma-ti-ya.* [7] *A ina libbi-ya.* [8] *A ki-ma ši-bi-im.* [9] *A uḳ-ṭa-ad-di-da-ni.* [10] *A bi-lum.* [11] *A ri-mi-nu-u.* [12] *A a-mi-lu-tu.* [13] *A na-bi-at.* [14] *A [a]-na ra-ma-ni-šá-ma.* [15] *A [a]-ra-ši.* [16] *A . . . . -i(?)-ma.* [17] The fragment K 6537, which exhibits a very similar text to ll. 16 ff., in the Transliteration is cited as *C.* [18] *C [šit]-tu-tú-um* . [19] *C [mudû]-ú u lâ mudû-ú mi-lim-[ma].* [20] *C pu-ṭur.* [21] Ll. 20 and 21 form one line in *C.* [22] *C nu-um-mir.*

21. *[dal]-ḫa-ti-ya zu-uk-ki*
22. [1]. . . . *.-ni abi-yà abu abi-yà ummi-yà ummu ummi-yà*
23. . . . . . . *-ti-yà ni-su-ti-yà*[2] *u sa-la-ti-yà*
24. *[a]-na ra-ma-ni-ya ai itiḫâ-a a-ḫi-tú-ma lil-lik*
25. *iḳ-ṭa-ba-an-ni-ma ili kîma* ^{šam}*KAN.KAL ubbib-an-ni*
26. *a-na ḳâti*^{pl} *damḳâti*^{pl} *ša ili-yà šal-mu ti-pi-iḳ-da-ni*
27. *ina ik-ri-bí taṣ-li-ti u tí-mí-ki da-riš lu-ziz-ku*
28. *ni-šu di-ša-a-tum(?) mâti ša ina áš-ri šak-na-át*
29. *li-na-du-ka an-ni pu-ṭur an-ni pu-šur*
30. *ḳarrâdu* ^{ilu}*Marduk an-ni pu-ṭur an-ni pu-šur*

Rev.

31. *bîltu rabîtum(tum)* ^{ilu}*Irûa an-ni pu-uṭ-ri*
32. *šú-mu ṭa-a-bu* ^{ilu}*Nabû an-ni pu - ṭur*
33. *bîltu rabîtum(tum)* ^{ilu}*Taš-mi-tum an-ni pu-uṭ-ri*
34. *ḳarrâdu* ^{ilu}*Nirgal an-ni pu - ṭur*
35. *ilâni*^{pl} *a-ši-bu* ^{ilu}*A-nim an-ni pu-uṭ-ra*
36. ^{ilu}*NA.GAL.A ša ul-tu ṣi-ḫi-ri-yà i-pu-šu*
37. *su-up-pi-iḫ-ma adî* VII-*ŠU pu - ṭur*
38. *lib - ba - ka ki - ma a - bi a - lid - ya*
39. *ù ummi a-lit-ti-ya a-na aš-ri-šú li-tu-ra*
40. *[ḳăr]-ra-du* ^{ilu}*Marduk dá-lí-li-ka lud-lul*

---

41. *INIM.INIM.MA ŠU IL.LA* ^{ilu}*Marduk.KAN*

---

42. *[AG].AG BÍ ana pân* ^{ilu}*Marduk ŠA.NA burâši tašakan(an)*
43. . . . . *.(an) ŠA šamni niḳû mû dišpu ḫimîtu tašakan(an)*
44. . . . . *zîr* ^{šam}*maštakal ana libbi šamnu? tanadi(di)*
45. . . . . *tašakan(an) mînûtu munu-ma šamnu tapašaš(áš)*

---

46. . . . . *ṣi - i - ru git - ma - lu ši-tar-ḫu*
47. *[ikal* $^{m\,ilu}$*Aššur-ban-apli] šarru etc.*

The incantation contained by No. 11 (K 235 + K 3334) is addressed to the god *Marduk* and is mainly concerned with petitions for the removal of sin. Though some of the lines are broken and portions of the incantation are obscure, the line of thought running through the composition is clear. The

---

[1] L. 22 is expanded into three lines in *C*, which read: . . . . *abi-ya* . . . ., ... *ummi-ya* . . . ., ... *aḫi-ya* . . . . [2] *C* . . . . *.-ti-ya ni-šú-*. . . . .

suppliant commences with an invocation of the god as "the hero *Marduk*, whose anger is the storm-flood", and whose word the disobedient and rebellious cannot disregard. In l. 5 f. he complains that, though *Marduk* has granted him eloquence, he has also afflicted him ("My words in my heart he bringeth forth! Like an old man hath he bowed me down!"). Therefore, after praising the righteous among mankind and stating his own aspirations ("whoever hath learnt the way of god let me praise, wickedness I have not possessed; the sanctuaries of life let me seek!"), he asks in ll. 19 ff. to be purified from his sin and delivered into the favourable hands of his god. Then follows a sort of litany for the removal of his sin, in which he successively addresses *Irûa*, *Nabû*, *Tašmîtu*, *Nirgal*, *Anu etc.* In the last three lines he returns to the god *Marduk*, for the renewal of whose favour he prays in the following terms: "Let thy heart like my father my begetter and the mother who bore me return into its place! O hero *Marduk*, let me bow in humility before thee!"

After the incantation there follow four lines of directions for ceremonies intended to accompany its recitation. "Do the following. Before *Marduk* a *ŠA.NA* of incense shalt thou set, ... a *ŠA* of oil, a drink-offering, water, honey (and) butter shalt thou offer, ... the seed of the *maštakal*-plant in the middle of the oil cast, ..., recite the incantation and anoint with oil." The catch-line commences a prayer to a god whom it hails as "the exalted, the perfect, the powerful!"

1. The duplicate A commences the text with the words *šiptu bît nu-ru* "incantation of the house of light", a title that is omitted in the text itself. For other incantations with this heading *cf.* No. 22, l. 35, K 2587, Obv. l. 30 (IV R 60 [67]), K 54 (Bezold, *Catalogue* p. 14 and Vol. II p. XXIII), K. 157, l. 9 (*ibid.* p. 41), K 2425, l. 1 (*ibid.* p. 442), K 7866, l. 1 (*ibid.* p. 880), K 9004, l. 10, Rm. 581, l. 5, *etc.*

i-zis-su, (var. *i-zi-su*) for *izzît-su*, *izzîtu* being prob. a synonym of *uzzu* and *uzzatu* "anger".

20 f. These lines have been restored from K 3927, Rev. l. 3 f.

27. It is possible that *-ku* in *lu-ziz-ku* = 2 s. m. suffix, *cf.* Delitzsch, *Grammar*, § 56, *Addenda*.

44. The plant ^{šam}*IN.NU.UŠ* is rendered in IV R² 26 l. 36*b* by  i. e. *maš-ta-kal* (not  as IV R¹ and Brünnow, *List*, no. 6049).

46. *ši-tar-ḫu* by *metathesis* for *šitraḫu*.

No. 12.

Transliteration.

1. *inuma lumun murṣi DI.PAL.A ZI.TAR.RU.DA KA.LU.BI.DA dubbubu ana amîlu úl iṭiḫi*

---

2. *DU.DU.BI ina mûši gušuru arḳu mû illu tasalaḫ ana pân* ^{ilu}*Marduk GI.GAB tukân(an)*
3. *suluppu KU.A.TIR tašapak(ak) ŠA šamni niḳû mû dišpu ḫimîtu tašakan(an)*
4. ^{karpatu}*a-da-gùr tukân(an) ši-am na-aḫ-la tašapak ŠA.NA burâši tašakan(an)*
5. *KAS.SAG tanaki(ki) ana pân KIŠDA arî*^{pl} ^{iṣu} *arî*^{pl} ^{iṣu}*MA arî*^{pl} ^{iṣu}*ŠID mà-kan-na*
6. *tanadi(di)* ^{ṣubâtu}*ḫuššû ina ili SIR.AD arka KIŠDA* ^{šam}*GIŠ.ŠAR tanadi(di)*
7. ^{immiru}*niḳi tanaḳi* ^{šîru}*ZAG* ^{šîru}*MI.ḪI u* ^{šîru}*KA.IZI tašakan(an)*
8. *šamnu ina* ^{iṣu}*napšaštu* ^{iṣu}*urkarinnu talaki(ki)-ma ana libbi šamnu šú-a-tu*
9. *gaṣṣu ḫurâṣu* ^{iṣu}*bînu* ^{šam}*maštakal* ^{šam}*IL burâšu*
10. ^{iṣu}*NIM* ^{iṣu}*ašâgu* ^{šam}*KUD.SIR* ^{šam}*ŠI.ŠI* ^{šam}*ŠI.MAN ARA(rad)*
11. *ana libbi šamnu*[1] *tanadi(di) ina DA.ŠAR tašakan(an) ša AN.ḪUL.MIŠ* I *ša* ^{abnu}*parûtu*
12. I *ša*[2] *ḫurâṣu* I *ša* ^{abnu}*uknû* I *ša* ^{iṣu}*kunukku tîpuš(uš)* ^{abnu}*parûtu* ^{abnu}*ḫurâṣu*
13. ^{abnu}*uknû* ^{abnu}*kunukku ina bi-rit AN.ḪUL.MIŠ ina GU.GAD tašakak(?)(ak)*
14. *ina DA.ŠAR ina* ^{karpatu}*bur-zi-gal tašakan(an) KU ša AN.ḪUL.MIŠ ša-šu-nu*

---

[1] *A šamnu šú-a-[tu].* [2] *A šá.*

15. *ina šamni ^{isu}šurmînu tubbal ina ^{isu}napšaštu [^{isu}urkarinnu ina DA].ŠAR tašakan(an)*
16. *ḳât ^{amîlu}marṣi ṣubut-ma šiptu ^{ilu}Marduk* . . . . III *šanîtu munu-šu*

17. *šiptu ^{ilu}Marduk bîl mâtâti šal-[ba-bu]* . . . . *-ru-bu*
18. *šar-ḫu id-diš-šú-u*[1] *git-ma-[lu]* . . . . *-ú-um*
19. *tiz-ḳa-ru ṣîru šá úl*[2] *uttakkaru(ru)* . . . . *-šar-šu*
20. *li-ʾ-ú šarru ša*[3] *uz-nu ṣil-* . . . . *-lum*
21. *^{ilu}Marduk*[4] *kabtu šú-tu-ru šá ša-* . . . . *-su*
22. *gaš-ru b(p)u-un-gu-lu a-[li]-* . . . . *kabtu*
23. *a-bu-ub ^{isu}kakku ḳa-bal la* . . . . *-iz-zu*
24. *^{ilu}DU.KIRRUD.ḲU git-mal-* . . . . *^{pl}*
25. . . . . *^{ilu}LUGAL.KIRRUD* . . . . *rabûti^{pl}*
26. . . . . *^{ilu}Marduk bîlu* . . . . *-ik*
27. *^{ilu}Marduk bîl mu-di-i(?)* . . . . *-nin nuḫšu*
28. *bîl šamî^{pl} šá-di-i u tâmâti^{pl} ḫa-i-du ḫur-sa-a-ni*
29. *bîl ú g(ḳ)up-pi u bi-ra-a-ti muš-ti-iš-ru nârî^{pl}*
30. *ḫa-ai-ád ^{ilu}aš-na-an u ^{ilu}la-ḫar(?) ba-nu-u ši-am u ki-i mu-diš-šú-u ^{šam}urḳîtu*
31. *ta-ba-an-na ša ilu u ^{ilu}iš-tar ba-nu-u ki-rib* . . . . *-mi(?)-šu-nu at-ta*
32. *ušumgal ^{ilu}A-nun-na-ki a-ši-ru ^{ilu}Igigi^{pl}*
33. *ir-šú bu-kur ^{ilu}Ia ba-nu-u ti-[mi]-šit gim-ri*
34. *bîlu at-ta-ma kîma a-bi u um-mi ina* . . . . *^{pl} ta-ba-áš-ši*
35. *at-ta-ma kîma ^{ilu}Šamaš iḳ-lu-si-[na?] tuš-nam-mar*
36. *ku-la u riš-ša* . . . . *-šir-ši-na* . . . . *^{ilu}UD.DA GAN*
37. *tuš-ti-šir i-ku-tu* . . . . *-tum* . . . . *-ri-bu*
38. *bi-rit uznâ^{du}-ši-na* . . . .
39. *mâtâti u nišî^{pl} rapšâti[^{pl}]* . . . .
40. *ri-mi-na-ta* . . . .
41. . . . . *-rum an-ḫa šú-nu* . . . .
42. . . . . *nam-ta-ru* . . . .
43. . . . . *-bat ḳât-su ša* . . . .
44. . . . . *u bît ṣi-* . . . .

---

[1] *A id-di-šú-ú.* [2] *A [ti]-iz-ḳa-ru si-ru ša la.* [3] *A [li]-ʾ-ú rap-šu.* [4] *A* here inserts *bîlu.*

45. *[ana-ku arad]-ka pulânu apil [pulâni ša ilu-šu pulânu ^{ilu}ištar-šu pulânîtum(tum)]*

46. *AKA . . . . ḳâtâ^{du}-šu ib- . . . .*

47. *ú-ma- . . . .*

48. *ana nîš ḳâti-[yà] . . . .*

49. *maruštu . . . .*

50. *ú-ban-ni kîma . . . .*

51. *alû di-ḫu u ta-ni-ḫu la-'-bu ta- . . . .*

52. *murṣu lâ ṭâbu ni-šú ma-mit ú-šaḫ- . . . .*

53. *šuk-lul balâṭ pag-ri-ya la-'-bu-ma lit-bu šà ku- . . . .*

54. *il-ḳu-u*[1] *ṣalmân^{pl}-ú-a šú- . . . .*

55. *ipir šîpî^{du}-yà šab-su man-da-ti-yà li - ḳa- . . . . .*

56. *ba-áš-ti tab-la-tú ina ip-ši limnîti^{pl} ša amîlûti^{pl}*[2] *lu-ub-ba-ku u lu-ub-bu-ta-ku-[ma]*

57. *mí-lat ili u amîlûti(ti)*[3] *ibašâ-a ili-yà BAR.DA šuttu-ú-a lim-na ḫa-da-a*

58. *idât^{pl}-ú-a ^{šir}utirtu-ú-a ri-ḫa-ma ul i-ša-a purus kit-ti*

59. *bí-lí ina ŭ-mi an-ni-í iziz-ma ši-mí*[4] *ḳa-ba-ai di-ni di-in purussa-ai purus(us)*[5]

60. [6]*muruṣ SAG NA nu-uk-kir-ma nu-us-si di-ḫu ša zumri-yà*

61. [7]*ili-yà ^{ilu}ištari-[yà?] amîlûtu dînû-ma aḫuzû(?)-ni*

62. *ina ki-bit pi-i-ka ai iṭiḫa-a mimma lim-nu ú-piš kaš-ša-pi u kaš-šap-ti*[8]

63. *ai iṭiḫu-ni imti imti imti aršašî^{pl}*[9] *limnûti^{pl} ša amîlûti^{pl}*[10]

64. *ai iṭiḫa-a lumun šunâti^{pl} idâti^{pl} ITI.MIŠ ša šamî-í u irṣitim(tim)*

65. *lumun ITI ali u mâti ai ikšuda-ni yá-ši*

66. *ina pî limni lišâni limnîti ša amîlûti^{pl} pâni-ka lu-uš-lim-ma*[11]

67. *šammu AN.ḪUL ša ina kišâdi-yà šaknu(nu) mimma limnu ai ú-šis-ni-ḳa*

68. *arrat limuttim(tim) pû ša lâ damḳu ana a-ḫi-ti li-is-kip*

69. *kîma ^{abnu}parûtu nu-ri lim-mir i-dir-tú ai ar-ši*[12]

[1] A gloss reads *iš-[ku-u]*. [2] *B -ša a-* . . . . [3] *B ili ^{ilu}ištari u amîlûtum(tum)*. [4] *B ši-mi*. [5] *B pu-ru-us*. [6] L. 60 is expanded in *B* and forms two lines which read . . . . *-ya nu-us-si*, and . . . . *-us-su di-ḫu ša zumri-yà*; *C*, which reads . . . . *-si*, and . . . . *-yà*, apparently had the same reading as *B*. [7] In place of l. 61 *B* reads . . . . *-ma li-ir-šú-ni liš-ku-nu-ni ri-í-ma*, *C* . . . . *-í-ma*. [8] *B kaš-šap-tum*, *C* . . . . *-tum*. [9] *B* . . . . *-ú aš-ša-šu-ú*. [10] *BC amîlûtum(tum)*. [11] *C* . . . . . *-uš-lim*. [12] *C* probably read *dr-ši*.

Rev.

70. *kîma* ^{abnu}*uknû na-piš-ti ina pâni-ka li-kir li-šak-na ri-i-mu*
71. *kîma ḫurâṣu ili-yà u* ^{ilu}*ištari-yà šulmu(mu) itti-yà*
72. *ina pî niši*^{pl} *ana damikti(ti) lu-ub-ši*
73. *kîma* ^{iṣu}*kunukku lu-ni-is-su-u*[1] *limnûti*^{pl}*-ya*
74. *arrat limutti(ti) lâ ṭâbtum(tum)*[2] *ai iṭiḫa-a ai ušisnika(ka)*
75. *ina pâni-ka šú-mi û pi-ir-i*[3] *li-šir*
76. *šammî*^{pl}[4] *u nap-šal-tum ša ina pâni-ka kun-nu lip-su-su lumnu(nu)-u-a*[5]
77. *ai ú-kàr-ri-bu-ni*[6] *uz-zu ul ug-gat ili*
78. [7]*itti šit-tú kil-la-tú ḫi-ṭi-tu lip-šú-ru ni-šu ma-mit*
79. *ni-iš kâti*[8] *zi-kir ilâni*^{pl} *rabûti*^{pl}
80. [9]*ina pi-ka dan-na lu-ba-ʾ ki-bi balâṭu*
81. [10]*kîma šamî-i lu-lil ina ru-ḫi-i ša ib-šú-u-ni*
82. *kîma irṣitim(tim)*[11] *lu-bi-ib ina ru-si-i lâ ṭâbâti*^{pl}[12]
83. *kîma*[13] *ki-rib šamî-i lu-ut-ta-mir lip-ta-aṭ-ṭi-ru ki-ṣir limnûti*^{pl}*-ya*
84. ^{iṣu}*bi-nu*[14] *ullil-an-ni* ^{šam}*DIL.BAD lip-šur-an-ni*[15] ^{iṣu}*ukuru(?) ar-ni-yà*[16] *lip-ṭur*
85. ^{karpatu}*a-gúb-ba ša*[17] ^{ilu}*Marduk li-šat-lim-ma*[18] *damiktu*
86. *li-ib-bi-bu-nin-ni*[19] *ŠA.NA dipâri ša* ^{ilu}*GIŠ.BAR* ^{ilu}*AZAG*[20]
87. *ina ki-bit* ^{ilu}*I-a*[21] *šar apsî a-bi ilâni*^{pl} ^{ilu}*[NIN.ŠI.KU]*
88. [22]*a-na nîš kâti-yà li-nu-uḫ libba(ba)-ka* ^{ilu}*Marduk maš-maš ilâni*^{pl} *rabûti[*^{pl} *abkal* ^{ilu}*Igigi]*
89. *a-mat* ^{ilu}*I-a*[23] *lu-ut-ta-ʾ-id û šar-ra-tum*[24] ^{ilu}*Dam-ki-[na lu-uš-li-šir]*
90. *ana-ku arad-ka pulânu apil pulâni lu-úb-luṭ lu-uš-[lim-ma]*
91. *lu-uš-tam-mar ilu-ut-ka lud-lu-la dá-[li]-li-[ka]*[25]

---

1 *C ki-ma* ^{abnu} ^{iṣu}*kunukku li-is-su-ú.* 2 *C arrat limuttum(tum) la ṭa-ab-tum.* 3 *C šumu u pi-ir-ʾ.* 4 *C*  for 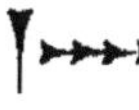. 5 *C ár-ni-ya.* 6 *C ai ú-kar-ri-bu-u-ni mimma lim-nu.* 7 *C* omits *itti* and reads *šit-ta kil-lat u ḫi-ṭi-tu* etc. 8 *C kâtâ*^{du}. 9 For l. 80 *C* reads  *i-dil-li-iš li-baʾ ki-bi balâṭu.* 10 For l. 81 *C* reads *ki-ma šamî-i lu-lil ina ru-ḫi-i kaš-ša-pi u kaš-šap-ti limnûti*^{pl} *ša ib-šu-ni.* 11 *C ki-ma ir-ṣi-tum.* 12 *C la ṭa-bu-tum.* 13 *C ki-ma.* 14 *C* ^{iṣu}*binu* (). 15 *C lipšur-an-ni.* 16 *C ár-ni-yà.* 17 *C* here inserts ^{ilu}*I-a u.* 18 *C li-ša-at-li-ma.* 19 *C lib-bi-bu- . . . .* 20 *C ša* ^{ilu}*GIŠ.BAR u* ^{ilu}*AZAG.IZU.* 21 *C* ^{ilu}*Ia* (). 22 *C niš kâtâ*^{du}*-yà li-kun | li-nu-uḫ etc.* 23 *C* ^{ilu}*Ia* (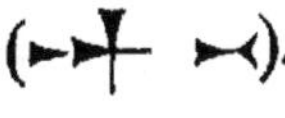). 24 *C u šar-rat.* 25 *C dá-li-li-ka lud-lul.*

92. *ili-yà lu-uš-tam-mar ḳur-di-[ka]*
93. *^{ilu}ištari-yà nar-bi-ka liḳ-[bi]*
94. *û ana-ku maš-maš arad-ka dá-lí-li-ka lud-lul*

---

95. *INIM.INIM.MA ŠU IL.LA ^{ilu}Marduk.KAN*

96\. . . . . . *KIŠDA it-tu-ḫu-*. . . . .*-pat-su BI-u*[1] *ḳaḳḳad immiri KI ŠA NU la*[2] *uttakkar(?)(ár)*
97\. . . . . .*-bu-ti-šu tanasaḫ(?)-ma lu ana ili šammu-ka lu*[3] *ana ili šá*[4] *iš-šub-ba-a*
98\. . . . . *u tanadi(di) gim-ru-ú ma-'am-ma ina pân ^{ilu}Marduk iš-pur-an-ni*
99. *[^{ilu}]Î-a ú-ma-'-ir-an-ni* III *šanîtu ḳibi-ma riksu tapaṭar(ár)*
100. *^{amilu}marṣu ana bîti-šu lîšir-ma ana arki-šu úl lîmur*

---

101. *DUR.DUR šammu AN.ḪUL.MIŠ ša ištu-šu-nu ^{šam}NI.KUL.LA ^{šam}UGU.KUL.LA*
102. *ARA ina šamni ^{išu}šurmînu tubbal ina TI.ŠAR tašakan(an) pušuš zumru*

---

103. *ipuš an-nam* III *šanîtu munu u ša AN.ḪUL.MIŠ niši-ma*
104. *abnî^{pl} šú-nu-ti itti šammu AN.ḪUL.MIŠ muḫur(?) ana ili ḪUR ki'âm ḳibi*
105. *šiptu at-ta AN.ḪUL ma-ṣar šulmi(mi) ša ^{ilu}Î-a u ^{ilu}Marduk*
106. *i-tam-mur kiš-pi ru-ḫi-i zi-ru-ti*
107. *mi-lat ilu u ^{ilu}ištar a-mì-lu-ti*[5]
108\. [6]. . . . . *ḪUR ZI.TAR.RU.DA DI.PAL.A KA.LU.BI.DA*
109\. . . . . *ú-piš kiš-pi lim-*. . . . .*-[i]-tú ša-as-ni-ḳa yá-ši*[7]
110. *^{ilu}šîdu damḳu ^{ilu}lamassu damiḳtu[(tú)] | šukna(na)*[8]
111. *ilu zi-na-a ^{ilu}[ištar zi-ni-ti(?)] û a-mì-lu-ta*
112. *šul-li-ma-am-ma [ki-niš li-ta]-mu-u*[9] *itti-yà*
113. *ina ma-ṣar šul-mi* . . . . . *u kâl* . . . . *luṭ-ṭul*[10]
114. *ina ki-bit ^{ilu}Marduk abkal [ilâni^{pl} rabûti^{pl}] ^{ilu}Marduk*

---

115. *ipuš an-nam ana ili šammu AN.ḪUL.MIŠ tak-ta-bu-u*[11]

---

[1] *D* . . . . .*-ú.* [2] *D lá.* [3] *D lû-u.* [4] *D ša.* [5] *E u amîlûtu.* [6] L. 108 forms two lines in *E* which read: . . . . *paris(is) napištim(tim)* |, and . . . . *KA.LU.BI.DA* |. [7] *E* . . . .*-i-tu ša-as-ni-ḳa a-na ya-a-ši.* [8] *E šuk-na.* [9] *E li-tam-mu-ú.* [10] For 113 *E* reads: . . . . *šutta damiḳta(ta) lu-mur luṭ-ṭul.* [11] *E* . . . .*-ú.*

116. *ina kišâdi-šu tašakan(an) ana libbi šamni ša ina* ^{iṣu}*napšaštu* ^{iṣu}*urkarinnu šaknu(nu)*
117. *šiptu iz-zi-tu* III *šanîtu munu(nu)-ma ka-ai-an dumum*
118. *ina ŭ-mi-šu-ma* ^{karpatu}*a-gúb-ba ŠA.NA*[1] *dipâri tuš-ba-'-šú-ma*
119. *šamû-ú šal-la-tú mimma ín-šú mimma lim-nu úl iṭiḫi-šu*
120. *šum-šu ana damikti(ti) tazakar(âr)*

---

121. *înuma amîlu kakkadu zumru akil-šu karṣi-šu ú-zak-kat-su*
122. *ikal* $^{m\ ilu}$*Aššur-bân-apli etc.*

The text of No. 12 (K 163 + K 218) has been published in IV R[1], pl. 64 and revised in IV R[2], pl. 57, the Reverse of K 2379, which is duplicate of ll. 76—96, being given on p. 11 of the *Additions* to the latter volume. It is here republished with restorations and variant readings from five duplicates.[2] The text as given in IV R[1] has been transliterated into Hebrew characters by HALÉVY, *Documents religieux*, p. 179 ff. and a translation of ll. 76—82 is given by LENORMANT, *La divination*, p. 212 f. and of ll. 1—24, 30—35, 61—95, 101—107 by SAYCE, *Hibbert Lectures*, p. 536 ff. (*cf.* BEZOLD, *Catalogue*, p. 42). The tablet is concerned entirely with the worship of the god *Marduk*, the object of its petitions and ceremonies being the cure of the suppliant who is suffering from sickness. The greater part of the tablet is occupied by the prayer or incantation addressed to the god, which is, however, preceded and followed by directions for ceremonies. The incantation is to be recited by the *mašmašu* or priest who also carries out the ceremonies that accompany it, for l. 16 contains a definite injunction to this effect, while in the last line of the prayer (l. 94) the *mašmašu* speaks in his own name. The prayer is, however, composed from the point of view of the sick man, on whose behalf the priest recites it.

---

1 *ŠA.NA* is apparently omitted by *E*.

2 After the plates had been lithographed the duplicate cited as *C* was increased by the addition of a fresh fragment, K 3289, Prof. ZIMMERN having last summer (1894) recognised it as a duplicate of K. 163, ll. 73—90. The variant readings of *C* therefore, which are given on pll. 29 f., though correct as for as they go, are not exhaustive. In the footnotes to the transliteration of the tablet however the fresh variants of *C* have been incorporated, and in all cases where the transliteration would leave the exact reading doubtful the cuneiform has been added in brackets.

The first line of the tablet forms a sort of heading or introduction, and, while stating the occasion of the prayer, contains a general direction to the effect that when the sickness has fallen on the man nothing evil or inauspicious is to be allowed to approach him. Then follows the first section on the tablet, containing 14 ll. of directions for ceremonies, which commence as follows: — "Perform the following. In the night sprinkle a green bough with pure water. Before *Marduk* the . . . . . drink-offering shalt thou set. Dates (and) . . . . . shalt thou heap up. A *ŠA* of oil, a drink-offering, water, honey (and) butter shalt thou offer; thou shalt set there an incense-burner, corn . . . . . shalt thou heap up; a *ŠA.NA* of incense shalt thou offer. The . . . . . -drink shalt thou pour out." The rites in the next line and a half are obscure; at l. 7 offerings of flesh are prescribed, three preparations of flesh being specified. In l. 8 the command is given to take the oil of certain woods, and the next two lines contain a list of substances that are to be cast into the oil, including gold, fragments of various kinds of wood and plants, and incense. In ll. 11 ff. certain offerings are specified in honour of the *AN.ḪUL.MIŠ*, the offerings consisting of one piece of alabaster, one piece of gold, one piece of lapis-lazuli and one seal. In the principal prayer of the tablet reference is made to each of these four offerings (*cf.* ll. 69—73), and, as the prayer is addressed throughout to *Marduk*, it is obvious that *AN.ḪUL.MIŠ* is merely a title of the god *Marduk*.[1] The ceremonies conclude with an injunction to the officiating priest to hold the hand of the sick man and recite the incantation. This incantation, which occupies ll. 17—94, reads as follows.

Translation.

17. O *Marduk*, lord of lands, the mighty . . . . .
18. Powerful, unique, perfect . . . . .
19. The exalted hero, who suffers no change . . . . .
20. The strong one, the king who . . . . .
21. O *Marduk* the illustrious, the great one who . . . . .

[1] The group is prob. a compound ideogram and is not to be transliterated *ilu hidûti*^{pl}; the rendering "the god of joys" is therefore tentative.

22. The mighty . . . . the illustrations!
23. The storm of the weapon, the battle . . . . .
24. O . . . . .! the perfect . . . . .! 25. . . . . the great . . . . .! 26. . . . . . . *Marduk*, the lord . . . . 27. O *Marduk*, the lord . . . . .
28. Lord of the heavens, of mountains and of oceans, who . . . . . the hills!
29. Lord of . . . . . and fortresses, who guideth the rivers!
30. Who bestoweth corn and grain(?), who createth wheat and barley, who reneweth the green herb!
31. Who createth the handiwork of god and goddess; in the midst of their . . . . . art thou!
32. The ruler of the *Anunnaki*, the director of the *Igigi*!
33. The wise, the first-born of *Ia*, the creator of the whole of mankind!
34. Thou art lord, and like my father and my mother among the . . . . . art thou!
35. Thou art like the Sun-god also: their darkness thou dost lighten!
36. A cry and a shout of joy . . . . . 37. Thou guidest him that is in need . . . . . 38. Their wisdom . . . .
39. Lands and distant peoples . . . . .
40. Thou art compassionate . . . . . 41. . . . . . I am weak . . . . .
42. . . . . 43. Thou holdest his hand . . . . . 44. . . . . .

At l. 45 the suppliant makes a formal statement of his own name along with that of his father, after which the tablet continues broken for several lines, only disconnected words having been preserved. When the lines once more become connected we find the suppliant imploring that the life of his body may be restored, the disease from which he is suffering being put down to the influence of magic. He concludes a description of his symptoms with the words: "My powers and my soul are bewitched and there is no righteous decision!" He therefore makes a direct appeal to the god in the following words:—

59. O lord, at this time stand beside me and hearken to my cries, give my judgment, make my decision!
60. The sickness . . . . . do thou destroy, and take thou away the disease of my body!

61. O my god (and) goddess, judge ye mankind, and possess me!
62. By the command of thy mouth may there never approach anything evil, the magic of the sorcerer and of the sorceress!
63. May there never approach me the poisons of the evil . . . . . of men!
64. May there never approach the evil of dreams, of powers (and) portents of heaven and of earth!
65. Never may the evil of the portent of city and land overtake me!
66. In spite of the evil mouth, the evil tongue of men in thy sight let me be perfect!
67. Let nothing evil ever restrain the plant of the god of joy that is placed upon my neck!
68. The evil curse, the mouth that is unfavourable let it cast aside!
69. Like alabaster let my light shine, let me never have affliction!

Rev.

70. Like lapis-lazuli may my life be precious in the sight, let it establish mercy!
71. Like gold, O my god and my goddess, may prosperity be with me!
72. In the mouth of the peoples may I be blessed!
73. Like a seal may my sins be torn away!
74. May the evil curse, that is unfavourable, never draw nigh, may it never be oppressive!
75. Before thee may my name and posterity prosper!
76. May the plants and . . . . . that are set before thee loosen my sin!
77. Never may there approach me the wrath or anger of the god,
78. With misery, disgrace (and) sin; from the curse
79. May the raising of my hand, the invocation of the great gods, give release!
80. At thy mighty command let me approach! Command thou life!
81. Like heaven may I shine among the enchantments that possess me!
82. Like the earth may I be bright in the midst of spells that are not good!
83. Like the heart of heaven may I be bright; may the power of my sins be destroyed!

84. May the *bînu*-wood purify me, may the .....-plant deliver me, may the *ukuru*-wood remove my sin!
85. May *Marduk*'s vessel of purification bestow favour!
86. May the flaming censer(?) of the god ..... make me bright!
87. At the command of *Ia*, king of the Abyss, father of the gods, the Lord of wisdom,
88. At the raising of my hand may thy heart have rest, O *Marduk*, the priest of the great gods, the arbiter of the *Igigi*!
89. The word of *Ia* let me glorify, and, O queen *Damkina*, let me have dominion!
90. May I thy servant so and so, the son of so and so, live, let me be perfect,
91. Let me revere thy divinity, and let me bow in humility before thee!
92. O my god, let me revere thy power!
93. O my goddess, let me tell of thy greatness!
94. And may I the priest, thy servant, bow in humility before thee!

On the conclusion of the prayer there follow three short sections of ceremonies, an incantation of ten lines, and a final section of ceremonial directions. After the first of these sections the sick man himself ceases to take part in the ritual, for the section concludes with the injunction that he shall go straight to his house without looking behind him. The remainder of the tablet deals with the due disposal of some of the offerings and objects, that have been used in the ceremonies at the commencement of the Obverse and in the course of the incantation.

Ll. 101—104 form two sections of two lines each which contain directions concerning the stones and the plant of "the god of joy" mentioned in ll. 11 ff., 66 ff. Then follows a short incantation addressed to "the god of joy" himself, in which he is besought to make the *šêdu* and *lamassu* propitious and restore by his command the favour of the angry god and goddess. The last section on the tablet contains directions concerning the plant of "the god of joy", the recital of the incantation and the offering of a vessel of purification and a censer. L. 121 gives the catch-line for the next tablet which probably contained similar prayers and ceremonies to be recited and performed for the relief of some other form of sickness.

1. In K 2513, a tablet containing directions for ceremonies, the first section of Col. IV commences: *înuma amîlu lumun murṣi ZI.TAR.RU.DA DI.PAL.A | KA.LU.BI.DA ú-pi-šu lim-nîti*[pl] (*cf.* BEZOLD, *Catalogue*, p. 449), while the second section contains ceremonies for a similar occasion; it is therefore probable that the ceremonies attached to the incantation in No. 12 form an extract from some larger work devoted entirely to ceremonial observances. The disease itself, with which the tablet deals, would appear to be of the nature of possession or bewitchment, *cf.* K 2572,[1] l. 8 *înuma a-na amîlu ZI.TAR.RU.DA šá* [ilu]*NIN.KILITI i-pu-us-su*, and l. 13 f. *amîlu šá ZI.TAR.RU.DA ip-šu-šu | ana pân* [kakkab]*MAR.BU.DA likmisu(su)*, and the somewhat similar texts K 3278, ll. 1 ff., 8 ff., and K 6172, ll. 1 ff., 11 (*cf. op. cit.* pp. 519 and 768); *see* also K 9612 + K 10760, ll. 10 ff., *etc.*

3. For a discussion of the *KU.A.TIR cf. supra* p. 22 f.

4 f. For *ŠA.NA burâši* and *KAS.SAG tanaki(ki) cf. supra* p. 20 f.

5. That = *aru* (BRÜNNOW, *List*, no. 5570) = the flower (of a palm) *cf.* JENSEN, ZK II, p. 26. The tablet clearly reads , not as in IV R[1], nor as in IV R[2]. The is possibly to be identified with the plant [šam] , which occurs in Sm. 8, Col. I, l. 14 f., where it is rendered by *ḫa-aš-ḫu-ra-ku*, and *ḫa-aš-ḫu-ur* (*cf.* BRÜNNOW, *List*, no. 4193).

6. According to BRÜNNOW, *List*, no. 8613 *ruššu* is also a possible rendering of the group *KU.ḪUŠ.A.*

7. The three forms of flesh here enumerated may represent the flesh of three different beasts, or flesh in general prepared in three different ways. The [širi]*KA.IZI* was poss. so named from its appearance, *KA.IZI* being = *ḫamâṭu, ša išâti* (*cf.* BRÜNNOW, *List*, no. 651).

---

[1] For the text of this tablet *cf.* BOISSIER, *Documents assyriens*, Paris, 1894, p. 42. For at the beginning of l. 6 read, according to the tablet, *i. e. ina mûši šú-a-tum etc.*

8. 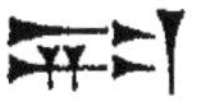 is to be here taken as = *šamnu* (*cf.* LATRILLE, ZK II, p. 356 f.). In ritual texts *šamnu* "oil" is rendered by ,  and  almost indiscriminately. No clear distinction in their use can be observed, though perhaps  is more often used for "oil" in general,  or  when the oil of some particular tree is specified.

That  should be read, not  as IV R^2, *cf.* l. 116.

9. That  is a material used in building is clear from the *East India House inscription*, Col. II, l. 45 (*cf.* SCHRADER'S *Keilins. Bibl.*, Bd. III, Hft. II, p. 14 and DELITZSCH, *Wörterbuch*, p. 110, note 1). The ideogram is transliterated in the text as *gaṣṣu*, in accordance with a communication from Dr. BEZOLD, who has come across the group in K 4864, l. 16 f. rendered by  and who compares the Arabic جصّ. *Cf.* also BRÜNNOW, *List*, no. 8470.

10.   cannot here = *ṣitaš*, but is prob. the name of a plant or tree,  being the determinative; *cf.* the plant  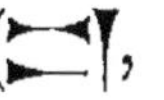, which occurs in Sm 8, Col. II, l. 5 and possibly in K 4354, Col. II, l. 12 (II R, pl. 43, no. 2), *etc.*

11 ff. The sign  in the phrases  ^{abnu}*parûtu*,  *ḫurâṣu*, *etc.* is to be taken as the relative, not as a numeral, the duplicate A giving the variant reading  In ll. 12 and 73 *kunukku* is written with the determinative , in l. 13 with , while in l. 73 the duplicate C writes the word with both determinatives.

16. The end of this line should probably be restored *šiptu* ^{ilu}*Marduk [bîl mâtâti]* III *šanîtu munu-šu* from l. 17, the incantation being cited by the words with which it commences. In this common rubric the suffix is not generally appended to the verb *munu*, so that it is possible the second  is merely an error, through ditography on the part of the scribe, for  the phonetic complement that is commonly found with the ideogram .

20. For   *šarru ša* of the text A gives the variant

reading [cuneiform] *rap-šu*, which has probably arisen from the misreading of a badly written [cuneiform].

27. The characters in this line are rubbed; if [cuneiform] the reading of IV R[1 and 2] be adopted, the phrase should be translitarated *mudaḫḫidi(di) nuḫšu*, (*i. e.* [cuneiform]), "who giveth great abundance".

30. [cuneiform]-*nu-u* should be read with IV R[1], not [cuneiform]-*nu-u* as in IV R[2].

32. The title *ušumgallu* in this passage is clearly not used in the sense of "dragon". The parallelism of *a-ši-ru* in the second half of the line suggests some general term implying authority.

50. The first sign in this line should probably be read [cuneiform] as in IV R[2], although [cuneiform] is all that is at present visible.

52. The signs [cuneiform], which occur frequently in a formula on the 6th tablet of the *šurpu*-series (*cf.* IV R, pl. 7, Col. II, ll. 2, 12, 22, 32, 42, 52; pl. 8, Col. III, ll. 3, 16), are explained by Jensen (ZK II, p. 20) as a verb (*i. e. nisû* III 1) with the 3 m. s. suffix, and as instances of the occurrence of the phrase he quotes the present passage and [cuneiform] in l. 79 (*see* below). It is more probable that the signs [cuneiform] should be transliterated phonetically *ni-šú*, a word that is not, however, to be identified with the *nišu* "spirit(?)", which occurs in the phrase *ma-mit niš* (= [cuneiform]) *šamî-i . . . nis irṣitim(tim)* (*ibid.* Col. I, l. 50; *see* also Brünnow, *List* no. 2326). In the passages cited above, as in the present line, *ni-šú* is followed, not preceded, by *ma-mit*, and is to be regarded as I 1, Inf. from *našû*, the two words being probably taken together in the sense of an "oath" or "curse" (lit. "the raising of an oath or curse"). *ni-šu*, however, sometimes occurs by itself (*cf.* No. I, l. 48: *li-in-ni-is-si ma-mit li-tá-kil ni-[šu(?)]*, *etc.*) so that in the phrase *ni-šú ma-mit* the two words are perhaps to be taken as separate synonymous phrases in apposition.

67. [cuneiform] *i. e. šâkinu(nu)* is to be read for [cuneiform] of IV R.

71 f. It is possible that these two lines should be taken together without a break.

73. The application of the metaphor in this line is not at first sight apparent. The *kunukku* may, however, refer to the seal-impression, and as seal-impressions have been found on small clay cones, which were originally attached to the documents they attested by means of a strip of reed (*cf.* BUDGE, ZA III, p. 214), it is probable that the tearing off or removal of such a seal-impression is the basis of the metaphor in the text.

77 ff. The division of ll. 77—79, as given in the translation is based on the duplicate C, which reads as follows:—

Rev. 5. Never may there approach me any thing evil, neither the wrath nor anger of the god, misery, disgrace and sin!

6. From the curse may the raising of my two hands, the invocation of the great gods, give release!

Here the general phrase *mimma limnu* is introduced and defined by the substantives that follow.  has been explained by JENSEN (ZK II, p. 20) as =  = *lušisišu* or *lišisišu* (*cf. supra sub* l. 52). The reading of C, however, proves that the phrase is to be transliterated *ni-iš ḳâti*, in apposition to *zi-kir ilâni*^{pl} *rabûti*^{pl}.

98.  is written over an erasure; the scribe had probably begun to write  omitting , but corrected his mistake.

99. On the rendering of  by *riksu tapatar(âr) cf. supra* p. 22 and *infra sub* No. 16, l. 11.

No. 13.

Transliteration.

1. . . . . 2. *lil-*. . . . . 3. *ša-ḳâ-a i-*. . . . . 4. *a-lik tap-pu-ti la li-ʾ-*. . . . . 5. *ana-ku pulânu apil pulâni ša ilu-šu pulânu [ilu ištar-šu pulânîtum(tum)]* 6. *azzaz(az) ina pân ilu-ti-ka rabîti(ti)* . . . . 7. *ina bikît nišî*^{pl} *ša la ma-*. . . . . 8. *mimma šumšu ḳa-ba-a u ma-ga-[ra]* . . . . 9. *lul-lik ruḳ-ka(?) a-mi-ri* . . . .

. . . . . . 10. *lu taš-lim ina ṣil-li-ka ni-mi-ki* . . . .
11. *ina pi-ka ša la na-kar li-*. . . . .

12. *INIM.INIM.MA* *ŠU IL.[LA* ^{ilu}*Marduk.KAN]*

13. *DU.DU BI* *ana pân* ^{ilu}*Marduk* . . . .
14. *[ŠA].NA* *burâši* *tašakan(an)* *nîš ḳâti* . . . .

15. *[šiptu]* *bi-lum* ^{ilu}*Marduk* *mu-di-i* . . . .
16. . . . . *-la-at nišî*^{pl} *a-pa-[a-ti]* . . . .
17. . . . . *-ba šit-ka-*. . . . .

Rev.

18. . . . . *-šap balâṭu iš-šak-na* . . . .
19. . . . . *šá iš-šak-nam-[ma]* . . . . 20. *[šá?]*
a-na ya-ši kîma šamî-i ana-ku a-na ša-a-šu . . . .
21. *[*^{ilu}*]šîdu damḳu ú-ši-is-sa* . . . . 22. *ú-ṣab-bit šap-*
ti-ya lib-bi ú-. . . . . 23. *ú-ka-as-si a-ḫi-ya* . . . . . .
. . . . 24. *bir-ki-ya ú-mal-li ṭâbti-*. . . . . 25. *gám-ma-*
al mâti-ya . . . . 26. *šú-mi ú-šat-bi ina ûmi*
[an-ni-i(?)] . . . . 27. *bí-lí aḳ-ri-dak-ka ši-mí* . . .
. . . . 28. *šur-ši di-ni* *purus* . . . . 29. *bi-*
il-la-an-ni . . . . 30. *ki-i la in-*. . . . .
31. ^{ilu}*Marduk* . . . . 32. *ina pi-i-*. . . . .
33. *maḫ-*. . . . .

No. 13 (K 3229) forms the bottom left corner of a large tablet similar to No. 12. The Obverse contains the conclusion of a prayer to *Marduk*, in which, after giving his own names and those of his god and goddess in the usual formula, the suppliant states that he stands before the god whom he adjures by the tears of the people; he prays that he may enjoy the god's favour, remaining in his deep shadow (*i. e.* protection) through his mighty command that does not change. This prayer is followed by two lines of directions for ceremonies, and at l. 15 a fresh prayer commences, which is continued on the Reverse of the tablet. The second prayer begins with an invocation of *Marduk*, who at l. 20 is described as "like the heavens" in his relation to the suppliant. In l. 21 the *šîdu* or divine colossus is addressed, probably as the minister who carries out the will of the greater god; at l. 27 the suppliant turns once more to *Marduk*, petitioning him for judgment. As both hymns are addressed to *Marduk*, it may be inferred that the tablet was somewhat similar in its arrangement to No. 12, and that it contained prayers and ceremonies in honour of this god only.

No. 14.

Transliteration.

1. . . . . *ili-yà* 2. . . . .*-lim-man-ni* 3. . . . . *taṣ-li-ti* 4. . . . . *gi-mil napišti(ti)* 5. . . . .*-tum ina ḳâti-yà li-kin* 6. . . . . *ḫi-ṭi-ti* 7. . . . . *si-lim itti-yà* 8. . . . . *I.SAG.ILA* 9. . . . . *bîlu-ut-ka* 10. . . . . *pa-nu-uk-ka li-sa-lik(?)*

11. *[INIM.INIM.MA ŠU IL.LA [ilu]]Marduk.KAN*

12. . . . . *[[ilu]] Marduk tašakan(an)*
13. . . . . *- lit - su magrat(at)*

14. . . . .*-ḫu* 15. . . . . *ḳar-du* 16. . . . . *ra-šub-bu* 17. . . . . *ul ib-ši* 18. . . . . *[pl]-šu*

No. 14 (K 2793) is a fragment of a large tablet and preserves the ends of a few lines only. It contains the conclusion of a prayer to *Marduk* (ll. 1—10), followed by two lines of directions for ceremonies and the commencement of a second prayer or incantation.

10. The last 3 characters in the line (*li-sa-lik* = *lištalik?*) may poss. be read *li-ir-ur*.

No. 15.

Transliteration.

1. . . . . *-yà* 2. . . . . *- tum* 3. . . . . *-ku* 4. . . . . *ár-ši* 5. . . . . *ár-ši* 6. . . . .*-tuk* 7. . . . . *ki-i-nu* 8. . . . . *arki-yà* 9. . . . . *limuttu ai a-mur* 10. . . . . .

. . . . . *yá-ši* 11. . . . . *šîmâti*^{pl} 12. . . . .
-šut-ka 13. . . . . *-mu ši-mat-ka* 14. . . . .
-bu-ka 15. . . . . *ina šú-bat ta-ni-iḫ-ti-yá* 16. . . . . . .
. . . . . *damiḳti(ti)-yà liḳ-bi-ka*

17. *[INIM.INIM.MA ŠU IL.LA]* ^{ilu}*Marduk.KAN*

18. . . . . *mû a-gúb-ba tukân(an)* 19. . . . .
GI.GAB tukân(an) 20. . . . . *[KU.A].TIR tašapak(ak)*
21. . . . . *-bu-ḳu* 22. . . . . *tukân(an)* 23. . .
. . . . *šiptu* III *šanîtu munu(nu)*

24. . . . . *[burâši] tašakan(an)* 25. . . . . *-az*
26. . . . . *-ḳu-nu* 27. . . . . *tanaki(ki)*
28. . . . .

Like the preceding fragment, No. 15 (K 2586 + K 7185) preserves a portion of the right side of what was originally a large tablet. The conclusion of a prayer to *Marduk*, a section of six lines giving directions for ceremonies, and the beginning of a second ceremonial section represent its present contents.

No. 16.

Transliteration.

Obv.
1. . . . . 2. . . . . *šipat-*. . . . . 3. . . . . .
. . . . . *ši-pir-*. . . . . 4. . . . . *-nam-ru* 5. . . . . .
. . . . . *-tú* 6. . . . .

Rev.
7. . . . . *[lu]-ú-ša-pi* . . . . 8. . . . . .
. . . . . *-ka I.SAG.ILA* 9. . . . . *si-lim liḳ-bi-ka*

10. *[INIM.INIM.MA ŠU IL].LA* ^{ilu}*Marduk.KAN*

11. *[DU.DU BI lu ina KIŠDA lu ina ŠA].NA ipuš(uš)*

12. . . . . *šamî u irṣiti*
13. *[ikal* ^{m} ^{ilu}*Aššur-bân-apli] etc.*

Of the Obverse of No. 16 (K 11681) a few characters only have been preserved, while the Reverse contains the concluding phrases of a prayer to *Marduk*, the last one on the tablet. The colophon-line that gives the title of the prayer (l. 10) is here accompanied by a rubric or direction contained in a single line (l. 11), which occurs frequently in the present class of texts. For other instances of its occurrence, *cf.* No. 18, l. 19; No. 21, l. 92; No. 22, l. 69; No. 28, l. 6; No. 34, l. 6; No. 38, l. 4; No. 39, l. 5; No. 41, l. 2; No. 46, l. 10; No. 47, l. 7. It will be seen that the line is never found by itself, but, when it occurs, always follows the colophon-line *INIM.INIM.MA ŠU IL.LA* etc. It commences with the phrase *DU.DU BI i. e. ipuš annam*, "do the following", which generally precedes any directions for ceremonies or ritual (*cf. supra* p. 19). The direction itself consists of the words *lû ina KIŠDA lû ina ŠA.NA ipuš*, a set formula that rarely varies.[1] No substantive is mentioned for the imperative *ipuš* to govern; hence it may be inferred that the object of the verb is to be supplied from the previous line, *i. e.* that the rubric refers to the manner in which the preceding prayer or incantation is to be recited. Two methods of recitation are in fact given as alternatives, the line reading: "Perform (the incantation) either *ina KIŠDA* or *ina ŠA.NA*.

In the course of a prayer to *Ninib* contained by No. 2, l. 27 reads: *ar-kus-ka rik-sa KU.A.TIR áš-ruk-ka*, "I have bound for thee a cord, the *KU.A.TIR* have I offered thee!" (*cf. supra* p. 17). The *KU.A.TIR* is of common occurrence among the offerings that are prescribed in the ceremonial directions that accompany the present class of incantations (*cf. supra* p. 22 f.). It would not therefore be surprising if the *riksu* mentioned in the first half of the line should also be found in the directions for ceremonies. It was suggested above (p. 58) that in l. 99 of No. 12 the phrase 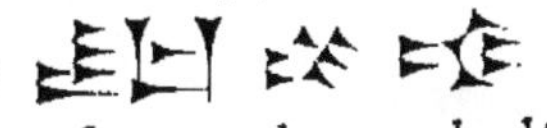 should be transliterated *riksu tapaṭar(ar)*, "the knot thou shalt loosen", and it is not improbable that in the phrase *ina* 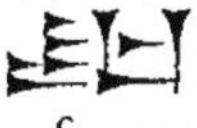 in the rubric under discussion we may see a further reference to the rite of the knotted cord (*riksu*). The second ideogram *ŠA.NA* has been already discussed on p. 19 f., where the suggestion was made that the word denoted a vessel for containing incense. The

[1] *See* below, *sub* No. 42, l. 25, and No. 52, l. 4.

rubric therefore is to the effect that the incantation must be accompanied either with the rite of the knotted cord, or with the offering of incense.

No. 17.

Transliteration.

1\. . . . . 2. . . . . *balâṭu* . . . .
3\. . . . . *ri-ša-a-ti u GUR.UD* . . . . 4. . . .
. . . . *ka-a-ša pa-li-ḫi-ka lu-*. . . . .

5\. *[INIM.INIM.MA ŠU] IL.LA ^{ilu}[Marduk(?).KAN]*

6\. . . . . *-mi ašar(?) šîpâ^{du} TAR(at)* . . . .
7\. . . . . *-za tanadi(di) ina ili* . . . . 8. . . .
. . . . *ina ili ša* . . . . 9. . . . .

The fragment No. 17 (K 5668) contains a few words of a prayer followed by some directions for ceremonies. The name of the god to whom the prayer is addressed, though broken, is in all probability *Marduk*; hence the fragment is included under the prayers addressed to that god.

No. 18.

Transliteration.

1\. . . . .
2\. *i - na - ṭa - lu* *pa - nu - uk - [ka]*[1]
3\. *a-na gi-biš ta-ma-a-ti pa-nu-ka ma-a-*. . . . .
4\. *ša - ḳá - ta* *ina* *ša - ma - mi*
5\. *kul - lat* *nišî^{pl}* *ta - bar - ri*
6\. *šur - ba - ta - ma* *ina irṣitim(tim)*
7\. *^{šiṛu}tîrti^{pl} - šu - nu* *[ta - bar - ri*[2]
8\. *ša ḫi - ṭu iḫ - ṭu - ú* *ta - ga - mil - šu at - ta*
9\. *ṣab - ta - ku - ma* *ki - i ti - i - ri*
10\. *ina*[3] *ḳa - an - ni - ka*

---

[1] Ll. 1 and 2 probably formed one line in *A*, which gives traces of two preceding lines, of which the second reads: . . . . *-ku-[ti?]*. [2] For l. 7 *A* reads: *^{šir}i^{pl}-šu-nu ta-na-[ṭal]*. [3] *A i-na*.

11\. *ki - i izakara(ra) - ni* ^{ilu}*Marduk*
12\. *a - la - su - um ur - ki - [ka]*

Rev.

13\. *na - ša - ku nindabû a - sa - rak . . . .*
14\. *pu - ṭur maruští*[1] *li - ki un - ni - [ni - yà]*[2]
15\. *šâru - ka ṭâbu li - zi - ḳa - am - [ma]*[3]
16\. *napištim(tim)*[4] *li - - ri - ik*
17\. *la-ta-am nar-bi-ka ana*[5] *niši*^{pl} *rapšâti*^{pl}

18\. *INIM.INIM.MA ŠU IL.LA* ^{ilu}*Marduk.GI*[6]

19\. [7]*DU.DU BI lu ina KIŠDA lu ina ŠA.NA ipuš(uš)*

20\. *šiptu ga-aš-ru šú-pu-u i-dil* ^{ilu}*Igigi*

No. 18 (K 8009) is the lower portion of a comparatively small tablet, of which about one third has been preserved. It probably contained only one prayer, the end of which is represented by ll. 1—17. L. 20 gives the catch-line to the next tablet, while l. 21 evidently marks the commencement of a colophon. The prayer is carefully written and several of the longer lines have been split up into two halves, each of which occupies one line of the tablet (*cf.* ll. 1 f., 4 f., 6 f., 9 f., 11 f., 15 f.), ll. 3—8, for instance, reading:—

Unto the ocean-flood thy face is . . . . .!
Thou art exalted in heaven:
 All nations thou dost behold!
Thou art mighty upon earth:
 Their spirits thou dost behold!
The man that hath sinned thou requitest!

This metrical arrangement of the lines is not to be found, however, in the duplicates A and B. On the Reverse of the tablet the suppliant states that he has offered a present and poured out a libation, and he therefore prays for the removal of his sorrow and sighing and for length of days, concluding

[1] *B marušti-yà.* [2] *A [un-ni]-ni-ya.* [3] *A [li]-zi-ḳam-ma.* [4] *B [napišti](ti).* [5] *A [a]-na.* [6] *iluMarduk.KAN.* [7] After l. 18 *A* ceases to be a duplicate giving three lines of directions for ceremonies, which read: . . . . *[ana pân ilu]Marduk ŠA.NA burâši* | . . . . *tašakan(an)* | . . . . III *ša-nîtu munu(nu)* |.

with the desire that he may declare the greatness of the god unto distant peoples.

10 ff. Between ll. 8 and 9 of A an insertion or a gloss is written in smaller characters of which only  has been preserved, the tablet reading: —

19. The duplicate A in place of l. 19 gives a ceremonial section of three lines prescribing the offering of incense and the repetition of the incantation three times.

20. This catch-line which gives the first line of the next tablet is to be found in the list of incantations, K 2832 + K 6680, col. I, l. 7 (*see* above p. 15).

No. 19.

Transliteration.

1. . . . .
2. . . . .-*šú* . . . .
3. *ilu ma-*. . . . .
4. *bîlu bîlu bîlu* . . . .
5. *a - bu* . . . . *rabûti*^{pl}
6. *bîl šimâti*^{pl} . . . . . . ^{isu}*uṣurâti*^{pl}
7. *mu - ma - ʾ - ir šamî - i u irṣiti(ti) bîl mâtâti*
8. *[ga] - mir di - ni ša úl inû - ú ki - bit - su*
9. *[mu] - šim šimâti* . . . . *kala(?)ma*
10. *[ina] lumun* ^{ilu}*atalî* ^{ilu}*Sin ša ina arḫi ûmi išakna(na)*
11. *[lumun] idâti*^{pl} *ITI.MIŠ limnîti*^{pl} *lâ ṭâbâti*^{pl}
12. *[ša] ina ikalli - yà u mâti - yà ibašâ - a*
13. *[ina ki] - bi - ka - ma ú - tal - la - da tí - ni - ší - î - ti*
14. *[a-na?] šarru šagganakku šú-mi-šú-nu ta-za-kar*
15. *áš-šum ba-ni-i ilu û šarru*
16. *ba - šú - ú itti - ka*

17. *û bîlu* ^{šam}*TU* ^{šam}*RIG* ^{šam}*GA dan - ni*

18. *ina ma - ' - du - ti kakkab ša - ma - mi*

19. *bí - lí ad - dan - ka*

20. . . . . *.-rat-ti-ka ip-ša-ku uznâ*^{du}*-ai*

Rev.

21. *šim - ti ba - la - ṭi - ya ši - im*

22. *ba - ni - i šu - mí - ya ki - bi*

23. *mi - ni - ta PAL - ma dumḳu šur - ka*

24. *šú - kun - ma ili - yà ba - áš - ta - ka rabîtu(tu)*

25. *[ilu] u šarru li - ša - ki - ru - in - ni*

26. . . . . . *u rubû ḳár - bu - ni - ya li - pu - šu*

27. . . . . *- ri li - ba - ša - an - ni*

28. *ina puḫri lu ši - mat ki - bi balâṭu*

29. ^{ilu}*šîdu likbi magâra u magâra*

30. *ŭ - mi - šam lit - tal - lak ìtti - yà*

31. *[ina] ki - bit - ka ṣir - ti ša úl uttakkaru(ru)*

32. *û an - ni - ka ki - nim ša úl inû - ú*

---

33. *INIM.INIM.MA ŠU IL.LA* ^{ilu}*BÎL.KAN*

---

34. *šiptu ru - ba - tú rabîtu(tu) i - lat ši - ma - a -ti*

As is the case in the preceding tablet, some of the longer lines in No. 19 (K 34) are divided into halves, which together occupy two lines on the tablet (*cf.* ll. 4 f., 15 f., 18 f., 29 f.). No. 19 contains only one prayer and this is addressed to the god *Bîl* and was intended for use after an eclipse of the moon (*cf.* ll. 10 ff.). The beginning of the prayer, with which the Obverse commenced, has been broken off; it probably contained, however, an invocation of the god, of which the conclusion, describing his power as ruler and creator, has been preserved.

4. O Lord! O Lord! O Lord! . . . .
5. Father of the great [gods?]!
6. The lord of destinies, the [god?] of charms!
7. The ruler of heaven and earth, the lord of lands!
8. Perfect in judgment, whose word is not altered!
9. Director of destinies . . . .
10. In the evil of the eclipse of the moon which in the month (*space*) on the day (*space*) has taken place,
11. In the evil of the powers, of the portents, evil and not good,

12. Which are in my palace and my land!
13. At thy command created was mankind!
14. Unto king and noble their names thou didst name!
15. Since to create god and king
16. Rests with thee!

In ll. 17 ff. the suppliant states he has made an offering to the god consisting apparently of three plants, and he therefore seeks the god's protection for himself and for his posterity ("The destiny of my life decree! The making of my name do thou command!"). The prayer concludes with the desire that the god will confer blessings through his attendant minister, the *šîdu*.

29. May the *šîdu* command favour upon favour,
30. Daily may he go with me,
31. Through thy exalted command which is not altered,
32. And thy sure mercy which changeth not!

No. 20.

Transliteration.

Obv.

1. . . . . - *ka* . . . . 2. . . . .
3. . . . . 4. . . . . - *tim* . . . .
5. . . . .*-riš-ka* . . . .*-da ši-*. . . . .
6. . . . . *MIN.NA DAGAL MA SUR* . . . .
7. *[INIM].INIM.MA* *ŠU IL.LA* . . . .
8. *[šiptu] šur - bu - ú* *git - ma - lu* . . . .
9. *[ú]-mu* *la* *a-ni-ḫu* *mut-tab-bil* . . . .

Rev.

10. *^{ilu}Rammânu* *šur-bu-ú* *git-ma-lu* . . . .
11. *ú-mu* *la* *a-ni-ḫu* *mut-tab-bil* . . . .
12. *ša - kin* *ú - mì - í* . . . .
13. *[mu] - šab - rik* *birku* *AN.ZA* . . . .
14. *[kaš] - ka - šú* *git - ma - lu* . . . .
15. *[la?]* *pa-du-ú* *a-ša-[rid?]* . . . .
16. *[^{ilu}]Rammânu* *kaš-ka-šú* *git-ma-[lu]* . . . .
17. *[la?]* *pa-du-ú* *a-[ša-rid?]* . . . .

18. . . . . . . - *kip* *ik* - *du* . . . .
19. . . . . . . - *ni* - *bu* *la* - ' - . . . .
20. . . . . . . - *su* *šar* - . . . . 21. . . . .

The Obverse of No. 20 (K 10406) contains the end of one prayer and the beginning of another. The name of the god to whom the first is addressed has not been preserved, but the second, which is continued on the Reverse of the tablet, is addressed to *Rammân* and is somewhat similar to the commencement of the prayer to the same god in No. 21, ll. 34 ff. In ll. 12 ff. the god is described as "the establisher of days . . . . ., who causeth the lightning to shine . . . . ., the strong one, the perfect . . . . ., the unconquerable, the prince . . . . .!"

No. 21.

Transliteration.

Obv.

[1.] [1]. . . . . [2.] . . . . *i-tar-ra-* . . . .
1. *bi-*. . . . .*-ru-šu ú-nam-ma-*. . . . . 2. *ga-*
. . . . *ša úl inû-ú* . . . . 3. *tik-*. . . . .*-tim*
mu-ša-as-. . . . . 4. *pa-*. . . . . *mu-diš-šú-[u]* . . .
. . . . 5. *ša* . . . . *aḫî^pl-šu šur-*. . . . .
6. *na-*. . . . .*-ti ša ina šamî-i* . . . . 7. *ša* . . .
. . . . . . *-ti-yà nir-bi ana nap-*. . . . . 8. . . . .
. . . *ša i-mu-ḳu* . . . . 9. *mu-*. . . . . *-nu ŭ-mu*
la [a-ni-ḫu?] . . . . 10. *al-*. . . . . *ina ki-rib šamî-i*
. . . . 11. *ana-ku* . . . . *[ana ma]-ḫar-ka*
az-ziz a-ši-'-ka ša-. . . . . 12. *ilu*. . . . . *ši-mat*
nišî^pl i-. . . . . 13. . . . . *ilu ṣalmu da-*. . . .
. . . . . . 14. . . . . *tu-ur-dam-ma ina ali-ya ta-*. . . .
. . . . . . 15. . . . .*-ka* . . . . *šamî-i tu-ur-*
[dam-ma] 16. . . . . *GAR* . . . .*-lu*

[1] Since the plates have been lithographed I have joined to No. 21 two small fragments K 6612 and K 6588. The former, while giving additions to ll. 1—12, adds two lines to the text which in the *Transliteration* are numbered [1] and [2]; the latter completes portions of ll. 37—47. For the present text of ll. [1]—12 and 37—47 *cf. Additions* to the plates.

sa-mid dûru ru- . . . . 17. . . . . di-bi- . . . .
. . . . . .-an u abnî^{pl} birḳu . . . . 18. ilu ali-ya . . .
. . . .-am-ma u-kal-lu . . . . 19. ^{ilu}Rammânu
bîlu . . . .-ka a-ta-ta-ma . . . . 20. [a-na?]
ya-a-ši . . . . a-ta-ta-ma . . . . 21. . . . . . .
. . . . . an-ni-i ma-ḫar- . . . . li-ki un-ni-ni-ya mu-gu-ur
su-[pi-ya] 22. . . . . pî-ka lu la itiḫâ-a . . . .
i-piš ri-ba lu la ikšud-an-ni ya-[a-ši?] 23. [nar]-bi-ka lu-ša-pi
[dalili-ka] ana nišî^{pl} rapšâti^{pl} lud-[lul]

24. [INIM].INIM.MA ŠU [IL.LA] ^{ilu}Rammânu.[KAN]

25. . . . . ^{ilu}Rammânu pû-šu ittanandû . . . .
alu lu bît ilu ali uš-tál-pi? . . . . 26. . . . .
libit bît ili lu . . . . lu sa-mi-id dûru ru- . . . .
27. . . . .-iḫ . . . .-in-na- . . . .

28. [DU].DU BI ina mûši gušûru [arḳu mû illu tasalaḫ GI].GAL
ana pân ^{ilu}Rammânu tukân(an) 29. suluppu KU.[A.TIR taša-
pak(ak) ŠA šamni niḳû mû dišpu ḫimîtu tašakan(an) 30. ^{immiru}niḳû
tanaki[(ki)] . . . .-taḫ-ḫa-ma 31. ŠIT . . . .
-i-ri- . . . . . 32. ki- . . . . . ^{ilu}Rammânu . . . . 33. . .
. . . .-ni . . . .

34. [šiptu] šur-bu-ú . . . . 35. [ŭ]-mu la a-ni-ḫu . . . .
. . . . . . 36. [^{ilu}]Rammânu šur-bu-ú . . . . 37. ŭ-mu
la a-ni-ḫu . . . . 38. ša-kin ú-mì-i . . . .-bu-
. . . . 39. kaš-kaš-šú git-ma-[lu] . . . .-a-lá-
. . . . 40. šam-ru la li-'- . . . . tam-ḫa- . . .
. . . . 41. ^{ilu}Rammânu kaš-kaš-šú git-ma-[lu šam]-ru la li-[']-
. . . . . 42. la-id muk-tap-lu . . . .-ri aš-ṭu- . . . . .
43. šá-giš(?) ga-aš-ru . . . .-i-di muš-tar- . . . . .
44. mu-ur-ṣi ín-ni- . . . .-pal-lu-u šal- . . . .
45. ší- . . . . du- . . . .-iz ta-šib- . . . .
46. ni- . . . . í-dan-ni ḳar-da mí- . . . . 47. ^{ilu}
. . . .-ší(?) . . . . 48. ina . . . .
49. tu- . . . . 50. . . . .

Rev.
51. . . . .^{pl} bír-tum ab- . . . . 52. . . . . .
. . . . . [kul]-lat ilâni^{pl} ša . . . . 53. . . . .
-taḳ-ḳu-ú . . . . 54. . . . . ya-ú aš-rat ta-
. . . . 55. ilû u šaplû ib-ni- . . . . 56. . . . .

. . . . . . *a-bi ilâni*^{pl} . . . . 57. . . . . *apsû ni-mi-ki* . . . . 58. *^{ilu}Bîlit banat(at) ilâni^{pl} ša-lum-ma-ta* . . . . 59. *^{ilu}Marduk tu-šir uš-mal-la ḳat-ta-ka na-mur-ra-ta* . . . . 60. *ina I.KUR bît šimâti^{pl} ša-ḳa-a [ri-ša-a-ka?]* 61. *bîlu ri-mi-nu-ú ina ilâni^{pl}* . . . . 62. *ip-ša-ku uznâ^{du}-ai ma-ḫar-ka ut-nin ša bal-*. . . . . 63. *ri-man-ni-ma bîlu ši-mí taṣ-[li-ti?]* 64. *[ḫul]-lik ai-bi-ya ṭu-ru-ud lim-*. . . . . 65. *[ai] iṭiḫû-ni imti imti imti aršašî^{pl}* . . . . 66. . . . . *naplisa-ni-ma ki-bi dum-ki-*. . . . . 67. *[ili-yà] u ^{ilu}ištari-yà šulma(ma) itti-ya* 68. . . . . *[líb]-ba-ka li-nu-ḫa lippašra(ra) ka-bit-ta-ka šulma(ma) šuk-[na]*

69. . . . . *li-ri-man-ni* . . . .*-yà lišâ-a rîmu*

70. . . . . *nikî an-ni-ma* . . . . *lù-ta-id ilu-ut-ka*

71. *[nar - bi] - ka lu - [ša] - pi dalili - ka lud - lul*

---

72. *[INIM].INIM.MA ŠU IL.LA ^{ilu}Rammânu.KAN*

---

73. *[DU DU] BI í-nu-ma ^{ilu}Rammânu ina ki-rib šamî-í pû-šu it-ta-na-an-du-ú*

74. . . . .*-ta ša* . . . . *illu tasalaḫ ŠA.NA burâši ina išâti ^{işu}ašâgi ta-šár-raḳ*

75. *[ŠU?] IL.LA* . . . .*-raš-ši-ma ši-ma-a-at*

---

76. *[šiptu] ^{ilu}Rammânu* . . . .*-ta-az-nu šú-pu-u ilu gaš-ru*

77. . . . .*-ḫi-*. . . . .*-ul-ḫu da-pi-nu ḳu-ra-du*

78. . . . .*-pi-í-ti mu-ṣal-lil ŭ-mi*

79. . . . . .*-tu-*. . . . . *áš-li-i-ti nu-uk-ka gam-ra-a-ti*

80. *[ba?]-šú-ú bir-ki bîl a-bu-bi*

81. *[mu] - ut - tab - bil šamî - í šadî^{pl} ta - ma - a - ti*

82. . . . . . . *- mu - ka* . . . . *ší - mu - ú zi - kir - ka*

83. . . . . . *- šim - mí* . . . . *- du - ú ḫur-sa-a-ni*

84. . . . .*-bi-í* . . . . *da-a-ri-šú u-ga-ru*

85. . . . .*-ḫi it-bu-*. . . . . *i-dal-la-la ḳur-di-ka*

86. . . . . .*-ša-am iz-*. . . . .*-ti-ma mûši u ú-mi*

87. . . . . . *U.A ur-ki-tú(?) tu-sal-lam šab-sa*

88. *[ana] ya-a-ši arad-ka ana ṭu-ub-ba-ti si-di-ir-ma*

89. *[mimma] šumšu ri-í-ma dá-li-li-ka lud-lul*

90. . . . . . .*-ka ṭâbu lul-tam-ma-ra ana niši^{pl} rapšâti^{pl}*

---

91. *INIM.INIM.MA ŠU IL.LA ^{ilu}Rammânu.KAN*

---

92. *[DU].DU BI lu ina [ŠAR] lu ina ŠA.NA ipuš(uš)*

93. *ilu bîlu šú-pu-u git-ma-lum ilâni*^{pl} *ra-šub-bu*
94. *ikal* ^{m} ^{ilu}*Aššur-bân-apli etc.*

Like No. 6 (*cf. supra* p. 33 f.) No. 21 has been built up of several fragments of the K. Collection (K 2741 + K 3180 + K 3208 + K 5043 + K 6588 + K 6612 + K 6672 + K 6908 + K 7047 + K 8498 + K 9157 + K 10219 + K 10497 + K 13431 + K 13793). The tablet at present contains traces of ninety-five lines; about six or seven lines however are missing from the beginning, and eight or nine from the end of the Obverse. It will be seen therefore that the tablet is somewhat similar in size to Nos. 6 and 12. The text commences with a prayer or incantation which is followed by two ceremonial sections, the first of three lines, the second being six lines in length. Then follows a second long prayer, which is in all probability continued without a break on the Reverse of the tablet. This is in turn followed by a section of three lines of ceremonies and a third incantation of fifteen lines. All the prayers and ceremonies are to be recited and performed in honour of the god *Rammân*.

The first prayer is much broken; it concludes with the desire that *Rammân* will accept his suppliant's sighing and receive his supplication: let no evil approach or possess him and he will proclaim the greatness of the god unto distant nations. The rubric in ll. 25—27 contains the statement that the prayer is to be repeated during a certain state of the wind, while ll. 28—33 recount the ceremonies that are to accompany its recitation. The commencement of this latter section is identical with that of the first ceremonial section in No. 12, for a translation of which *cf. supra* p. 60.

The beginning of the second prayer is very similar to No. 20, ll. 8 ff. (*see* above p. 76). At l. 58 the goddess *Bîlit* is addressed, and in the following line the god *Marduk*. After allusions to his power and mercy the suppliant states that he is petitioning before him, and the prayer concludes (ll. 61 ff.): "Have mercy on me, and, O Lord, hear my prayer! Destroy my foes and drive away the wicked! Never let there approach me the poisons, the enchantments . . . : .! . . . . . pity me and command favour! O my god and my goddess, may peace be my portion! . . . . . may thy heart have rest, may thine anger be loosened, and do thou establish prosperity! Thy greatness let me praise, let me bow in humility before thee!" The directions for ceremonies that follow this prayer enjoin that "when the Storm-god has set his mouth (*i. e.* has spoken) in the midst of heaven", among other offerings "a vessel of incense with fire of the *ašâgu*-wood" shall be presented.

The last prayer on the tablet commences with the following invocation of the Storm-god: "O *Rammân* . . . . . powerful one, O mighty god! . . . . . strong one, O hero! . . . . . who darkenest the day! . . . . . Possessor of the lightning, Lord of the storm-flood! Who destroyest the heavens, the mountains, and the seas!" The prayer concludes with general petitions for mercy and blessings. The colophon-line in l. 91 is followed by the rubric which has been already discussed on p. 71 f.

25. That  is probably to be transliterated *ittanandû*, *cf.* l. 73.

67. As *-ma* is evidently the phonetic complement, 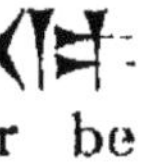 cannot = *lislimû* (*cf.* No. 1, l. 23 f. *etc.*); it should rather be transliterated by the subs. *šulmu* as in l. 68.

89. *lul-tam-ma-ra* for *luštammar*, *cf.* *lu-uš-tam-mar ilu-ut-ka* (or *-ki*), No. 8, l. 17, No. 9, l. 11, *etc.*

No. 22.

Transliteration.

Obv.

1. *šiptu rubû ašaridu bu-kur ^{ilu}Marduk*
2. *massû-u*[1] *i-ti-ip-šu i-lit-ti ^{ilu}Zarpanîtu*
3. *^{ilu}Nabû na-aš duppu ši-mat ilâni^{pl} a-šir I.SAG.ILA*
4. *bîl I.ZID.DA ṣu-lul ^{dûru}Borsippa^{KI}*
5. *na - ram ^{ilu}Ia ḳa - i - šu balâṭu*
6. *ašarid Bâbili na - ṣi - ru na - piš - ti*

[1] A [*massû*]-*ú*.

7. *ilu du-ul da-ád-mi - kar nišî^{pl} bîl iš-ri-ti*
8. *zi - kir - ka ina pî nišî^{pl}* ŠU.DUB.BA *^{ilu}šîdu*
9. *mâr rubî(?) rabî(?) ^{ilu}Marduk ina pî - ka kit - ti*
10. *ina si-ik-ri-ka*[1] *kabti ina ki-bit ilu-ti-ka rabîti(ti)*
11. *ana-ku pulânu apil pulâni mar-ṣu šum-ru-ṣu arad-ka*
12. *ša ḳât utukki-ma imat* BUR.RU.DA *nam-kil-lu-ni-ma naḳ-šušu(?)-ni*
13. *lu-úb-luṭ lu-uš-lim-ma* . . . . GUB.BU.DU *lukšud(?)(ud)*
14. *šú - uš - kin kit - [ti] ina pî - yà*[2]
15. *šup - ši - ka [damiḳti(ti)] ina libbi - yà*
16. *ti - i - ru u*[3] *man - za - [za liḳ - bu - u] damiḳti(ti)*
17. *li-iz-ziz [ili-yà] ina imni-yà*
18. *li-iz-ziz [^{ilu}ištari-yà] ina šumîli-yà*
19. *^{ilu}šîdu damiḳtu ^{ilu}[lamassu damiḳtu]* . . . .*-kiš itti-yà*
20. *šú-ut-li-ma-am-[ma]* . . . . *u ma - ga - [ra]*
21. *sí - kir*[4] *a - ta -* . . . . *- ti liš -* . . . . .
22. *mâr rubî(?) rabî-i*[5] *[^{ilu}]* . . . . *la ki-*. . . . .
23. *pânu - ka ki - niš* . . . . *lit - uš - bi(?)*
24. *^{ilu}Marduk* KAN . . . . KAN.SIR - *[ka?]*
25. *^{ilu}*. . . . . *lik - ru - bu - ka*
26. *^{ilu}*. . . . . *- ka*
27. *ilâni^{pl}* . . . .
28. *^{ilu}Nabû* . . . .
29. *ina* I. . . . .

---

30. INIM.INIM.[MA ŠU IL.LA *^{ilu}Nabû*].KAN

---

31. DU.DU BI II ḲA *ḳîmi* . . . .
32. *iṣu tanitti itti ḳîmu* ARA . . . .
33. KAS.SAG *tanaki(ki) tubbal-ma šiptu* . . . .
34. *kurmat-su tašakan-ma maḫ-rat* . . . .*-i*

---

35. *šiptu bît nu-ru ab-kal* . . . .*-ú*
36. *ilu ṣîru [a] - pil ^{ilu}Marduk*
37. *^{ilu}Nabû abkallu ašaridu ir - šú mudû - u*
38. *ilu ṣîru a - pil ^{ilu}Marduk*
39. . . . .*-mar-raš šamî-i u irṣitim(tim)*
40. . . . .*-tu-ú ša* I.SAG.ILA

[1] *B ina zik-ri-ka.* [2] *B ina pî-ya.* [3] Omitted by *B.* [4] *B zi-kir.* [5] *B mâr rubî(?) rabî(?).*

41. . . . . *^{ilu}Marduk šar ilâni^{pl}*
42. . . . . *ḫur-ša-nu illûti^{pl} tamâti^{pl} rapšâti^{pl}*
43. . . . . *'i-ták-ku* . . . .
44. . . . .

Rev.

45. . . . .
46. . . . . *ki-di-*. . . . .
47. . . . . *.'-a-tu šak-*. . . . .
48. . . . . . . *-na ik-ṣa-* . . . . *ana DI.DI(iš)*
49. *UGU-ma ki-í* . . . . *ta-ša-kan ^{ilu}ṣalmu*
50. *šá in-ši kil-lim-* . . . . *ta-da-an*
51. *ana-ku pulânu apil pulâni* . . . . *-ka*
52. *maruštu im-mur-* . . . . *-sa-ku*
53. *ina ku-u-ru u* . . . . *-a-ni*
54. *ina lu-mun* . . . . *-ti*
55. *pû u lišânu ka-* . . . . *-yà*
56. *ina ŭ-mí an-ni-í* . . . . *.-šid*
57. *az-ziz ma-ḫar-ka* . . . . *.-ka*
58. *[ṣu]-lul-ka ṭâbu ta-ai(?)-*. . . . . *.-a ili-yà*
59. *[ur]-ḫi lid-mi-iḳ* . . . . *li-šir*
60. *[kib]-sa i-ša-ra šú-kun ina šîpî^{du}-yà*
61. *bîlu ili-yà si-lim it-ti-yà*
62. *^{ilu}Nabû bîlu ili-yà si-lim it-ti-yà*
63. *i-na šat mu-ši lid-mi-ḳa šunât^{pl}-u-a*
64. *ri-í-ma un-ni-na bal-ta ^{ilu}šîdu*
65. *ḳa-ba-a ši-ma-a šuk-na ya-ši*
66. *ina ki-bit ilu-ti-ka rabîti[(ti)] lu-úb-luṭ lu-di-ma*
67. *dalîli^{pl}-ka ana nišî[^{pl} rapšâti^{pl}] lud-lu!*

68. *INIM.INIM.MA [ŠU IL.LA] ^{ilu}Nabû.KAN*

69. *DU.DU BI [lu ina ŠAR lu ina ŠA].NA ipuš(uš)*

70. *šiptu ^{ilu}[Na-bi-um a-ša-ri-du bu-kur] ^{ilu}Marduk*
71. *ikal [^{m} ^{ilu}Aššur-bân-apli etc.*

No. 22 (K 140 + K 3352 + K 8751 + K 10285) forms the upper portion of a large tablet, from which about a quarter is at present missing. The tablet contains portions of three prayers and of one ceremonial section, all of which are composed in honour of the god *Nabû*. The first prayer on the tablet contains petitions for life and prosperity, and was intended for the relief of a man suffering from sickness and demoniacal possession. The end of the prayer is broken; the first 20 ll., however, read as follows.

Translation.

1. O hero, prince, first-born of *Marduk*!
2. O prudent ruler, offspring of *Zarpanitu*!
3. O *Nabû*, Bearer of the tablet of the destiny of the gods, Director of *Isagila*!
4. Lord of *Izida*, Shadow of Borsippa!
5. Darling of *Ia*, Giver of life!
6. Prince of Babylon, Protector of the living!
7. God of the hill of dwelling, the fortress of the nations, the Lord of temples!
8. Thy name is . . . . . in the mouth of the peoples, O *šîdu*!
9. O son of the mighty prince *Marduk*, in thy mouth is justice!
10. In thy illustrious name, at the command of thy mighty godhead,
11. I so and so, the son of so and so, who am smitten with disease, thy servant,
12. Whom the hand of the demon and the breath of the . . . . .
13. May I live, may I be perfect . . . .
14. Set justice in my mouth!
15. . . . . . mercy in my heart!
16. Return and be established! May they command mercy!
17. May my god stand at my right hand!
18. May my goddess stand at my left hand!
19. May the favourable *šîdu*, the favourable *lamassu* . . . . . with me!

On the conclusion of the prayer there follows a section of four lines containing directions for the making of certain offerings, and the commencement of an incantation, both of which are much broken. On the Reverse of the tablet is inscribed the conclusion of a prayer, which may possibly be the continuation of that which commences at the end of the Obverse. The sick man, after making a formal statement in l. 51 of his own name and of that of his father, concludes the prayer with the following petitions.

56. At this time . . . . . 57. I stand before thee . . . . .!
58. Good is thy shadow . . . . .!
59. May my way be propitious . . . . .!
60. Set a pleasant path for my feet!
61. O lord, my god, deal graciously with me!
62. O lord *Nabu*, my god, deal graciously with me!
63. In the night season may my dreams be propitious!
64. Mercy, compassion, (and) life, O *šîdu*,
65. Command, grant my petition and establish me!
66. At the command of thy mighty godhead let me live, let me have knowledge!
67. In the sight of(?) wide-spread peoples may I bow in humility before thee!

The catch-line for the next tablet reads: "O *Nabû*, the prince, the first-born of *Marduk*!"

2. *i-ti-ip-šu* probably for *itpîšu* an adj. of the form فِتْعَال from √אפשׁ.

9. That the beginning of this line is not to be read *mâr abgalli* ^ilu^*Marduk* appears from l. 22, in which *-i* is added to the sign [cuneiform]; *mâr rubî rabî* ^ilu^*Marduk* seems therefore to be the only reading admissible.

12. [cuneiform] here poss. = *bušû*, *i. e.* "prey of the demon", but the transliteration *ša ḳât* appears to me better, as it balances *imat* in the following phrase.

14. For this and the following petitions *cf.* No. 9, ll. 13 ff. The present prayer is composed throughout on somewhat similar lines to the first prayer of No. 9.

No. 23.

Transliteration.

1. . . . . 2. . . . . *li-ši-rib* . . . .
3. . . . . *li-ki un-ni-[ni-yà]* 4. . . . . *-ďa-ar-ti*
. . . . 5. . . . . *[nar] - bi - ka lu - [ša - pi]*

6. *[INIM.INIM.MA ŠU IL.LA* ^ilu^*]Sin.KAN*

7. . . . . *niš* . . . . 8. . . . .

[^{ilu}]*Sin* . . . . 9. . . . .^{pl} *ša* . . . .
10. . . . . 11. . . . .

No. 23 (K 13277) contains a few phrases from the end of a prayer to *Sin* and from the beginning of a section of ceremonies to be performed in honour of the same god.

No. 24.

Transliteration.

1. . . . . -*id* . . . . 2. . . . . -*bit*
ik-. . . . . 3. . . . . *šar-ra-ti ra*-. . . . .

4. *[INIM].INIM.MA* *ŠU IL.[LA* ^{ilu}*Sin.KAN]*

5. *[AG].AG BI i-nu-ma* ^{ilu}*Sin* . . . . 6. . . . . .
. . . . . *tanaki(ki) ana pân* ^{ilu}*Sin* . . . . 7. . . . . .
. . . . . *munu(nu)* . . . .

The name of the god to whom the prayer on No. 24 (K 13922) is addressed has not been preserved in the colophon-line. As, however, the ceremonies that follow it are to be observed in honour of *Sin* during a certain phase or position of the moon (*cf.* l. 5), it is clear that the preceding prayer is also addressed the Moon-god.

No. 25.

Transliteration.

1. . . . . 2. . . . . *dir* - . . . .
3. . . . . *a-ṭi-ra*-. . . . . 4. . . . .
ma-ḫar-ka lu-. . . . .

5. *[INIM.INIM.MA* *ŠU IL.LA]* ^{ilu}*Sin.[KAN]*

6. . . . . -*ki-im aburriš nârî*^{pl}*(?)* 7. . . . . -*ti*
III *šanîtu munu[(nu)]* 8. . . . . *ŠA šamni hurâṣu* VII
. . . . 9. . . . .

Like the two preceding fragments No. 25 (K 13296) contains the conclusion of a prayer to *Sin* and the commencement of a ceremonial section.

No. 26.

Transliteration.

Obv.

1\. . . . . 2. . . . . -*bil*

3\. [*INIM.INIM.MA* *ŠU*] *IL.LA* ^{ilu}*Sin.KAN*

4\. . . . . *ana* ^{ilu}*Sin*

5\. . . . . -*ši* *ina* *ûmi* *magâri* *gušuru* *ta* - *ša* - *bit*

Rev.

6\. . . . .-*šal-tú* 7. . . . . *kîmu* *tubbal-ma*

8\. . . . . - *an* - *ma* 9. . . . . *rabû*

10\. . . . .-*ḫur*

11\. . . . .-*tim* 12. . . . .

No. 26 (K 10550) preserves portions of a prayer to *Sin* and a ceremonial section of seven lines, which runs over onto the Reverse of the tablet, and was probably followed by a second prayer or incantation.

No. 27.

Transliteration.

1\. *šiptu bi-lum gaš-ru ti-iz-ḳa-[ru bu-kur* ^{ilu}*NU.NAM.NIR*]

2\. *a-ša-rid* ^{ilu}*A-nun-na-[ki bîl tam-ḫa-ri*]

3\. [1]*i-lit-ti* ^{ilu}*KU.TU.ŠAR* [*šar-ra-tum*[2] *rabîtum(tum)*]

4\. ^{ilu}*Nirgal kaš-kaš ilâni*^{pl} [*na-ram* ^{ilu}*NIN.MIN.NA*]

5\. *šú-pa(?)-ta ina šamî-i illûti*[^{pl} *šá-ku*[3] *man-za-az-ka*]

6\. *ra-ba-ta ina arallî-*[*ma âšira(ra) LA.TI-šu*]

7\. *it-ti* ^{ilu}*Í-a ina puḫur*[4] [*ilâni*^{pl} *mi-lik-ka*[5] *šú-ṭur*]

8\. *it-ti* ^{ilu}*Sin ina šamî-i* [*ta-ši-'*[6] *gim-ri*]

9\. *id-din-ka-ma*[7] ^{ilu}*Bîl abu-[ka ṣal-mat ḳakḳadu pu-ḫur napišti(ti)*]

10\. *bu-ul* ^{ilu}*Nirgal nam-maš-[ši-i ḳa-tuk-ka ip-ḳid*]

---

1 Sm. 398, cited as *C*, is duplicate of ll. 3—16. 2 *C* [*šar*]-*ra-ti*. 3 *C* [*šá*]-*ḳu-ú*. 4 *A* [*ina pu*]-*ḫur*. 5 *mi-lik-ka* has been restored from *C*. 6 *C ti-ši-'*. 7 *A iddin-ka-ma*.

11. [1]*ana-ku pulânu apil pulâni [arad-ka]*
12. *mi-lat ili u ^{ilu}ištari [iš - šak - nu - nim - ma]*
13. *nasâḫu u ḫu-lu-uḳ-ḳu-[u*[2] *bašû-u*[3] *ina bîti-yà]*
14. *ḳa-bu-u*[4] *la ši-mu-[ú it - tal - pu - nin - ni]*
15. *áš-šum gam-ma-la-ta bi-li*[5] *[as-sa-ḫar ilu-ut-ka]*
16. *áš-šum ta-ai-ra-ta*[6] *[iš - ti - ' - ú - ka(?)]*
17. *áš-šum mu-up-pal-sa-ta [a - ta - mar . . . .]*
18. *áš-šum ri-mi-ni-ta*[7] *[at - ta - ziz pâni - ka(?)]*
19. *ki-niš naplis-an-ni-ma [ši - mi ḳa - ba - ai]*
20. *ag-gu lib-ba-ka*[8] *[li - nu - ḫa]*
21. *[pu]-ṭur an-ni ḫi-[ṭi-ti*[9] *. . . . .]*
22. *. . . . . .-ṣir lib-bi ilu-ti-ka . . . .*
23. *ilu u ^{ilu}ištaru zi-nu-ti šab-. . . . .*
24. *nir-bi-ka lu-uḳ-bi [dá-li-li-ka lud-lul]*

25. *[INIM.INIM.MA] ŠU [IL.LA ^{ilu}Nirgal.KAN]*

26. [10]. . . . .

No. 27 (K 2371 + K 13791) contains the first prayer of what was originally a large tablet. It has been restored chiefly from the duplicate which is cited as A. This tablet is a comparatively small one and contains nothing more than the prayer in ll. 1—25 of the text, followed by a catch-line, its Obv. giving ll. 1—15 in 22 lines, its Rev. ll. 16—25 in 10 or 11 lines, while the end of the Reverse is left blank. It is inscribed in rather coarse characters, and was copied from one of the larger texts for Ashurbanipal, who substituted his own name in place of the general formula in l. 11. Moreover the insertion of the eclipse-formula in A changes the general character of its petitions and proves that the copy was required for use during or after an eclipse of the moon. Thus restored, not much is missing from the prayer. Ll. 1—10 contain the invocation of the god, at l. 11 the suppliant states his name and goes on to

---

[1] For l. 11 *A* reads *ana-ku ^{m}Aššur-bân-apli arad-ka*, which is followed by the formula *ina lumun ^{ilu}atalî etc.* in three lines; ll. 11 and 12 form one line in *B* and *C*. [2] *A ḫul-ḳu-u.* [3] *C bašû-ú.* [4] *A ḳá-bu-ú u, B ḳá-bu-. . . . .* [5] *A [^{ilu}]Nirgal.* [6] *A [ta]-ai-rat.* [7] *A [ri-mi]-na-ta.* [8] *A libba-ka.* [9] *A ḫi-ṭi-ti.* [10] Of the catch line, with which the text of *B* concludes, only the end has been preserved: . . . . *IN.DUL-ki.*

describe his cause of complaint, and the conclusion of the prayer contains his various petitions.

Translation.

1. O mighty lord, hero, first-born of *NU.NAM.NIR*!
2. Prince of the *Anunnaki*, lord of the battle!
3. Offspring of *KU.TU.ŠAR* the mighty queen!
4. O *Nirgal*, strong one of the gods, the darling of *NIN.MIN.NA*!
5. Thou treadest in the bright heavens, lofty is thy place!
6. Thou art exalted in the Under-world and art the benefactor of its . . . . .
7. With *Ia* among the multitude of the gods inscribe thy counsel!
8. With *Sin* in the heavens thou seekest all things!
9. And *Bîl* thy father has granted thee that the black-headed race, all living creatures,
10. The cattle of *Nirgal*, created things, thy hand should rule!
11. I so and so, the son of so and so am thy servant!
12. The . . . . . of god and goddess are laid upon me!
13. Uprooting and destruction are in my house! 14. . . . .
15. Since thou art beneficent, I have turned to thy divinity!
16. Since thou art compassionate, I have sought for thee!
17. Since thou art pitiful, I have beheld . . . . .!
18. Since thou art merciful, I have taken my stand before thee!
19. Truly pity me and hearken to my cries!
20. May thine angry heart have rest!
21. Loosen my sin, my offence . . . . . 22. . . . .
23. O god and angry goddess . . . . .
24. Let me talk of thy greatness, let me bow in humility before thee!

4. The title ^{ilu}*NIN.MIN.NA*, *i. e.* "Lady of the crown", is evidently an abbreviated form of ^{ilu}*NIN.MIN.AN.NA*, *i. e.* "Lady of the crown of heaven", since the former occurs as a variant of the latter in l. 48 of the Cylinder-inscription of Sargon, *cf.* LYON, *Sargon*, p. 8, n. 2 and p. 71.

6. For the rendering of  by the Part. of *ašâru* *cf.* BRÜNNOW, *List*, no. 8211 and No. 12, l. 32, *a-ši-ru* ^{ilu}*Igigi*^{pl}. 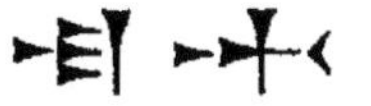 is apparently a compound ideogram. 

i. e. ina ma-ti-šu cannot be read, as the duplicate A clearly reads .

7. *šú-tur* might poss. be read for *šú-ṭur i. e.* "mighty is thy counsel".

19 f. L. 19 has been restored from No. 2, l. 32, *etc.*, though poss. some other synonym for "prayer" or "cry" may have been employed. L. 20 is restored from No. 21, l. 68, No. 46, l. 5, *etc.*

No. 28.

Transliteration.

1. . . . . 2. . . . .*-ḫar-ra* 3. . . . .
lislimu(mu) itti-ya 4. . . . . *[dá-li-li-ka] lud-lul*

5. *[INIM.INIM.MA ŠU IL.LA]* *ilu Nirgal.KAN*

6. *[DU.DU BI lu ina ŠAR lu ina] ŠA.NA ipuš(uš)*

7. . . . .*-ú ilu ri-mi-nu-ú* 8. . . . .*mu-bal-liṭ*
amilu mîtu 9. . . . .*-gu-ú iḫ-ṭu-ú* 10. . . . .
-liḫ a-du-ur-ma 11. . . . .*-ub-la* 12. . . . .
-ka li-nu-ḫa 13. . . . .

No. 28 (K 3355) is a small fragment from the right side of a large tablet. It preserves a few phrases from the end of a prayer to Nirgal and from the beginning of a prayer to a god who is addressed as "a merciful god . . . ., the quickener of the dead!

Section III.

Prayers addressed to Goddesses.

Like the preceding division, Section III is made up of tablets containing prayers addressed only to one deity. While the prayers in Section II, however, are composed in honour of gods, those in the present Section are addressed to goddesses. Nos. 30 and 33, and possibly Nos. 29 and 35, contain but one prayer, which is accompanied, in the case of the two former, by directions for ceremonies. The tablets are comparatively small and are inscribed in a somewhat large and coarse character, and, like others in Section II, may perhaps be regarded as forming extracts from the larger compositions. The question whether any large tablet existed, containing a series of prayers and ceremonies addressed only to one goddess, and in its arrangement corresponding to Nos. 12, 21, and 22, is one that cannot be answered with certainty. It is true that Nos. 31, 32, and 34 are fragmentary portions of large tablets, and, as their present contents refer only to one goddess, they have been classified under the present Section. It is not impossible, however, that the tablets of which they are fragments originally contained prayers addressed to other deities. Their inclusion, therefore, under this Section must be regarded as provisional.

No. 29.

Transliteration.

1. . . . . *[du?]-um-mu-ḳu ku-um-ma* . . . .

2. *[INIM.INIM.MA]* *ŠU IL.LA* ^{ilu}*Ša-la.[KAN]*

3. . . . . *ti-iz-ḳa-ru bu-kur* ^{ilu}. . . . .

No. 29 (K 13907) has preserved three lines from the Reverse of a small tablet, which represent the last line of a prayer followed by its colophon-line, and apparently the catch-line for the next tablet. The latter should possibly be restored from No. 27, l. 1: *[šiptu bi-lum gaš-ru] ti-iz-ḳa-ru bu-kur* ^{ilu}*[NU.NAM.NIR]*. If this is so, the sign  must have been written over an erasure.

No. 30.

Transliteration.

1. . . . .
2. ^{karpatu}*GU.ZI* *karâni* *ib-bi(?)* . . . .
3. *as-ruk-ki* *si-riḳ* . . . .
4. . . . . *in-na-*. . . . .
5. *a-ku-*. . . . .*-a-ba* *ši-*. . . . .
6. *linuḫ(uḫ)* *libbu-ki* *ka-bit-ta-*. . . . .
7. *ana-ku pulânu apil pulâni ša maruštu* . . . .
8. *da-ya-na-ti* *di-ni* *di-*. . . . .
9. *muš-ti-ši-ra-a-ti* *a-lak-ti* *ki-*. . . . .
10. *li-saḫ-ra* *ili* *ša* *iz-nu-ú* *itti-[ya?]*
11. *in-nin-ti* *ḳab-ri* *ka-si-ti* *li-*. . . . .
12. *linasiḫ(iḫ) murṣu ša zumri-ya linasi(si) MUN.GU ša da-*
13. *lip-ta-ṭi-ru* *a-di-ra-tú* *ša* *lib-bi-ya*
14. *šur-dim-ma šumu u zîru lu rîmu si-li-ti*  *lu-ša-pa zi-kir-ki*
15. *lubluṭ(uṭ)* *lu-uš-lim-ma* *nir-bi-ki* *lu-ša-pi*
16. *da-li-li-ki* *lud-lul*
17. *a-mi-ru-ú-a* *nir-bi-ki* *li-ša-pu-ú*
18. *a-na* *niši*^{pl} *rapšâti*^{pl}

Rev.

19. *[INIM].INIM.MA ŠU IL.LA ^{ilu}[Ištar.KAN]*

---

20. *AG.AG BI ina ûmi magâri URU TI ana pân ^{ilu}Ištar ummu* . . . .
21. *mû illu tasalaḫ GI.GAB tukân(an) suluppu KU.A.TIR [tašapak(ak)]*
22. *ŠA šamni niḳû mû dišpu ḫimîtu tašakan[(an)]*
23. *^{karpatu}a - da - gùr tukân(an) KAS.SAG tanaki(ki)*
24. *SID(di) SIR.AD KU.DUB.DUB.BU ŠUB.[ŠUB(di)]*
25. *KU.KU ^{isu}irinu ^{isu}ŠID ^{šam}IL.LA ARA* . . . . .
26. *ina šamni ^{isu}šurmîni MU.ŠAL ^{isu}urkarinnu talaki MI ina TI.ŠAR [tašakan(an)]*
27. *šiptu an-ni-tú* III *šanîtu munu-ma* . . . .
28. *riksu tapaṭar - ma šamnu šuatu(?)* . . . .
29. *an-nu-ú ki-. . . . . tu-.* . . . .

---

30. *šiptu ĭl-ti ^{ilu}Igigi bu - uk - rat* . . . .
31. *duppu* CXXXIV^{KAN} *šiptu* . . . .
32. *ikal ^{m} ^{ilu}Aššur-bân-apli etc.*

A little over one third of the original tablet has been preserved by No. 30 (K 3448). The text contains a single prayer addressed to the goddess *Ištar*, followed by a ceremonial section, and, according to the colophon, forms the 134th tablet of a certain series. Of the prayer to *Ištar* only the latter part has been preserved. The suppliant cries that he has poured out a libation to the goddess and prays that her heart may therefore have rest and that her anger may abate. After stating his name in l. 7 and the fact that he is suffering from sickness, he continues:—

8. Thou art the judge of my cause . . . . .
9. Thou art the director of my path . . . . .
10. May my god who is angry with me turn!
11. Sorrow, the grave, and bonds may he . . . . .!
12. May he remove the sickness of my body, may he tear away the . . . . . of . . . . .
13. May he loosen the grief of my heart!
14. Cause name and posterity to advance; let there be mercy and compassion; let me praise thy name!
15. Let me live, let me be perfect, let me praise thy greatness!

16. Let me bow in humility before thee!
17. May my . . . . . praise thy greatness
18. Unto the distant peoples!

The Reverse of the tablet begins with the colophon-line referring to the prayer contained by the Obverse. Then follows a section of ten lines of directions for ceremonies, which are to be performed before *Ištar* "on a favourable day". "Pure water shalt thou sprinkle. The . . . . . drink-offering shalt thou present. Dates (and) . . . . . shalt thou heap up. A *ŠA* of oil a drink-offering, water, honey (and) butter shalt thou offer. An incense-burner shalt thou set there. The . . . . .-drink shalt thou pour out." Ll. 24—26 prescribe certain rites to be performed with various woods and oil, and are followed by the injunction to recite the incantation three times and to unloose "the knotted cord".[1] The end of the first line of the colophon (l. 31), which contained the title of the series to which the tablet belonged, is broken away.

24. This line has been restored from No. 40, l. 12 (*q. v.*). That the signs *KU.DUB.DUB.BU* are to be taken together, *cf.* No. 62, l. 29.

25. The character [cuneiform sign] is somewhat spread out on the tablet, so that it might almost be taken for two signs and read *ištiniš(niš)*. As however other characters on the tablet are carelessly written, it is preferable to regard it as one sign, as in No. 12, l. 10, *etc.*

No. 31.

Transliteration.

1. . . . .
2. *šá* . . . .
3. *šá* . . . .
4. *ana-ku pulânu [apil pulâni ša] ilu-šu [pulânu ^{ilu}ištar-šu pulânîtum](tum)*
5. *a-na ka-a-ši* . . . . *-dan*
6. *ina pušķi u dannâti šú-zi-bi* . . . . *[dá-lí-lí]-ki lud-lul*

[1] *See* above, p. 22.

7. *INIM.INIM.MA ŠU IL.LA ilu. . . . . šamî-i*

8. *ina mûši ana pân ilu Ištar gušuru arku mû illu tasalaḫ*
9. *GI.GAB tukân(an)* VII TA.A.AN *kurmatîpl tar-bi(?)*
10. . . . . *burâši ta-šár-raḳ i-ṭi-ra u gi-mil-tú kun-ni*

11. . . . . *GI.GI bu-uk-rat ilu Sin ti-li-tú*

No. 31 (K 7207 + K 9675 + K 13274) represents the end of the Obverse of a tablet containing prayers and ceremonies addressed to the goddess *Ištar*. Ll. 1—6 give the concluding phrases of a prayer, in the last three lines of which the suppliant states his own name, and, after probably referring to the offerings he has made to the goddess, concludes with a petition for deliverance "in misery and distress". The prayer is succeeded by three lines of ceremonies to the following effect: "In the night before *Ištar* thou shalt sprinkle a green bough with pure water. The . . . . . drink-offering shalt thou present. Seven times the food shalt thou . . . . . A . . . . . of incense shalt thou offer. Place thou there a garment and a gift." L. 11 commences an incantation that was continued on the Reverse of the tablet.

No. 32.

Transliteration.

1. . . . . *.-bu*

2. *[INIM.INIM.MA ŠU] IL.LA ilu Ištar.KAN*

3. *[DU.DU BI ana pân ilu Ištar ŠA].NA burâši tašakan KAS.SAG tanaki(ki)*

4. . . . . III *šanîtu munu(nu) i-il-ta-šu* . . . .
5. . . . . *[ilu]ištar-[šu?] itti-šu sâlimu(mu?)*

6. . . . . *.-na ilu Ištar ḳá-rid-ti i-lá-a-[ti]*
7. . . . . *man-za-az-ki ina ki-rib šamî-i illûti[pl]*
8. . . . . *.-ti-ma ki-ma ilu Šamaš* . . . .
9. . . . . *šamîpl šadîpl u tâmâti[pl]*
10. . . . . *.-piš-ti na-maš-ti ḳaḳ-ḳa-ri ta-bar-ri-i* . . . .

11. . . . . *nišî^pl sa-pi-iḫ-ti tuš-ti-ši-ri* . . . .
12. . . . .*-ni-ki-ma kul-lat-si-na ba-*. . . . .
13. . . . . .*-ru-ki na-maš-šú-ú* . . . .
14. *[at]-ti-ma ^ilu^ Ištar li-ʾ-at* . . . .
15. . . . .*-ki-ma bîltu ina ki-rib [šamî-i illûti^pl ?]*

Like the preceding fragment, No. 32 (K 3358 + K 9047) represents the lower portion of the Obverse of a tablet. Only one sign remains of the incantation to which the colophon-line (l. 2) refers. Then follow three lines of directions prescribing the offering of incense, the pouring out of a libation, and the due recital of the incantation three times. At l. 6 there commences a fresh prayer to the goddess *Ištar*, containing the invocation of the goddess and a description of her power. The beginning and end of most of the lines are broken.

6. . . . . . : O *Ištar*, heroine among goddesses!
7. Thy seat is . . . . . in the midst of the bright heavens!
8. Thou art . . . . ., and like the Sun-god . . . . .!
9. [Lady?] of the sky, the mountains and the ṣeas!
10. Thou . . . . . the handiwork of creatures of the ground, thou beholdest . . . . .!
11. Thou scatterest the nations . . . . ., thou directest . . . . .!
12. . . . . . all of them . . . . . 13. . . . . . creation . . . . .!
14. Thou, O *Ištar*, art powerful . . . . .,
15. And thy . . . ., O Lady, is in the midst of the bright heavens!

No. 33.

Transliteration.

1. . . . .*-zu-zu i-lat mu-na-*. . . . .
2. *[muš(?)]-ti(?)-iš-ma-at a-mat-sa ša-ki-na-at* . . . .
3. *[muš] - ti - ni - iḫ uz - zi ili u* . . . .
4. *ši - mat taṣ - li - ti u su - pi - i*
5. *li - ḳat ik - ri - bi u un - ni - ni*
6. *im - šir ʾ - pa - a - ti a - pil ^ilu^ Marduk*
7. *dan(?)* - . . . . *IL du - ru* - . . . . *šadû-ú kib-ra-a-ti*

8. *zîr I.ZID.DA bît ši-kin na-piš-ti šá ilâni^{pl} rabûti^{pl}*
9. *[šar] - rat Borsippa^{KI} ba - ' - lat da - ád - mi*
10. *[^{ilu}]Taš-mi-tum bi-il-tum ša ki-bi-sa gaš-[rat?]*
11. . . . . *^{ilu}ištarâti^{pl} [rabâti^{pl}(?)]* . . . .
12. . . . . *ina ilâni^{pl} a - bi kib - ra - a - ti*
13. . . . . *- i - kiš - ki ka - a - ši*
14. . . . . *-ri* . . . . *-si-na azkur(ur) pâni-ki*
15. . . . . *taš-ma-a u sa - li - ma*
16. . . . . *-at ma-gi-ri [ta-ša?]-ka-ni taš-ma-a u sa-li-ma*
17. . . . . . *-riš-ma* . . . . *-nu tu-ša-aš-mi-i ki-bit-su-un*
18. . . . . *lib-ba-šu-nu tu-ši-iš-ši-ri iš-* . . . .
19. . . . . . *^{pl} ru-ku-tu tu-šak-na pânu-ki* . . . .
20. *^{ilu}Taš-mi-tum i-lat*[1] *su-pi u da-di bi-[lit* . . . . *]*
21. *[ana]-ku pulânu apil pulâni ša ilu-šu pulânu ^{ilu}ištar-šu [pu-lanîtum(tum)]*
22. [2]*as - ḫur - ki bîlti - yà ši - mi - i su - [pi - ya]*
23. *[a]-na ^{ilu}Nabû ḫa-i-ri-ki*[3] *bîlu ašaridu mâri riš-[ti-i]*
24. *[ša Ĭ.SAG.ILA a-bu-[ti ṣab-ti-ma]*
25. *[liš-mi zik]-ri-ya*[4] *[ina ki-bit pi-ki]*
26. *[lil - ki un] - ni - ni - ya [lil - ma - da su - pi - ya]*
27. *[ina zik-ri-šu kabti](ti)] ilu [u ^{ilu}ištar lislimu(mu) itti-ya]*

Rev.

28. *[li-in-ni-is]-si [murṣu ša zumri-ya]*
29. *[lit-ta-kil*[5]*] ta-[ni-ḫu ša šîri^{pl}-ya]*
30. *[lit-ta-bil] ašakku [ša bu'âni^{pl}-ya]*
31. [6]. . . . . *ru-ḫu-u ru-[su-u?]* . . . .
32. *[li-in]-ni-is-si ma-mi-tu*[7] *lit-[ta-kil*[5] *ni* - . . . . . *]*
33. . . . . *gallû*[8] *li - ṣal - ' [irat - su]*
34. *[a-na(?)] niši^{pl} a-pa-a-ti*[9] *liš-ša-kin ba-ni-[ti]*
35. *[ilu] û*[10] *šarru lik - bu - u damikti[(ti)]*
36. *[ina ki-bit]-ki ṣir-ti ša úl uttakkaru(ru)*[11] *u an-ni-ki ki-[nim]*[12]
37. *[^{ilu}Taš - mi] - tum bi - il - tum*[13]

38. *[INIM.INIM.MA ŠU] IL LA ^{ilu}Taš-mi-tum.KAN*

---

[1] *A ilat(at).* [2] After l. 21 *A* inserts the formula *ina lumun ^{ilu}atalî etc.* in two lines, and for l. 22 reads: *asḫur-ki imid-ki ši-mi-i a-ra-ti.* [3] *A ḫa-'-i-ri-ki.* [4] *A zik-ri.* [5] *A li-tá-kil.* [6] For l. 31 *A* reads: *lip-pa-aš-ru imti^{pl} imti^{pl} imti^{pl} šá ibašû-ú ili-yá.* [7] *A mu-mit.* [8] *A lit-lu-ud ^{ilu}NAM.TAR.* [9] *A ina pi-ki.* [10] *A u.* [11] *A uttakkarum(rum).* [12] *A* inserts *ša úl inû-u.* [13] *A bîltu.*

39. . . . . *mû illu tasalah ŠA.NA burâši harri*
40. . . . . *GA ina kîmi tašapak(ak)*
41. *munu(nu)-ma šukki?(ki)-ma*
42. . . . . *šâlimu(mu)*
43. . . . .

---

44. . . . . *ina rik-si TAG-ma* . . . . :
45. . . . . *i-nu-ma tîpuš(uš) šûmu lil(?)-*. . . . .
46. . . . . *[KAM] ŠAH(?) úl takalu(lu) ú-*. . . . .

---

47. . . . . *šar-rat kib-ra-a-ti i-lit bi-li-i-ti*
48. *ikal* *m ilu* *Aššur-bân-apli etc.*

No. 33 (K 3432 + K 8147) is a small tablet inscribed with rather coarse characters, which are in places much broken. It contains a prayer to the goddess *Tašmîtu*, the latter half of which is preserved in duplicate on the Reverse of No. 1 (*see* pp. 4, 6 f.). The prayer is followed by two short ceremonial sections, which with the catch-line and a short colophon complete the text of the tablet. The prayer commences as follows.

Translation.

1. . . . . . . O goddess . . . . .
2. Who causeth her word to be obeyed, who establisheth . . . . .!
3. Who appeaseth the anger of god and . . . . .!
4. Who heareth prayer and supplication!
5. Who accepteth petition and sighing! . . . .
8. O seed of *Išida*, the house of the living creature of the great gods!
9. Queen of Borsippa, Lady of the Dwelling!
10. O lady *Tašmîtu*, whose command is mighty!

The next few lines are broken. After stating (l. 14) that he is crying before the goddess, the suppliant describes her merciful character, as the giver of peace and prosperity. At l. 20 he once more addresses her by name and proceeds to make his request.

20. O *Tašmîtu*, goddess of supplication and love, lady of. . . . .!
21. I so and so, the son of so and so, whose god is so and so, whose goddess is so and so,
22. Have turned towards thee, O lady! Hearken to my supplication!

23. Before *Nabû* thy spouse, the lord, the prince, the first-born son
24. Of *Isagila*, intercede for me!
25. May he hearken to my cry at the word of thy mouth!
26. May he remove my sighing, may he learn my supplication!
27. At his mighty word may god and goddess deal graciously with me!
28. May the sickness of my body be torn away!
29. May the groaning of my flesh be consumed!
30. May the consumption of my muscles be removed!
31. [1]. . . . . sorcery, poison, ...
32. May the ban be torn away may the . . . . . be consumed
33. May . . . .
34. May mercy be established among men (and their) habitations!
35. May god and king ordain favour
36. At thy mighty command that is not altered, and thy true mercy,
37. O lady *Tašmîtu*!

Of the two ceremonial sections a few phrases only have been preserved. The first prescribes that the sprinkling of pure water and the offering of incense of *ḫarru*-wood shall accompany the recital of the incantation, while the second apparently deals, among other matters, with the rite of the knotted cord (*cf. supra* p. 71, *etc.*).

24. On the restoration of the end of this line, *see* above p. 14).

29. The verb *lit-ta-kil* is here restored from l. 32 and No. 1, ll. 46, and 48 (*cf. supra* p. 14).

32. The last sign in this line is probably to be restored as  (*cf.* Pl. 3, No. 1, Rev. (*cont.*), l. 48). For the explanation of *nišû* (= I 1, Inf. from *našû*) as a synonym of *mâmîtu*, *cf. supra*, p. 66.

41. The sign  is written over an erasure; it is clearly however to be read as , not .

46. The reading , suggested in the transliteration is not certain.

[1] For l. 31 *A* reads: "May the poisons that are upon me be loosened!"

No. 34.

Transliteration.

1. . . . . 2. . . . . *a-ta-mar* . . . .
3. . . . . *pár(?)-da-a ya-ši* 4. . . . .
dá-lí-lí-ki lud-lul

5. [*INIM.INIM.MA ŠU IL*].*LA* *ilu MI.MI*

6. [*DU.DU BI lu ina ŠAR*] . *lu ina ŠA.NA ipuš(uš)*

7. . . . .

The fragment No. 34 (K 11876) contains a few phrases from a prayer to the goddess *ilu MI.MI* (*cf.* Brünnow, *List*, no. 10449), the two colophon-lines being followed by a second prayer or perhaps the catch-line for the next tablet. Of this line, however, only traces of signs remain.

3. If the rendering of  by *pár* is correct *pár-da-a* must = 3 f. pl. *Prms.* I 1, from √פרד. For another instance of the use of the verb in I 1, *cf.* Lotz, *Tiglathpileser*, Col. II, l. 67 (p. 22) *li-par-du* (), and for its use in IV 1 with the meaning, according to Zimmern, *Busspsalmen* p. 110, of "to shine to the bright", *cf.* IV R 60* [67], C. Rev. l. 20 *ka-bit-ta-šu ip-par-du* (), whence the epithet *nipirdû*, "shining" (*see* Delitzsch in Lotz's *Tigl.* p. 106 and Zimmern, *op. cit.* p. 110). Perhaps also from this root are to be derived the subs.  (= *pár*?)-*da-a-ti* in the phrase *šunâti*^{pl} *pár-da-a-ti lâ ṭâbâti* (IV R 17, 16 *b*), and 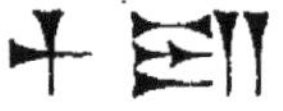 in No. 12, l. 57.

No. 35.

Transliteration.

1. . . . . *ša bi(?)-lu-*. . . . . 2. . . . .
ina . . . . . 3. . . . . *balâṭu ši-*. . . . . 4. . . . . .
. . . . . *ina pa-ni-* . . . . . 5. . . . . *nap-li-* . . . . .
6. . . . . *libbu ḫidûti-*. . . . . 7. . . . .
DIM. . . . . 8. . . . .

Rev.

9\. . . . . II . . . . 10. . . . .
GIŠ.TUK . . . . 11. . . . . *ŠAG.GA* . . . . .
. . . . . 12. . . . . *ik-ri-*. . . . . 13. . . . . .
. . . . .*-mi-ik-ti* *id-*. . . . .

14\. . . . . *ni - iš* *ka - a - ti* *šá* *ilu Bîlit*

15\. . . . . *saḫ(?)* *ki-bit* *ana* *arkat(?)* L *DA.RA*
16\. . . . .

No. 35 (K. 2757) contains portions of a prayer to the goddess *Bîlit*, at the end of which there follows the catch-line for the next tablet and traces of the first line of the colophon (l. 16). The interest of the fragment centres in l. 14, where we find the colophon-line, which is characteristic of the present class of texts, written phonetically (*see* above p. 13).

Section IV.

Prayers to deities whose names are not preserved.

Section IV is composed of fragments of tablets, which contain the colophon-line that is characteristic of the present collection of texts, but from which the names of the deities addressed are missing. It is generally possible to distinguish whether a god or goddess is addressed. In some cases, however, in addition to the colophon-line, only a few signs have been preserved.

No. 36.

Transliteration.

1. . . . . *-ki* . . . . 2. . . . . *-zi-*
. . . . 3. . . . . *ḫi-ṭi-ti(?)* . . . .
4. . . . . *šur-*. . . . . 5. . . . . *'-il-ti*
. . . .

---

6. *[INIM.INIM.MA]* *ŠU IL.LA* *ilu*. . . . .

---

7. . . . . *burâši* *ina* *išâti* . . . .
8. . . . . *ŠU* *IL.LA* . . . .
9. . . . . - *ma* *tiṣlitu* . . . .

---

10. . . . . *[ilu]Igigi* *butuktu* *ḫa-si-*. . . . .
11. *[ikal m ilu Aššur]-bân-apli etc.*

The fragment No. 36 (K 9125) contains the end of a prayer, followed by three lines of directions for ceremonies, which prescribe that the burning of incense and the rite of raising the hand are to accompany its recitation. L. 10 gives the catch-line for the next tablet.

No. 37.

Transliteration.

1. . . . . *ilu*. . . . . 2. . . . . *napiš-tim(tim)* . . . . 3. . . . . *pl libbi-*. . . . . 4. . . . . *ḫi-ir-tu* . . . . 5. . . . . *[ši?]-kin na-piš-ti* . . . .

6. *[INIM.INIM.MA ŠU] IL.LA* . . . .

7. *[šiptu]* . . . .[1] *[bîltu] šur-bu-tum ummu ri-mi-ni-tum*[2] *a-[ši-bat šamî-í illûti*pl*]*

8. *[al-si-ki* *bîlti-yà i-]ziz-zi-im-ma ši-mi-i*[3] *[ya-a-ti]*

9. *[iš-í-ki ašḫur-ki*[4] *kîma] ulinnu ili-yà u* *ilu* *ištari-yà ulinnu-[ki aṣ-bat]*

10. *[áš - šum di - ni*[5] *da] - a - ni purus [parasi(si)*[6]*]*

11. *[áš-šum bul-lu-ṭu]*[7] *šul-lu-mu bašû-u*[8] *[itti-ki]*

12. *[*[9]*áš-šum iṭîra gamâla] ti - [di - í]*

13. . . . .[1] *[bîltu ša-ḳu]-tum*[10] *ummu ri-[mi-ni-tum*[11]*]*

No. 37• (K 9087) contains a few words from the end of one prayer and the first seven lines from the commencement of another. The second prayer is addressed to a goddess and is partly duplicate of the prayer to *Ba'u* in No. 6, ll. 71 ff., and of that to the goddess, who bears the title *Bîlit ili*, in No. 7, ll. 9 ff. For a translation *see* above, p. 34 f.

---

1 Possibly to be restored from *B* *iluBi-lit ili*; *A* *iluBa'u*. 2 *A ri-mi-[ni-tum]*. 3 *A [ši-mi]-í*. 4 *A as-ḫur-ki*. 5 *A di-in*. 6 *D [pa]-ra-su*. 7 *A* here inserts the copula *u*. 8 *AD ba-šú-ú*. 9 For l. 12 *A* reads *áš-šum i-ṭi-ra ga-ma-* . . . . *šú-zu-ba ti-di-í*, *D* . . . . *-ma-la u šú-zu-ba ti-di-í*. 10 *A šur-[bu-tum]*. 11 *D um-mu ri-mi-ni-tum*.

No. 38.

Transliteration.

1\. *ana di-*. . . . . 2. *dá - li - [li -]* . . . .

3\. *INIM.INIM.[MA ŠU IL.LA]* . . . .

4\. *DU.DU [BI lu ina ŠAR lu ina ŠA.NA ipuš(uš)]*

5\. *šiptu šur-*. . . . .

6\. *û* . . . .

7\. . . . .

No. 38 (Bu. 91—5—9, 16) is a fragment from the left side of a tablet and preserves the beginnings of two lines from the end of a prayer, which is followed by the two common colophon-lines, the catch-line, and the beginning of the colophon.

No. 39.

Transliteration.

1\. . . . . 2. . . . . *[a]-na ka-*. . . . .

3\. . . . . ^{ilu}*Ištar* . . . .

4\. *[INIM.INIM].MA ŠU IL.LA* . . . .

5\. *[DU.DU BI] lu ina ŠAR lu ina ŠA.NA [ipuš(uš)]*

6\. . . . . *kakkabâni*^{pl} *i-lat šar-*. . . . .

7\. . . . . *- i - ti i-lat i-*. . . . .

8\. . . . . *ilâni*^{pl} *DI.BAR šamî-i* . . . .

9\. . . . . *[damiktu](tu)* ^{ilu}*Igigi nu-úr ma-*. . . . .

10\. . . . . *muš-na-mi-rat* . . . .

11\. . . . . *-bu-u di - pa - ru -* . . . .

12\. . . . . *it - ta - na - an - bi - ṭu* . . . .

13\. . . . . *-ki bi-il-ti ina ki-* . . . .

14\. . . . . *- ya ku - ši - ma* . . . .

15\. . . . . *- ni - ma ma -* . . . .

16\. *[ana-ku pulânu apil] pulâni ša šum-ru-*. . . . .

17\. . . . . *-maḫ-ra dan-*. . . . .

18\. . . . .

Of the first prayer to which the two colophon-lines (l. 4 f.) on No. 39 (K 8930) refer, a few characters only remain. The prayer that commences at l. 6 is addressed to a goddess. The first eight lines contain the invocation, and ascribe to her the power of giving light (to the world); the beginning and end of every line, however, is broken off.

No. 40.

Transliteration.

1. . . . . *DI* . . . .

---

2. *[INIM.INIM.MA]* *ŠU IL.LA* . . . .

---

3. . . . .*pl-šu ša IM.IL ilu*. . . . .
4. . . . . - *at isu irinu a - [na?]* . . . .
5. . . . .*KUR.NA TU.UD.TA dipâru* . . . .
6. . . . .*-niš-su-un-nu SIR ina lubuštu piṣâti lubuštu*. . . . .
7. . . . .*-rit-ta-šú* VII *bâbâti pl tu-*. . . . .
8. . . . . *isu paššuru tašakan(an)* XXXVI *ŠA AŠ.A.AN ŠIR (. . . . .)*
9. . . . .*-na ša ZU.DU tukân(an) immiru niḳî tunam-mar(?) kap-ra tunikis(?)(is)*
10. . . . . *širu KA.IZI SI.IL(ḳa) nîš îni*
11. . . . . *[isu]irinu û upuntu tu-nam-mar*
12. *[mi - iḫ - ḫa?] tanaḳi(ki) KU.DUB.DUB.BU ŠUB.ŠUB(di)*
13. . . . .*-su nîš îni-ma* III *šanîtu mînûtu(tú) an-ni-tú*
14. . . . .*-šu DIM.ŠID šam AN.IRIM u riksu tapaṭar(ar)*
15. . . . . *- bu-ma ina šumi šuati tudammiḳ(iḳ)*.
16. *ana damiḳti(ti) tazakar(ar)*

---

17. . . . .

The principal contents of No. 40 (K 2567) consist of fourteen lines of directions for ceremonies. These were preceded by a prayer, of which only a few traces of signs remain. Bezold (*Catalogue*, p. 454) suggests that this fragment belongs to K 2487 (= No. 2, *see* above, p. 18). The character of the writing on both tablets is very similar.

8. For the explanation of the sign-group  as = *irrit zunni*, *see* Jensen, *ZA* I, p. 308 (*cf.* Brünnow, *List*, no. 6767). What meaning attaches to the group in the present passage is not clear.

12. The suggested restoration of the beginning of this line is based on No. 8, l. 21 (*cf. supra*, p. 42 f.).

No. 41.

Transliteration.

1. . . . .

2. *[DU.DU BI] lu ina KIŠDA lu ina ŠA.NA [ipuš(uš)]*

3. . . . . *šarru ni - mi - ki ba - nu - u ta - šim - ti*

4. . . . . *m ilu Aššur-bân-apli etc.*

In No. 41 (K 7916) the first line is probably to be restored as the colophon-line *INIM.INIM.MA ŠU IL.LA etc.* L. 3 gives the catch-line for the next tablet.

No. 42.

Transliteration.

Obv.

1. . . . . 2. *na-*. . . . . 3. *kul-lat* . . . . 4. *ú-tag-ga(?)-*. . . . . 5. . . . . . *-ri-ʾ ki-*. . . . . 6. *ta-ta-na-ru-*. . . . . 7. *a-na ri-i-*. . . . . 8. *šak-na-ta* . . . . 9. *ša ZIG.GIR-ka* . . . . 10. *a-lik ḫar-ra-ni* . . . . 11. *la DIM.KU la ir-*. . . . . 12. *ša paḳ-du pi-*. . . . . 13. *dannu ina dan-na-*. . . . . 14. *i-lul mun-nap-*. . . . . 15. *ina kâri dan-na* . . . . 16. *mu-šap-šiḳ UD* . . . . 17. *ina pî-ka ki-*. . . . . 18. *ša la* . . . . 19. *a-zu-*. . . . .

Rev.

20. . . . . 21. *ul-*. . . . . 22. *ḫidûtu-ka* . . . . 23. *ilu NIN.A.KU.KUD.[DU]* . . . .

24. *INIM.INIM.MA ŠU [IL.LA]* . . . .

25. *înu(?)-ma ina KIŠDA înu(?)* . . . .

26. *šiptu* ^{ilu}*Marduk bîlu rabû* . . . .
27. *ikal* $^{m\ ilu}$*Aššur-bân-[apli] etc.*

No. 42 (K 3221) preserves part of the left side of a large tablet, about four lines being missing from the beginning of the Obverse. L. 25 gives an unusual form of one of the common colophon-lines (*see* above, p. 71).

No. 43.

Transliteration.

1. . . . .*-bu-*. . . . . 2. ^{ilu}*Marduk* . . . . 3. *[ilâni]*^{pl} . . . . 4. *ilâni*^{pl} . . . . 5. *ilâni*^{pl} *a-šib* . . . . 6. ^{ilu}*A-nim* ^{ilu}*Bîl* . . . . 7. *ana-ku arad-ki* . . . .

8. *[INIM].INIM.MA ŠU [IL.LA]* . . . .

. . . .

The end of a prayer to a goddess has been preserved by No. 43 (K 13355).

No. 44.

Transliteration.

1. . . . . ^{ilu}*NIN* . . . .

2. *[INIM.INIM].MA ŠU IL.[LA]* . . . .

3. . . . .*-tu an-na* . . . . 4. . . . . *KU*^{pl} . . . . 5. . . . .*-nu* . . . .

6. . . . .

No. 44 (K 14210) contains traces of a prayer and three lines of directions for ceremonies.

No. 45.

Transliteration.

Obv.

1. . . . .*-ti* . . . . 2. . . . . *-luṭ lu-*
. . . . 3. . . . .*-um taḳ-bu-u* ^{ilu}*Šamaš* . . . .

4. *[INIM.INIM].MA ŠU IL.LA* ^{ilu}. . . . .

5. . . . .

Rev.

6. . . . . *-ra-ka* . . . . 7. . . . . *-ma*
a-na . . . . 8. . . . . *-na ši-it-*. . . . .
9. . . . . *ba-la-tu* . . . . 10. . . . .
-bil . . . .

The fragment No. 45 (82—3—23, 119) contains traces of prayers; so little however has been preserved that it is impossible to decide with certainty which side is the Obverse of the tablet.

Section V.

Prayers to Astral Deities.

Section V contains prayers to certain stars, which are not regarded as inanimate, but are personified as deities. This personification of the stars and planets is not surprising, for there are not lacking proofs that the greater gods, even when addressed by name in prayer, were regarded as astral powers. To mention three instances in the present collection of texts, in No. 19, l. 17 f. the god *Bîl* is selected from "the multitude of the stars of heaven" to receive a gift, while in No. 6, l. 77 f. the goddess *Ba'u*, and in No. 7, l. 15 f. the goddess *Bîlit ili*, are sought by the suppliant among the stars. Moreover the astral deities here addressed are invoked in terms as exalted as those employed in prayers to the greater gods, and in No. 50, if my restoration of the passage is correct, the fixed star *Sibziana* is even credited with the creation of mankind.

The majority of the tablets in this section are of the larger class, and contained, when complete, several prayers, interspersed in some cases with directions for ceremonies.

No. 46.

Transliteration.

1\. . . . . - *gu - u* *iḫ - ṭu - u*
2\. . . . . - *liḫ* *a - du - ur - ma*
3\. . . . . - *[ka]* *rabîti(ti)* *ub - la*
4\. . . . . *lim - ḫu - ru - ka - ma*
5\. *[ag - gu* *lib - ba - ka]* *li - nu - ḫa*

6. . . . .-*[ka ra-bu]-u*[1] *ta-ai-ra-tu-ka kab-ta-a-tum*
7. . . . .-*ši lib-ša-nim-ma*
8. *[dá - lil ilu - ti - ka] rabîti(ti) lud - lul*

9. *INIM.INIM.[MA ŠU IL].LA* ^{kakkabu}*Muštabarrû-mûtânu(a-nu).KAN*

10. *DU.DU BI [lu ina KIŠDA] lu ina ŠA.NA ipùš(uš)*

11. *šiptu* ^{ilu}*Nirgal bîl* . . . . ^{kakkabu}*Piṣû ṭi-iḫ šamî-i u irṣitim(tim)*
12. *sa-ni-ku* . . . . - *ti bu-kur* ^{ilu}*KU.TU.ŠAR*
13. *ma-am-lu git-ma-lum pa-ki-du gi-mir KIRRUD.AZAG.GA*
14. *i - lit - ti* ^{ilu}*A - nim mâru riš - tu - ú*
15. *ḫa - lip ša - lum - ma - ti ša lit - bu - šú nam - ri - ri*
16. *dan - dan - nu ḳit - ru - du bîl a - ba - ri*
17. *ša - kin taḫ - tí - [í] mu - ša - aš - ki - nu li - i - ti*
18. *šarru tam - ḫa - [ri ir?] - šú ik - du la pa - du - ú*
19. . . . . *[mu-hal-liḳ?] za-ai-ri*
20. . . . . *[šal?]-ba-bu muḳ-tab-lum*
21. . . . .-*tú ḳarrâdu*
22. . . . .-*ti*
23. . . . .

The upper portion of No. 46 (K 11153 + Rm 582) contains the end of a prayer to the ^{kakkabu}*Muštabarrû-mûtânu*,[2] addressed as a male deity, which, after the double colophon (l. 9 f.), is followed by a prayer to *Nirgal*, who is invoked as follows:—

11. O *Nirgal*, lord of . . . . . *Piṣu*, near to heaven and earth!
12. Who harasses the . . . . ., the first-born of *KU.TU.ŠAR*!
13. The strong, the perfect, who careth for the whole of the *Kirrud-azaga*!
14. The offspring of *Anu*, the first-born son!
15. Who is clad with brightness, who is clothed with light!
16. The mighty, the valiant, the lord of power!
17. Who giveth the victory, who establisheth strength!

---

[1] *A ra-bu-ú.*

[2] One of the seven names of the planet Mercury, see JENSEN, *Kosmologie* p. 120 f.

18. King of the battle, the wise, the courageous, the invincible!
19. . . . . who destroyeth the foe!
20. . . . . the impetuous, the warrior!
21. . . . . the hero!

9. That the *kakkabu NI-BAT-a-nu* is phonetically written *kakkabu Muštabarrû-mûtânu*, *cf.* BRÜNNOW, *List*, no. 5347, and JENSEN, *Kosmologie*, p. 119.

12. For the identification of -*azaga* with -*azaga*, and the explanation of the latter as "the lordly chamber" of the Lower World, *see* JENSEN, *op. cit.*, p. 234 f.

15. The word *šalummatu* expresses the idea of light viewed as an object of terror (JENSEN, *op. cit.*, p. 155).

19. This line is restored from I R 17, l. 8 where *Ninib* is described as *mu-hal-lik za-ya-a-ri*. Several of the epithets in this prayer are to be found in *Aššurnaṣirpal*'s dedication.

No. 47.

Transliteration.

1. . . . .-*i* *ru-*. . . . . 2. . . . . *lim - nu -*. . . . . . 3. . . . . *KA.LU.BI.DA* . . . . 4. . . . .-*na-ku-nu balâṭu ba-a-ni* 5. . . . . *dâ-li-li-ku-nu lud-lul*

6. *[INIM.INIM.MA ŠU IL].LA Mul-mul.KID*

7. *[DU.DU BI lu ina KIŠDA lu] ina ŠA.NA ipuš(uš)*

8. . . . . *gaš - ru - ú - ti*
9. . . . . *ŠU IL.LA KAN* . . . . .
10. *[ikal m ilu Aššur-bân]-apli etc.*

The end of a prayer has been preserved by No. 47 (K 8808). In l. 6 the signs   I have taken as the *Mul-mul*-star (*cf.* JENSEN, *Kosmologie*, p. 152) and not as the plural of *kakkabu* (*see* No. 8, l. 22), though the suffix in *dâ-li-li-ku-nu* suggests that the prayer is addressed to more than one deity.

The tablet apparently formed one of a series, part of the title of which is contained by l. 9.

No. 48.

Transliteration.

Obv.

1. . . . . *-ni-ti* 2. . . . . *-a-ti* 3. . . . . *in-ši* 4. . . . . *-ša* 5. . . . . *-a-ti* 6. . . . . *-li-ku* 7. . . . . *MIN* 8. . . . . *-ri* 9. . . . . *-šu* 10. . . . . *-yà* 11. . . . . *ziz* 12. . . . . *-ši* 13. . . . . *-ziz* 14. . . . .

Rev.

15. *ki-*. . . . .

---

16. *INIM.INIM.MA* *ŠU IL.LA* *Mul-mul.KAN*

---

17. *šiptu bêlu šur-bu-u ša ina šamê-i šú-luḫ-ḫu-šu illu*
18. VIII-*ú par-su Bît sa-la-mi-i ikal* [m ilu]*Aššur-bân-apli etc.*

According to the first line of the colophon (l. 18), No. 48 (K 8116) forms the eighth part of a composition entitled the *Bît sa-la-mi-i* (*cf.* Bezold, *ZA* V, p. 112 and *Catalogue*, p. 896). The Obverse of No. 48 preserves a few ends of lines from the beginning of the tablet, the Reverse the end of a prayer to the *Mulmul*-star. According to the catch-line the next part of the composition commenced with the words: "O mighty lord, whose . . . . . is brilliant in heaven!"

18. With the composition entitled the *Bît salamî* may be compared the incantations that commence *šiptu bît nu-ru* (*see* above, p. 53), and the Series *Bît rimki* (*supra*, pp. 14 ff.). The *bît rim-ki* and the *bît ša-la-mi-i* are mentioned together in the letter K 168, l. 13 (*cf.* Lehmann, *Šamaššumukin*, Pt. II, p. 76 and pl. XLV).

No. 49.

Transliteration.

Obv.

1. . . . . 2. . . . . *-ú-ti* 3. . . . .
-mar 4. . . . . *-a-ti* 5. . . . . *ilâni*^{pl} ^{ilu}*Igigi*
6. . . . . *ṭa-ab-tú* 7. . . . . *-ai-ti* 8. . . . .
. . . . *-li-ti* 9. . . . . *-lu at-mu-ú-a* 10. . . . .
-pú(?) ya-a-ši 11. . . . . *-ni ú-mi-šam* 12. . . . .
-ru-sa-a-ti 13. . . . . *-ú lim-nu-ti* 14. . . . . *-ú*
ina zumri-yà 15. . . . . *[šar]-ra-tum rabîtum(tum)*
16. . . . . *ka - ru - bu* 17. . . . . *- ma - ' - ú*
18. . . . . *- ši - la - ku* 19. . . . . *ri - ši - ka*

---

20. *[INIM.INIM.MA ŠU IL.LA* ^{kakkabu}*KAK].SI.DI.KAN*

---

21. . . . . *-ṭur* . . . .

Rev.

22. . . . . 23. . . . . *i-mu-ki* 24. . . . . . .
. . . . *-ru-ti* 25. . . . . *ra-šub-bu* 26. . . . .
-ša-an-nu 27. . . . . ^{pl} *u išâtu* 28. . . . .
abnî^{pl} 29. . . . . *šamî-i* 30. . . . . *[mu-ša?]-*
az-nin nuḫšu 31. . . . . *ḫa-ra-ár-ra* 32. . . . . . .
. . . . . *il - lu ṣîru* 33. . . . . *ḫa - ra - ár - [ra]*

The Obverse of No. 49 (D.T. 65) preserves part of a prayer to the star *KAK.SI.DI* (*cf.* JENSEN, *Kosmologie*, p. 49 ff., *etc.*), addressed as a male deity. This prayer is followed by a second, which is continued on the Reverse of the tablet.

No. 50.

Transliteration.

Obv.

1. *[šiptu* ^{kakkabu}*SIB.ZI.AN.NA]* . . . .
2. *[mu - na - kir]* . . . .
3. *[ina šamî-i]* . . . .
4. *[kan - su maḫ - ra - ka?]* . . . .
5. *[ilâni*^{pl} *rabûti*^{pl} *i - ṣal - lu - ka - ma?]* . . . .
6. *[ina ba - li - ka* ^{ilu}*A - nim]* . . . .
7. ^{ilu}*Bêl ma - [li - ku?]* . . . .

8. *^{ilu}Rammânu ašarid šamî-i u irṣitim(tim) ul . . . .*
9. *ina ki - bit - ka*[1] *izzakara(ra) ti - [ni - ši - i - ti?]*[2]
10. *ši - si - ma itti - ka*[3] *ilâni^{pl} rabûti^{pl} li - zi - [zu]*
11. [4]*di - ni di - in purussa - ai purus(us)*
12. *a - na - ku arad - ka ^{m}Aššur - bân - apli mâr ili - šu*
13. *šá ilu - šu Aššur ^{ilu}iš - tar - šu ^{ilu}Aš - šú - ri - i - tú*
14. *ina lumun ^{ilu}atalî ^{ilu}Sin ša ina arḫi ûmi ^{KAN}*
išakna(na)
15. *ina lumun idâti^{pl} ITI.MIŠ limnîti^{pl} lâ ṭâbâti^{pl}*
16. *ša ina ikalli - yà u mâti - yà ibašâ - a*
17. *ás - šum ú - piš limutti(ti) murṣu lâ ṭâbu ar - ni*
18. *ḳil-la-ti ḫi-ṭi-ti ša ina zumri-yà . . . .*
19. *ikimmu lim-nu ša itti-yà rak-su-ma ú-šaḫ- . . . .*
20. *am - ḫur - ka ú - sa - pi - [ka]*
21. *niš ḳâti - yà mu - ḫur ši - mi taṣ - [li - ti]*
22. *pu - šur kiš - pi - ya pu - si - si ḫi - ṭa - ti - [ya]*
23. [5]*linnasiḫ(iḫ) mimma lim-nu ša ana na-kàs napišti-ya illika[(ka)]*
24. *^{ilu}šidu damḳu lu ka - ai - an ina rîši - yà*
25. *ilu ^{ilu}ištar amîlûti sa - li - mu . li - ir - šú - ni*

Rev.

26. *ina ḳibît - ka lu - úb - luṭ*
27. *ludlul - ka nar - bi - ka lu - ša - pi*[6]

---

28. *INIM.INIM.MA ŠU IL.LA ^{kakkabu}SIB.ZI.AN.NA.KAN*
29. *šiptu at-ta ^{kakkabu}KAK.SI.DI ^{ilu}NINIB a-ša-rid ilâni^{pl} rabûti^{pl}*

No. 50 (K 2801 + K 9490) is a comparatively small tablet inscribed for *Aššurbanipal* with a prayer to be recited on the occasion of an eclipse of the Moon. The prayer is evidently extracted from one of the larger compositions, which contain several prayers and ceremonial sections. Such a text, similar in size to Nos. 12, 21, and 22, must have been the tablet of which the duplicates A and B are parts. These two fragments do not join but from the style of the writing and character of the clay it may be assumed that they are parts of the same

[1] *A ina ḳibît-ka.* [2] Restored from the similar expression in No. 19, l. 13. [3] *A it-[ti-ka].* [4] For l. 11 *A* reads: . . . . -*zi* . . . . [5] For l. 23 *B* reads: *ú-šur-*. . . . . [6] After l. 27 *B* ceases to be a duplicate and reads: | *šiptu kakkabu*. . . . . , | *^{ilu}DUMU* . . . . , | *ki-ma* . . . . , | . . . . . -*ti-*. . . . . , | . . . .

tablet. The prayer in the present text, however, was not extracted from the original of A and B, for the incantation that follows in B commences 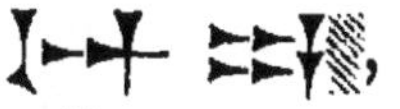, and does not agree with the catch-line of No. 50. The prayer is inscribed to the star *Sibziana*,[1] addressed as a male deity, and invoked in ll. 1—9 in somewhat extravagant terms. The object of the prayer is to induce *Sibziana* to remove the evil spells, bewitchments, possession by spectres *etc.*, that have followed in the train of the lunar eclipse. The prayer reads as follows.

Translation.

1. O *Sibziana* . . . . 2. Thou that changest the . . . . .
3. In the heavens . . . . . 4. They bow down before thee . . . . .
5. The great gods beseech thee and . . . . .
6. Without thee *Anu* . . . . . 7. *Bîl* the arbiter . . . .
8. *Rammân* the prince of heaven and earth . . . . .
9. At thy command mankind was named![2]
10. Give thou the word and with thee let the great gods stand!
11. Give thou my judgement, make my decision!
12. I, thy servant, *Aššurbanipal*, the son of his god,
13. Whose god is *Aššur*, whose goddess is *Aššurîtu*,
14. In the evil of the eclipse of the moon which in the month (*space*) on the day (*space*) has taken place,
15. In the evil of the powers, of the portents, evil and not good,
16. Which are in my palace and my land,
17. Because of the evil magic, the disease that is not good, the iniquity,
18. The transgression, the sin that is in my body . . . . .,
19. [Because of] the evil spectre that is bound to me and . . . . .,
20. Have petitioned thee, I have glorified thee!
21. The raising of my hand accept! Hearken to my prayer!
22. Free me from my bewitchment! Loosen my sin!

[1] For the identification of *Sibziana* with Regulus, and the explanation of the name as "the true shepherd of heaven" (*Rî'u kînu ša šamî*), *see* JENSEN, *ZA* I, p. 266, and *Kosmologie*, pp. 36 f., 48 f. *etc.*

[2] *I. e.* created. It is possible that  should be rendered by the Qal, not the Nifal, of *zakâru*, *šumu* being understood; in either case the meaning of the line remains the same.

23. Let there be torn away whatsoever evil may come to cut off my life!
24. May the favourable *šidu* be ever at my head!
25. May the god, the goddess of mankind grant me favour!
26. At thy command let me live!
27. Let me bow down and extol thy greatness!

The catch-line for the next tablet reads: "Thou, O *KAK.SI.DI* art *Ninib*, the prince of the great gods!" This line is discussed by Jensen (*Kosmologie*, pp. 53 f., 150), Bezold having published the fragment K 9490 (*cf. ZA* III, p. 250), which contains the conclusion of the text.

No. 51.

Transliteration.

1\. . . . . 2. *[i]-ṭi-ir* . . . . 3. . . . . . -*pal*
ár - ša - . . . . 4. . . . . . *amîlûtu* . . . .
5\. . . . . . -*ma* . . . . 6. *[aṣ]-bat ṣubâta(?)-ka ú-*. . . . .
. . . . . 7. *gi-mil balâṭi ili-*. . . . . 8. *dalili-ka* . . . . .

9\. II *INIM.INIM.MA ŠU IL.LA* *kakkabu[SIB.ZI.AN.NA.KAN]*

10\. *AG.AG BI ana pân* *kakkabu SIB.ZI.AN.NA* II . . . .
11\. *[ŠA.NA] burâši tašakan(an) KAS.SAG tanaḳi(ki) šiptu an-ni-[ti]* . . . .
12\. . . . .-*za-za aḫarriḳânu(?) itti(?)* *iṣu bînu* . . . . .
13\. . . . . *šamni* *iṣu šurmînu* *pušuš* . . . .
14\. . . . . *ŠI* *šam IGI.MAN.ĜIRI* *iṣu NAM*. . . . .
15\. . . . . *[tašakan?](an) ina ulṣi(?)* . . . .
16\. . . . . *lim - nu* *úl* . . . .
17\. . . . .

In No. 51 (K 8190) the colophon-line (l. 9) seems to refer to two prayers, of which the end of the second has been preserved. At l. 10 a ceremonial section of seven lines commences, prescribing the offering of incense and the pouring out of a libation before *Sibziana*. Ll. 12 ff. contain certain rites to be performed with various plants and woods, including anointing with the oil of *šurmînu*-wood.

No. 52.

Transliteration.

1\. . . . . 2. *ina an-ni-ka ki-nim* . . . .

3\. *AG.AG BI ana pân* ^{kakkabu}*SIB.[ZI.AN.NA]* . . . .
4\. *lu ina KIŠDA lu ina ŠA.NA* III *šanîtu munu[(nu)]*

5\. *šiptu šarru ilâni*^{pl} *gaš-ru-ú-ti ša nap-ḫar ma-a-ti šú-pu-u* ^{ilu}*IMINA.BI at-tu-nu-ma*
6\. *ikal* ^{m} ^{ilu}*Aššur-[bân]-apli etc.*

Part of the last line of a prayer has been preserved by No. 52 (K 6395 + K 10138), followed by a rubric of two lines which presents a variant form of a common ceremonial direction. Elsewhere the injunction *DU.DU BI lû ina KIŠDA lû ina ŠA.NA ipuš* follows the colophon-line *INIM.INIM.MA ŠU IL.LA etc.* In the present tablet, however, it is directly preceded by the incantation, and is expanded so as to form two lines. It is possible that nothing followed the name of the star in l. 3. In that case l. 4 would not commence a new sentence, but would run on without a break: "Do the following. Before *Sibziana* either *ina KIŠDA* or *ina ŠA.NA* three times recite (the incantation)".[1]

The catch-line (l. 5) reads: "O king of the mighty gods of all the land! Powerful, O Seven-fold one, are ye!" While citing the passages in which the 𒀭 𒅓 𒁉 is found, E. T. Harper (*Beiträge zur Assyr.*, Bd. II, Hft. 2 (1892) p. 436), has attempted to distinguish its use as applied to a single divinity from those instances in which the context shows a plurality of deities are referred to. In l. 5 of No. 52, however, we have a remarkable instance of the combination of sing. and plur. with reference to the ^{ilu}*IMINA.BI*, the plur. of the pers. pron. occurring by the side of *šarru* and *šupû*. There is no doubt, therefore, that the name 𒀭 𒅓 𒁉 was applied to a group of gods who were so closely connected, that, though addressed in the plural, they could in the same sentence be regarded as forming a single personality.

---

[1] *See* above p. 71 f.

Section VI.

Prayers against the evils attending an eclipse of the Moon.

The sixth and final Section might be more strictly termed an appendix, for the texts it contains are only indirectly connected with the series of tablets classified under Sections I—V. Throughout these five sections it will be observed that several of the prayers contain the formula, discussed on pp. 7 ff., in which it is stated that the prayer is offered in consequence of certain evils that have followed in the train of a lunar eclipse. The formula is to be found in No. 1, ll. 1—28, a prayer to *Sin*, and ll. 36—52, a prayer to *Tašmîtu*, in No. 4, ll. 9—22, a prayer to *Damkina*, and ll. 24—50, a prayer to *Ba'u*, in the concluding prayer of No. 6, according to the duplicate F, in No. 7, ll. 9—33, a prayer to the goddess *Bîlit ili*, and ll. 34—63, a prayer to *Išhara*, in No. 19, ll. 1—33, a prayer to *Bîl*, in the prayer to *Nirgal* in No. 27, according to the duplicate A, and in No. 50, ll. 1—28, a prayer to *Sibziana*. It is not, however, confined to the group of texts collected in Sections I—V, but is of somewhat common occurrence in various series and classes of prayers. In Section VI, therefore, I have collected those tablets and fragments in which I have come across the formula. The list, however, makes no pretence of being exhaustive, for it is probable that the eclipse-formula is contained by other tablets throughout the collections from Kouyunjik.

No. 53.

Transliteration.

Obv.

1\. . . . .

2\. . . . . gaš(?)-ru . . . . -ḫu

3\. abḳal kiš-ša-ti ^{ilu}Marduk šal-ba-[bu bîl?] I.ṬUR.RA

4\. ^{ilu}Í-a ^{ilu}Šamaš u ^{ilu}Marduk ya-a-ši ru-ṣa-nim-ma

5\. ina an-ni-ku-nu i-ša-ru-tú lul-lik

6\. ^{ilu}Šamaš ikimmu mu-pal-li-ḫi šá iš-tu ŭ-mí ma-'-du-ti

7\. arki-ya rak-su-ma lâ muppaṭiru(ru)

8\. ina kâl ŭ-mi ikšuš(?)-an-ni ina kâl mûši up-ta-na-laḫ-an-ni

9\. ri-du-su ušîzizu(zu) lubuštu(?) ili-yà uz-za-na-ḳa-pu

10\. pâni-yà i-ḫi-su-u ínipl-yà uz-za-na-ḳup

11\. ur-ka-yà ub-ba-lu šîripl-yà i-šam-ma-mu

12\. kal pag-ri-ya ub-ba-lu

13\. lu í-kim-mu kim-ti-ya u sa-la-ti-ya

14\. lu í-kim-mu ša ina di-ik-ti di-ku

15\. lu ikimmu GUṘ TAP.PI DU an-nu-ú šú-ú an-nu-u . . . . -šu

Rev.

16\. ^{ilu}Šamaš ina pâni-ka íš-tí-'-šú-ma lubuštipl ana lit-bu-ši-šu
miširu ana kabti(?)

17\. miširu ana ḳabli-šu SU.A.RU.LA mîpl ana šatî-šu

18\. ^{kimu} í-šiḫ-šu ŠA.KASKAL addin-šu

19\. a-na í-rib ^{ilu}Šamši(ši) lil-lik

20\. a-na ^{ilu}NÍ.DU.NI DU.GAL ša irṣitim(tim) lu-pa-ḳid

21\. ^{ilu}NÍ.DU.NI DU.GAL ša irṣitim(tim) maṣartu-šu li-dan-nin

22\. li-iz-ziz ^{isu}šigaru nam-ṣa-ki-šu-nu(?)

23\. ^{ilu}Šamaš ina ki-bi-ti-ka ṣir-ti ša [úl] uttakkaru(ru)

24\. ina lumun ^{ilu}atalî ^{ilu}Sin ša ina arḫi pulâni ûmi pulâni išakna(na)

25\. lumun idâtipl ITI.MIŠ limnîtipl lâ ṭâbâtipl

26\. ša ina ikalli-yà u mâti-yà ibašâ-a

27\. [ina] ki-bit abḳalli ilânipl ^{ilu}Marduk ina zumri-yà . . . . .
. . . . -kis-su

28\. . . . . -yà ipparasu(su) ina zumri-yà . . . . .
. . . . -pal-šu

29\. . . . . lu-ta-mí napšat ^{ilu}Í-a . . . . lu-ta-mí

30\. . . . . pl . . . . lu-ta-mí

31\. . . . .

No. 53 (K 3859 + Sm. 383) preserves the bottom portion of a tablet and contains a prayer to *Ia*, *Šamaš*, and *Marduk*, of which both the beginning and end are missing. The suppliant states that he is praying after an eclipse of the Moon, and he implores these three deities to rescue him from the clutches of a spectre, by whom he is continually haunted. What remains of the Obverse commences as follows: —

3. O arbiter of the world, *Marduk*, the mighty, the lord of *Iṭura*!
4. O *Ia*, *Šamaš*, and *Marduk* deliver me,
5. And through your mercy let me come to prosperity!
6. O *Šamaš*, the spectre that striketh fear, that for many days
7. Has been bound on my back, and is not loosed,
8. Through the whole day hath . . . . . me, through the whole night hath stricken me with terror!

The suppliant then describes the ways in which he is tormented by the spectre, who defiles him and attacks his face, his eyes, his back, his flesh and his whole body. On the Reverse of the tablet he recounts to *Šamaš* how he has tried to appease and to restrain his tormentor. Apparently his efforts have met with no success for he now turns to the Sun-god for relief, which he prays he may receive through his mighty command that is not altered, and through the command of *Marduk*, "the arbiter of the gods".

10. After the form *uz-za-na-ḳa-pu* in l. 9 one might perhaps assign to  in *uz-za-na-* the new value *ḳap*.

18. The character  is not quite accurately rendered on pl. 68, for the small perpendicular wedge should project slightly above the long horizontal one. Elsewhere the forms of this character are somewhat various. While the beginning of the sign () remains constant, together with the small perpendicular wedge (), the number and position of the small diagonal wedges above the long horizontal line vary considerably. In K 2971, Col. III, l. 22 three wedges () occur above the horizontal line (not two as in IV R[2] 56, l. 55 *b*), in V R 18, l. 35 f. (as corrected in *ZK* I, p. 349) two wedges only occur, and in V R 11, l. 10 f. four wedges () are to be found,

which in the duplicate K 4410 are written . In all these passages, however, only one diagonal wedge is written below the long horizontal wedge.

23. In the transliteration before the sign  I have restored , which has been apparently omitted by the scribe in error.

No. 54.

Transliteration.

1. *[ana-ku] pulânu apil pulâni šá ilu-šu pulânu ^{ilu}[ištar-šu pulânîtum(tum)]*
2. *[ina] lumun ^{ilu}atalî ^{ilu}Sin šá ina arḫi pulâni ûmi pulâni [išakna(na)]*
3. *[ina] lumun idâti^{pl} ITI.MIŠ limnîti^{pl} [lâ ṭâbâti^{pl}]*
4. *[šá] ina ikalli - yà u mâti - yà [ibašâ - a]*
5. *[ina] ḳibît - ka kit - ti lu - [úb - luṭ]*
6. *[lu - uš] - lim - ma lu - uš - tam - mar [ilu - ut - ka]*
7. *[í - ma] ú - ṣa - am - ma - ru lu - [uk - šú - ud]*
8. . . . . *kit - tum* . . . .
9. . . . . *[damiḳtim](tim)* . . . .
10. . . . .

No. 54 (Sm. 512) is a fragment from the centre of a prayer, and, in addition to the eclipse-formula, contains some of the common petitions for life, success, *etc.* Ll. 8 and 9 are possibly to be restored according to No. 9, l. 13 f.

No. 55.

Transliteration.

1. . . . . 2. *ana-[ku ^{m}]Aššur-bân-apli ^{ilu}BAR* . . . . 3. *ina lumun ^{ilu}atalî ^{ilu}Sin ša ina arḫi [ûmi ^{KAN}išakna(na)]* 4. *ina lumun idâti^{pl} ITI.MIŠ [limnîti^{pl} lâ ṭâbâti^{pl}]* 5. *šá ina ikalli - yà u mâti - yà ibašâ - [a]* . . . .

Part of a prayer of Ashurbanipal has been preserved by No. 55 (K 6792). The fragment is from the left side of one of the class of smaller tablets.

No. 56.

Transliteration.

1. *ša* . . . .
2. *ilu Šamaš ilu* . . . .
3. *mâru* . . . .
4. *ik - ka - ru ki -* . . . .
5. *mu - ša - ri in -* . . . .
6. *i - ṭi - ir* . . . .
7. *a-na-ku m Aššur-[bân-apli]* . . . .
8. *šá ilu - šu [Aššur ilu iš - tar - šu ilu Aš - šú - ri - i - tú]*
9. *ina lumun ilu [atalî ilu Sin ša ina arḫi ûmi KAN išakna(na)]*
10. *[ina] lumun idâti[pl ITI.MIŠ limnîtipl lâ ṭâbâtipl]*
11. *[ša ina] ikalli[-yà u mâti-yà ibašâ-a]*

Like the preceding fragment No. 56 (K 2810) contains part of a prayer written for Ashurbanipal. The tablet is one of the smaller kind and is written in somewhat coarse characters; what has been preserved of the Reverse is uninscribed.

No. 57.

Transliteration.

Obv.

1. . . . .
2. *ilu Iš-ḫa-ra ummu ri-[mi-ni-tum šá nišîpl* . . . .
3. *ana-ku pulânu apil pulâni ša ilu-šu [pulânu ilu ištar-šu pulânîtum(tum)]*
4. *ina lumun ilu atalî ilu Sin ša [ina arḫi pulâni ûmi pulâni išakna(na)]*
5. *lumun idâtipl ITI.[MIŠ limnîtipl lâ ṭâbâtipl]*
6. *ša ina ikalli - yà u [mâti - yà ibašâ - a]*

7. *a - na šú - a - ti ashur - ki al - [si - ki]* . . . .
8. *áš - šum gi - mil dum - ki* . . . .
9. *as - ruk - ki si - riḳ* . . . .
10. *za - ka - a da - aš - pa ku - ru - [un - na]* . . . .
11. *ú - ma - ḫir - ki mu -* . . . .
12. *napišti(ti) ub - lak - ki* . . . .
13. *ilu Iš - ḫa - ra ina šap -* . . . .
14. *bi - lit mâtâti ina šap -* . . . .
15. *dup - pi - ri mimma* . . . .
16. *mimma lim - nu* . . . .
17. *šú -* . . . . 18. . . . .

Rev.

19. . . . . *- mi -* . . . . 20. . . . .
21. . . . . 22. . . . .

The commencement of No. 57 (K 9909) is very similar to the end of the Reverse of No. 7. Each tablet is addressed to *Išḫara*, No. 57, ll. 2 and 4—7 corresponding to No. 7, ll. 59—62. L. 63 of No. 7, however, does not agree with l. 8 of No. 57, so that the texts, through closely parallel, are apparently not duplicates.

No. 58.

Transliteration.

Obv.

1. . . . . *.pl mu-šim šîmâti pl* 2. . . . . *.-šú-ú nuḫšu* 3. . . . . *.pl ta-pa-ḳid* 4. . . . . *lim-na-ti šú-ul-ma* 5. . . . . *[ana-ku pulânu apil] pulâni ša ilu-šu pulânu ilu ištar-šu pulânîtum(tum)* 6. *[ina lumun ilu atalî ilu Sin ša ina arḫi pulâni] ûmi pulâni išakna(na)* 7. *[lumun idâti pl ITI.MIŠ limnîti pl lâ ṭâbâti pl ša ina] ikalli-yà u mâti-a ibašâ-a*
8. . . . . *pa-ša-šu* 9. . . . . *- an -* . . . . .
10. . . . . *.-ka* . . . . 11. . . . . *na* . . . . 12. . . . . *ḫu* . . . .
13. . . . .

Rev.

14. . . . . 15. . . . . *- ši - ru šú - luḫ - ḫi*
16. . . . . *.-mí ilâni pl mu-tál-lum* 17. . . . . *mu-na-mir uk-li* 18. . . . . *- ki mu - riš I.ṬUR.RA*

To judge from the thickness of the tablet, No. 58 (K 6644) may possibly have contained two columns on either side. In that case, the beginning of Col. II and the end of Col. III have been preserved, inscribed with portions of two separate incantations.

No. 59.

Transliteration.

1. . . . .^{pl} *ina kal* . . . .
2. . . . .*-ni ša ipri*^{pl} *DUB* . . . .
3. . . . . *šadâni*^{pl}*(ni) ḫarrâni*^{pl} *NUN* . . . .

---

4. . . . . *bîl ilâti*^{pl} *šaplâti*^{pl} *BUR* . . . .
5. . . . . *-ú taṣ-lit* . . . .
6. . . . . *bîl ridûti(ti)* . . . .
7. . . . . *ár-ni u ma-mit ilâni*^{pl} . . . .
8. . . . . ^{ilu}*Šamaš kaspu ḫurâṣu nu-*. . . . .
9. . . . . *[kam]-sa-ku a-na-kar ir-*. . . . .
10. . . . . *lit-ba-lu* . . . .
11. . . . .*-ti-ka rabîti(ti) ša úl uttakkaru(ru)* . . . . .
12. *[ina lumun]* ^{ilu}*atalî* ^{ilu}*Sin ša ina arḫi pulâni [ûmi pulâni išakna(na)]*
13. *[lumun idâti]*^{pl} *ITI.MIŠ [limnîti*^{pl} *lâ ṭâbâti*^{pl}*]*
14. *[ša ina ikalli]-yà u mâti-yà [ibašâ-a)*
15. . . . .*-yà liš-*. . . . .
16. . . . .*-li-na-an-ni ma-ḫi(?)-*. . . . .
17. . . . . *mâr ili-šu in - an - na* - . . . .
18. . . . . ^{ilu}*Šamaš* ^{ilu}*Rammânu u* ^{ilu}*Marduk* . . . . .
19. . . . . *-tab-ba-la-ka ta* - . . . .
20. . . . . *rîk - ku - ti* . . . .
21. . . . . ^{amîlu}*mîtu lâ itûr* . . . .
22. . . . . *iribu* . . . .

The upper portion of a tablet has been preserved by No. 59 (K 7978), consisting of a heading or introduction of three lines, and the beginning of an incantation to a male deity.

No. 60.

Transliteration.

Obv.

1\. . . . .

2\. *[LUGAL?] BI KA.TAR.ZU GA.AN.SIL* ⊱ *šar-[ru? šú]-ú dá-[lí-lí-ka lud-lul?]*

3\. *û anaku ^{amîlu}MU.MU aradka dalilika ludlul*

4\. *INIM.INIM.MA KI ^{ilu}Šamaš.KAN maš-maš limnu(nu)*

5\. *šiptu ^{ilu}Šamaš daiân šamî-í u irṣitim(tim) la-iṭ irṣiti(ti) ra-paštim(tim)*

6\. *bîlu pi-tu-ú uz-ni na-ram ^{ilu}Bîl*

7\. *daiânu ṣîru ša ki-bit-su la ut-tak-ka-ru*

8\. *an-na-šú ilu ma-am-man la í-nu-u*

9\. *bîlu at-ta-ma šur-bat a-mat-ka*

10\. *ki-bit-ka ul im-maš-ši ut-nin-ka ul iš-ša-na-an*

11\. *kîma ^{ilu}A-nim abu-ka ki-bit-ka ṣi-rat*

Rev.

12\. . . . . ^{pl}*-ka šú-tu-rat a-mat-ka*

13\. . . . . *ša í - mu - ka ra - aš - bu*

14\. . . . . *[í] - mu - ki ṣîrâti^{pl} at-ta-*. . . . .

15\. . . . . *-di-ri-ka ša šit-mu-ru la sa-*. . . . .

16\. . . . . *amâti^{pl} ŠI.MIŠ lim-ḫu-ru-*. . . . .

17\. . . . . *-mat lik-ru-bu-*. . . . .

18\. . . . ? . . . . . . *-ri NI.RUŠ lizziza(za)* . . . .

19\. *[ina lumun ^{ilu}]atalî Sin ša ina arḫi pulâni ûmi pulâni išakna[(na)]*

20\. *[lumun idâti^{pl}] ʾITI.MIŠ limnîti^{pl} lâ ṭâbâti[^{pl}]*

21\. *[ša ina ikalli]-yà mâti-yà ibašâ-[a]*

22\. . . . . *-us šú-ut-li-ma-am-ma [damiḳtim](tim)*

. . . .

No. 60 (K 3463) consists of the lower portion of a tablet. After three colophon-lines there follows a prayer to *Šamaš*, which is continued on the Reverse of the tablet. The prayer opens with the following invocation:—

5\. O *Šamaš*, judge of heaven and earth, that burnest the broad earth!

6\. O Lord, that openest the ear, the darling of *Bîl*!

7\. Exalted judge, whose command is not altered,

8. Whose mercy no god has ever annulled!
9. A lord art thou, and mighty is thy word!
10. Thy command is not forgotten, thy intercession is unequalled!
11. Like *Anu*, thy father, thy word is exalted!

On the Reverse of the tablet, which is somewhat broken, the suppliant continues his invocation of the god, and in ll. 19 ff. states the occasion of the prayer.

2. The second half of this line is probably a semitic translation of the Sumero-Akkadian phrases with which it commences. For my conjectural restoration, *cf.* Brünnow, *List*, no. 561, and Zimmern, *Busspsalmen*, p. 73.

No. 61.

Transliteration.

1\. . . . .
2\. - *šat - ki* . . . .
3\. *[. . . . . IN]TI šik-nat matâti nu* - . . . .
4\. [III] *šanîtu kibi - ma limuttu* . . . .

5\. *[šiptu] mârat ^{ilu}A-nim ša šamî-i* . . . . .
6\. *[bi] - nu - ut tâmti ta - ma - ti rapšâti(ti)*
7\. *[^{ilu}]A - nim a - bu - ni ib - na - na - ši - [ma?]*
8\. *[šamû]-ú u irṣitim(tim)*[1] *ib-ba-nu-ú it-ti-[ni]*
9\. *[û] ma - mi - tu ib - ba - ni it - ti - ni - [ma?]*
10\. *[at]-ti ma-mit ŠA.LA*[2] *^{karpatu}GU.ZI u ^{iṣu}paššuru*
11\. *[ina ûmi]* II^{KAN} *ûmi* VII^{KAN} *ûmi* XV^{KAN} *ûm nu-bat(?)-ti ûm AB.AB ûmi* XIX*[^{KAN}]*
12\. *[ûmi* XX*]^{KAN} bubbulum ûm rim-ki ûm limutti*[3] *ûmi* XXX^{KAN}
13\. *[a-na] nap-šat ili u šarri ka-ti at-ta-ra-[am?]*
14\. *[ni] - iš ilâni^{pl} rabûti^{pl} az - za - [kar?]*
15\. *[a-na] mûdû - ú lâ mûdû - ú at - ta* - . . . .
16\. *[*[4]*ina lumun] ^{ilu}atalî ^{ilu}Sin ša ina arhi pulâni ûmi pulâni išakna[(na)]*

[1] *A irṣitum(tum).* [2] After  *A* reads in smaller characters:  *it-ti.* [3] *A higalli.* [4] *A* apparently omits l. 16, reading in its place: *lumun idâti^{pl} ITI.MIŠ limnîti^{pl} [lâ ṭâbâti^{pl}] | [ša ina ikalli]-yà u mâti-yà [ibašâ-a].*

17. . . . . *muḫ-ra-an-ni* GU.ZUR-*ki u-kul-li-*. . . . .
18. . . . .-*pi-ka pu-šur ina la ḪI-ka šú-ṣa-a-*. . . . .
19. . . . . [*ka?*]-*bu-ut-ta-ka-ma taš-ma-a an-*. . . . .
20. . . . . - *tu - un   šipat* ^{ilu}*I - a* . . . .
21. . . . . ^{ilu}*Ba'u   šipat* ^{ilu}*NIN.A* . . . .

22. . . . . MA   GU . . . .

23. . . . .

No. 61 (K 8293) contains traces of four lines of directions for ceremonies, which are followed by a short incantation of seventeen lines, addressed to a goddess, "the daughter of *Anu*". Only the first line of the eclipse-formula is included in the text, while in the duplicate A this is replaced by the second and third lines of the formula.

11. For the *ûm nu-bat(?)-ti*, cf. DELITZSCH, *Beiträge zur Assyr.*, Bd. I, p. 231, and JENSEN, *Kosmologie*, p. 106 f. A similar sequence of days occurs in K 2866, 1. 25 f. (S. A. SMITH, *Miscellaneous Assyrian Texts*, p. 17); cf. also III R 56, No. 4.

No. 62.

Transliteration.

Obv.
1. . . . . *kiššat   ilâni*^{pl}   *rabûti*^{pl}
2. . . . . *šîmâti*^{pl}   *mu-uṣ-ṣi-ru* ^{isu}*uṣurâti*^{pl}
3. . . . . *šamî-i u irṣitim*(*tim*) *at-tu-nu-ma*
4. . . . .^{pl}   *uṣ - ṣu - ru   bušû - ku - nu - ma*
5. . . . . [*ta*]-*ṣim-ma* ^{isu}*uṣurâti*^{pl} *balâṭu at-tu-nu-ma tu-uṣ-ṣa-ra*
6. . . . . *ta-par-ra-sa   šipat-ku-nu   balâṭu*
7. . . . .-*la-mu   i-piš pî-ku-nu   ba-la-ṭu-um-ma*
8. . . . . *ka - bi - su   irṣiti*(*ti*)   *rapašti*(*ti*)
9. . . . .-*bu ka-bi-su ki-rib šamî-i rûḳûti*^{pl} *at-tu-nu-ma*
10. . . . . *lum-ni ša-ki-nu dum-ki mu-pa-si-su idâti*^{pl}
      ITI.MIŠ *limnîti*^{pl}
11. . . . .-*da-a-ti limnîti*^{pl} *lâ ṭâbâti mu-šal-li-tu ki-i lum-ni*
12. . . . .-*ši-ru* NAM.BUL.BI.I *i-ma idâti*^{pl} ITI.MIŠ
      ma-la ba-ša-a

13. [ana-ku pulânu] apil pulâni ša ilu-šu pulânu ^{ilu}ištar-šu pulânîtum(tum)

14. . . . . .^{pl} ITI.MIŠ limnîti^{pl} it-ta-nab-ša-nim-ma

15. [pal]-ḫa-ku-ma ad-ra-ku u šú-ta-du-ra-ku

---

16. ina lumun ^{ilu}atalî ^{ilu}Sin ina lumun ^{ilu}atalî ^{ilu}Šamaš

17. ina lumun kakkabâni^{pl} ša šú-ut ^{ilu}I-a šú-ut ^{ilu}A-nim šú-ut ^{ilu}Bîl

18. ina lumun . . . .^{pl} ša ana kakkabâni^{pl} ḫarrâni^{pl} iṣ-ṣal-. . . . .

19. ina lumun . . . .^{pl} ša ana a-ḫa-miš it-ti-iḫ- . . . .

20. . . . . ina lumun ali . . . .

Rev.

21. . . . . ^{ilu}I-a . . . .

22. . . . . rabîti(ti) ana . . . .

---

23. . . . . kalû . . . .

---

24. . . . .-ak-ki ŠAR mî^{pl} illûti^{pl} . . . .

25. . . . . [^{ilu}]Marduk tukân(an) III ḲA$^{TA.A.AN}$ . . . . .

26. [suluppu KU.A].TIR tašapak(ak) ŠA šamni niḳû mû [dišpu ḫimîtu tašakan(an)]

27. . . . . tukân(an) ŠA.NA burâši tašakan(an) . . . .

28. [^{immiru}niḳî] tanaki(ki) ^{šiṛu}ZAG ^{šiṛu}MI.ḪI [u ^{šiṛu}KA.IZI tašakan(an)

29. . . . . [ta ?]-sal-laḫ III KU.DUB.DUB.BU ŠUB.[ŠUB(di)]

30. . . . . minûtu(tú) an-ni-tú III šanîtu munu-ma uš-ki-in-ma . . . .

---

31. [šiptu bîl] bîlî šar šarrâni . . . .

32. [ikal] $^{m\ ilu}$Aššur-bân-apli šarri kiššati šarri $^{mâtu\ ilu}$[Aššur^{KI}]

33. [šá a] - na ^{ilu}Aššur ù ^{ilu}Bîlit tàk - lum

34. [šá] ^{ilu}Nabû ù ^{ilu}Taš-mi-tum uznâ^{du} rapaštum(tum) iš-ru-ku-uš

35. [i-ḫu]-zu înâ^{du} na-mir-tum ni-siḳ dup-šar-ru-ti

36. [šá ina] šarrâni^{pl}(ni) a - lik maḫ - ri - ya

37. [mimma šip - ru] šú - a - tu la i - ḫu - zu

38. [ni-mi-iḳ ^{ilu}Nabû] ti-kip sa-an-tàk-ki ma-la ba-aš-mu

39. [ina dup-pa-a-ni aš] - ṭur as - niḳ ab - ri - i - ma

40. [a-na ta-mar-ti ši-ta]-as-si-ya ki-rib ikalli-ya ú-kin

41. [itillu mudû nu - ur] šarri ilâni^{pl} ^{ilu}Aššur

42. [man-nu šá itabbalu ù lu-u] šuma-šu it-ti šumi-ya i-šaṭ-ṭa-ru

43. [^{ilu}Aššur ù ^{ilu}Bîlit ag]-giš iz-zi-iš lis-ki-pu-šu-ma

44. [šuma - šu zîra - šu] ina mâti li - ḫal - li - ḳu

No. 62 (K 7593) is the upper portion of a large tablet. Its Obverse contains a prayer, which is addressed to more than one deity, and is offered with the object of obtaining help on several occasions of distress. The line that is ruled between ll. 15 and 16 does not mark the commencement of a second incantation, but rather a fresh section of the first prayer. For at that point the suppliant ceases his invocation and the statement of his own condition of alarm, and prays for deliverance from various evil powers and influences. As the first of these evils is that caused by a lunar eclipse the tablet is included in the present Section. The other evils, that are enumerated in ll. 17—20, appear to be of an astral nature. The Reverse of the tablet concludes with a ceremonial section of seven lines.

12. The compound ideogram *NAM.BUL.BI* appears to be a somewhat general term for evil or unpropitious influences, *cf.* IV R 17, Rev., l. 15 f., K 2277, Obv., ll. 3 ff., Rev., ll. 1, 4, *etc.* For the Series of incantations entitled the  , *see* Bezold, *Catalogue*, p. 456, *sub* K 2587.

29. For the restoration of the end of this line, *cf.* No. 40, l. 12; *see* also No. 30, l. 24.

32. The most recent translation of this colophon has been given by Tallqvist, *Die Assyrische Beschwörungsserie Maqlû*, Leipzig 1895, pp. 41, 53 f., *etc.*

VOCABULARY

א

א$_2$ = ה; א$_3$ = ח, ح; א$_4$ = ע$_1$, ع; א$_5$ = ע$_2$, غ

אאל îltu "spell, charm": *'-il-ti* **36**, 5; *i-il-ta-šu* **32**, 4.

אב abu "father": *a-bu* **11**, 2; **19**, 5; *a-bi* **6**, 24; **11**, 38; **12**, 34, 87; **21**, 56; **33**, 12; *abu* **11**, 22; *abu-ka* **2**, 17; **3**, 15; **27**, 9; **60**, 11; *abi-ya* **11**, 22 *C*; *abi-yà* **11**, 22bis; *a-bu-ni* **61**, 7.

אבב I 1 "to shine, be bright": *lu-bi-ib* **12**, 82; — II 1 "to make bright, to purify": *li-ib-bi-bu-nin-ni* **12**, 86; *lib-bi-bu* . . . . . **12**, 86 *C*; *ubbib-an-ni* (ideogr. LAḪ.LAḪ) **11**, 25.

ibbu "pure": *ib-bi* **30**, 2.

אבב abûbu "deluge, inundation": *a-bu-bu* **11**, 1; *a-bu-ub* **12**, 23; *a-bu-bi* **21**, 80.

AB.AB a festival?: *(ûm)* AB.AB **61**, 11.

אבן abnu "stone": *abnî^{pl}* **12**, 104; **49**, 28.

aban birḳi "thunderbolt": *abnî^{pl} birḳu* **21**, 17.

abḳallu "arbiter": *ab-kal* **22**, 35; *abḳallu* **22**, 37; *abḳalli* **53**, 27; *abḳal* **12**, 88, 114; **53**, 3.

אבר abâru "to be strong": ? *a-bì-rum* **6**, 97; **10**, 7.

abâru "strength": *a-ba-ri* **46**, 16.

אבר$_3$ aburriš "in security": *aburriš* (ideogr. U.SAL) **25**, 6.

אבת$_4$ abbuttu "chain, fetter" (*see* ṣabâtu): *a-bu-ti* **1**, 42; **9**, 45; **33**, 24.

agubbû "pure water; vessel of purification": ^{karpatu}*a-gúb-ba* **12**, 85, 118; *a-gúb-ba* **15**, 18.

אגג agâgu "to be enraged": *i-gu-ga* **4**, 46; **6**, 89; **7**, 27.
aggu "angry": *ag-gu* **6**, 12; **27**, 20; **46**, 5.
uggatu "anger": *ug-gat* **12**, 77.

אגה igû "sin": *[i]-gu-u* **46**, 1; *[i]-gu-ú* **28**, 9.
UGU.KUL.LA(*šam*): **12**, 101.
IGI.MAN.GIRI(*šam*): **51**, 14.

אגר ugaru "plain, country": *ú-ga-ru* **21**, 84.
adaguru "incense-burner, censer": *karpatu a-da-gúr* **12**, 4; *karpatu a-da-gùr* **30**, 23.

אדה adî "up to": *adî* **11**, 37.

אדל idlu "hero": *i-dil* **9**, 1; **18**, 20.

אדם admu "child": ? *ad-mi-ki* **7**, 40.

אדר adâru "to fear": I 1 *a-du-ur-ma* **28**, 10; **46**, 2; *ad-ra-ku* **4**, 42; **62**, 15; — III 2 *šú-ta-du-ra-ku* **4**, 42: **62**, 15.

אדר adiru "trouble, distress": *a-di-*. . . . . **5**, 6.
idirtu "affliction": *i-dir-tú* **12**, 69.
adirtu "grief": ? *a-di-ra-tú* **30**, 13.

אדש₃ mudiššû "renewer, renovator": *mu-diš-šu-u* **9**, 5; *mu-diš-šú-u* **12**, 30; **21**, 4.
iddiššû, iddišû "newly shining": *id-diš-šú-u* **12**, 18; *id-diš-šú-ú* **1**, 2; **6**, 98; *id-di-šú-ú* **12**, 18 *A*.

אום ûmu "storm": *ŭ-mu* **20**, 9, 11; **21**, 9, 35, 37.

אור urru "light": *urru-ka* **1**, 5, 10.

אזב₄ izîbu III 1 "to save, to deliver": *šú-zi-bi* **31**, 6; *šú-zu-ba* **4**, 31; **6**, 76.

אזז₄ izîzu "to be angry": *i-zi-za* **6**, 89; **7**, 27; *i-zi-za-ma* **7**, 41.
izzu "mighty, terrible": *iz-zi-tú* **12**, 117.
uzzu "anger": *uz-zu* **12**, 77; *uz-zi* **33**, 3.
izzîtu? "anger": *i-zis-su* **11**, 1; *i-zi-su* **11**, 1 *A*.

אזן uznu "ear": *uz-nu* **12**, 20; *uz-ni* **60**, 6; *uznâdu-ai* **4**, 34; **6**, 79; **7**, 16; **19**, 20; **21**, 62; *uznâdu-ši-na* (*cf.* bîrtu) **12**, 38.

אח aḫu "brother": *aḫi-ya* **11**, 22 *C*; *aḫîpl-šu* **21**, 5.
aḫamiš "together": *a-ḫa-miš* **62**, 19.

אח aḫu "side": *a-ḫi-ya* **13**, 23.
aḫîtu "side": *a-ḫi-ti* **12**, 68.

אחה aḫû "hostile": ? *a-ḫi-tú-ma* 11, 24.

אחז aḫâzu "to hold, to grasp": *a-ḫu-zu* 8, 6.

aḫarriḳânu a disease of the eye: *aḫarriḳânu* (ideogr. IGI.IGI) 51, 12.

$אטר_4$ iṭîru "to protect": *i-ṭi-ir* 56, 6; *[i]-ṭi-ir* 51, 2; *iṭ-ri-nì-in-ni-ma(?)* 4, 34; *iṭ-ṭi-rat* 9, 35; *i-ṭi-ra-ta* 6, 64; *i-ṭi-ra* 4, 31; 6, 76; *iṭîra* (ideogr. KAR) 7, 14; 37, 12.

iṭiru a garment: *i-ṭí(?)-ra* 31, 10.

אי ai "not, never": *ai* 2, 45; 6, 124; 7, 57bis; 10, 22; 11, 19, 24; 12, 62, 63, 64, 65, 67, 69, 74bis, 77; 15, 9; 21, 65.

אי ya'u "where?": *ya-ú* 11, 10; 21, 54.

איב aibu "foe": *ai-bi-ya* 21, 64.

$אין_4$ înu "eye": *îni* 40, 10; *îni-ma* 40, 13; *îni*pl*-yà* 53, 10.

איר âru I 2 "to lead, rule": *mu-ut-ta-'-ir* (or I 2 fr. $מאר_2$?) 6, 20.

tîrtu "command, law": *ti-rit* 2, 18; 3, 15.

אכד ikdu "mighty, courageous": *ik-du* 20, 18; 46, 18.

אכה ikû "needy": *i-ka-a* 2, 20; 3, 16.

ikûtu "need, want": *i-ku-tú* 12, 37; *i-ku-tum* 2, 20 *B*; *i-ku-ti* 2, 20; 3, 16.

אכל akâlu "to eat, to consume": I 1 *ikkal-šu* (ideogr. KU.KU) 12, 121; *takalu(lu)* ideogr. KU 33, 46; — IV 2 *li-tá-kil(?)* 1, 45, 48; *lit-[ta(?)-kil(?)]* 33, 29, 32.

mâkalû "eating": *ma-ka-li-i* 7, 52.

$אכל_3$ iklitu "darkness": *ik-lit-si-[na]* 12, 35.

uklu "darkness": *uk-li* 58, 17.

ukallu?: *ú-kal(gal?)-lu* 21, 18.

ikallu "palace": *ikal* 9, 32; *ikalli-yà* 1, 13, 40; 4, 19, 41; 6, 113 *F*; 7, 22, 61; 19, 12; 27, 11 *A*; 50, 16; 53, 26: 54, 4; 55, 5; 56, 11; 57, 6; 58, 7; 59, 14; 60, 21; 61, 16 *A*.

$אכם_4$ ikimmu "spectre": *i-kim-mu* 53, 13, 14; *ikimmu* (ideogr. GIDIM) 50, 19; 53, 6, 15; GIDIM(UTUG?).MA 22, 12.

uknû "lapis-lazuli": *abnu*uknû 12, 12, 13, 70.

אכר ikkaru "husbandman": ? *ik-ka-ru* 56, 4.

אל alu "city": *alu* 21, 25; *ali* 12, 65; 21, 25; 62, 20; *ali-ya* 21, 14, 18; *ali-yà* 4, 37, 46; 6, 82, 88; 7, 19, 26.

אל ilu "god": *ilu* **1**, 25, 44, 50; **4**, 37, 46; **6**, 3, 4, 82, 88, 121, 122, 132; **7**, 19, 26; **10**, 20, 21, 27; **11**, 7, 11, 15, 17; **12**, 31, 107, 111; **19**, 3, 15, 25; **21**, 18, 25, 76, 93; **22**, 7, 36, 38; **27**, 23; **28**, 7; **33**, 27, 35; **50**, 25; **60**, 8; *ili* **12**, 57, 77; **21**, 26; **27**, 12; **33**, 3; **61**, 13; *ili* (NI.NI) **4**, 45; **6**, 67; **11**, 25; **30**, 10; *ilu-šu* **1**, 38; **2**, 24, 26; **3**, 3; **6**, 27, 55, 83 *E*; **10**, 32; **12**, 45; **13**, 5; **31**, 4; **33**, 21; **50**, 13; **54**, 1; **56**, 8; **57**, 3; **58**, 5; **62**, 13; *ili-šu* **2**, 26 *D*; **50**, 12; **59**, 17; *ili-yà* **1**, 23; **2**, 40; **4**, 29, 36; **6**, 73, 81, 87, 123; **7**, 11, 18, 25; **9**, 16, 18; **10**, 21; **11**, 26; **12**, 61, 71, 92; **21**, 67; **22**, 17, 61, 62; **37**, 9; *ili-*. . . . . **6**, 11; *ilâni*^{pl} **1**, 11, 14, 16, 17; **2**, 2, 15, 18, 25, 30, 31, 45, 47; **3**, 6bis, 13, 15; **4**, 9, 11, 12; **5**, 1; **6**, 39, 65, 91, 111, 127, 129, 130; **7**, 5, 6, 29; **8**, 19bis, 23; **9**, 25, 26, 29, 30, 32; **10**, 3, 5, 15, 23; **11**, 14, 35; **12**, 79, 87, 88, 114; **21**, 52, 56, 58, 61, 93; **22**, 3, 27, 41; **27**, 4, 7; **33**, 8, 12; **39**, 8; **43**, 3, 4, 5; **49**, 5; **50**, 5, 10, 29; **52**, 5; **53**, 27; **58**, 16; **59**, 7; **61**, 14; **62**, 1.

iltu "goddess": *il-tum* **7**, 35; *ìl-ti* **30**, 30; *'i-lat* **2**, 43; **19**, 34; **33**, 1, 20; **39**, 6, 7; *ilat(at)* **1**, 37; *i-lá-a-ti* **1**, 29; **5**, 11; **32**, 6.

ilûtu "godhead, divinity": *ilu-ti-ka* **1**, 18; **13**, 6; **22**, 10, 66; **27**, 22; **46**, 8; *ilu-ut-ka* **9**, 11; **12**, 91; **21**, 70; **27**, 15; **54**, 6; *ilu-*. . . . . **6**, 16; *i-lut-ka* **6**, 68; *ilu-ut-ki* **4**, 34; **8**, 17.

אל ul "not": *ul* **6**, 26; **12**, 58; **14**, 17; **50**, 8; **60**, 10bis; *úl* **1**, 50, 51; **4**, 44; **6**, 86; **7**, 24; **12**, 1, 19, 77, 100, 119; **19**, 8, 31, 32; **21**, 2; **33**, 36, 46; **51**, 16; **53**, 23; **59**, 11.

אל ultu "from": *ul-tu* **6**, 58; **11**, 36.

אלה alû a demon: *alû* **12**, 51.

אלה$_4$ ilû "lofty, situated above"; that which is in heaven (opp. to šaplu, *q. v.*): . . . . .*-lá-a* **2**, 16 *B*; *ilû* **21**, 55; *ilâti*^{pl} **59**, 4.

ili "on, upon": *ili* **7**, 58; **12**, 6, 97bis, 104, 115; **17**, 7, 8; *ili-ka* **2**, 34; *ili-ya* **6**, 58; **10**, 4; *ili-yà* **1**, 22, 47; **12**, 57; **14**, 1; **19**, 24; **22**, 58; **53**, 9; *ili-*. . . . . **6**, 93; **7**, 31; **51**, 7.

? *mi-lat* (?): **12**, 57, 107; **27**, 12.

? *ti-li-tú*: **31**, 11.

אלך₂ alâku "to go": I 1 *illika(ka)* ideogr. DU 50, 23; *lil-li-ki* 5, 4; *lil-lik* 11, 24; 53, 19; *lul-lik* 6, 117; 10, 18; 13, 9; 53, 5; *a-lik* 13, 4; 42, 10; *a-li-kăt* 8, 12; — I 2 *lit-tal-lak* 19, 30; *lit-tal-*. . . . . 6, 123; 10, 21; — III 2 *li-sa-lik* (= **lištalik?*) 14, 10.

alaktu "path, way": *a-lak-ti* 4, 30; 6, 113; 10, 16; 11, 11; 30, 9.

IL.(LA) a plant: ^{šam}IL 12, 9; ^{šam}IL.LA 30, 25.

אלל alâlu "to bind, to gird, to hang up": *i-lul* 42, 14.

אלל I 1 "to shine, be bright": *lu-lil* 12, 81; — II 1 "to make bright, purify": *ullil-an-ni* (ideogr. AZAG) 12, 84.

illu "bright, pure": *il-lu* 49, 32; *illu* 12, 2; 21, 28, 74; 30, 21; 31, 8; 33, 39; 48, 17; *illûti*^{pl} 4, 24; 6, 21, 71; 7, 9; 22, 42; 27, 5; 32, 7, 15; 37, 7; 62, 24.

ulinnu "robe, vestment": *ulinnu* 4, 29; 6, 73; 7, 11; 37, 9; *ulinnu-ka* 5, 2; *ulinnu-ki* 4, 29; 6, 73; 7, 11; 37, 9.

אלץ₄ ulṣu "joy, pomp": *ul-ṣi* 6, 121; 10, 20; *ulṣi* (ideogr. UL) 51, 15.

אם ima "when; in, among": *i-ma* 8, 18; 9, 12, 20 *B*; 54, 7; 62, 12.

אמד₄ imîdu "to stand; to establish": *îmid-ki* (ideogr. ḲI.ḲI) 1, 41; *li-im-id* 5, 4.

אמה "to speak": III 2 *uš-ta-mu-ú* 1, 15.

amâtu "word, speech": *a-mat* 4, 43; 6, 85; 7, 23; 8, 15; 9, 20; 12, 89; *a-mat-sa* 33, 2; *a-mat-ka* 60, 9, 12; *am-ma-ti-ya* 11, 5 *A*; *am-ma-ti-ya* 11, 5; *amâti*^{pl} (KA.A.MIŠ) 60, 16.

atmû "speech, word": *at-mu-ú-a* 49, 9.

mâmîtu "ban, curse": *ma-mi-tu* 33, 32; 61, 9; *ma-mit* 1, 48; 12, 52, 78; 59, 7; 61, 10; *ma-*. . . . . 39, 15.

אמל amîlu "man": *amîlu* 11, 15; 12, 1; *amîlu* (NA) 12, 121; *a-mì-lu-tu* 11, 8 *A*; *a-mì-lu-tum* 11, 8; *a-*. . . . . 12, 56 *B*; *amîlûti*^{pl} 7, 51; 12, 56, 63, 66; *amîlûtum(tum)* 12, 57 *B*, 63 *BC*; *amîlûti(ti)* 12, 57.

amîlûtu "mankind": *amîlûtu* 12, 107 *E*; 51, 4; *amîlûti* 12, 61; 50, 25; *a-mì-lu-ti* 12, 107; *a-mi-lu-ta* 12, 111.

אמם ummu "mother": *um-mu* **6**, 77 *D*; *ummu* **4**, 47; **6**, 71, 77; **7**, 9, 15, 59; **11**, 22; **30**, 20; **37**, 7, 13; **57**, 2; *um-mi* **12**, 34; *ummi* **11**, 39; *ummi-ya* **11**, 22*C*; *ummi-yà* **11**, 22bis.

אמן ummâtu "host": *um-mat* **2**, 47.

אמק₄ imûḳu "might, strength": *i-mu-ḳu* **21**, 8; *i-mu-ḳa* **60**, 13; *i-mu-ki* **49**, 23; **60**, 14; *i-muḳ* **1**, 19.

nîmîḳu "wisdom": *ni-mi-ki* **13**, 10; **21**, 57; **41**, 13.

tîmîḳu "supplication": *ti-mi-ki* **11**, 27.

אמר amâru "to see": I 1 *a-mur* **15**, 9; *lîmur* (ŠI.BAR) **12**, 100; *lu-mur* **12**, 113 *E*; *a-ma-ri-ka* **1**, 8; — I 2 *i-tam-mur*(?) **12**, 106; *a-ta-mar* **2**, 36; **3**, 4; **27**, 17; **34**, 2.

אמר amîru "deafness(?)": *a-mi-ru-ú-a* **30**, 17; *a-mi-ri-*. . . . . **4**, 4; *a-mi-ri* **13**, 9.

אמר immiru "lamb, sheep": *immiru* **6**, 110; *immiri* **12**, 96.

אן ana "to, for, towards, according to"; also compounded with *aḫamiš, ili, arki, libbi, maḫar, pâni* (*qq. v.*): *a-na* **1**, 3, 42; **2**, 22; **6**, 23; **7**, 29, 50, 52, 62; **8**, 24; **11**, 9, 24, 26, 39; **12**, 88, 109 *E*; **13**, 20bis; **18**, 3, 17 *A*; **19**, 14; **21**, 20; **30**, 18; **31**, 5; **33**, 23, 34; **39**, 2; **40**, 4; **42**, 7; **45**, 7; **53**, 19, 20; **57**, 7; **61**, 13, 15; *ana* **1**, 4, 8, 27; **2**, 10; **4**, 36, 37; **6**, 23 *A*, 34, 81, 82, 91, 116; **7**, 18, 19, 58; **8**, 20; **10**, 18, 33; **11**, 15, 42, 44; **12**, 1, 2, 5, 8, 11, 48, 68, 72, 97bis, 100bis, 104, 115, 116, 120; **13**, 13; **18**, 17, 19 *A*; **21**, 7, 11, 23, 28, 88bis, 90; **22**, 48, 67; **24**, 6; **26**, 4; **30**, 20; **31**, 8; **32**, 3; **35**, 15; **38**, 1; **40**, 16; **50**, 23; **51**, 10; **52**, 3; **53**, 16bis, 17bis; **62**, 18, 19, 22.

aššum (= *ana šum*) "since, because of": *áš-šum* **4**, 31, 32; **6**, 74, 75, 76; **7**, 12, 13, 14; **19**, 15; **27**, 15, 16, 17, 18; **37**, 10, 11, 12; **50**, 17; **57**, 8.

אן ina "in, through, among, during"; also compounded with *ili, balû, bîrit, kirib, pâni, šapli* (*qq. v.*): *i-na* **18**, 10*A*; **22**, 63; *ina* **1**, 5, 11, 12bis, 13, 15, 24, 26, 39bis, 40, 43, 44, 49, 50; **2**, 2, 15, 16; **3**, 13, 14; **4**, 5, 7, 12, 17bis, 19, 38, 39bis, 41, 43bis; **5**, 1, 18; **6**, 21, 22, 24, 26, 37, 41, 47, 65, 78, 83*D*, 84*E*, 85bis, 113 *F*ter, 120, 122; **7**, 16, 19, 20bis, 22, 23bis, 38, 44, 56, 60bis, 61; **8**, 16, 24; **9**, 8, 10, 13, 14, 16, 17, 18, 35; **10**, 21; **11**, 5, 14, 27, 28; **12**, 2, 6, 8, 11, 13bis,

14bis, 15ter, 34, 56, 59, 62, 66, 67, 70, 72, 75, 76, 80, 81, 82, 87, 98, 102bis, 113, 114, 116bis, 118; **13**, 6, 7, 10, 11, 26, 32; **14**, 5; **15**, 15; **16**, 11bis; **17**, 7, 8; **18**, 4, 6, 10, 19bis; **19**, 10bis, 12, 13, 18, 28, 31; **21**, 6, 10, 14, 28, 48, 60, 61, 73, 74, 92bis; **22**, 8, 9, 10bis, 14, 15, 17, 18, 29, 53, 54, 56, 60, 66, 69bis; **26**, 5; **27**, 5, 6, 7, 8, 11 *A*^{ter}, 13; **28**, 6bis; **30**, 20, 26bis; **31**, 6, 8; **32**, 7, 15; **33**, 12, 25, 27, 36, 40, 44; **34**, 6bis; **35**, 2, 4; **36**, 7; **38**, 4bis; **39**, 5bis, 13; **40**, 6, 15; **41**, 2bis; **42**, 13, 15, 17, 25; **46**, 10bis; **47**, 7bis; **48**, 17; **49**, 14; **50**, 3, 6, 9, 14bis, 15, 16, 18, 24, 26; **51**, 15; **52**, 2, 4bis; **53**, 5, 8bis, 14, 16, 23, 24bis, 26, 27bis, 28; **54**, 2bis, 3, 4, 5; **55**, 3bis, 4, 5; **56**, 9bis, 10, 11; **57**, 4bis, 6, 13, 14; **58**, 6bis, 7; **59**, 1, 12bis, 14; **60**, 19bis, 21; **61**, 11, 16bis, 16 *A*, 18; **62**, 16bis, 17, 18, 19, 20.

אן$_4$ înuma "when": *i-nu-ma* **6**, 56; **21**, 73; **24**, 5; **33**, 45; *înu-ma* **12**, 1, 121; *înu(?)-ma* **42**, 25; *înu(?)* . . . . . **42**, 25.

אנה$_4$ inû "to annul; to be annulled, to be altered, to become invalid": *i-nu-u* **60**, 8; *inû-u* **1**, 51; **19**, 32; *inû-ú* **4**, 44; **6**, 86; **7**, 24; **19**, 8; **21**, 2.

אנח tânîḫu "sighing, groaning": *ta-ni-ḫu* **1**, 45; **12**, 51; **33**, 29; *ta-ni-[ḫi?]* **5**, 7.

tânîḫtu "sighing": *ta-ni-iḫ-ti-yá* **15**, 15.

אנח "to faint, to be weary": *a-ni-ḫu* **20**, 9, 11; **21**, 9, 35, 37.

אנך anaku "I": *a-na-ku* **50**, 12; **56**, 7; *ana-ku* **1**, 38; **2**, 26, 36; **4**, 16; **6**, 27, 83 *E*; **11**, 16; **12**, 45, 90, 94; **13**, 5, 20; **21**, 11, 51; **27**, 11; **30**, 7; **31**, 4; **33**, 21; **39**, 16; **43**, 7; **54**, 1; **55**, 2; **57**, 3; **58**, 5; **62**, 13; *anaku* **60**, 3.

INIM.INIM.MA "prayer": **1**, 28, 52; **2**, 9, 42; **3**, 9; **4**, 8, 23; **5**, 10; **6**, 17, 35, 70, 95, 131; **7**, 8, 33; **8**, 20; **9**, 27; **10**, 6, 26, 34; **11**, 41; **12**, 95; **13**, 12; **14**, 11; **15**, 17; **16**, 10; **17**, 5; **18**, 18; **19**, 33; **20**, 7; **21**, 24, 72, 91; **22**, 30, 68; **23**, 6; **24**, 4; **25**, 5; **26**, 3; **27**, 25; **28**, 5; **29**, 2; **30**, 19; **31**, 7; **32**, 2; **33**, 38; **34**, 5; **36**, 6; **37**, 6; **38**, 3; **39**, 4; **40**, 2; **42**, 24; **43**, 8; **44**, 2; **45**, 4; **46**, 9; **47**, 6; **48**, 16; **49**, 20; **50**, 28; **51**, 9; **60**, 4.

אנן annu "sin": *an-ni* **2**, 38; **11**, 19, 29bis, 30bis, 31, 32, 33, 34, 35; **27**, 21.

אנן$_8$ "to be merciful"; II 2 "to weep, to pray": *ut-nin* **21**, 62; *ut-nin-ka* **60**, 10.

annu "mercy": *an-na-šú* **60**, 8; *an-ni-ka* **19**, 32; **52**, 2; *an-ni-ki* **1**, 51; **4**, 44; **6**, 86; **7**, 24; **33**, 36; *an-ni-ku-nu* **53**, 5.

unninu "mercy, compassion; sighing, prayer": *un-ni-na* **22**, 64; *un-ni-ni* **9**, 39; **33**, 5; *un-ni-ni-ya* **1**, 43; **2**, 33; **6**, 80; **7**, 17; **8**, 4; **18**, 14 *A*; **21**, 21; **33**, 26; *un-ni-ni-yà* **4**, 35; **18**, 14; **23**, 3.

? innintu "sorrow (?)": *in-nin-ti* **30**, 11.

annû "this": *an-nu-u* **53**, 15; *an-nu-ú* **30**, 29; **53**, 15; *an-ni-i* **7**, 38; *an-ni-í* **12**, 59; **13**, 26; **21**; 21; **22**, 56; *an-ni-ma* **21**, 70; *an-nam* **12**, 103, 115; BI (= *annam*) **2**, 9; **6**, 95; **11**, 42; **12**, 2; **13**, 13; **16**, 11; **18**, 19; **21**, 28, 73, 92; **22**, 31, 69; **24**, 5; **28**, 6; **30**, 20; **32**, 3; **34**, 6; **38**, 4; **39**, 5; **41**, 2; **46**, 10; **47**, 7; **51**, 10; **52**, 3; *an-na(?)* ..... **44**, 3; *an-ni-tú* **2**, 10; **30**, 27; **40**, 13; **62**, 30; *an-ni-[ti]* **51**, 11; *a-nu-ti-ma* **1**, 33; *a-na-ti-ma* **5**, 15.

AN.IRIM*(šam)*: **40**, 14.

אנש inšu "weak": *in-šú* **12**, 119; *in-ši* **2**, 21; **22**, 50; **48**, 3; *in-ši* **9**, 37, 45.

אנש altu "wife": *al-ti* **4**, 10, 11.

אנש tînišîtu "men, mankind": *ti-ni-ši-i-ti* **2**, 19; **3**, 16; **19**, 13; **50**, 9; *ti-ni-ši-i-ti* **2**, 19 *B*; *ti-ni-ši-ti* **9**, 52; *ti-ni-šit* **12**, 33.

אנת atta; attî "thou": *at-ta* **2**, 25; **6**, 43; **12**, 31, 105; **18**, 8; **50**, 29; *at-ta-ma* **6**, 112; **10**, 15; **12**, 34, 35; **60**, 9; *at-ti* **4**, 10, 11; **61**, 10; *[at]-ti-ma* **32**, 14.

attunu "ye": *at-tu-nu* **7**, 46; **8**, 22; *at-tu-nu-ma* **52**, 5; **62**, 3, 5, 9.

אסן isinnu "festival": *i-sin-na-ka* **1**, 18.

אסר mîsiru "band, fetter": *mîsiru* (ideogr. SU.I.BU) **53**, 16; *mîsiru* (ideogr. SU.I.TUM) **53**, 17.

אף aptu "dwelling, habitation": *a-pa-a-ti* **13**, 16; **33**, 34; *'-pa-a-ti(?)* **33**, 6.

אפה$_4$ upû "clouds": *ú-pi-i* **20**, 12; **21**, 38.

אפל apâlu: I 1 *a-pa-lu* 11, 4; *a-pa-lum* 11, 4 *A*.

אפל aplu "son": *ap-lu* 2, 11; 3, 10; *a-pil* 2, 47; 9, 31; 22, 36, 38; 33, 6; *aplu* (ideogr. TUR.UŠ) 9, 38; *apil* (ideogr. A) 1, 38; 2, 26; 4, 16; 6, 27, 83 *E*; 10, 31; 12, 45, 90; 13, 5; 22, 11, 51; 27, 11; 30, 7; 31, 4; 33, 21; 39, 16; 54, 1; 57, 3; 58, 5; 62, 13.

upuntu a plant: *upuntu* 6, 80; 7, 17; 40, 11.

apsû "the deep, the abyss": *apsû* 3, 5; 4, 15; 8, 18; 21, 57; *apsî* 5, 18; 12, 87.

אפר ipîru "to support, sustain": *[i?]-pi-rat* 9, 37.

אפר₄ ipru "dust": *ipir* 12, 55; *ipri*^{pl} (IŠ.ZUN) 59, 2.

אפשׁ apšânu "yoke": *ap-ša-na-ki* 8, 7.

אפשׁ ipîšu "to do, to make, to perform": *i-pu-šu* 11, 36; *tî-puš(uš)* ideogr. DU 12, 12; 33, 45; *i-pu-uš* 11, 16; *li-pu-šu* 19, 26; *ipuš(uš)* ideogr. DU 8, 21; 16, 11; 18, 19; 21, 92; 22, 69; 28, 6; 34, 6; 38, 4; 39, 5; 41, 2; 46, 10; 47, 7; *ipuš* (ideogr. DIM) 12, 103, 115; DU.DU (= *ipuš*) 2, 9; 6, 95; 12, 2; 13, 13; 16, 11; 18, 19; 21, 28, 73, 92; 22, 31, 69; 28, 6; 32, 3; 34, 6; 38, 3; 39, 5; 41, 2; 46, 10; 47, 7; AG.AG (= *ipuš*) 11, 42; 24, 5; 30, 20; 51, 10; 52, 3; *i-piš* 62, 7.

ipištu "handiwork": *[i]-piš-ti* 32, 10.

אפשׁ ipîšu "to practise magic"; part. "sorcerer, sorceress": *i-pi-ši* 7, 58; *i-piš-ti* 7, 58.

ipšu "magic, sorcery": *ip-ši* 12, 56.

upîšu "magic, sorcery": *ú-piš* 12, 62, 109; 50, 17.

אפשׁ itpîšu "prudent": *[it]-pi-[ši]* 4, 15; *i-ti-ip-šu* 22, 2.

אצר₄ "to surround, confine, bewitch": II 1 *tu-uṣ-ṣa-ra* 62, 5; *mu-uṣ-ṣi-ru* 62, 2; *uṣ-ṣu-ru* 62, 4.

uṣurtu "charm, spell": ^{isu}*uṣurâti*^{pl} 6, 112; 10, 15; 19, 6; 62, 2, 5.

אקר uḳuru a plant or tree: ^{isu}*uḳuru* (? ^{isu}*libbi gišimmari*) 12, 84.

אר aru "blossom": *arî*^{pl} 12, 5ter.

אר irtu "breast": *irat-su* 1, 49; 33, 33.

ארב iribu "flight of locusts": *iribu* 59, 22.

ארב₅ irîbu I 1 "to enter": *i-rib* (Inf. with *Šamši* = "sunset") 53, 19; — III 1 "to bring in": *li-ši-rib* 23, 2.

ארד? ardu "servant; slave": *arad-ka* 2, 26 *D*; 12, 45, 90, 94; 21, 88; 22, 11; 27, 11; 50, 12; *aradka* (URU.ZU) 60, 3; *arad-ki* 43, 7.

ארח urḫu "way": *ur-ḫi* 1, 24; 22, 59.

ארח arḫiš "quickly": *ár-ḫiš* 2, 24.

ארך arâku I 1 "to be long": *li-ri-ik* 18, 16; — II 1 "to lengthen": *ur-ri-ki* 8, 17; — III 1 "to lengthen": *šú-ri-ka* 5, 3.

urkarinnu a precious wood: *iṣuurkarinnu* 12, 8, 15, 116; 30, 26.

arallû "the Lower World, the realm of the dead": *a-ra-al-li-i* 2, 22; *arallî[-ma]* 27, 6.

ארן arnu "sin": *ár-nu* 2, 23 bis; *ár-na* 2, 23 *B*; 6, 54; *ar-ni* 7, 48; 50, 17; *ár-ni* 59, 7; . . . . *-ni* 5, 6; *ar-nu(-ya?)* 7, 47; *ar-ni-yà* 12, 84; *ár-ni-ya* 12, 76 *C*; *ár-ni-yà* 1, 26; 12, 84 *C*.

ארן irinu "cedar": *iṣuirinu* 30, 25; 40, 4, 11.

ארץ irṣitu "earth": *ir-ṣi-tum* 12, 82 *C*; *irṣitum(tum)* 61, 8 *A*; *irṣita(ta)* 1, 7; *irṣiti(ti)* 1, 30; 19, 7; 60, 5; 62, 8; *irṣi-tim(tim)* 3, 8; 5, 12; 6, 100, 128; 10, 9, 24; 12, 64, 82; 18, 6; 22, 39; 46, 11; 50, 8; 53, 20, 21; 60, 5; 61, 8; 62, 3; *irṣiti* 4, 15; 16, 12.

ארר arratu "curse, incantation": *a-ra-ti* 1, 41; *arrat* 12, 68, 74.

ארש iršu "wise": *ir-šú* 12, 33; 22, 37; 46, 18.

ארש irîsu "scent, odour": *i-ri-šu* 2, 28; *i-ri-ša* 12, 28 *CD*.

ארש₃ aršašû "device, machination": *ár-ša-šu-ú* 12, 63 *B*; *ár-ša-šú[-u?]* 7, 57; *ár-ša-ši-i* 7, 51; *ár-ša-*. . . . . 51, 3; *aršašîpl* 12, 63; 21, 65.

אש išâtu "fire": *išâtu* 49, 27; *išâti* 21, 74; 36, 7.

אשב₄ išîbu "to sprout, to bear fruit": *iš-šub-ba-a* 12, 97.

אשג ašâgu a shrub: *iṣuašâgu* 12, 10; *iṣuašâgi* 21, 74.

אשה išîtu "trouble, confusion": *[i]-ša-ti-ya* **11**, 20.

ašakku "evil sickness, consumption": *ašakku* **1**, 46; **33**, 30.

áš-li-i-ti (? *ina li-i-tí*) **21**, 79.

ušumgallu "sovereign, ruler": *ušumgal* **9**, 7; **12**, 32.

ašnan "corn, grain": *aš-na-an* **2**, 29 *D*; *ilu aš-na-an* **12**, 30; *áš-na-an* **2**, 29.

אשר ašâru "to be favourable, to bless": I 1 *li-šú-[ru-u]* **3**, 6; *a-ši-ru* **12**, 32; *a-šir* **22**, 3; *a-šír* **6**, 43; *âšira(ra)* ideogr. ŠAR (? *[ma]-ḫi-ra*) **27**, 6; — II 1 *uš-šú-ru* **1**, 4.

aširtu "sanctuary, shrine": *aš-rat* **21**, 54; *áš-rat* **11**, 13.

iširtu "shrine": *íš-ri-ti* **22**, 7.

אשר ašru "place": *áš-ri* **11**, 28; *aš-ri-šú* **11**, 39; *ašar* (ideogr. KI) **17**, 6.

ašaridu "prince, chief": *a-ša-ri-du* **22**, 70; *a-ša-rid* **2**, 25; **6**, 39, 127; **9**, 5; **10**, 23; **20**, 15, 17; **27**, 2; **50**, 29; *ašaridu* (ideogr. SAG.KAL) **22**, 1, 37; *ašaridu* (ideogr. INI.DU) **1**, 42; **33**, 23; *ašarid* (ideogr. SAG.KAL) **22**, 6; *ašarid* (ideogr. TIK.GAL) **50**, 8.

ištu "from": *iš-tu* **1**, 23; **53**, 6; *iš-tú(?)* **9**, 44; *ištu-šu-nu* **12**, 101.

אשתר ištaru "goddess": *iš-ta-ri* **6**, 67; *ilu iš-tar* **12**, 31; *ilu iš-tar-šu* **50**, 13; **56**, 8; *ilu ištaru* **27**, 23; *ilu ištari* **12**, 57 *B*; **27**, 12; *ilu ištar* **1**, 44; **6**, 57; **12**, 61, 107, 111; **33**, 27; **50**, 25; *ilu ištar-šu* **1**, 38; **2**, 24 *D*, 26; **3**, 3; **6**, 27, 83 *E*; **12**, 45; **13**, 5; **31**, 4; **32**, 5; **33**, 21; **54**, 1; **57**, 3; **58**, 5; **62**, 13; *ilu ištari-yà* **2**, 40; **4**, 29, 36, 45; **6**, 73, 81, 87; **7**, 11, 18, 25; **9**, 17; **12**, 71, 93; **21**, 67; **22**, 18; **37**, 9; *ilu ištarî* **1**, 23; *ilu ištarâti pl* **7**, 43; **9**, 29; **33**, 11.

ITI *cf.* אתה.

את itti "with": *it-ti* **27**, 7, 8; *itti* **2**, 35; **12**, 78, 104; **22**, 32; **51**, 12; *itti-šu* **2**, 24; **32**, 5; *itti-*. . . . . **6**, 55; *it-[ti-ka]* **50**, 10 *A*; *itti-ka* **2**, 30, 31; **19**, 16; **50**, 10; *it-ti-ki* **4**, 32; *itti-ki* **6**, 75; **7**, 13; **37**, 11; *it-ti-yà* **4**, 37; **22**, 61, 62; *itti-ya* **1**, 44; **6**, 82, 88; **7**, 26; **21**, 67; **28**, 3; **30**, 10; **33**, 27; *itti-yà* **1**, 24; **6**, 82 *E*; **7**, 19; **12**, 71, 112; **14**, 7; **19**, 30; **22**, 19; **50**, 19; *it-ti-ni* **61**, 8; *it-ti-ni-[ma?]* **61**, 9.

אחה ittu "portent": *ittu* (ITI) **12**, 65; *ittâti*^{pl} (ITI.MIŠ) **1**, 13, 40; **4**, 18, 40; **6**, 113 *F*; **7**, 21, 61; **12**, 64; **19**, 11; **27**, 11 *A*; **50**, 15; **53**, 25; **54**, 3; **55**, 4; **56**, 10; **57**, 5; **58**, 7; **59**, 13; **60**, 20; **61**, 16 *A*; **62**, 10, 12, 14.

atalû "eclipse": ^{ilu}*atalû* **6**, 122; **10**, 21; ^{ilu}*atalî* **1**, 12, 39; **4**, 17, 39; **6**, 113 *F*; **7**, 20, 60; **19**, 10; **27**, 11 *A*; **50**, 14; **53**, 24; **54**, 2; **55**, 3; **56**, 9; **57**, 4; **58**, 6; **59**, 12; **60**, 19; **61**, 16; **62**, 16bis.

אחל$_4$ itillu "mighty, exalted": *i-til-lit* **9**, 30.

itilliš "mightily": *i-til-li-iš* **12**, 80 *C*.

אחק$_4$ itîḳu "to remove, tear away": *i-ti-iḳ* **11**, 17; *[i?]-ti-iḳ* **2**, 39.

ב

באל ba'âlu "to be great, mighty": *ba-'-lat* **9**, 41.

ba'altu "lady": *ba-'-lat* **9**, 41 *A*; **33**, 9.

באל$_4$ bîlu "to rule": *ti-bi-il-li* **1**, 33; *ta-bi-il-li* **5**, 15; *bi-il-la-an-ni* **13**, 29.

bîlu "lord": *bi-lum* **6**, 61; **11**, 7 *A*; **13**, 15; **27**, 1; *bi-li* **12**, 59; **13**, 27; **19**, 19; **27**, 15; *bîlu* **1**, 42, 53; **6**, 1, 91, 102; **7**, 29; **9**, 9, 21; **10**, 10; **11**, 7; **12**, 21 *A*, 26, 34; **19**, 4, 17; **21**, 19, 61, 63, 93; **22**, 61, 62; **33**, 23; **42**, 26; **48**, 17; **60**, 6, 9; *bîl* **6**, 111, 112; **9**, 4; **10**, 15bis; **12**, 17, 27, 28; **19**, 6, 7; **21**, 80; **22**, 4, 7; **27**, 2; **46**, 11, 16; **53**, 3; **59**, 4, 6; **62**, 31; *bi-li-i* **8**, 26; *bîlî* **19**, 4; **62**, 31.

bîltu "lady": *bi-il-tum* **33**, 10, 37; *bi-il-ti* **39**, 13; *bi(?)-lit* **3**, 1; *bi-lit* **1**, 37; **3**, 8; **4**, 14, 15; **9**, 33; **33**, 20; **57**, 14; *bîltu* **1**, 51; **4**, 24, 27, 33, 47; **6**, 71, 77, 85, 90; **7**, 9, 15, 16, 23, 28; **11**, 31, 33; **32**, 15; **37**, 7, 13; *bîlti-yà* **2**, 3; **6**, 72; **7**, 10; **33**, 22; **37**, 8; *bi-li-i-ti* **2**, 43; **33**, 47.

bîlûtu "lordship, dominion": *bi-lut-ki* **2**, 4; **8**, 11; *bi(?)-lu-*. . . . . **35**, 1; *bîlu-ut-ka* **14**, 9; *bîlu-ut-ki* **3**, 7.

בב bâbu "gate": *bâbâti*^{pl} **40**, 7.

בבל babâlu "to bring, supply": *ba-ba-lu* **11**, 15.

bubbulum the time of the moon's disappearance: *bub-bulum* **1**, 17; **61**, 12.

בוא bâ'u I 1 "to come": *lu-ba-'* **12**, 80; *li-ba-'* **12**, 80*C*; — III[II] 1 "to bring": *tuš-ba-'-šú-ma* **12**, 118.

בול bûlu "cattle": *bu-ul* **27**, 10.

בון bu'ânu "muscle, sinew": *bu'âni^{pl}-ya* **1**, 46; **33**, 30.

בין bînu a tree or shrub: *^{isu}bi-nu* **12**, 84; *^{isu}bînu* **12**, 9, 84*C*; **51**, 12.

בית bîtu "house": *bît* **1**, 54; **2**, 16; **3**, 14; **11**, 1*A*; **12**, 44; **21**, 25, 26, 60; **22**, 35; **33**, 8; **48**, 18; *bîti-šu* **12**, 100; *bîti-yà* **27**, 13.

בכה bikîtu "tears, weeping": *bikîtu* **4**, 33; *bikît* **13**, 7.

בכר bukru "first-born": *bu-kur* **2**, 11; **3**, 10; **9**, 2; **12**, 33; **21**, 1, 70; **27**, 1; **29**, 3; **46**, 12; *bu-uk-ri-*. . . . . **1**, 10.

bukratu "first-born daughter": *bu-uk-rat* **1**, 31; **5**, 13; **30**, 30; **31**, 11.

בלה balû, balî "without"; compounded with *ina*: *ba-li-ka* **6**, 24, 26, 41; **50**, 6; *balî-ka* (ideogr. NU.MI.A) **6**, 26*A*.

בלט balâṭu I 1 "to live": *lu-úb-luṭ* **8**, 17; **9**, 10; **12**, 90; **22**, 13, 66; **50**, 26; **54**, 5; . . . .*-luṭ* **45**, 2; *lubluṭ(uṭ)* ideogr. TI **30**, 15; — II 1 "to cause to live, to quicken": *mu-bal-liṭ* **28**, 8; *bul-lu-ṭu* **4**, 32; **6**, 75; **7**, 13; **9**, 34*A*; **37**, 11; *bul-lu-ṭa* **9**, 34.

balâṭu "life": *ba-la-ṭa* **8**, 17; *ba-la-ṭi* **11**, 13; *ba-lá-ṭi* **5**, 5; **6**, 93; **7**, 31; *ba-laṭ* **9**, 22; *balâṭu* (ideogr. TI) **12**, 80; **19**, 28; *balâṭu* (ideogr. TI.LA) **8**, 11; **9**, 5, 39; **12**, 80*C*; **13**, 18; **17**, 2; **22**, 5; **47**, 4; **62**, 5, 6; *balâṭu* (ideogr. NAM.TI.LA) **35**, 3; *balâṭu* (ideogr. NAM.TIN) **6**, 106; *balâṭi* (ideogr. TI.LA) **51**, 7; *balâṭ* (ideogr. TI) **12**, 53; *ba-la-ṭi-ya* **19**, 21.

balṭu "living": *^{amilu}balṭu* (ideogr. TI) **6**, 99; **10**, 8.

בלל "to pour out": *bulul* **12**, 15, 102; *bulul-ma* **22**, 33; **26**, 7 (ideogr. ŠAR.ŠAR).

בלת balâtu "to abound": *tab-la-tú* **12**, 56; *ba-la-tu* **45**, 9; *ba-la-tu-um-ma* **62**, 7.

baltu, baštu "abundance": *bal-ta* **22**, 64; *ba-áš-ti* **12**, 56; *ba-áš-ta-ka* **19**, 24.

bungulu: *b(p)u-un-gu-lu* **12**, 22.

בנה banû "to build, create": I 1 *ib-ni(-. . . . .)* **21**, 55; *ib-nu-ku-nu-ši* **8**, 24; *ib-na-na-ši-[ma?]* **61**, 7; *ba-nu-u* **12**, 30, 31, 33; **41**, 3; *ba-a-ni* **47**, 4; *ba-an-tú(?)* **1**, 35; **5**, 17; *[ba]-na-at* **9**, 40; *banat(at)* ideogr. DU **21**, 58; *ba-ni-i* **19**, 15, 22; — II 1 *ú-ban-ni* **12**, 50; — IV 1 *ib-ba-ni* **61**, 9; *ib-ba-nu(-u?)* **10**, 30; *ib-ba-nu-ú* **61**, 8.

binûtu "creature, offspring": *bi-nu-ut* **61**, 6.

nabnîtu "creation": *nab-ni-ti* **1**, 53; **2**, 48; *nab-ni-ta* **9**, 40.

tabannu "handiwork": *ta-ba-an-na* **12**, 31.

בנה banîtu "brightness, mercy": *ba-ni-ti* **1**, 49; **9**, 51, **33**, 34.

ברה barû "to see, perceive": *ta-bar-ri* **18**, 5, 7; *ta-bar-ri-i* **9**, 42; **32**, 10; *ba-ra-a-. . . . .* **6**, 42.

bîru "vision": *bi-ri* **4**, 38; **6**, 83 *D*; **7**, 19.

bîrtu "glance"; bîrit uzni "understanding"; compounded with *ina* "between, within"; *pl.* *bîrâti* "springs": *bîr-tum* **21**, 51; *bi-rit (uznâ^{du}-ši-na)* **12**, 38; *bi-rit* **12**, 13; *bi-ra-a-ti* **12**, 29.

burzigallu a vessel: ^{karpatu}*bur-zi-gal* **12**, 14.

ברך birku "knee": *bir-ki-ya* **13**, 24.

ברק "to lighten"; III 1 *do.*: *mu-šab-riḳ* **20**, 13.

birḳu "lightning": *bir-ki* **21**, 80; *birḳu* **20**, 13. (For *aban birḳi*, see *sub* abnu.)

ברש burâšu "pine-wood; incense": *burâšu* **12**, 9; *burâši* **2**, 9; **8**, 20; **11**, 42; **12**, 4; **13**, 14; **15**, 24; **18**, 19 *A*; **21**, 74; **31**, 10; **32**, 3; **33**, 39; **36**, 7; **51**, 11; **62**, 27.

בשה bašû "to be; to have": I 1 *ta-ba-áš-ši* **12**, 34; *ibašû-ú* **1**, 47; *ibašâ-a* **1**, 13, 40; **4**, 19, 41; **6**, 113 *F*; **7**, 22, 61; **12**, 57; **19**, 12; **27**, 11 *A*; **50**, 16; **53**, 26; **54**, 4; **55**, 5; **56**, 11; **57**, 6; **58**, 7; **59**, 14; **60**, 21; **61**, 16 *A*; *ib-ši* **14**, 17; *ib-šú-u-ni* **12**, 81; *ib-šu-ni* **12**, 81 *C*; *ib-ša-ku* **19**, 20; **21**, 62; *ib-ša-ki* **4**, 34; **6**, 79; **7**, 16; *lib-ša-nim-ma* **46**, 7; *li-ba-ša-an-ni* **19**, 27; *lu-ub-ši* **12**, 72; *[ba?]-šú-ú* **21**, 80; . . . . .*-šú-ú* **58**, 2; *ba-šú-ú* **4**, 32; **6**, 75; **19**, 16; *bašû-u* **6**, 75 *E*; **7**, 13; **27**, 13; **37**, 11; *bašû-ú* **27**, 13 *CD*; *ba-ša-a* **62**, 12; — IV 3 *it-ta-nab-ša-nim-ma* **62**, 14.

bušû "property, possession": *bušû-ku-nu-ma* **62**, 4.

בתק butuḳtu "flood, inundation": *bu-tuḳ-[tum]* **6**, 59; *butuḳtu* (ideogr. A.ḪUL) **36**, 10.

ג

GA a plant: *šam*GA **19**, 17.

גבש gibšu "mass, volume": *gi-biš* **18**, 3.

GI.GAB a drink(?)-offering: **12**, 2; **15**, 19; **21**, 28; **30**, 21; **31**, 9.

GU.ZI a vessel: *karpatu*GU.ZI **30**, 2; **61**, 10.

גלה gallû a demon: *gallû* **33**, 33.

גמל gamâlu "to complete, benefit, maintain, requite": *ta-ga-mil-šu* **18**, 8; *ga-mil* **9**, 6; *gam-ma-la-ta* **6**, 65; **27**, 15; *ga-ma-la* **4**, 31; **6**, 76; *gám-ma-al* **13**, 25; *gamâla* (ideogr. ŠU.KAR) **6**, 76 *E*; **7**, 14; **37**, 12.

gimillu "present, gift": *gi-mil* **6**, 93; **7**, 31; **14**, 4; **51**, 7; **57**, 8.

gimiltu "gift": *gi-mil-tú* **31**, 10.

gitmalu "perfect": *git-ma-lu* **2**, 12; **3**, 10; **6**, 97; **10**, 7; **11**, 46; **12**, 18; **20**, 8, 10, 14, 16; **21**, 39, 41; *git-ma-lum* **21**, 93; **46**, 13; *git-mal-. . . . .* **12**, 24.

גמר gamru "perfect": *ga-mir* **19**, 8; *gam-ra-a-ti* **21**, 79.

gimru "the whole, totality": *gi-mir* **1**, 53; **9**, 40; **46**, 13; *gim-ri* **12**, 33; **27**, 8.

gim-ru-ú(?) **12**, 98.

גצץ gaṣṣu "plaster": *gaṣṣu* (ideogr. IM.PAR) **12**, 9.

גשר I 1 "to strengthen; to be strong"; II 2 "to be mighty, powerful": I 1 *ga-šir* **6**, 37; *gaš-[rat?]* **33**, 10; — II 2 *ug-da-ša-ra* **1**, 8.

gašru "strong, mighty": *ga-aš-ru* **18**, 20; **21**, 43; *ga-áš-ru* **9**, 1; *gaš-ru* **2**, 11; **3**, 10; **12**, 22; **21**, 76; **27**, 1; **53**, 2; *gaš-ru-ú-ti* **47**, 8; **52**, 5.

gušûru "beam, branch": *gušûru* **12**, 2; **21**, 28; **26**, 5; **31**, 8.

GIŠ ŠAR(*šam*) **12**, 6.

ד

דאץ "to treat with injustice, to oppress": *id-da-ṣa-an-ni* **11**, 4.

דבב dabâbu "to plan, to intrigue": I,1 *da-ba-bi* **9**, 47; — II 1 *dubbubu* (ideogr. KA.ḪI.KUR.RA) **12**, 1.

dadmu "dwelling": *da-ád-mi* **22**, 7; *da-ád-mí* **33**, 9.

דוד dâdu "love": *da-di* **1**, 37; **33**, 20.

דוך dâku "to slay": *di-ku* **53**, 14.

dîktu "slaughter": *di-ik-ti* **53**, 14.

דור dârû "eternal": *dá-ra-ti* **1**, 27.

dâriš "for ever": *da-riš* **11**, 27; ? *da-a-ri-šú* **21**, 84.

דור dûru "wall, fortress": *dûru* **21**, 16, 26.

דחה dîḫu "pestilence, sickness": *di-ḫu* **12**, 51, 60.

דין dânu "to judge": *i-dan-ni* **21**, 46; *ta-da-an* **22**, 50; *ta-dan* **2**, 19; **3**, 16; *di-in* **12**, 59; **50**, 11; *di-ni* **4**, 30; **7**, 49; *da-a-ni* **6**, 74; **7**, 12; **37**, 10; *da-ni* **4**, 28.

dînu "judgment": *di-na* **7**, 49; *di-ni* **4**, 28, 30; **7**, 12; **12**, 59; **13**, 28; **19**, 8; **30**, 8; **37**, 10; **50**, 11; *di-in* **2**, 19; **3**, 16; **6**, 45, 74; *di-in* **2**, 19 *B*.

daiânu "judge": *da-ya-na-ti* **30**, 8; *daiânu* **60**, 7; *daiân* **6**, 111; **10**, 15; **60**, 5.

dulu "hill(?)": *du-ul* **22**, 7.

DIL.BAD a plant: *šam*DIL.BAD **12**, 84.

דלח dalâḫu "to disturb, to disorder": *da-li-ḫu* **8**, 27.

dalḫu "disturbed, confused": *dal-ḫa-ma* **12**, 58.

daliḫtu "disorder, confusion": *dal-ḫa-ti-ya* **11**, 21.

דלל dalâlu "to bow down, to humble oneself": *i-dal-la-la* **21**, 85; *a-dal-lu-ka* **9**, 23 *B*, *a-dál-lu-ka* **9**, 23 (or *a-tal-lu-ka*, *cf. supra* p. 47); *lud-lu-la* **12**, 91; *lud-lul* **1**, 27; **2**, 8, 41; **5**, 9; **6**, 69, 94; **7**, 32; **11**, 40; **12**, 91 *C*, 94; **21**, 23, 71, 89; **22**, 67; **27**, 24; **28**, 4; **30**, 16; **31**, 6; **34**, 4; **46**, 8; **47**, 5; **60**, 2; GA.AN.SIL (*ludlul*) **60**, 2, 3; *ludlul-ka* (KA.TAR.ZU-*ka*) **50**, 27.

dalîlu "submission, humility": *da-lil* **6**, 15; *dá-lîl* **46**, 8; *dá-lí-li-ka* **1**, 27; **2**, 41; **6**, 69; **11**, 40; **12**, 91, 94;

21, 89; **27**, 24; **28**, 4; **60**, 2; *dalîli-ka* (ideogr. KA.TAR) **21**, 23, 71; **51**, 8; *dalîli*^{pl}*-ka* (ideogr. KA.TAR.MIŠ) **22**, 67; KA.TAR.ZU (*dalîlika*) **60**, 2, 3; *da-li-li-ki* **30**, 16; *dá-lí-lí-ki* **2**, 8; **6**, 94; **7**, 32; **31**, 6; **34**, 4; *dá-lí-[lí]-. . . . .* **38**, 2; *dá-lí-lí-ku-nu* **47**, 5.

dallu "humble, submissive": *dal-la* **9**, 44.

דמא *ta-di(ti?)-im-mi* **1**, 34; **5**, 16.

דמם damâmu "to weep, lament": *dumum* (ideogr. ŠIŠ.ŠIŠ) **12**, 117.

דמק damâḳu I 1 "to be favourable": *lid-mi-iḳ* **1**, 24; **22**, 59; *lid-mi-ḳa* **10**, 17; *lid-mi-ḳa* **6**, 115; **22**, 63; — II 1 "to make favourable": *tudammiḳ(iḳ)* **40**, 15; *du-um-mi-iḳ* **6**, 113; **10**, 16; *[du]-um-mu-ḳu* **29**, 1.

damḳu "favourable"; f. damiḳtu as subs. "favour": *damḳu* **12**, 68; *damiḳtu(tu)* **39**, 9; *damiḳtu(tú)* **12**, 110; *damiḳta(ta)* **12**, 113 *E*; *damiḳti(ti)* **1**, 50; **4**, 7; **6**, 116, 118; **9**, 14 *B*, 15 *B*, 46, 53; **10**, 18, 19; **12**, 72, 120; **22**, 15, 16; **33**, 35; **40**, 16; *damiḳtim(tim)* **2**, 5, 40; **9**, 14, 15; **54**, 9; **60**, 22; *damiḳti(ti)-yà* **15**, 16; *damḳûti*^{pl} **9**, 50; *damḳâti*^{pl} **11**, 26.

dumḳu "favour": *dum-ki* **1**, 22; **6**, 93; **7**, 31; **57**, 8; **62**, 10; *dum-ḳa* **8**, 13; *dum-ki-. . . . .* **21**, 66; *dumḳu* **12**, 85; **19**, 23; *dumḳi* **8**, 12; **12**, 110; **13**, 21; **22**, 19bis; **50**, 24.

דנן danânu "to be strong": *li-dan-nin* **53**, 21.

dannu "strong, mighty": *dan-nu* **4**, 19; *dan-na* **12**, 80; **42**, 15; *dan-ni* **19**, 17; *dan-na-. . . . .* **42**, 13; *dannu* **42**, 13.

dannatu "distress": *dannati* (ideogr. SAL.KAL.GA) **9**, 35; **31**, 6.

dandannu "mighty": *dan-dan-nu* **46**, 16.

DI.PAL.A ideogr.: **7**, 53; **12**, 1, 108.

דפן dapinu "strong": *da-pi-nu* **21**, 77.

דפף duppu "tablet": *duppu* **1**, 54; **22**, 3.

דפר II 1 "to tear away, to remove": *dup-pi-ri* **57**, 15; IV 1 "to be torn away": *lid-dip-pìr* **1**, 49.

דפר dipâru "torch": *di-pa-ra-ka* **1**, 6; *di-pa-ru-. . . . .* **39**, 11; *di-par* **1**, 30; **39**, 8; *dipâru* (ideogr. GI.BIL.[LA]) **40**, 5; *dipâri* (ideogr. GI.BIL.LA) **12**, 86, 118.

דרר darru "strong": *dar-ri* **1**, 32; **5**, 14.

דשא dišû "abounding, numerous": *di-ša-a-tum* **11**, 28.

דשף dašpu "mead": *da-aš-pa* **57**, 10.

dišpu "honey": *dišpu* **11**, 43; **12**, 3; **21**, 29: **30**, 22; **62**, 26.

duššupu "mead": *du-uš-šú-pu* **2**, 29.

DA.ŠAR ideogr. **12**, 11, 14, 15.

ו

ו u "and": *u* **1**, 13, 22, 23, 24, 30, 37, 40, 44, 50, 51; **2**, 40; **3**, 3, 8; **4**, 3, 6, 15, 19, 29, 38, 41, 42, 44; **5**, 12; **6**, 32, 33, 67, 73, 75, 76, 83 *D*, 93, 99, 100, 113 *F*, 120, 121; **7**, 11, 19, 22, 61; **8**, 16; **9**, 19, 35, 38, 41, 43; **10**, 8, 9, 25, 30; **11**, 3, 4, 23, 27; **12**, 7, 28, 29, 30bis, 31, 34, 36, 39, 44, 51, 56, 57, 62, 64, 65, 71, 75 *C*, 76, 78 *C*, 81 *C*, 85 *C*, 86 *C*, 89 *C*, 98, 103, 105, 107, 107 *E*, 113; **13**, 8; **16**, 12; **17**, 3; **19**, 7, 12, 25, 26, 29; **21**, 17, 55, 67, 86; **22**, 20, 39, 53, 55; **27**, 11 *A*, 12, 13, 14 *A*, 23; **30**, 14; **31**, 6, 10; **32**, 9; **33**, 3, 4, 5, 15, 16, 20, 27, 36; **37**, 9; **40**, 14; **46**, 11; **49**, 27; **50**, 8, 16; **53**, 4, 13, 26; **54**, 4; **55**, 5; **56**, 11; **57**, 6; **58**, 7; **59**, 7, 14, 18; **60**, 5; **61**, 8, 10, 13, 16 *A*; **62**, 3, 15, 28; *û* **6**, 25, 86; **7**, 24, 31, 46, 52; **8**, 9, 11; **10**, 2, 20; **11**, 39; **12**, 75, 89, 94, 111; **19**, 15, 17, 32; **33**, 35; **38**, 6; **40**, 11; **60**, 3; **61**, 9.

ואם? imtu "breath, poison": *imti* c **12**, 63ter; **21**, 65ter; *imti*^{pl} **1**, 47ter.

ובל abâlu I 1 "to bring, to carry, to carry off, remove": *ub-ba-lu* **53**, 11, 12; *ú-bil* **8**, 7; *ub-la* **28**, 11; **46**, 3; *ub-lak-ki* **57**, 12; *lu-bi-il* **8**, 6; — I 2 Part. "leader, ruler": *mu-ut-tab-bil* **21**, 81; *mut-tab-bil* **20**, 9, 11; — IV 2 "to be removed": *lit-ta-bil* **1**, 46; **5**, 6; **33**, 30.

ולד alâdu "to bear, to beget": I 1 *a-lid-ya* **11**, 38; *a-lit-ti-ya* **11**, 39; *a-lit-tum* (*la-a-lit-tum?*) **6**, 47; — II 2 *ú-tal-la-da* **19**, 13.

ilittu "child, offspring": *i-lit-ti* **1**, 31; **2**, 12; **3**, 10; **5**, 13; **6**, 18; **22**, 2; **27**, 3; **46**, 14; *i-lit* **33**, 47.

וספא "to shine forth"; III 1 "to glorify": *lu-ša-pi* 2, 8, 41; 5, 8; 6, 69, 94; 7, 32; 21, 23, 71; 23, 5; 30, 15; 50, 27; [*lu*]-*ú-ša-pi* 16, 7; *lu-ša-pa* 30, 14; *li-ša-pu-ú* 30, 17.

šûpû "glorious, mighty": *šú-pu-u* 2, 15; 3, 13; 18, 20; 21, 76, 93; 52, 5; *šú-pu-ú* 1, 16; 6, 132; *šú-pú-ú* 9, 1; *šú-pa(?)-ta* 27, 5.

וצא aṣû "to go out": I 1 *a-ṣi-ka* 6, 23; *aṣi-ka* (ideogr. UD.DU) 6, 23 A; — III 1 *šú-ṣa-a-*..... 61, 18; — III 2 *uš-ti-ṣi-ma* 11, 5.

ṣîtu "exit; offspring": *ṣi-i-ti* 6, 59.

ṣîtaš "beginning, rising": *ṣi-ta-aš* 9, 41.

וקר aḳâru I 1 "to be of value": *li-ḳir* 4, 4; 12, 70; ? *li-ḳa-*..... 12, 55; — III 1 "to consider valuable, to esteem, to honour": *tu-šaḳ-ḳa-ri* 2, 21 B; *li-ša-ḳi-ru-in-ni* 19, 25; *li-ša-ḳi-ru-in-ni-ma* 2, 40.

ורד I 1 "to go down": *tu-ur-dam-ma* 21, 14, 15; — III 1 "to bring down": *šú-ru-du* 2, 22.

ורה arû I 2 "to bring, to carry, to rule": *i-tar-ri-in-ni* 8, 16; *i-tar-ra-*..... 21, [2].

ורח arḫu "month": *arḫi* 1, 12, 39; 4, 17, 39; 6, 84 E, 113 F; 7, 20, 60; 19, 10; 27, 11 A; 50, 14; 53, 24; 54, 2; 55, 3; 56, 9; 57, 4; 58, 6; 59, 12; 60, 19; 61, 16.

ורך arki "behind": *ár-ki-ki* 8, 12; *arki* 12, 6; *arki-šu* 12, 100; *arki-ya* 53, 7; *arki-yà* 15, 8.

urku "back": *ur-ki-ka* 18, 12; *ur-ka-yà* 53, 11.

ורק arḳu "green": *arḳu* 12, 2; 21, 28; 31, 8.

urḳîtu "green herb": *ur-ḳi-tú* 21, 87; ˢᵃᵐ*urḳitu* 12, 30.

ושב ašâbu "to dwell, to inhabit": *a-ši-bat* 4, 15, 24; 6, 71; 7, 9; 37, 7; *a-ši-bu* 11, 35; *a-šib* 43, 5.

šubtu "place, dwelling-place": *šú-bat* 15, 15.

ושן šuttu "dream": *šuttu* 6, 116; *šutta* 12, 113 E; *šutti* 4, 38; 6, 83 DE; 7, 19; *šuttu-ú-a* 12, 57; *šunâti*ᵖˡ 1, 25; 6, 7; 10, 18; 12, 64; *šunât*ᵖˡ*-ú-a* 22, 63; *šunât*ᵖˡ*-ú-a* 6, 115; 10, 17.

ושף šiptu "incantation": *šiptu* 1, 1, 29, 53; 2, 11; 3, 10; 4, 9, 24; 5, 11; 6, 1, 18, 36, 71, 96, 97, 132; 7, 9, 34; 8, 22; 9,

1; **10**, 7, 27; **11**, 1; **12**, 16, 17, 105, 117; **13**, 15; **15**, 23; **18**, 20; **19**, 34; **20**, 8; **21**, 34, 76; **22**, 1, 33, 35, 70; **27**, 1; **30**, 27, 30, 31; **37**, 7; **38**, 5; **42**, 26; **46**, 11; **48**, 17; **50**, 1, 28 *B*, 29; **51**, 11; **52**, 5; **60**, 5; **61**, 5; **62**, 31; *šipat* **61**, 20, 21; *šipat-*. . . . . **16**, 2; *šipat-ku-nu* (ideogr. MU) **62**, 6.

ותר šûturu "mighty, prodigious": *šú-tu-ru* **12**, 21; *šú-tu-rai* **1**, 10; **60**, 12.

ז

ZAG a species of flesh: *šîru*ZAG **12**, 7; **62**, 28.

זיק "to break loose, to burst forth": *li-zi-ḳa-am-ma* **18**, 15; *li-zi-ḳam-ma* **18**, 15 *A*.

זיר zaiâru "foe": *za-ai-ri* **46**, 19.

zîrûtu "hate": *zi-ru-ti* **12**, 106.

זכה I 1 "to be bright, to be pure": *za-ka-a* **57**, 10; — II 1 "to brighten, to purify": *zu-uk-ki* **11**, 21.

זכר zakâru "to name, call, speak, command": I 1 *izaka-ra(ra)-ni* **18**, 11; *ta-za-kar* **19**, 14; *tazakar(ár)* **12**, 120; **40**, 16; *az-za-[kar?]* **61**, 14; — IV 1 *izzakara(ra)* **50**, 9.

zikru "name, word, cry": *zik-ri* **2**, 34; **8**, 14; *zík-ri* **1**, 43; *zi-kir* **12**, 79; **22**, 21 *B*; *sí-kir* **22**, 21; *zík-ri-šu* **1**, 44; **33**, 27; *zi-kir-ka* **5**, 8; **21**, 82; **22**, 8; *zík-ri-ka* **22**, 10 *B*; *sí-ik-ri-ka* **22**, 10; *zi-kir-ki* **30**, 14; *zík-ri-ya* **33**, 25.

זלף zaliptu "wickedness": *[za?]-lip-tû* **11**, 12.

זמה? zîmu "appearance, countenance": *zi-mu-ú-a* **8**, 10.

זמר zumru "body": *zumru* **12**, 102; *zumri-ya* **1**, 45; **30**, 12; **33**, 28; *zumri-yà* **12**, 60; **49**, 14; **50**, 18; **53**, 27, 28.

זנה zinû "to be angry": *iz-nu-ú* **30**, 10; *iz-*. . . . . **6**, 55.

zinû "angry": *zi-nu-u* **2**, 24 *D*; *zi-nu-ú* **2**, 24; *zi-ṇa-a* **12**, 111; *zi-ni-i* **4**, 36; **6**, 81; **7**, 18; *zi-ni-tú* **4**, 45; *zi-ni-tum* **6**, 87; **7**, 25; *zi-ni-ti* **4**, 36; **6**, 81; **7**, 18; **12**, 111; *zi-nu-ti* **6**, 67; **27**, 23.

זנן zanânu "to rain": III 1 *[mu-ša]-az-nin* **49**, 30; . . . . .*-nin* **12**, 27.

זקף zaḳâpu I 1 "to erect"; II 1 "to impale"; — I 3 *uz-za-na-ḳa-pu* **53**, 9; *uz-za-na-ḳup* **53**, 10.

זקר tizḳâru "lofty, noble": *ti-iz-ḳa-ru* **12**, 19 *A*; **27**, 1; **29**, 3; *ti-iz-ḳá-ru* **9**, 2; *tiz-ḳa-ru* **12**, 19.

זקת "to sting": II 1 *ú-zak-ḳat-su* **12**, 121.

זרא₄ zîru "seed": *zîru* (ideogr. KUL) **30**, 14; *zîru* (ideogr. ŠÍ.KUL) **9**, 37, 38; *zîr* (ideogr. KUL) **11**, 44; **33**, 8.

ZI.TAR.RU.DA ideogr.: **7**, 54; **12**, 1, 108.

ח

ḫigallu "abundance": *ḫigalli* **61**, 12 *A*.

חדה ḫadû I 1 "to rejoice"; II 1 "to make joyful": *ḫu-ud* **8**, 16.

ḫadû "joyful": *ḫa-da(ṭa?)-a* **12**, 57.

ḫadiš "joyfully": *ḫad-iš(?)* **1**, 24.

ḫidûtu "joy": *ḫidûtu-ka* **6**, 128; **10**, 4, 24; **42**, 22; *ḫi-dûtu-.....* **7**, 3; *ḫidûtu-ki* **3**, 5; **8**, 18; *ḫidûti-.....* **35**, 6.

חטא ḫaṭû "to sin": *iḫ-ṭu-u* **46**, 1: *iḫ-ṭu-ú* **18**, 8; **28**, 9.

ḫiṭṭu, ḫîṭu "sin": *ḫi-iṭ-ṭi* **9**, 42; *ḫi-ṭu* **18**, 8.

ḫiṭîtu "sin": *ḫi-ṭi-tú* **12**, 78; *ḫi-ṭi-ti* **2**, 39; **14**, 6; **27**, 21; **50**, 18; *ḫi-ṭi-ti* **27**, 21 *A*; **36**, 3; *ḫi-ṭa-ti-[ya]* **50**, 22.

חיד ḫaiadu "giver, bestower": *ḫa-ai-ád* **12**, 30.

חיד "to rule, to govern": *ḫa-i-du* **12**, 28.

חיר ḫâ'iru "spouse, husband": *ḫa-'-i-ri-ki* **1**, 42; *ḫa-i-ri-ki* **33**, 23.

ḫîrtu "spouse, wife": *ḫi-ir-tu* **6**, 126; **37**, 4; *ḫir-tú* **10**, 23.

חלף ḫalâpu "to be clad": *ḫa-lip* **46**, 15.

חלק ḫalâḳu I 1 "to perish"; II 1 "to destroy": *ḫul-liḳ* **21**, 64; *ḫul-li-ki* **2**, 6; *[mu-ḫal-liḳ]* **46**, 19; *ḫul-lu-ḳu* **8**, 24.

hulḳû "destruction": *ḫul-ḳu-u* **27**, 13 *A*.

hulukḳû "destruction": *ḫu-lu-uḳ-ḳu-u* **27**, 13.

חמא ḫimîtu "butter": *ḫimîtu* **11**, 43; **12**, 3; **21**, 29; **30**, 22; **62**, 26.

חסא *i-ḫi-su-u(?)* **53**, 10.

ḫarbašu "storm, fury": *ḫar-ba-šu* **2**, 13; **3**, 11.

חרן ḫarrânu "way, road": *ḫar-ra-ni* **42**, 10; *ḫarrâni*^{pl} **59**, 3; **62**, 18.

חרץ ḫurâṣu "gold": *ḫurâṣu* **12**, 9, 12, 71; **25**, 8; **59**, 8; *abnu ḫu-râṣu* **12**, 12.

חרר ḫarâru "to dig, to plough": ? *ḫa-ra-ár-ra* **49**, 31, 33.

חרר ḫarru a wood: *ḫarri* (ideogr. ŠIM.ŠIŠ) **33**, 39.

חרש ḫuršu, ḫursu "mountain, hill": *ḫur-ša-nu* **22**, 42; *ḫur-sa-a-ni* **12**, 28; **21**, 83.

חשש ḫuššû a ceremonial robe: *ṣubâtu ḫuššû* **12**, 6.

חתח taḫtû "victory": *taḫ-ti-i* **46**, 17.

ט

טחח ṭiḫû "to approach": I 1 *iṭiḫi* **12**, 1; *iṭiḫi-šu* **12**, 119; *iṭi-ḫa-a* **12**, 62, 64, 74; *iṭiḫû-ni* (*iṭḫû-ni?*) **7**, 57; **12**, 63; **21**, 65; *iṭiḫâ-a* **11**, 24; **21**, 22; — II 1 *lu-ṭaḫ-ḫi* **6**, 14.

ṭîḫi "near": *ṭi-iḫ* **46**, 11.

טיב ṭâbu I 1 "to be good, to be acceptable": *li-ṭib* **2**, 34; **8**, 25; *li-ṭi-ba* **10**, 4; — II 1 "to make good, to gladden": *li-ṭib-ka* **10**, 5; *li-ṭib-bu* **6**, 130; **8**, 19; **9**, 26; *ṭu-ub* **8**, 6, 16.

ṭâbu "good": *ṭa-a-bu* **8**, 1; **11**, 32; *ṭa-a-ba* **2**, 28 *D*; *ṭa-a-ab* **9**, 8; . . . . .*-a-ba* **30**, 5; *ṭâbu* (ideogr. DUG.GA) **2**, 28; **12**, 52; **18**, 15; **21**, 90; **22**, 58; **50**, 17; *ṭa-ab-tú* **49**, 6; *ṭa-ab-tum* **12**, 74 *C*; *ṭâbtu(tú)* ideogr. DUG **7**, 53; *ṭâb-tum(tum)* ideogr. DUG.GA **12**, 74; *ṭa-bu-tum* **12**, 82 *C*; *ṭâbûti*pl (ideogr. DUG.GA) **12**, 82; *ṭâbâti*pl (ideogr. DUG) **1**, 13, 40; **27**, 11 *A*; *ṭâbâti*pl (ideogr. DUG.GA) **4**, 18, 40; **6**, 84 *E*, 113 *F*; **7**, 21, 61; **19**, 11; **50**, 15; **53**, 25; **54**, 3; **55**, 4; **56**, 10; **57**, 5; **58**, 7; **59**, 13; **60**, 20; **61**, 16 *A*; **62**, 11.

ṭâbtu "blessing": *ṭâbti-*. . . . . **13**, 24.

ṭubtu "friendliness, kindness": *ṭu-ub-ba-ti* **21**, 88.

טרד ṭarâdu "to expel": *ṭu-ru-ud* **21**, 64.

יד idu "hand, side": *i-di-a* **10**, 32; *idi-yà* **9**, 18; *i-da-ai* **9**, 18 *B*.
Pl. idâti "forces, powers": *i-da-tu-ú-a* **6**, 114; **10**, 17; *idât^{pl}-ú-a* **12**, 58; *idâti^{pl}* **1**, 13, 40; **4**, 18, 40; **6**, 113 *F*; **7**, 21, 61; **12**, 64; **19**, 11; **27**, 11 *A*; **50**, 15; **53**, 25; **54**, 3; **55**, 4; **56**, 10; **57**, 5; **58**, 7; **59**, 13; **60**, 20; **61**, 16 *A*; **62**, 10, 12.

ידא idû "to know": *ti-di-í* **4**, 31; **6**, 76; **7**, 14; **37**, 12; *lu-di-ma* (fr. ודה?) **22**, 66.
mûdû "understanding, wise": *mu-di-í* **13**, 15; *mu-di-i(?)* **12**, 27; *mûdû-u* **11**, 18bis; *mûdû-ú* **11**, 18 *C*^{bis}; **22**, 37; **61**, 15bis; *mu-da-at* **4**, 13.

יום ûmu "day": *ú-mi* **21**, 86; *ŭ-mi* **6**, 5, 6; **7**, 38; **12**, 59; **21**, 78; **53**, 8; *ŭ-mí* **22**, 56; **53**, 6; *ŭ-um* **1**, 17, 18, 23; *ûm* **61**, 11bis, 12bis; *ûmu* **1**, 18; *ûmi* **1**, 12, 39; **4**, 17, 39; **6**, 84 *E*, 113 *F*; **7**, 20, 60; **13**, 26; **19**, 10; **26**, 5; **27**, 11 *A*; **30**, 20; **50**, 14; **53**, 24; **54**, 2; **55**, 3; **56**, 9; **57**, 4; **58**, 6; **59**, 12; **60**, 19; **61**, 11^{quater}, 12bis, 16; *ŭ-mi-šu-ma* **12**, 118; *ŭ-mi-ya* **6**, 118; *ŭ-mi-yà* **10**, 19; *ûmi^{pl}-ya* **5**, 3; **8**, 17.
ûmišam "daily": *ŭ-mi-šam* **19**, 30; **49**, 11; *ŭ-mi-šam* **8**, 16.

יממא immu "day, daylight": *im-ma* **9**, 43.

ימן imnu "right, right side": *im-nu-uk-ki* **8**, 13; *im-ni-ya* **9**, 16 *B*; *imni-yà* **6**, 122; **9**, 16; **10**, 21; **22**, 17.

יצף iṣîpu "to add to, augment, increase": II 1 *lu-uṣ-ṣip* **8**, 13.

יש yâši, yâti "me": *ya-a-ši* **12**, 109 *E*; **21**, 20, 22, 88; **49**, 10; **53**, 4; *ya-ši* **7**, 50; **13**, 20; **22**, 65; **34**, 3; *yá-ši* **12**, 65, 109; **15**, 10; *ya-a-ti* **2**, 7; **6**, 72; **7**, 10; **37**, 8; *ya-a-tu-ú(?)* **2**, 35.

ישה išû "to have; to be": *lîšâ-a* (ideogr. TUK) **21**, 69; *i-šú-ú* **2**, 23; *i-ša-a* **12**, 58.

ישר I 1 "to go straight, to advance, to succeed, be prosperous": *li-šir* **12**, 75; **22**, 59; *lîšir-ma* (ideogr. SI DI) **12**, 100; *li-ši-ra* **8**, 8; *lu-ši-ra* **2**, 36; *li-ši-ra* **6**, 114; **10**, 17; — II 1 ? *mu-ša-ri* **56**, 5; — III 1 "to guide, to bless": *tu-ši-iš-ši-ri* **33**, 18; *šú-šú-ru* **2**, 20; *šú-šú-ra* **3**, 16; — III² 2 "to lead, to direct, to rule": *tuš-ti-ši-ri* **32**, 11; *tuš-ti-šir* **2**, 20; **3**, 16; **12**, 37; *lu-uš-ti-šir* **12**, 89; *muš-ti-iš-ru* **12**, 29; *muš-ti-šir* **1**, 53; **6**, 99; **10**, 8; *muš-ti-ši-ra-a-ti* **30**, 9.

išaru "straight, right": *i-ša-ra* **22**, 60; *i-ša-ru-tú* **53**, 5.

išariš "rightly": *i-ša-riš* **6**, 117; **10**, 18.

mîšaru "righteousness": *mi-ša-ri* **1**, 22; *mîšari* (ideogr. ŠA.SI.DI) **1**, 24.

mîšariš "rightly": *miš-šár-riš* **11**, 18.

כאא : *u-ki-'* **8**, 8.

כאן III[II] 1 "to pay homage, to humble oneself": *uš-ki-in-ma* **62**, 30; *uš-kin-ma* **33**, 41.

KU.A.TIR a species of grain: **2**, 27; **12**, 3; **15**, 20; **21**, 29; **30**, 21; **62**, 26.

כבס kabâsu "to tread": *ka-bi-su* **62**, 8, 9.

kibsu "path": *kib-sa* **22**, 60.

כבר kibratu "quarter of heaven, region": *kib-ra-a-ti* **2**, 43; **5**, 12; **6**, 38; **33**, 7, 12, 47; *kibrâti[pl]* **1**, 30.

כבת kabtu "weighty, important, powerful": *kab-tu* **12**, 21; *kab-[ta?]* **6**, 92; **7**, 30; *kabti(ti)* ideogr. DUGUD **1**, 44; **33**, 27; *kabtu* (ideogr. DUGUD) **12**, 22; *kabti* (ideogr. DUGUD) **22**, 10; *kabti* (ideogr. ILIM) **53**, 16; *ka-bit-ti* **9**, 10 *B*; *kab-ta-a-tum* **46**, 6.

kabittu "disposition": *ka-bit-ta-ka* **21**, 68; *ka-bit-ta-*. . . . . **30**, 6.

kabuttu?: *[ka?]-bu-ut-ta-ka-ma* **61**, 19.

KU.DUB.DUB.BU: **30**, 24; **40**, 12; **62**, 29.

KUD.SIR (*šam*): **12**, 10.

כו kummu "thy, thine": *ku-um-ma* **29**, 1.

כון kânu I 1 "to be firm, to stand fast": *li-kun* **12**, 88 *C*; II 1 "to establish, to place, to set": *tukân(an)* **12**, 2, 4; **15**, 18, 19, 22; **21**, 28; **30**, 21, 23; **31**, 9; **40**, 9; **62**, 25, 27; . . . . . *(an)* **11**, 43; *li-kin* **14**, 5; *mu-kin* **2**, 47; *kun-nu(?)* **12**, 76.

kînu "sure, certain, true": *ki-i-nu* **15**, 7; *ki-ni* **6**, 86 *D*; *ki-nim* **1**, 51; **4**, 44; **6**, 86; **7**, 24; **19**, 32; **33**, 36; **52**, 2.

kîniš "truly": *ki-niš* **2**, 32, 37; **6**, 62; **7**, 46; **8**, 4; **12**, 112; **22**, 23; **27**, 19.

kittu "truth, righteousness": *kit-tu* **9**, 13; *kit-tú* **9**, 13 *B*; *kit-tum* **54**, 8; *kit-ti* **1**, 24; **6**, 45; **7**, 56; **12**, 58; **22**, 9, 14; **54**, 5.

kaianu "continual, constant": *ka-ai-an* **9**, 18; **50**, 24.

kaian "continuously": *ka-ai-an* **12**, 117.

כי kî "when, as, according to": *ki-i* **8**, 1; **10**, 35; **13**, 30; **18**, 9, 11.

ki'âm "thus": *ki'âm* **12**, 104.

kîma "like, when, as": *ki-ma* **8**, 15; **9**, 20; **11**, 6 *A*, 38; **12**, 73 *C*, 81 *C*, 82 *C*, 83 *C*; **32**, 8; **50**, 28 *B*; *kîma* **1**, 6, 10; **4**, 29; **6**, 73; **7**, 11; **11**, 6, 25; **12**, 34, 35, 50, 69, 70, 71, 73, 81, 82, 83; **13**, 20; **37**, 9; **60**, 11.

KA.IZI a species of flesh: *širu*KA.IZI **12**, 7; **40**, 10; **62**, 28.

כך? kakku "weapon": *iṣu*kakku **12**, 23.

KU.KU ideogr.: **12**, 101; **30**, 25.

ככב kakkabu "star": *kakkab* **7**, 16; **19**, 18; *kakkabâni*pl **6**, 78; **39**, 6; **62**, 17, 18; *kakkabâni* (MUL.MUL) **8**, 22.

KA.ḶU.BI.DA ideogr.: **7**, 53; **12**, 1, 108; **47**, 3.

כלה kalû "all": *kal* **53**, 12; *kalû* (ideogr. KAK) **7**, 54; *kalû* (ideogr. KAK.A.BI) **62**, 23; *kal* (ideogr. KAK) **4**, 9, 11; **12**, 113; **53**, 8bis; **59**, 1.

kalâmu "all, of every kind": *ka-la-ma* **10**, 27; *kalâ-ma* (KAK.A-*ma*) **19**, 9.

kališ "altogether, completely": *ka-liš* **9**, 7, 8.

כלל "to be complete"; III 1 "to make complete": II 1 *ú-kâl-lil* **11**, 10; — III 1 *šuk-lul* **12**, 53.

kullatu "the whole": *kul-lat* **2**, 18; **3**, 15; **18**, 5; **21**, 52; **42**, 3; *kul-lat-si-na* **32**, 12.

כמה kimtu "family": *kim-ti-ya* **53**, 13; . . . . .*-ti-yà* **11**, 23; . . . . .*-ti-ya* **11**, 23 *C*.

כמל kamâlu "to be angry": *kam-lu* 4, 87; 6, 82 *E*; 7, 19; *kám-lu* 6, 82, 88; 7, 26.

כמס kamâsu "to bow down, to humble oneself": *kan(kám?)-su* 1, 11; 50, 4; *kam-sa-ku* 59, 9; *kan(kám?)-sa-ku* 1, 21; . . . . . *-sa-ku* 22, 52; — I 2 *kit-mu-ša* 9, 43.

כנה II 1 "to prepare carefully": *kun-ni* 31, 10.

kanû "strong(?)": *ka-nu-tú* 2, 45; *ka-nu-ut* 1, 29; 4, 14; 5, 11; 9, 30.

כנך kunukku "seal": *abnu kunukku* 12, 13; *iṣu kunukku* 12, 12, 73; *abnu iṣu kunukku* 12, 73 *C*.

KAN.KAL a plant: *šam*KAN.KAL 11, 25.

כסה kasû "to bind"; II 1 "to bind fast, to fetter": *ú-ka-as-si* 13, 23.

kasîtu "fetter, bonds": *ka-si-ti* 30, 11.

KAS.SAG a drink-offering: 2, 10; 6, 96; 12, 5; 22, 33; 30, 23; 32, 3; 51, 11.

כסף kaspu "silver": *kaspu* 59, 8.

כפף kuppu "well, source": *kup-pi* 12, 29.

כפר kapru "bowl": *kap-ra* 40, 9.

kâru "wall, fortress": *kar* 22, 7; *kâri* 42, 15.

כרב karâbu "to be favourable, to bless": *lik-ru-bu-ka* 6, 129; 9, 25; 22, 25; *lik-ru-bu-*. . . . . 60, 17; *lik-ru-bu-ki* 3, 6; 8, 19.

ikribu "prayer": *ik-ri-bi* 7, 36, 45; 33, 5; *ik-ri-bí* 11, 27; *ik-ri-*. . . . . 35, 12.

kirûbu(?) "favourable(?)": *ki-ru-ub* 8, 1.

כרב karûbu "great, mighty": *ka-ru-bu* 49, 16.

כרה I 2 "to draw near": *ik-tar* 11, 19.

כרה kûru "need, distress": *ku-u-ru* 22, 53.

כרם kurmatu "food": *kurmat-su* 22, 34; *kurmati*pl 31, 9.

כרן karânu "wine": *karâni* 30, 2.

kurunnu a drink made from sesame-seed: *ku-ru-[un-na]* 57, 10.

כש kâša, kâši "thee, thyself": *ka-a-ša* 6, 49; 17, 4; *ka-*. . . . . . . 1, 21; *ka-ša* 1, 22; *ka-a-ši* 31, 5; 33, 13; *ka-*. . . . . 7, 16; 39, 2.

כשד kašâdu "to attain to, to capture, to overcome": *iksud-an-ni* **21**, 22; *ikšuda-ni* **12**, 65; *lu-uk-šú-ud* **8**, 18; **9**, 12, 48; **54**, 7; *lu-uk-šú-da* **8**, 13; *lukšud(ud)* **22**, 13.

כשד kišâdu "neck": *kišâdi-šu* **12**, 116; *kišâdi-yà* **12**, 67.

KIŠDA i. e. *riksu* "knot": **12**, 5(?), 6(?), 96(?); **16**, 11; **18**, 19; **21**, 92; **22**, 69; **28**, 6; **34**, 6; **38**, 3; **39**, 5; **41**, 2; **42**, 25; **46**, 10; **47**, 7; **52**, 4.

כשף kišpu "magic, enchantment": *kiš-pi* 7, 50; **12**, 106, 109; *kiš-pi-ya* **50**, 22; UḪ **22**, 12.

kaššapu "sorcerer": *kaš-ša-pi* **12**, 62, 81*C*.

kaššaptu "sorceress": *kaš-šap-ti* **12**, 62, 81*C*; *kaš-šap-tum* **12**, 62*BC*.

כשש kašâšu: I 1 *ikšuš(?)-an-ni* (ideogr. UŠ.UŠ) **53**, 8; — IV 1 *nakšušu(?)-ni* (ideogr. UŠ.UŠ) **22**, 12.

כשש kiššatu "host, multitude, the whole": *kiš-ša-ti* **3**, 6; **6**, 129; **8**, 19; **9**, 25; **53**, 3; *kiš-šat* **1**, 53; *kiššat* (ideogr. ŠAR) **62**, 1.

kaškaššu "strong": *kaš-kaš-šú* **21**, 39, 41; *kaš-ka-šú* **20**, 14, 16; *kaš-kaš* **27**, 4.

ל

לא lâ "not": *la* **1**, 9, 19bis; **2**, 14, 20, 21; **3**, 12, 16; **5**, 9; **6**, 47(?), 66bis, 122; **10**, 21; **11**, 3, 4, 10bis, 12; **12**, 19*A*, 23(?), 74*C*, 82*C*, 96; **13**, 4, 7, 11, 30; **20**, 9, 11, 15, 17; **21**, 9, 22bis, 35, 37, 40, 41; **22**, 22; **27**, 14; **42**, 11bis, 18; **46**, 18; **60**, 7, 8, 15; **61**, 18; *lâ* **1**, 13, 40; **4**, 18, 40; **6**, 84*E*, 113*F*; 7, 21, 53, 61; **11**, 18; **12**, 52, 68, 74, 82, 96*D*; **19**, 11; **27**, 11*A*; **50**, 15, 17; **53**, 7, 25; **54**, 3; **55**, 4; **56**, 10; **57**, 5; **58**, 7; **59**, 13, 21; **60**, 20; **61**, 15, 16*A*; **62**, 11.

לאב la'âbu "to oppress": *la-'-bu* **12**, 51; *la-'-bu-ma* **12**, 53.

לאה li'û "strong": *li-'-ú* **12**, 20; *li-'-a* **2**, 21; *li-'-. . . . .* **13**, 4; **21**, 40, 41(?); *li-'-at* **32**, 14.

la'û? "strong": *lá-ú* **4**, 12; *lá-tú* **4**, 9, 11.

lîtu "strength": *li-i-ti* **46**, 17.

לאט "to burn": *la-iṭ* **21**, 42; **60**, 5.

לבב libbu "heart": *lib-bi* **8**, 16; **13**, 22; **27**, 22; *libbu* **6**, 11; **35**, 6; *libbi* **11**, 44; **12**, 8, 11, 116; *libbu-šu* **4**, 37; **6**, 88; **7**, 26; *lib-ba-ka* **11**, 38; *lib-ba-ka* **6**, 130; **9**, 26; **12**, 88; **21**, 68; **27**, 20; **28**, 12; **46**, 5; *lib-bi-ka* **4**, 7; *libba-ka* **9**, 26 *B*; **27**, 20 *A*; *lib-ba-ki* **8**, 19; *libbu-ki* **3**, 6; **30**, 6; *libbi-*. . . . . **8**, 6; **37**, 3; *lib-bi-ya* **11**, 5; **30**, 13; *libbi-ya* **9**, 14 *B*; **11**, 5 *A*; *libbi-yà* **9**, 14; **22**, 15; *lib-ba-šu-nu* **33**, 18.

לבה "to enclose, to surround": II 1 *lu-ub-ba-ku* **12**, 56.

לבן labânu "to cast down": IV 2 *it-tal-bu-nin-ni* **11**, 3 *A*; **27**, 14; *it-tal-ban-ni* **11**, 3.

libittu "brick": *libit* **21**, 26.

לבש labâšu "to clothe oneself, be clothed": I 2 *lit-bu-šu* **3**, 11; *lit-bu-šú* **2**, 13; **46**, 15; *lit-bu-ša* **12**, 53; *lit-bu-ši-šu* **53**, 16.

lubuštu "clothing": *lubuštu* (ideogr. SIG) **53**, 9; *lu-bušti*^{pl} (KU.ZUN) **53**, 16.

לו lû precative particle; "or": *lu-u* **6**, 118; **9**, 18, 20, 21 *B*; **10**, 19; *lu-ú* **8**, 9, 11, 15; **12**, 97 *D*; *lu* **8**, 12bis; **11**, 16, 17; **12**, 97bis; **13**, 10; **16**, 11bis; **18**, 19bis; **19**, 28; **21**, 22bis, 25, 26bis, 92bis; **22**, 69bis; **28**, 6bis; **30**, 14; **34**, 6bis; **38**, 4bis; **39**, 5bis; **41**, 2bis; **46**, 10bis; **47**, 7bis; **50**, 24; **52**, 4bis; **53**, 13, 14, 15.

לוא$_3$ li'û "tablet": ^{iṣu}*li-'-um* **10**, 35.

LA.ḪAR (*la-ḫar?*) "grain(?)": ^{ilu}*la-ḫar(?)* **12**, 30.

ללר lallartu "wailing, loud crying": *lallartu* **1**, 20.

למד lamâdu "to learn": *i-lam-ma-du* **1**, 9, 19; *i-lam-mad* **11**, 9, 11; *lil-ma-da* **1**, 43; **33**, 26; *lim-[da]* **4**, 30.

למן limnu "evil": *lim-nu* **12**, 62, 77 *C*, 119; **50**, 19, 23; **51**, 16; **57**, 16; *lim-na* **12**, 57; *lim-*. . . . . **21**, 64; *limnu* **12**, 67; *limni* **12**, 66; *limuttum(tum)* **12**, 74 *C*; *limutti(ti)* **12**, 74; **50**, 17; *limuttim(tim)* **2**, 6; **12**, 68; *limuttu* **15**, 9; **61**, 4; *limutti* **12**, 66; *limutti* (ideogr. ḪUL.GAL) **61**, 12; *lim-nu-tú* **10**, 3; *lim-nu-ti* **8**, 24; **49**, 13; *lim-nu-*. . . . . **47**, 2; *limnûti*^{pl} **12**, 63, 81 *C*; *limnûti(ti)* **7**, 51; *limnîti*^{pl} **1**, 13, 40; **4**, 18, 40; **6**, 84 *E*, 113 *F*; **7**, 21, 61; **12**, 56; **19**, 11; **27**, 11 *A*; **50**, 15; **53**, 25; **54**, 3; **55**, 4; **56**, 10; **57**, 5; **58**, 7; **59**, 13; **60**, 20; **61**, 16 *A*; **62**, 10, 11, 14; *limnîti*^{pl}*-ya* **12**, 73; *limnîti*^{pl}*-yà* **12**, 83; *lim-na-ti(?)* **58**, 4.

lumnu "evil": *lum-ni* 62, 10, 11; *lu-mun* 22, 54; *lumun* 1, 12, 13, 39, 40; 4, 17, 18, 39, 40; 6, 113 F^bis; 7, 20, 21, 60, 61; 12, 1, 64, 65; 19, 10, 11; 27, 11 A^bis; 50, 14, 15; 53, 24, 25; 54, 2, 3; 55, 3, 4; 56, 9, 10; 57, 4, 5; 58, 6, 7; 59, 12, 13; 60, 19, 20; 61, 16, 16 A; 62, 16bis, 17, 18, 19, 20; *lumnu(nu)-u-a* 12, 76.

למס lamassu "guardian deity": ^ilu *lamassu* 8, 12; 12, 110; 22, 19.

לסם lasâmu: ? *a-la-su-um* 18, 12.

לפת lapâtu "to surround": II 1 *lu-up-pu-ta-ku-ma* 12, 56; — III 2 ? *uš-tál-pi-. . . .* 21, 25.

לקא liḳû "to receive, to take": *talaki(ki)-ma* 12, 8, *talaki* 30, 26 [? *tiliḳi*]; *lil-ki* 1, 43; 33, 26; *li-ki* 18, 14; 21, 21; 23, 3; *li-ki-ma* 2, 33; *liḳi-ma* 2, 33 D; *li-ki-i* 6, 80; 8, 4; *liḳî-i* 3, 2; 4, 35; 6, 80 E; 7, 17; *li-ḳat* 9, 39; 33, 5.

לשן lišânu "tongue": *li-ša-[nu]* 6, 33; *lišânu* 22, 55; *lišâni* 12, 66; *lišânu-šu* 12, 121; *lišâni-. . . .* 4, 20.

מ

MA: ^iṣu MA 12, 5.

מאד ma'du "many": *ma-'-du* 7, 47.

ma'dûtu, mâdûtu "great quantity": *ma-'-du-ti* 6, 78; 7, 16; 19, 18; 53, 6; *ma-du-ti* 1, 23.

מאר₁ mâru "son": *mâru* (ideogr. DU.UŠ) 46, 14; 56, 3; *mâri* (ideogr. DU) 1, 42; 4, 48; 33, 23; *mâr* (ideogr. DU) 2, 26 D; 22, 9, 22; 50, 12; 59, 17.

mârtu "daughter": *mârat* (ideogr. DU.ŠAL) 61, 5.

מאר₂ II 1 "to send, despatch; to rule": *ú-ma-'-ir-ma* 1, 25; *ú-ma-'-ir-an-ni* 12, 99; *mu-ma-'-ir* 19, 7.

מגר magâru "to be favourable; to listen to, receive favourably": *mu-gu-ur* 21, 21; *ma-ag-rat* 8, 15; 9, 20; *magrat(at)* 14, 13; *ma-ga-ru* 8, 9; *ma-ga-ra* 9, 19; 13, 8; 22, 20; *magâra* 19, 29bis; *magâri* (? *simî*) 26, 5; 30, 20; GIŠ.TUK 35, 10.

mâgiru "favourable, willing, obedient": *ma-gi-ri* 33, 16; *ma-gir* 6, 120.

מן mû "water": *mû* **11**, 43; **12**, 2, 3; **15**, 18; **21**, 28, 29; **30**, 21, 22; **31**, 8; **33**, 39; **62**, 26; *mî*^{pl} **53**, 17; **62**, 24.

מוש mûšu "night": *mu-ši* **22**, 63; *mûši* **1**, 20, 26; **9**, 43; **12**, 2; **21**, 28, 86; **31**, 8; **53**, 8.

מות mîtu "dead": ^{amîlu}*mîtu* **6**, 99; **10**, 8; **28**, 8; **59**, 21.

MI.ḪI a species of flesh: ^{šîru}MI.ḪI **12**, 7; **62**, 28.

miḫḫu a drink(?)-offering: *mi-iḫ-ḫa* **8**, 21; **40**, 12.

מחר I 1 "to oppose; to take, accept; to implore": *am-ḫur-ka* **50**, 20; *lim-ḫu-ri* **10**, 31; *lim-ḫu-ru-*. . . . . **60**, 16; *lim-ḫu-ru-ka-ma* **46**, 4; *mu-ḫur* **2**, 33; **50**, 21; *muḫ-ra-an-ni* **61**, 17; *muḫ-ri-ma* **4**, 35; *muḫ-ri-in-ni-ma* **6**, 80; **7**, 17; *ma-ḫi-rat* **9**, 39; *maḫ-rat* **22**, 34; — II 1 *ú-ma-ḫir-ki* **57**, 11; — IV 1 *im-maḫ-ḫa-ru* **2**, 14; **3**, 12.

maḫru "before": ? . . . . .*-ḫar* **6**, 30; *maḫ-ra-ka* **50**, 4; *ma-ḫar-ka* **9**, 23; **21**, 11, 62; **22**, 57; **25**, 4; *ma-ḫar-*. . . . . **21**, 21; *ma-ḫar-ku-nu* **7**, 48.

tamḫaru "battle": *tam-ḫa-ri* **27**, 2; **46**, 18; *tam-ḫa-*. . . . . **21**, 40.

מלא malû "to fill; to be full": *ma-lu-u* **2**, 13; *ma-lu-ú* **1**, 7; **2**, 13 *B*; **3**, 11; — II 1 *ú-mal-li* **13**, 24; — III^{II} 1 *uš-mal-la* **21**, 59.

mâla "as many as": *ma-la* **11**, 8; **62**, 12.

? *mi-lim-ma* **11**, 18.

מלך maliku "arbiter, prince": *ma-li-ku* **6**, 25; **50**, 7; *ma-li-ki* **1**, 34; **5**, 16; **6**, 19.

milku "counsel": *mil-ka* **1**, 14; *mi-lik-šu* **1**, 19; *mi-lik-šu* **1**, 9; *mi-lik-ka* **27**, 7.

MU.MU a priest: ^{amîlu}MU.MU **60**, 3.

מם mamma, mimma "whosoever, whatsoever": *ma-am-ma* **12**, 98; *ma-am-man* **60**, 8; *ma-*. . . . . **1**, 9, 19; *mimma* (ideogr. NIN) **12**, 62, 67, 77 *C*, 119bis; **50**, 23; **57**, 15, 16.

mimma šumšu "of whatever kind; anyone, anything": *mimma šum-šu* **7**, 52; *mimma šumšu* (ideogr. ŠA.NAM.MA) **7**, 55; **13**, 8; **21**, 89.

mamlu "strong": *ma-am-lu* **46**, 13.

מן **mạnnu** "who": *man-nu* 11, 9, 10, 11.

מנה **manû** "to repeat, recite": *limnu(nu)* 60, 4; *munu(nu)* 2, 10; 15, 23; 18, 19 *A*; 24, 7; 25, 7; 32, 4; 52, 4; *munu(nu)-ma* 12, 117; 33, 41; *munu* 12, 103; *munu-ma* 6, 96; 11, 45; 30, 27; 62, 30; *munu-šù* 12, 16.

minûtu "repetition, recital, incantation": *minûtu(tú)* 2, 10; 11, 45; 40, 13; 62, 30.

minîtu: *mi-ni-ta* 19, 23.

massû "ruler(?)": *massû-u* 22, 2; *[massû]-ú* 22, 2 *A*.

מצר **maṣṣaru** "watch, guard": *ma-ṣar* 12, 105, 113.

maṣartu "watch": *maṣartu-šu* (ideogr. IN.NUN) 53, 21.

מקת **maḳâtu** "to fall": *ma-aḳ-tum* 6, 44.

מרץ **marṣu** "sick": *mar-ṣu* 22, 11; *amîlumarṣu* 12, 100; *amîlumarṣi* 12, 16.

murṣu "sickness, disease": *mu-ur-ṣi* 21, 44; *murṣu* 1, 45; 4, 19; 7, 53; 12, 52; 30, 12; 33, 28; 50, 17; *murṣi* 12, 1; *muruṣ* 12, 60; *murṣi-yà* 5, 5.

šumruṣu "diseased": *šum-ru-ṣu* 22, 11; *šum-ru-. . . . .* 39, 16.

מרש **maruštu** "misfortune, disaster, sickness": *maruštu* 7, 53; 12, 49; 22, 52; 30, 7; *marušti* 18, 14; *marušti-yà* 18, 14 *B*.

משה **mašû** "to forget": I 1 *ma-ši-i* 6, 66; — IV 1 *im-maš-ši* 60, 10; . . . . *.-ṃa-ši* 5, 7.

mašmašu a priest: *maš-maš* 12, 88, 94; 60, 4.

משר *im-šir(?)* 33, 6.

מת **mâtu** "land": *ma-a-ti* 9, 6; 52, 5; *mâti* 6, 112; 10, 15; 11, 28; 12, 65; *mâti-ya* 13, 25; *mâti-yà* 1, 13; 4, 19, 41; 6, 113 *F*; 7, 22, 61; 19, 12; 50, 16; 53, 26; 54, 4; 55, 5; 56, 11; 57, 6; 59, 14; 60, 21; 61, 16 *A*; *mâti-a* 1, 40; 27, 11 *A*; 58, 7; *ma-ta-a-ti* 9, 33; *ma-. . . . .* 39, 9; *mâtâti* 1, 11; 12, 17, 39; 19, 7; 57, 14; 61, 3.

נאא *li-ni-'* 1, 49; 33, 33.

נאד nâdu I 1 "to be exalted; to praise(?)": ? *li-na-du-ka* 11, 29; — I 2 "to exalt, to praise": *lu-ut-ta-'-id* 12, 89; *lù-ta-id* 21, 70; *lut-ta-id* 5, 8; *lu-ut-ta-id-ma* 11, 12.

tanittu: *iṣutanitti* (*iṣutikniti?*, ideogr. ŠIM.GIG) 22, 32.

נא₂ר nâru "stream": *nârî^pl* 12, 29; 25, 6.

נבא nabû "to name"; šuma nabû "to exist, to be": *na-bat* 11, 8; *na-bi-at* 11, 8 *A*.

נבט nabâṭu "to shine"; I 3 do.: *it-ta-na-an-bi-ṭu* 39, 12.

nubattu a festival: *(um) nu-bat(?)-ti* 61, 11.

נדב nindabû "offering": *nindabû* 18, 13.

נדה nadû "to cast, to place": I 1 *tanadi(di)* 11, 44; 12, 6bis, 11, 98; 17, 7; — I 3 *it-ta-na-an-du-ú* 21, 73; *ittanandû* 21, 25.

נדן nadânu "to give": *tanadin(in)* 1, 14, 16; *id-din-ka-ma* 2, 17; 3, 15; 27, 9; *iddin-ka-ma* 27, 9 *A*; . . . . .*-dan* 31, 5; *ad-dan-ka* 19, 19; *ad-dan-ki* 4, 33; *addin-šu* 53, 18; *naduat(at)* 9, 38.

mandatu "tribute": *man-da-ti-yà* 12, 55.

נוח nâḫu I 1 "to be weak; to rest": *an-ḫu* 4, 16; *an-ḫa* 12, 41; *li-nu-uḫ* 12, 88; *li-nu-ḫa* 6, 89; 7, 27; 21, 68; 27, 20; 28, 12; 46, 5; *linuḫ(uḫ)* 30, 6; — III 2 "to appease, to pacify": *muš-ti-ni-iḫ* 33, 3.

נור nûru "light": *nu-ú-ru* 6, 108; *nu-ú-ra* 8, 2; *nu-ru* 11, 1 *A*; 22, 35; *nu-ri* 12, 69; *nu-úr* 6, 100; 39, 9.

נזז nazâzu "to stand": I 1 *az-za-az* 1, 21; *azzaz(az)* ideogr. GUB 13, 6; *az-ziz* 21, 11; 22, 57; *izzizû* (ideogr. GUB.BU) 1, 15; *li-iz-ziz* 6, 122; 9, 16, 17; 10, 21; 22, 17, 18; 53, 22; *li-iz-zi-zu* 2, 30, 31; 7, 42; *li-zi-zu* 50, 10; *li-ziz-zu* 2, 30 *D*, 31 *D*; *lizziza(za)* ideogr. GUB 60, 18; *iziz-ma* (ideogr. GUB) 12, 59; *i-ziz-zi-im-ma* 6, 72; 7, 10; 37, 8; *i-ziz-zi-ma* 4, 27; ? *lu-ziz-ku* (*lu-bat-tuk?*) 11, 27; — III 1 *ušîzizu(zu)* ideogr. GUB.GUB 53, 9; — IV 1 *na-an-za-zu* 9, 15; — I 2 *at-ta-ziz* 27, 18.

manzazu "place, station": *man-za-za* 2, 15; 3, 13; 22, 16; *man-za-az-ka* 27, 5; *man-za-az-ki* 32, 7.

נחל naḫlu "date-palm(?)": *na-aḫ-la* 12, 4.

נחש naḫâšu "to abound": *na-ḫa-ši* 8, 3.

nuḫšu "abundance": *nuḫšu* 12, 27; 49, 30; 58, 2.

נטל naṭâlu "to see, behold": *i-na-ṭa-lu* 18, 2; *ta-na-ṭal* 18, 7 A; *aṭ-ṭu-la* 6, 116; 10, 18; *luṭ-ṭul* 12, 113.

נכל "to be cunning": I 1 *ak-kil(?)* 6, 29; — IV 1 ? *nam-kil-lu-ni-ma* 22, 12.

NI.KUL.LA(*šam*) 12, 101.

נכם nakâsu "to cut off": I 1 *na-kás* 50, 23; — II 1 *tunikis(is)* ideogr. KUD 40, 9.

נכר nakâru I 1 "to rebel, be hostile"; II 1 "to alter"; II 2 "to be altered": I 1 *a-na-kar* 59, 9; *na-kar* 13, 11; — II 1 *nu-uk-kir(kir?)-ma* 12, 60; *mu-na-kir* 50, 2; — II 2 *ut-tak-ka-ru* 60, 7; *uttakkaru(ru)* 12, 19; 19, 31; 33, 36; 53, 23; 59, 11; *uttakkarum(rum)* 1, 50; *uttakkar(ár)* 12, 96.

NIM a tree: *isu*NIM 12, 10.

NAM.BUL.BI ideogr.: NAM.BUL.BI.I 62, 12.

נמר namâru "to shine, to be bright"; II 1 "to make bright"; III^II 1 do.; II 2 "to be bright": I 1 *lim-mir* 12, 69; *lim-mi-ru* 8, 10; *nam-rat* 1, 5; — II 1 *ú-nam-ma-......* 21, 1; *tu-nam-mar* 40, 11; *tunammar(?)* ideogr. LAḪ.LAḪ 40, 9; *nu-um-mi-ir* 11, 20; *nu-um-mir* 11, 20C; *mu-nam-mir* 1, 2; *mu-na-mir* 58, 17; *mu-na-......* 33, 1; — III^II 1 *tuš-nam-mar* 12, 35; *muš-na-mi-rat* 39, 10; — II 2 *lu-ut-ta-mir* 12, 83.

namru "bright": *nam-ru* 16, 4; *nam-ri(?)* 10, 27; *nam-ru-ti* 8, 23.

namriš "brightly": *nam-riš* 9, 23.

namrîru "brightness, splendour": *nam-ri-ri* 46, 15; *nam-ri-ru-ka* 1, 7; *nam-ri-ir-ri-ki* 8, 10.

namirtu "brightness": *na-mir-ti* 1, 3.

namurratu "brightness": *na-mur-ra-ta* 21, 59.

נמש nammaššû "reptile, creature": *na-maš-šu-ú* 32, 13; *nam-maš-ši-i* 27, 10.

nammaštu "reptile, creature": *na-maš-ti* **32**, 10.

namtaru: *nam-ta-ru* **12**, 42.

נסא nisû "to remove, to tear away; to be removed": I 1 *li-is-su-ú* **12**, 73*C*; — II 1 *lu-ni-is-su-u* **12**, 73; *nu-us-si* **12**, 60; . . . . .*-us-su* **12**, 60 *B*; — IV 1 *li-in-ni-is-si* **1**, 45, 48; **33**, 28, 32; *linnisi(si)* ideogr. BAD **30**, 12.

nisûtu "male relatives": *ni-su-ti-yà* **11**, 23; ? *ni-šú-*. . . . . **11**, 23 *C*.

נסח nasaḫu "to remove, to tear away": I 1 *tanasaḫ(?)-ma* (ideogr. ZI) **12**, 97; *nasâḫu* (ideogr. ZI.GA) **27**, 13; — IV 1 *linnasiḫ(iḫ)* ideogr. ZI **30**, 12; **50**, 23.

נפש napištu "life": *na-piš-ti* **12**, 70; **22**, 6; **33**, 8; **37**, 5; *na-pišti(ti)* **7**, 37; **9**, 5, 21 *B*, 38; **14**, 4; **18**, 16 *B*; **27**, 9; **57**, 12; *napištim(tim)* **6**, 60; **9**, 21; **12**, 108 *E*; **18**, 16; **37**, 2; *nap-šat* **61**, 13; *napsat* **53**, 29; *napišti(tim)-ya* **9**, 22; *napišti-ya* **9**, 22 *B*; **50**, 23.

נצר naṣâru "to keep, preserve": *aṣ-ṣur* **8**, 9; *na-ṣi-ru* **22**, 6; *na-ṣi-rat* **9**, 38.

נקה niḳû "to offer": *tanaki(ki)* [? *tiniḳi*] **6**, 96; **12**, 5, 7; **15**, 27; **21**, 30; **22**, 33; **24**, 6; **30**, 23; **32**, 3; **40**, 12; **51**, 11; **62**, 28; *tanaki(ki)-ma* **2**, 10; **8**, 21; *ak-ki(?)* **2**, 45; *ak-ki-ka* **1**, 20; *aḳḳi-ka* **2**, 29; — II 1 ? *nu-uk-ka* **21**, 79.

niḳû "offering": *niḳû* ideogr. DIM (? *tanaḳi*) **11**, 43; **12**, 3; **21**, 29; **30**, 22; **62**, 26; *niḳî* (ideogr. DIM) **21**, 70; *immiru niḳû* **21**, 30; *immiru niḳî* **12**, 7; **40**, 9; **62**, 28.

nirtu: *ni-ir-tú* **6**, 58.

נשא nišû "to raise": *niši-ma* **12**, 103; *na-aš* **22**, 3; *na-ša-ku* **18**, 13; *ni-šu* **12**, 78; *ni-*. . . . . **1**, 48; **33**, 32; *ni-šú* **12**, 52; *ni-iš* **12**, 79; **35**, 14; *niš* **12**, 88*C*; **50**, 21; *niš* (ideogr. IL) **4**, 35; **12**, 48, 88; **13**, 14; **23**, 7; **40**, 10, 13; IL.LA (= *niš*) **1**, 28, 52; **2**, 9, 42; **3**, 9; **4**, 8, 23; **5**, 10; **6**, 17, 35, 70, 95, 131; **7**, 8, 33; **8**, 20, 21; **9**, 27; **10**, 6, 26; **11**, 41; **12**, 95; **13**, 12; **14**, 11; **15**, 17; **16**, 10; **17**, 5; **18**, 18; **19**, 33; **20**, 7; **21**, 24, 72, 75, 91; **22**, 30, 68; **23**, 6; **24**, 4; **25**, 5; **26**, 3; **27**, 25; **28**, 5; **29**, 2; **30**, 19; **31**, 7; **32**, 2; **33**, 38; **34**, 5; **36**, 6, 8; **37**, 6; **38**, 3; **39**, 4; **40**, 2; **42**, 24; **43**, 8; **44**, 2; **45**, 4; **46**, 9; **47**, 6, 9; **48**, 16; **49**, 20; **50**, 28; **51**, 9.

nišu "spirit(?)": *niš* **8**, 1.

nišu "people": *ni-šu* **11**, 28; *ni-ši* **9**, 6; *niši^pl* **1**, 3, 4, 8, 53; **4**, 5; **7**, 59; **9**, 8, 40; **12**, 39, 72; **13**, 7, 16; **18**, 5, 17; **21**, 12, 23, 90; **22**, 7, 8, 67; **30**, 18; **32**, 11; **33**, 34; **57**, 2.

נשך našku "weak(?)": *na-aš-ki* **9**, 36.

סבס sabâsu "to be angry": *is-bu-su* **1**, 23.

סדר "to arrange": *si-di-ir-ma* **21**, 88.

סחר saḫâru "to turn towards": *is-saḫ-ru* **6**, 52; *as-sa-ḫar* **27**, 15; *is-ḫu-ra* **7**, 54; *as-ḫur* (*az-mur?*) **8**, 11; *as-ḫur-ka* **6**, 28; *as-ḫur-ki* **6**, 73, 79; **33**, 22; *asḫur-ki* **1**, 41; **4**, 29; **7**, 11, 62; **37**, 9; **57**, 7; *li-saḫ-ra* **30**, 10.

סכל sukkallu "messenger": *suk-kal-lu* **6**, 20; *sukkallu* **6**, 20 *A*.

סכף sakâpu "to cast down, overthrow": *li-is-kip* **12**, 68.

סלה II 1 "to implore, to beseech": *i-sal-lu-ka-ma* **1**, 14, 16; **50**, 5.

silîtu "compassion": *si-li-ti* **30**, 14.

salâtu "female relatives": *sa-la-ti-ya* **53**, 13; *sa-la-ti-yà* **11**, 23.

סלח salâḫu "to sprinkle": *[ta]-sal-laḫ* **62**, 29; *tasalaḫ* **12**, 2; **21**, 28, 74; **30**, 21; **31**, 8; **33**, 39.

סלם salâmu I 1 "to be favourable"; II 1 do.: I 1 *tas-lim* **8**, 12bis; *tas-lim* **13**, 10; *lis-li-mu* **1**, 24; *lislimu(mu)* **1**, 44; **28**, 3; **33**, 27; *si-lim* **2**, 35; **14**, 7; **16**, 9(?); **22**, 61, 62; *sal-li-mu* **9**, 18; *sal-li-. . . . .* **6**, 123; **10**, 21; *sâlimu(mu)* **33**, 42; **32**, 5 (*lislimu?*); *sâlimu* **6**, 122; **10**, 21; ? *sa-la-mi-i* **48**, 18; — II 1 *tu-sal-lam* **2**, 24; **21**, 87; . . . . .*-sal-lam* **6**, 55; *tu-sál-lam(?)* **2**, 24 *B*.

salimu "favour": *sa-li-mu* **4**, 6; **8**, 8; **50**, 25; *sa-li-ma* **33**, 15, 16; . . . .*-ma* **12**, 61 *B*: *salima(ma)* **12**, 61.

suluppu "date": *suluppu* **12**, 3; **21**, 29; **30**, 21; **62**, 26.

סמד *sa-mi-id* **21**, 26; *sa-mid* **21**, 16.

סנק sanâḳu "to harass; to shut up, to fetter": I 1 *sa-ni-ḳu* **46**, 12; — III 1 *ú-šis-ni-ḳa* **12**, 67; *ušisniḳa(ḳa)* **12**, 74; *tu-ša-as-ni-ḳa* **12**, 109 *E*; *tú-ša-as-ni-ḳa* **12**, 109.

ספה sipû "to beseech": II 1 *ú-sa-pi-[ka]* **50**, 20.

supû, suppû "supplication": *su-pi-í* **33**, 4; *su-pí* **1**, 37; **33**, 20; *su-pi-ya* **1**, 43; **21**, 21; **33**, 22, 26; *su-up-pu-ú-ki* **8**, 1.

ספח sapâḫu I 1 "to scatter, to loosen"; II 1 do.: I 1 *su-pu-uḫ* **5**, 7; *sa-ap-ḫi* **6**, 53; *sa-pi-iḫ-ti* **32**, 11; *su-up-pi-iḫ-ma* **11**, 37.

SIR.AD ideogr.: **12**, 6; **30**, 24.

סרק sarâḳu "to pour out": *a-sa-raḳ* **18**, 13; *as-ruk-ka* **1**, 20; *as-ruk-ki* **30**, 3; **57**, 9.

sirḳu "libation": *si-riḳ* **1**, 20; **30**, 3; **57**, 9.

פגר pagru "body, corpse": *pa-gar-šu* **2**, 22; *amîlu pagar-šu* **2**, 22 *B*; *pag-ri-ya* **12**, 53; **53**, 12.

פדה padû "to set free, to spare": *pa-du-ú* **20**, 15, 17; **46**, 18; *pa-da-a* **5**, 9.

פו pû "mouth": *pu-ú* **6**, 33; *pû* **12**, 68; **22**, 55; *pî* **4**, 5; **9**, 8; **10**, 35; **12**, 66, 72; **22**, 8; *pu-šú* **11**, 14; *pû-šu* **21**, 25, 73; *pi-i-ka* **12**, 62; *pi-i-. . . .* **13**, 32; *pi-ka* **12**, 80; **13**, 11; *pî-ka* **21**, 22; **22**, 9; **42**, 17; *pi-ki* **1**, 43; **33**, 25; *pî-ki* **1**, 49; *pi-ya* **9**, 13 *B*, 49; *pî-ya* **6**, 57; **22**, 14 *B*; *pî-yà* **9**, 13; **22**, 14; *pî-ku-nu* **62**, 7.

פחר puḫru "totality, the whole": *pu-ḫur* **27**, 7 *A*, 9; *puḫur* **27**, 7; *puḫri* **19**, 28; *pu-ḫur-šu-nu* **1**, 15.

napḫaru "the whole": *nap-ḫar* **6**, 40; **52**, 5.

פטר paṭâru "to tear, to loosen, to remove": I 1 *ta-paṭ-ṭár* **2**, 23; *ta-pa-. . . .* **2**, 23 *D*; *tapaṭar(ár)* **12**, 99; **40**, 14; *tapaṭar-ma* **30**, 28; *lip-ṭur* **12**, 84; *pu-ṭur* **2**, 38; **11**, 19 *C*, 29, 30, 32, 34, 37; **18**, 14; **27**, 21; . . . . *-ṭur* **49**, 21; *pu-ṭur-ma* **11**, 19; *pu-uṭ-ri* **11**, 31, 33; *pu-uṭ-ra* **11**, 35; — II 1 *tu-paṭ-ṭár* **2**, 23 *B*; *li-paṭ-ṭir* **10**, 3; — IV 1 *lip-pa-ṭir* **5**, 6; **7**, 48; *muppaṭiru(ru)* **53**, 7; — II 2 *lip-ta-aṭ-ṭi-ru* **12**, 83; *lip-ta-ṭi-ru* **30**, 13.

פלח palâḫu "to fear, to reverence"; II 1 "to terrify"; I 3 do.: I 1 *pa-li-ḫi-ka* **17**, 4; *pa-liḫ-ka* **2**, 35; *pa-liḫ-ki* **2**, 7;

. . . . . -liḫ **28**, 10; **46**, 2; pal-ḫa-ku **4**, 42; pal-ḫa-ku-ma **62**, 15; — II 1 mu-pal-li-ḫi **53**, 6; — I 3 up-ta-na-laḫ-an-ni **53**, 8.

puluḫtu "terror": pu-luḫ-tú **2**, 13; **3**, 11.

פלן pulânu "such and such": pulânu **1**, 38bis; **2**, 26bis; **4**, 16; **6**, 27bis, 83 E^bis; **10**, 31; **12**, 45bis, 90; **13**, 5bis; **22**, 11, 51; **27**, 11; **30**, 7; **31**, 4bis; **33**, 21bis; **39**, 16; **54**, 1bis; **57**, 3bis; **58**, 5bis; **62**, 13bis; pulâni **1**, 12bis, 38, 39bis; **2**, 26; **4**, 16, 17bis, 39bis; **6**, 27, 83 E, 84 E^bis, 113 F^bis; **7**, 20bis, 60bis; **10**, 31; **12**, 45, 90; **13**, 5; **22**, 11, 51; **27**, 11; **30**, 7; **31**, 4; **33**, 21; **39**, 16; **53**, 24bis; **54**, 1, 2bis; **57**, 3, 4bis; **58**, 5, 6bis; **59**, 12bis; **60**, 19bis; **61**, 16bis; **62**, 13; pulânîtum(tum) **1**, 38; **2**, 26; **6**, 27, 83 E; **12**, 45; **13**, 5; **31**, 4; **33**, 21; **54**, 1; **57**, 3; **58**, 5; **62**, 13.

פלס IV 1 "to look at, to regard favourably, to pity, to show mercy": nap-lis-an-ni **2**, 37; nap-lis-an-ni-ma **2**, 32; **6**, 62; naplis-an-ni **2**, 37 D; naplis-an-ni-ma **27**, 19; naplisa-ni-ma **2**, 32 D; **21**, 66; nap-li-. . . . . **35**, 5; nap-li-si-in-ni-ma **8**, 4; naplisû-nin-ni **7**, 46; mu-up-pal-sa-ta **2**, 37; **27**, 17; mu-up-pal-sa-at **2**, 37 D; [nap]-lu-us-sa **4**, 26; [nap]-lu-us-ki **8**, 2.

פנה pânu "face": pân **2**, 10; **8**, 20; **11**, 42; **12**, 2, 5, 98; **13**, 6, 13; **18**, 19 A; **21**, 28; **24**, 6; **30**, 20; **31**, 8; **32**, 3; **51**, 10; **52**, 3; pa-nu-uk-ka **14**, 10; **18**, 2; pa-nu-ka **18**, 3; pa-ni-ka **2**, 36; **27**, 17 D; pânu-ka **10**, 33; **22**, 23; pâni-ka **1**, 11bis; **6**, 34; **12**, 66, 70, 75, 76; **27**, 18; **53**, 16; pa-ni-ki **8**, 12; pânu-ki **1**, 36; **33**, 19; pâni-ki **33**, 14; pa-ni-. . . . . **35**, 4; pâni-yà (ideogr. SAG.KI) **53**, 10.

פסס pasâsu "to loosen, to forgive (sin)": I 1 lip-su-su **12**, 76; pu-si-si **50**, 22; — II 1 mu-pa-si-su **62**, 10.

פצא piṣâtu a brightly-coloured(?) robe: ˡᵘᵇᵘˢᵗᵘ piṣâti **40**, 6.

פקד pakâdu I 1 "to take care of, to rule, to entrust to"; II 1 "to visit, to resort to": I 1 ta-pa-ḳid **58**, 3; ip-ḳid **27**, 10; ti-pi-iḳ-da-ni **11**, 26; pa-ḳi-du **46**, 13; paḳ-du **42**, 12; — II 1 lu-pa-ḳid **53**, 20.

פרא parûtu "alabaster": ᵃᵇⁿᵘ parûtu **12**, 11, 12, 69.

פרא pir'u "offspring, posterity": pi-ir-i **12**, 75; pi-ir' **12**, 75 C.

פרד *par(maš?)-da-a* **34**, 3.

פרך parakku "shrine": *parakkâni^pl* **9**, 7.

פרכה IV 1 "to cease, to yield": *ip-par-ki* **6**, 124; **10**, 22.

פרס parâsu "to separate, to decide": I 1 *ta-par-ra-sa* **62**, 6; *pu-ru-us* **12**, 59 *B*; *purus(us)* **12**, 59; **50**, 11; *purusi(si)* **4**, 30; **7**, 49; *paris(is)* **12**, 108 *E*; *[pa]-ra-su* **6**, 74 *D*; *parâsi(si)* **4**, 28; **6**, 74; **7**, 12; **37**, 10; — IV 1 *ipparasu(su)* **53**, 28.

parsu "part": *par-su* **48**, 18.

piristu "decision"; *pi-ris-ti* **1**, 17.

purussu "decision": *purus* **1**, 11; **4**, 28; **6**, 74; **7**, 12; **12**, 58; **13**, 28; **37**, 10; *purussa-ai* **4**, 30; **7**, 49; **12**, 59; **50**, 11.

פרץ parṣu "command": *par-ṣu-[ki]* **4**, 12.

פשח pašâḫu "to be pacified, to be consoled": *pa-ša-ḫa* **8**, 7.

פשק? III 1 *šup-ši-ka* **9**, 14; **22**, 15; *mu-šap-šiḳ(pik?)* **42**, 16.

פשק pušḳu "sorrow, misery": *pušḳi* **9**, 35; **31**, 6.

פשר pašâru "to loosen, to free, to interpret": I 1 *lip-šú-ru* **12**, 78; *lip-šur-an-ni* **12**, 84; *lipšur-an-ni* **12**, 84 *C*; *pu-šur* **2**, 38; **11**, 19, 29, 30; **50**, 22; **61**, 18; *pa-šir* **6**, 5, 6, 7; BUR.RU.DA **22**, 12; — II 1 ....*-ši-ru* **62**, 12; — IV 1 *lip-pa-aš-ru* **1**, 47; *lip-pa-aš-*...., **6**, 13; *[lip]-pa-aš-[ra]* **27**, 21 *D*; ....*-aš-ra* **28**, 2; *lippašra(ra)* **21**, 68; *nap-šur-šú* **11**, 2.

paššuru "dish, vessel": *^išu paššuru* **40**, 8; **61**, 10.

פשש pašâšu "to rub, to anoint": *tapašaš(áš)* **11**, 45; *pušuš* **12**, 102; **51**, 13; *pa-ša-šu* **58**, 8.

napšaštu "ointment; vessel for ointment": *nap-šal-tum* **12**, 76; *^išu napšaštu* **12**, 8, 15, 116.

פתא₃ pitû "to open": I 1 *pi-tu-ú* **60**, 6; *pi-tu-*..... **6**, 98; *pitû-ú* **12**, 29; — II 1 *tu-pat-ti* **6**, 107.

צ

צאר₂ ṣîru "mighty": *ṣi-i-ru* 6, 20; 11, 46; *ṣi-ru* 12, 19 *A*; *ṣîru* 12, 19; 22, 36, 38; 60, 7; *ṣir-tum* 9, 28; *ṣir-ti* 1, 50; 4, 43; 6, 85; 7, 23; 9, 10; 19, 31; 33, 36; 53, 23; *ṣi-rat* 60, 11; *ṣîrâti*^{pl} 60, 14.

צאר₄ ṣîru "field": *ṣîru* 8, 27; 49, 32.

צבת ṣabâtu "to grasp, to seize"; abbuttu ṣabâtu "to intercede for": I 1 *ta-ṣab-bat* 2, 21; . . . .*-bat* 12, 43; *aṣ-bat* 4, 29; 6, 73; 7, 11; 37, 9; 51, 6; *ṣabat-ma* (ideogr. DIB) 12, 16; *ṣab-ti-ma* 1, 42; 33, 24; *ṣa-bi-ta* 9, 36; *ṣa-bi-ta-at* 6, 90; 7, 28; 9, 36 *A*; . . . .*-at* 9, 45; *ṣab-ta-ku-ma* 18, 9; — II 1 *ú-ṣab-bit* 13, 22.

ṣubâtu "garment": *ṣubâta-ka* (ideogr. TUG) 51, 6.

ṣibittu "imprisonment": *ṣi-bit-ti-ka* 10, 29.

צחר "to be small": *aṣ-ṣa-ḫar (az-za-mur?)* 2, 3.

ṣiḫru "small": *ṣi-ḫi-ri-yà* 11, 36.

צלה taṣlîtu, tiṣlîtu "prayer": *taṣ-li-ti* 11, 27; 14, 3; 21, 63; 27, 19 *D*; 33. 4; 50, 21; *taṣ-lit* 2, 33; 9, 39; 59, 5; *ta-ṣil-ti* 1, 18; . . . . .*-li-ti* 49, 8; *tiṣlîtu* (ideogr. A.RA.ZU) 36, 9.

צלל II 1 "to cover over, to darken": *mu-ṣal-lil* 21, 78.

ṣillu "shadow, protection": *ṣil-lu* 6, 120; *ṣil-li-ka* 13, 10.

ṣulûlu "shadow, protection": *ṣu-lul* 9, 6, 33; 22, 4; *ṣu-lul* 9, 6 *B*; *ṣu-lul-ka* 22, 58; *ṣu-lul-ki* 6, 92; 7, 30.

צלם ṣalmu "darkness": ^{ilu}*ṣalmu* 21, 13; 22, 49.

ṣalmu "dark"; ṣalmat ḳakḳadi "the black-headed (race), mankind": *ṣal-mat* 1, 4; 27, 9.

ṣalmu "image": *ṣalmân*^{pl}*-ú-a* 12, 54.

צמר II 1 "to think, to devise, to plan": *ú-ṣa-am-ma-ru* 8, 18; 9, 12; 54, 7.

ṣirgarru a stone: ^{abnu}ṢIR.GAR.RA-*ki* 8, 25.

ḲA a measure: **22**, 31; **62**, 25.

קאת ḳâtu "hand": *ḳa-a-ti* **35**, 14; *ḳa-ti* **61**, 13; *ḳâti* **12**, 79; **13**, 14; *ḳât* **2**, 21; **9**, 36 *A*; **12**, 16; ŠU (*ḳâti*) **1**, 28, 52; **2**, 9, 42; **3**, 9; **4**, 8, 23; **5**, 10; **6**, 17, 35, 70, 95, 131; **7**, 8, 33; **8**, 20, 21; **9**, 27; **10**, 6, 26; **11**, 41; **12**, 95; **13**, 12; **14**, 11; **15**, 17; **16**, 10; **17**, 5; **18**, 18; **19**, 33; **20**, 7; **21**, 24, 72, 75, 91; **22**, 12, 30, 68; **23**, 6; **24**, 4; **25**, 5; **26**, 3; **27**, 25; **28**, 5; **29**, 2; **30**, 19; **31**, 7; **32**, 2; **33**, 38; **34**, 5; **36**, 6, 8; **37**, 6; **38**, 3; **39**, 4; **40**, 2; **42**, 24; **43**, 8; **44**, 2; **45**, 4; **46**, 9; **47**, 6, 9; **48**, 16; **49**, 20; **50**, 28; **51**, 9; *ḳât-su* **12**, 43; *ḳa-tuk-ka* **2**, 18; **3**, 15; **27**, 10; *ḳat-ta-ka* **21**, 59; *ḳâti-yà* **4**, 35; **12**, 48, 88; **14**, 5; **50**, 21; *ḳâtâ*[du] **9**, 36; **12**, 79 *C*; *ḳâtâ*[du]*-šu* **12**, 46; *ḳâtî*[pl] **11**, 26; *ḳâtî*[du]*-yà* **12**, 88 *C*.

קבא₄ "to speak, to command": I 1 *a-ḳab-bu-ú* **8**, 15bis; **9**, 20bis; *taḳ-bu-u* **45**, 3; *liḳbi* **19**, 29; *liḳ-bi* **12**, 93; *lu-uḳ-bi* **27**, 24; *liḳ-bi-ka* **15**, 16; **16**, 9; *liḳ-bu-u* **1**, 50; **2**, 40; **9**, 15; **22**, 16; **33**, 35; *ki-bi* **5**, 5; **9**, 21, 22; **12**, 80; **19**, 22, 28; **21**, 66; *ḳibi* **12**, 104; *ḳibi-ma* **12**, 99; **61**, 4; *ki-bi-i* **2**, 5; **4**, 49; **8**, 3; **9**, 46; *ki-bi-ma* **8**, 14; *ḳa-bu-u* **27**, 14; *ḳa-bu-ú* **11**, 3; *ḳá-bu-ú* **27**, 14 *A*; *ḳá-bu-*. . . . . **27**, 14 *B*; *ḳa-bat* **11**, 14; *ki-bi-ka-ma* **19**, 13; *ḳa-ba-a* **9**, 19; **13**, 8; **22**, 65; *ḳa-ba-ai* **2**, 32; **4**, 27; **12**, 59; **27**, 19; — I 2 *iḳ-ṭa-ba-an-ni-ma* **11**, 25; *tak-ta-bu-u* **12**, 115; . . . .*-ú* **12**, 115 *E*.

ḳibîtu "word, command": *ki-bit* **1**, 43; **12**, 62, 87, 114; **22**, 10, 66; **33**, 25; **35**, 15; **53**, 27; *ki-bit-su* **19**, 8; **60**, 7; *ki-bit-sa* **4**, 26; *ki-bi-sa* **33**, 10; *ki-bi-ti-ka* **9**, 10; **53**, 23; *ki-bit-ka* **6**, 21; **19**, 31; **50**, 9; **60**, 10, 11; *ḳibît-ka* **9**, 10 *B*; **50**, 9 *A*, 26; **54**, 5; *ki-bit-ti-*. . . . . **7**, 44; *ki-bi-ti-ki* **4**, 43; **6**, 85; **7**, 23; *ki-bit-ki* **1**, 50; **8**, 2; **33**, 36; *ki-bit-su-un* **33**, 17; *ki-bit-[ku-nu]* **7**, 56.

קבל I 2 "to oppose"; Part. "warrior": *muḳ-ṭab-lu* **21**, 42; *muḳ-ṭab-lum* **46**, 20.

ḳablu "battle; middle. waist": *ḳa-bal* **12**, 23; *ḳa-bal-šu* **2**, 14; **3**, 12; *ḳabli-šu* **53**, 17.

קבר ḳabru "grave": *ḳab-ri* **30**, 11.

קדד ḳadâdu "to bow down"; II 2 "to make bow down, to bend": *uk-ta-ad-di-da-an-ni* **11**, 6; *uḳ-ṭa-ad-di-da-ni* **11**, 6 *A*.

קדקד ḳakḳadu "head": *ḳakḳadu* (ideogr. SAG.DU) **1**, 4; **27**, 9; *ḳakḳad* (ideogr. SAG) **12**, 96; *ḳakḳad-su* (ideogr. SAG.DU) **12**, 121; *ḳakḳadu-ki* (ideogr. SAG) **8**, 8.

קו ḳû "barley(?)": *ki-i* **12**, 30.

קו ḳû "cord": ? *ki-i* **22**, 49; **62**, 11.

קול ḳûlu "voice": *ku-la* **12**, 36.

קיש "to bestow": *ḳu-ši-ma* **39**, 14; *ḳa-i-šu* **22**, 5; *ḳa-i-šat* **4**, 25; **7**, 37; *[ka?]-i-sat* **9**, 39.

$קלא_4$ II 1 "to take, to seize": ? *mu-ḳil-lu* **7**, 40.

קלל ḳillatu "sin, disgrace": *ḳil-la-tú* **12**, 78; *ḳil-lat* **12**, 78 *C*; *ḳil-la-ti* **5**, 7; **27**, 21*D*; **50**, 18; *ḳil-la-ti-ma* **2**, 39; *ḳil-la-a-ti* **9**, 54.

$קמא_3$ ḳîmu "grain": *ḳîmu* **22**, 32; **26**, 7; *ḳîmi* **22**, 31; **33**, 40.

קנה ḳanû "reed": ? *ḳa-an-ni-ka* **18**, 10.

קצר ḳiṣru "might, strength": *ki-ṣir* **12**, 83.

קרב "to approach": I 1 *i-ḳăr-ri-ba* **21**, 22; *iḳ-ru-bu-ni* **7**, 57;— II 1 *ú-ḳar-ri-bu-u-ni* **12**, 77 *C*; *ú-ḳar-ri-bu-ni* **12**, 77.

ḳirbu "midst": *ki-rib* **12**, 31, 83; **21**, 10, 73; **32**, 7, 15; **62**, 9; *ki-*. . . . . **39**, 13.

ḳár-bu-ni-ya **19**, 26.

קרד ? *aḳ-ri-dak-ka* **13**, 27.

קרד ḳardu, f. ḳaridtu "brave, valiant": *ḳar-du* **14**, 15; *ḳar-da* **21**, 46; *ḳa-rid-tú* **4**, 10, 11; *ḳá-rid-tú* **1**, 29; *ḳá-rid-tum* **5**, 11; *ḳá-rid-ti* **32**, 6.

ḳarradu do.: *ḳar-ra-du* **11**, 1*A*; *ḳăr-ra-du* **11**, 40; *ḳarradu* **11**, 1, 30, 34; **46**, 21.

ḳurâdu do.: *ḳu-ra-du* **2**, 25; **5**, 14; **21**, 77; *ḳu-ra-di* **1**, 32.

ḳitrudu do.: *ḳit-ru-du* **46**, 16.

ḳurdu "valour, might": *ḳur-di-ka* **12**, 92; **21**, 85; *ḳu-ru-ud-ká* **5**, 9.

קרקר kaḳḳaru "ground": *ḳak-ḳa-ri* **32**, 10.

ר

ראם râmânu ". . . . . self": *ra-ma-ni-ša* **11**, 9; *ra-ma-ni-šá-ma* **11**, 9 *A*; *ra-ma-ni-ya* **11**, 24.

ראם₃ râmu "to love, to pity": *i-ram-mu* **9**, 34; *li-ri-man-ni* **21**, 69; *ri-man-ni-ma* **21**, 63; . . . . *.-man(min?)-ni-ma* **2**, 5; *ri-min-ni-ma* **8**, 3; *ra-im* **9**, 4.

rîmu "mercy": *ri-i-mu* **12**, 70; *ri-i-ma* **12**, 61 *BC*; **21**, 89; **22**, 64; *rîmu* **21**, 69; **30**, 14.

rîmnu, rîmînu "merciful": *ri-mi-nu-u* **11**, 7 *A*; *ri-mi-nu-ú* **11**, 2, 7; **28**, 7; *ri-mi-nu-ú-um* **11**, 2 *A*; *ri-mi-nu-ú* **21**, 61; *ri-mi-ni-ya* **6**, 91; **7**, 29; *ri-mi-na-ta* **12**, 40; **27**, 18 *A*; *ri-mi-ni-ta* **27**, 18; *ri-mi-ni-tum* **6**, 71 *E*, 77; **7**, 9, 15; **37**, 7, 13; **57**, 2; *ri-mi-ni-tum* **6**, 71, 77*D*; *rim-ni-tum* **4**, 25; *rim-ni-tum* **7**, 35, 59.

narâmu, f. narâmtu "darling": *na-ram* **6**, 19; **22**, 5; **27**, 4; **60**, 6; *na-ram-[ta?]* **6**, 126; **10**, 23.

ראק₃ rûḳu "distant": *ruḳ-ḳa(?)* **13**, 9; *ru-ḳu-tu* **1**, 36; **33**, 19; *rûḳûti*^{pl} **62**, 9.

rîḳûtu "distance": *riḳ-ḳu-ti* **59**, 20.

ראש rîšu "head": *ri-ši-ka* **49**, 19; *riši-yà* **50**, 24; *ri-ša-a* **5**, 1; **6**, 29; *ri-ša-a-ka* **2**, 16; **3**, 14; **21**, 60.

rîštû "former, original, preeminent": *riš-tu-ú* **46**, 14; *riš-ti-i* **1**, 42; **33**, 23; *riš-ti-i* **4**, 48.

ראש₄ rîšu I 1 "to shout for joy, to hail"; II 1 "to cause to rejoice": I 1 *li-riš-ka* **9**, 24; . . . . *.-riš-ka* **20**, 5; *li-riš-[ki]* **8**, 18; ? *riš-ša* **12**, 36; — II 1 *mu-riš* **9**, 3; **58**, 18.

rišati pl. "shouts of joy": *ri-ša-a-ti* **6**, 121; **10**, 20; **17**, 3.

ri-iš-ta-a (fr. rîštû?, *cf. supra*) **1**, 20.

רבה "to be great"; III 1 "to make great": *li-šar-bu-u* **3**, 7; . . . . *.-bi* **5**, 3.

rabû "great": *ra-bu-u* **46**, 6; *ra-bu-ú* **46**, 6 *A*; *rabû-ú* **9**, 9, 21; **11**, 7; *rabû* **9**, 21 *B*; **26**, 9; **42**, 26; *rabî-i* **22**,

22; *rabî* **22**, 9, 22 *B*; *ra-ba-ta* **27**, 6; *ra-bít* **2**, 44; **9**, 29; *rabîtu(tu)* **19**, 24, 34; *rabîtum(tum)* **11**, 31, 33; **27**, 3; **49**, 15; *rabîta(ta)* **6**, 68; *rabîti(ti)* **13**, 6; **22**, 10, 66; **27**, 3 *D*; **46**, 3, 8; **59**, 11; **62**, 22; *rabûti*^{pl} **1**, 11, 14, 17; **2**, 15; **3**, 6, 13: **6**, 130; **7**, 6; **8**, 19, 23; **9**, 26: **10**, 5; **12**, 25, 79, 88, 114; **19**, 5; **33**, 8; **50**, 5, 10, 29; **61**, 14; **62**, 1; *rabâti*^{pl} **33**, 11.

rubû "prince": *rubû* **9**, 2; **10**, 3; **19**, 26; **22**, 1; *rubî* **22**, 9, 22.

rubâtu "princess": *ru-ba-tú* **19**, 34.

surbû "powerful, mighty": *šur-bu-u* **2**, 12; **48**, 17; *šur-bu-ú* **3**, 10; **6**, 1, 2, 18, 97; **10**, 7; **20**, 8, 10; **21**, 34, 36; *šur-bat* **60**, 9; *šur-ba-ta-ma* **18**, 6; *šur-ba-ti* **4**, 12; *šur-bu-tú* **4**, 24, 47; **6**, 85 *D*; *šur-bu-tum* **6**, 71, 77, 85, 90; **7**, 9, 23, 28; **37**, 7; *šur-*. . . . . **38**, 5.

narbû, nirbû "greatness, might": *nir-bi* **6**, 16; **21**, 7; *nar-bi-ka* **2**, 41; **5**, 8; **6**, 69; **7**, 2; **12**, 93; **18**, 17; **21**, 23, 71; **23**, 5; **50**, 27; *nir-bi-ka* **27**, 24; *nar-bi-ki* **2**, 8; **6**, 94; **7**, 32; *nir-bi-ki* **30**, 15, 17.

רבץ râbiṣu a demon: *râbiṣu* (ideogr. MAŠKIM) **6**, 124; **10**, 22.

RIG a plant: *šam*RIG **19**, 17.

רדה "to tread, to advance": I 1 *ir-di* **8**, 5; — III 1 *šur-dim-ma* **30**, 14.

ridûtu "copulation; dominion": *ri-du-su* **53**, 9; *ridûti(ti)* **59**, 6.

רום II 1 "to raise"; IV 2 do.: *at-ta-ra-[am]* **61**, 13.

רוץ "to help, to deliver": I 1 *ru-ṣa-nim-ma* **53**, 4.

רחה ruḫû "enchantment, sorcery": *ru-ḫu-u* **33**, 31; *ru-ḫi-í* **12**, 81, 106.

רכס rakâsu "to bind, to knot": *ar-kus-ka* **2**, 27.

raksu "bound": *rak-su-ma* **50**, 19; **53**, 7.

riksu "band, cord": *rik-sa* **2**, 27; *rik-si* **33**, 44; *riksu* (ideogr. KIŠDA) **12**, 99; **30**, 28; **40**, 14.

רמה "to be loose"; II 1 "to loosen": *ru-um-[mi]* **2**, 39.

רמך rimku "libation": *rim-ki* **1**, 54; **61**, 12.

רסה rusû "magic, sorcery": *ru-[su-u]* **33**, 31; *ru-si-í* **12**, 82.

רפש rapâšu "to be broad"; II 1 "to broaden, to enlarge": *ru-up-piš* **5**, 4.

rapšu "broad, wide-spreading, distant": *rap-šu* **7**, 30; **12**, 20 *A*; *rap-šú* **6**, 92; *rapašta(. . . . .)* **1**, 7; *rapašti(ti)* **62**, 8; *rapaštim(tim)* **60**, 5; *rap-ša-a-ti* **9**, 6; *rapšâti(ti)* **61**, 6; *rapšâti*^{pl} **10**, 11; **12**, 39; **18**, 17; **21**, 23, 90; **22**, 42, 67; **30**, 18.

רשב rašbu "mighty, powerful": *ra-aš-bu* **60**, 13.

rašûbu do.: *ra-šub-bu* **14**, 16; **21**, 93; **49**, 25.

rušûbu do.: *ru-šú-bu(?)* **1**, 1.

רשה "to possess; to grant": *a-ra-ši* **11**, 12 *A*; *a-ra-aš-ši* **11**, 12; . . . . .*-raš-ši-ma* **21**, 75: *ar-ši* **12**, 69; *ár-ši* **12**, 69 *C*; **15**, 4, 5; *li-ir-šú-ni* **12**, 61 *B*; **50**, 25; *liršû-ni* (ideogr. TUK) **12**, 61; — III 1 *šur-ši* **13**, 28.

ש

ש ša rel. pron., "who, which"; sign of the genitive: *ša* **1**, 9, 12, 13, 16, 19, 25, 38, 39, 40, 42, 45bis, 46, 50, 51; **2**, 14, 22, 23, 24, 26; **3**, 6, 12; **4**, 17, 19, 37, 38, 39, 41, 43, 44, 46, 48; **6**, 27, 40, 44, 49, 52, 53, 54, 55, 66, 82, 83 *E*, 85, 86, 88, 89bis, 113 *F*^{bis}, 118, 122, 129; **7**, 5, 19, 20, 22, 23, 24, 26, 27bis, 51bis, 54, 56, 60, 61; **8**, 12bis, 13bis, 19, 22, 23, 26; **9**, 25, 34 *A*; **10**, 19, 21, 35; **11**, 1, 17, 26, 28, 36; **12**, 11bis, 12ter, 14, 19 *A*, 20, 31, 43, 45, 56, 60, 63, 64, 66, 67, 68, 76, 81, 85, 86, 97 *D*, 101, 103, 105, 116; **13**, 5, 7, 11; **17**, 8; **18**, 8; **19**, 8, 10, 12, 31, 32; **21**, 2, 5, 6, 7, 8, 52, 62, 74; **22**, 12, 40; **23**, 9; **27**, 11 *A*^{bis}; **30**, 7, 10, 12bis, 13; **31**, 4; **33**, 10, 21, 24, 28, 29, 30, 36; **35**, 1; **39**, 16; **40**, 3, 9; **42**, 9, 12, 18; **46**, 15; **48**, 17; **50**, 14, 16, 18, 19, 23; **52**, 5; **53**, 14, 20, 21, 23, 24, 26; **55**, 3; **56**, 1, 9, 11; **57**, 3, 4, 6; **58**, 5, 6, 7; **59**, 2, 11, 12, 14; **60**, 7, 13, 15, 19, 21; **61**, 5, 16, 16 *A*; **62**, 13, 17, 18, 19; *šá* **1**, 23, 47; **2**, 13; **3**, 11; **6**, 48; **7**, 50, 52, 55, 59; **9**, 34; **10**, 30, 32; **12**, 12 *A*, 19, 21, 97; **13**, 19, 20; **22**, 50; **31**, 2, 3; **33**, 8; **35**, 14; **50**, 13: **53**, 6; **54**, 1, 2, 4; **55**, 5; **56**, 8; **57**, 2.

ש šû, šunu; šâšu, šâšunu pers. pron., "he, they; him, them": *šú-ú* **53**, 15; *šú-nu* **12**, 41; *ša-a-šu* **13**, 20; *ša-šu-nu* **12**, 14.

šu'atu; šû, šunuti dem. pron., "that, those": *šú-a-tu* **12**, 8, 11*A*; *šú-a-ti* 7, 62; **57**, 7; *šu'atu* (BI) **30**, 28; *šu'ati* (BI) **40**, 15; *šú-ú* **60**, 2; BI (= *šû*) **60**, 2; *šú-nu-ti* **12**, 104.

šut connective particle: *šú-ut* **2**, 30, 31; **62**, 17ter.

ŠA a measure: **11**, 43; **12**, 3; **21**, 29; **25**, 8; **30**, 22; **40**, 8; **62**, 26.

שאח₄ ši'û I 1 "to look, to look for, to seek"; I 2 "to seek, look for, concern oneself with"; I 3 do.: I 1 *ta-ši-'* **27**, 8; *ti-ši-'* **27**, 8*C*; *i-ši-'* **2**, 4; *a-ši-'-ka* **1**, 21; **21**, 11; *iš-i-ka* **6**, 28; *a-ši-'-ki* **4**, 29; *iš-i-ki* **6**, 73; **7**, 11; **37**, 9; — I 2 *iš-ti-'-ú* **8**, 10; *? áš-ti-i* (*? ina ti-i-. . . .*) **6**, 9; *iš-ti-'-šú-ma* **53**, 16; *iš-ti-'-ú-ka* **27**, 16; *[iš-ti]-'-i-ka* **27**, 16 *D*; *lu-uš-ti-'-ma* **11**, 13; . . . .*-i(?)-ma* **11**, 13 *A*; — I 3 *iš-ti-ni-'* **6**, 48.

šâtu "moment, time": *šat* **1**, 26; **22**, 63.

שאל tašiltu "decision(?)": *ta-ši-la-a-ti* **2**, 16; **3**, 14.

שאר šîru "flesh": *šîru* **6**, 110; *šîri* **8**, 16; *šîri[pl]-ya* **1**, 45; **33**, 29; *šîri[pl]-yà* **53**, 11; *šîri[pl]-šu-nu* **18**, 7 *A*.

שאר šîrtu "iniquity": *šír-ti* **1**, 26; *šĭr-ti* **2**, 38; **11**, 19; *šĭr-tim* **2**, 38 *DE*.

שאר₄ šâru "wind, breeze": *šâru-ka* **18**, 15.

שאח₈ "to flee, to escape": *i-ši-it* **11**, 10.

שבא₄ "to be satisfied": *lu-uš-bi* **9**, 23; **22**, 23.

שבס šabâsu "to be angry": *šab-su* **4**, 37, 45; **6**, 87; **7**, 25; *šab-sa* **21**, 87; *šab-su-ma* **6**, 82, 88; **7**, 19, 26.

שבס? *šab-su* **12**, 55.

ŠUB.ŠUB: ŠUB.ŠUB*(di)* **30**, 24; **40**, 12; **62**, 29.

שבת *ta-ša-bit(?)* **26**, 5.

šagganakku a governor or high official: *šagganakku* **19**, 14.

שגר šigaru "bolt": *išu šigaru* **53**, 22.

שגש *šá-giš(?)* **21**, 43.

ŠID a tree: *išu*ŠID **12**, 5; **30**, 25.

שדה šadû "mountain": *ša-du-ú* **9**, 32; *šadû-ú* **33**, 7; *šá-di-i* **12**, 28; *šadi[pl]* **21**, 81; **32**, 9; *šadâni[pl](ni)* **59**, 3.

שדח šadâḫu "to move along, to advance": *iš-di-ḫu* **8**, 5.

VOCABULARY

שׁוּד šîdu "guardian deity": ^{ilu}šîdu (AN.ALAD) 8, 12; 12, 110; 13, 21; 22, 19; 50, 24; ^{ilu}šîdu (AN.DAN) 6, 32; 19, 29; 22, 8, 64.

שׁוֹם šûmu "garlic": šûmu 33, 45.

שׁוּף šîpu "foot": šîpu(?)-. . . . . 4, 3; šîpâ^{du} 17, 6; šipî^{du}-ya 12, 55; 22, 60.

שׁטר šaṭâru "to write, to inscribe": ta-ša-ṭar 6, 110; šú-ṭúr 27, 7.

שׁי ší'u "corn, grain": ší-am 12, 4, 30.

שׁיב šîbu "old man": ši-bi 11, 6; ši-bi-im 11, 6 A.

שׁיח? I 1 i-šiḫ-šu 53, 18.

שׁים šâmu "to settle, to establish": I 1 ta-šim-ma 62, 5; . . . . .-šim-mi 21, 83; ši-im 6, 113; 19, 21; ši-i-mi 10, 16; — II 1 mu-šim 6, 19; 19, 9; 58, 1.

šîmtu "destiny": šim-ti 6, 113; 10, 16; 19, 21; ši-mat 6, 112; 10, 15; 22, 3; ši-mat-ka 15, 13; ši-ma-a-ti 19, 34; šîmâti^{pl} 6, 112 F; 15, 11; 19, 6, 9; 21, 60; 58, 1; 62, 2.

? tašimtu: ta-šim-ti 41, 3.

שׁכך šakâku: tašakak?(ak) ideogr. UD.DU 12, 13.

שׁכל maštakal a plant: ^{šam}maštakal 11, 44; 12, 9.

שׁכן šakânu "to set, to place, to establish; to lie, to be placed": I 1 išakna(na) 1, 12, 39; 4, 17, 39; 6, 84 E, 113 F; 7, 20, 60; 19, 10; 27, 11 A; 50, 14; 53, 24; 54, 2; 55, 3; 56, 9; 57, 4; 58, 6; 59, 12; 60, 19; 61, 16; ta-ša-kan 22, 49; ta-šak-kan 6, 108; tašakan(an) 2, 10; 8, 20; 11, 42, 43, 45; 12, 3, 4, 7, 11, 14, 15, 102, 116; 13, 14; 14, 12; 15, 24; 18, 19 A; 21, 29; 30, 22, 26; 32, 3; 40, 8; 51, 11, 15; 62, 26, 27, 28; tašakan-ma 22, 34; [ta-ša?]-ka-ni 33, 16; li-šak-na 12, 70; liš-ku-nu-ni 12, 61 B; šu-kun 22, 60; šú-kun-ma 19, 24; šuk-na 6, 116; 10, 18; 12, 110 E; 21, 68; 22, 65; šukun(un) 1, 22; šukna(na) 12, 110; šuk-. . . . . 8, 7; ša-ki-nu 62, 10; šâkin(in) 1, 11; šak-. . . . . 22, 47; šaknu(nu) 12, 67, 116; ša-ki-na-at 33, 2; šá-ki-in 1, 3; ša-kin 21, 38; ša-kin 20, 12; 46, 17; šak-na-át 11, 28; šak-na-ta 42, 8; — II 1 tu-šak-na 1, 36; 33, 19; — III 1 šú-uš-kin 22, 14; šú-uš-kin 9, 13; mu-ša-aš-ki-nu 46, 17; — IV 1 iš-šak-na 13, 18; iš-šak-nam-[ma] 13, 19; iš-šak-nu-nim-ma 27, 12; liš-ša-kin 1,

49; 4, 5; 33, 34; — IV 3 *it-ta-na-aš-ka-nam-ma* 6, 83 *DE*; 7, 19.

šiknu "creature": *ši-kin* 33, 8; 37, 5; *šik-nat* 10, 13; 61, 3.

שכר šikaru "drink": *ši-kar* 1, 20; 2, 29.

šalbabu "mighty, courageous(?)" fr. √לבב?: *šal-ba-bu* 9, 3, 31; 12, 17; 46, 20; 53, 3.

šuluḫḫu: *šú-luḫ-ḫi* 58, 15; *šú-luḫ-ḫu-šu* 48, 18.

שלל šallatu: ? *šal-la-tú* 12. 119.

שלם šalâmu I 1 "to be intact, perfect, complete, to be prosperous"; II 1 "to preserve intact, to cause to prosper": I 1 *lu-uš-lim-ma* 8, 17; 9, 10; 12, 66, 90; 22, 13; 30, 15; 54, 6; *lu-*. . . . . 45, 2; . . . .*-uš-lim* 12, 66 *C*; — II 1 *šul-li-ma-am-ma* 12, 112; *mu-šal-lim* 9, 5; *šul-lu-mu* 4, 32; 6, 75; 7, 13; 37, 11.

šalmu "intact, safe and sound": *šal-mu* 6, 10; 11, 26.

šulmu "peace, prosperity": *šú-ul-ma* 58, 4; *šul-mu* 4, 26; 6, 124; 8, 11; . . . . *-ma* 45, 7; *šul-mi* 12, 113; *šulmu(mu)* 10, 22; 12, 71; *šulma(ma)* 21, 67, 68; *šulmi(mi)* 12, 105.

šalummatu "light": *ša-lum-ma-ta* 21, 58; *ša-lum-ma-ti* 46, 15.

šilan "setting"; a point in heaven: *ši-la-an* 9, 41.

שלח (שלט?) II 1 *mu-šal-li-tu* 62, 11.

שם šumu "name": *šú-mu* 11, 32; *šú-ma* 11, 8; *šumu* 12, 75 *C*; 30, 14; *šumi* 40, 15; *šum-šu* 12, 120; *šumu-ka* 9, 8; *šumi-ka* 8, 1; *šumu-ki* 4, 33; *šú-mi-ya* 19, 22; *šú-mì(pi?)-í* 1, 32; 5, 14; *šú-mi* 5, 3; 12, 75; 13, 26; *šú-mi-šú-nu* 19, 14.

שמא simû "to hear": I 1 *liš-mi* 1, 43; 33, 25; *lu-uš-mi(?)* 1, 26; *ši-mi* 2, 32; 12, 59 *B*; 50, 21; *ši-mí* 12, 59; 13, 27; 21, 63; 27, 19; *ši-ma-a* 2, 32 *E*; *ši-mi-i* 1, 41; 6, 72 *E*; 7, 10; 33, 22; 37, 8; *ši-mi-i* 4, 27; *ši-mi-í* 6, 72; *ši-mu-ú* 7, 45; *ši-mu-u(?)* 10, 27; *ši-mu-ú* 21, 82; . . . .*-ú* 59, 5; *ši-mat* 7, 36; 21, 12; 33, 4; *ši-ma-a-at* 21, 75; *ši-mat* 19, 28; *ši-ma-a* 9, 19; 22, 65; — III 1 *tu-ša-aš-mi-ı* 33, 17; — IV 1 *liš-ši-mi* 8, 14; — III 2 *[muš]-ti(?)-iš-ma-at* 33, 2.

šimû "obedient, friendly": *ši-mu-ú* 11, 3; 27, 14.

tašmû "prosperity, success": *taš-mu-ú* 4, 26; 8, 2, 9; *taš-ma-a* 33, 15, 16; 61, 19; *taš-mi-i* 4, 6.

שמאל šumîlu "left": *šú-mi-lu-uk-ki* 8, 13; *šú-mi-li-ya* 9, 17 *B*; *šumîli-yà* 9, 17; 22, 18.

שמה šamû "heaven": *šamû-ú* 3, 5; 6, 128; 8, 18; 10, 4, 24; 12, 119(?); 61, 8; *šamî* 4, 15; 16, 12; *šamî-i* 1, 5, 9, 30, 33; 3, 8; 4, 24; 5, 12, 15; 6, 3, 4, 21, 71, 100, 107; 7, 5, 9; 10, 9; 12, 64, 81, 83; 13, 20; 19, 7; 21, 6, 10, 15, 73, 81; 22, 39; 27, 5, 8; 31, 7; 32, 7, 15; 37, 7; 39, 8; 46, 11; 48, 17; 49, 29; 50, 3, 8; 60, 5; 61, 5; 62, 3, 9; *šamî*^{pl} (ideogr. IDIN, *cf.* 21, 81) 12, 28; 32, 9; *ša-ma-mi* 6, 78 *DE*; 7, 16; 18, 4; 19, 18; *ša-ma-mi* 8, 24; *šá-ma-mi* 6, 78.

שמם I 1 *i-šam-ma-mu* 53, 11.

שמם šammu "plant": *šammu* 12, 67, 101, 104, 115; *šammu-ka* 12, 97; *šammî*^{pl} 12, 76.

שמן šamnu "oil": *šamnu* (ideogr. NI) 30, 28; *šamnu* (ideogr. NI.IṢ) 11, 45; 12, 8bis, 11; *šamni* (ideogr. NI) 11, 43; 12, 3, 15, 102, 116; 21, 29; 25, 8; 30, 22; 62, 26; *šamni* (ideogr. NI.IṢ) 11, 44; 30, 26; 51, 13.

ŠI.MAN a plant: ^{šam}ŠI.MAN 12, 10.

שמר šamâru II 2 "to revere, to worship": I 2 *? šit-mu-ru* 60, 15; — II 2 *lu-uš-tam-mar* 8, 17; 9, 11; 12, 91, 92; 54, 6; *lul-tam-ma-ra* 21, 90.

שמר šamru "violent": *šam-ru* 21, 40, 41.

ŠA.NA "vessel for incense; censer": 2, 9; 8, 20; 11, 42; 12, 4, 86, 118; 13, 14; 16, 11; 18, 19; 21, 74, 92; 22, 69; 28, 6; 32, 3; 33, 39; 34, 6; 38, 4; 39, 5; 41, 2; 46, 10; 47, 7; 51, 11; 52, 4; 62, 27.

שנה šanîtu ". . . . . times": *šanîtu* 6, 96; 8, 21; 12, 16, 99, 103, 117; 15, 23; 18, 19 *A*; 25, 7; 30, 27; 32, 4; 40, 13; 52, 4; 61, 4; 62, 30.

שנן šanânu "to oppose, to rival": I 1 *ša-na-an* 1, 19; — IV 1 *iš-ša-na-an* 60, 10.

שסה šasû "to speak, to call, to invoke, to command": I 1 *ta-ša-as-si* 6, 109; *al-si-ka* 6, 61; *al-*. . . . . 6, 34; *al-si-ki* 4, 27; 6, 72; 7, 10, 62; 37, 8; 57, 7; *ši-si-ma* 50,

10; *šá-su-ú* 11, 4; — III 1 *ú-št-is-sa* 13, 21; *mu-ša-as-*..... 21, 3.

שׂפת šaptu "lip": *šap-ti-ya* 13, 22.

שׁפך šapâku "to pour out": *tašapak(ak)* 12, 3; 15, 20; 21, 29; 30, 21; 33, 40; 62, 26; *tašapak* 12, 4; *ša-pi-kăt* 9, 37.

שׁפל šaplu "that which is beneath; beneath, under": *ša-ap-la* 6, 46; *šap-* .... 57, 13, 14; *šaplu* 21, 55; *šapli-ka* 1, 15; *šaplâti*[pl] 59, 4.

שׁפר šapâru "to send": *iš-pur-an-ni* 12, 98; *lu-uš-pur-ki* 4, 36; 6, 81; 7, 18.

šipru "letter, message": *ši-pír-* .... 16, 3.

שׁקה šakû "to be high": *il* (glossed *iš*)-*ku-u* 12, 54; *ša-ká-ta* 18, 4; — III 1 *tu-ša-aš-ka* 2, 21.

šakû "high, exalted": [*šá*]-*ku-ú* 27, 5 CD; *šá-ku* 27, 5; *ša-ka-a* 2, 16; 3, 14; 21, 60; *ša-ká-a* 13, 3; *ša-ku-tum* 6, 77 DE; 7, 15; 37, 13.

שׂרא mišrû "property, wealth": *miš-ra-a* 8, 13.

שׂרא mišrîtu: *miš-ri-tu-ú-a* 10, 4.

שׂרח šarḫu "powerful": *šar-ḫu* 12, 18.

šitraḫu do.: *ši-tar-ḫu* 11, 46.

שׂרח šarâḫu I 1 "to be bright(?)": *šar-ḫat* 1, 6; — II 1 "to make bright(?)": *šur-ru-ḫat* 6, 22.

šarḫu "bright(?)": *šar-ḫa* 1, 18; *šar-ḫu-tum* 8, 22.

שׂרט? *šar(?)-ṭa-a-ki* 8, 6.

šurmînu "cypress": [isu]*šurmînu* 12, 15, 102; 51, 13; [isu]*šurmîni* 30, 26.

שׂרק šarâku "to offer, to present": *ta-šár-rak* 21, 74; 31, 10; *áš-ruk-ka* 2, 27, 28; *šur-ka* 19, 23; *šur-kam-ma* 9, 19 B; *šur-kám-ma* 9, 19; *šur-ki* 8, 17.

שׂרר šarûru "splendour": *ša-ru-ru* 1, 30; *ša-ru-ur* 5, 12; *ša-ru-ra-ki* 8, 9.

šarru "king": *šar-[ru?]* 60, 2; *šarru* 1, 50 C; 12, 20; 19, 14, 15, 25; 33, 35; 41, 3; 46, 18; 52, 5; *šarru* (ideogr. MAN) 1, 50; *šarri* 61, 13; *šar* 6, 38, 91; 7, 29; 22, 41; 62, 31; *šar* (ideogr. MAN) 12, 87; LUGAL 60, 2; *šarrâni* 62, 31.

šarratu "queen": *šar-ra-tum* **12**, 89; **27**, 3; **49**, 15; *šar-ra-ti* **24**, 3; **27**, 3 *C*; *šar-rat* **4**, 9, 11; **9**, 31, 32; **12**, 89 *C*; **33**, 9, 47.

ŠI.ŠI a plant: ^{šam}ŠI.ŠI **12**, 10.

שתה šatû "to drink": *šatî-šu* (ideogr. NAK) **53**, 17.

שתח šittu "misery": *ši-it-ti* **6**, 8; *šit-tú* **12**, 78; *šit-ta* **12**, 78 *C*.

šittutu(?): *šit-tu-tú* **11**, 16; *šit-tu-tú-um* **11**, 16 *C*.

ת

TU a plant: ^{šam}TU **19**, 17.

תא₂ם tâmtu "ocean": *tâmti* **61**, 6; *ta-ma-a-ti* **18**, 3; **21**, 81; *ta-ma-ti* **61**, 6; *tâmâti*^{pl} **12**, 28; **22**, 42; **32**, 9.

תאר tîrtu "soul, spirit": ^{šîru}*tîrtu-ú-a* (ŠIR.UR.UŠ) **12**, 58; ^{šîru}*tîrti*^{pl}*-šu-nu* (ŠIR.UR) **18**, 7.

תב₄א tibû "to come": III 1 *ú-šat-bi* **13**, 26.

תבל "to carry off, to take away": *lit-ba-lu* **59**, 10.

תור târu I 1 "to turn, to return"; II 1 "to bring back, to restore": I 1 *itûr* **59**, 21; *li-tu-ra* **6**, 87; **7**, 25; **11**, 39; *litûra(ra)* **4**, 45; -- II 1 *ti-i-ru-u* **9**, 15; **22**, 16; *ti-i-ru* **22**, 16 *B*; *ti-ru-u* **9**, 15 *B*; *tutîra(ra)* **2**, 22.

tairu "pitiful, compassionate": *ta-ai-ra-ta* **6**, 63; **27**, 16; *ta-ai-rat* **27**, 16 *A*.

tairatu "compassion": *ta-ai-ra-tu-ka* **46**, 6; *ta-ai-*. . . . . **22**, 58; *ta-ai-ra-tu-ki* **6**, 92; **7**, 30.

? *ti-i-ri* **18**, 9.

תחז taḫâzu "battle": . . . . .*-ḫa-zi* **2**, 49.

תכל tukultu "help, aid": *tukulti(ti)* **2**, 46; **9**, 4.

תלה II 1 ? *mu-tál-lum* **58**, 16.

תלם III 1 "to entrust, to bestow": *li-ša-at-li-ma* **12**, 85 *C*; *li-šat-lim-ma* **12**, 85; *šú-ut-li-ma-am-ma* **6**, 119; **10**, 19; **22**, 20; **60**, 22; . . . .*-ma-am-ma* **6**, 68.

תמה tamû "to speak, to declare": I 1 *li-ta-mi-ka* **6**, 125; **10**, 22; *lu-ta-mi* **53**, 29bis, 30; *lu-ta-*. . . . . **1**, 26; *la-ta-am*

18, 17; *li-ta-mu-u* 12, 112; *li-tam-mu-ú* 12, 112 *E*; — IV 2 ? *a-ta-ta-ma* (= **attatmu*?) 21, 19, 20.

tamîtu "word, oracle": *ta-mit* 1, 16; *ta-mit-ti-ka* 1, 17.

תמח tamâḫu "to hold, to grasp": *tam-ḫat* 2, 18; 3, 15.

tappû "helper": *tap-pi-í* 6, 117; 10, 18.

tapputu "help": *tap-pu-tí* 13, 4.

tarrinnu a sacrificial feast: *tar-rin-nu* 2, 28; *tar-rin-na* 2, 28 *CD*.

TI.ŠAR ideogr. 12, 102; 30, 26.

APPENDIXES.

I.— LIST OF PROPER NAMES.

Ai *(ilu)*:  6, 126; 10, 23.

AZAG *(ilu)*:  12, 86.

AZAG.IZU *(ilu)*:  12, 86 *C*.

Anu *(ilu)*:  1, 9; 6, 2, 4, 6, 24; 7, 7; 8, 24; 10, 25; 11, 35; 43, 6; 46, 14; 50, 6; 60, 11; 61, 5, 7; 62, 17.

AN.ḪUL.[(LA.)MIŠ]:  12, 67, 105;  12, 11, 13, 14, 101, 104, 115;  12, 103.

Anunnaki *(ilu)*:  12, 32; 27, 2;  4, 13.

Aššur:  2, 26 *D*; 50, 13; 56, 8.

Aššur *(alu)*: 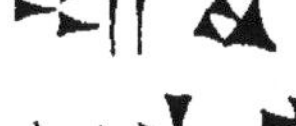 9, 1.

Aššurîtu *(ilu)*: 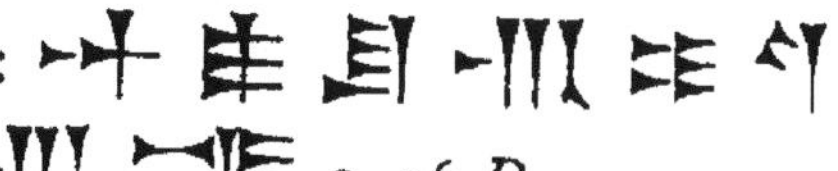 50, 13; 56, 8;  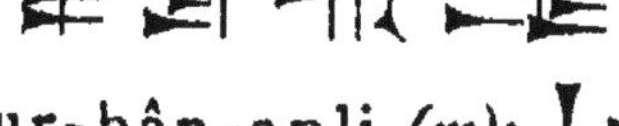 2, 26 *D*.

Aššur-bân-apli *(m)*:  2, 26 *D*; 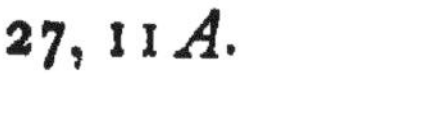 50, 12; 55, 2; 56, 7; 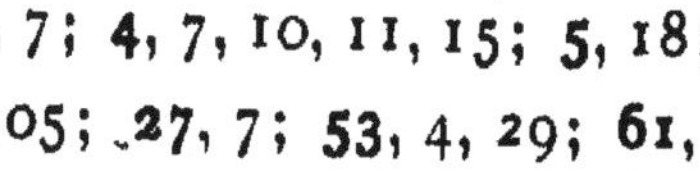 27, 11 *A*.

Ía *(ilu)*: 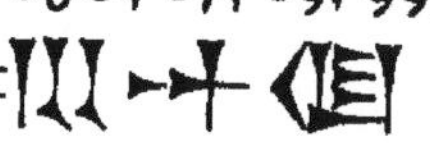 3, 7; 4, 7, 10, 11, 15; 5, 18; 9, 24; 10, 25; 12, 85 *C*, 87, 89, 99, 105; 27, 7; 53, 4, 29; 61, 20; 62, 17, 21; 12, 33; 9, 2; 22 5;

12, 87; 4, 8; 12, 87 *C*, 89 *C*.

I.A . . . . .: 4, 14.

Igigi (*ilu*): 2, 44; 31, 11 (?); 4, 13; 6, 111; 10, 15; 12, 88; 18, 20; 30, 30; 36, 10; 39, 9; 49, 5; 12, 32.

Îzida: 2, 46; 7, 4; 9, 4; 22, 4; 33, 8.

Îṭura (*Apsû*): 4, 14; 9, 3; 53, 3; 58, 18.

Îkur: 1, 16; 2, 16, 31; 3, 14; 4, 43; 6, 85; 7, 23; 21, 60.

I.MAḪ.TIL.LA: 9, 5.

IMINA.BI (*ilu*): 52, 5.

Îsagila: 1, 42; 7, 3; 9, 4, 32; 14, 8; 16, 8; 22, 3, 40; 33, 24.

Irûa (*ilu*): ? 11, 31.

IR.NI.NA (*ilu*): 4, 11.

Išḫara (*ilu, kakkabu*): 7, 59; 57, 2, 13; 7, 34.

Išum (*ilu*): 7, 39.

Îšara: 2, 12; 3, 10; 6, 22.

Ištar (*ilu*): 1, 29, 33; 5, 11, 15; 8, 3; 8, 20; 30, 19, 20; 31, 8; 32, 6, 14; 39, 3; 8, 20; 32, 2, 3.

UD.ḌA.GAN (*ilu?*): 12, 36.

Utgallu (*ilu*): 2, 14; 3, 12.

Ba'u (*ilu*): 4, 24, 47; 6, 71, 77, 85, 90, 95; 61, 21.

BU . . . . . (*ilu*): (*i. e.* ?) 6, 125; 10, 22.

Bâbilu: 9, 4, 33; 22, 6.

Bîl (*ilu*): 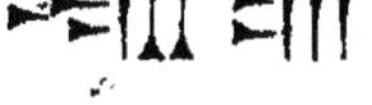 1, 34; 2, 11, 17, 30; 3, 10, 15; 5, 16; 6, 19, 25, 30; 7, 7; 9, 24; 10, 25; 27, 9*B*; 43, 6; 60, 6;  19, 33;  27, 9;  9, 41; 50, 7; 62, 17.

Bîlit (*ilu*):  35, 14;  21, 58.

Bîlit-ili (*ilu*):  6, 71*E*; 7, 9, 15, 23, 28; 9, 34.

Borsippa:  33, 9;  22, 4.

Gibil (*ilu*):  1, 6.

GIŠ.BAR (*ilu*):  12, 86.

Dagân (*ilu*):  2, 44; 5, 9(?).

DU.DUL.KU (*ilu*):  9, 31.

DI.KUD (*ilu*):  5, 10.

DU.KIRRUD.KU (*ilu*):  12, 24.

Damkina (*ilu*):  3, 8, 9; 4, 9; 12, 89.

Dûr-ilu:  6, 18.

ZA.GAR (*ilu*):  1, 25.

Zarpanîtu (*ilu*):  22, 2.

KAK.SI.DI (*kakkabu*): 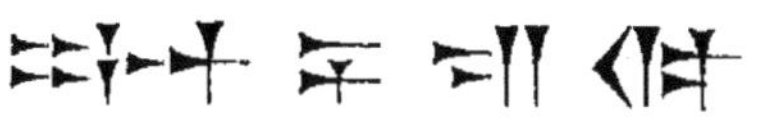 49, 20; 50, 29.

KIRRUD.AZAG.GA:  46, 13.

KU.TU.ŠAR (*ilu*): 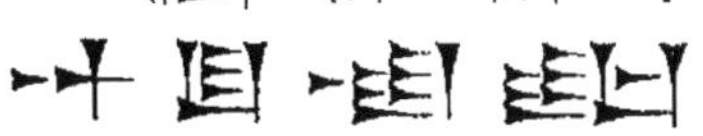 21, 59; 46, 12; 
 27, 3.

LUGAL.KIRRUD (*ilu*):  12, 25.

MUL.MUL:  47, 6; 48, 16.

MI.MI (*ilu*):  34, 5.

Marduk (*ilu*):  4, 46, 48; 6, 91, 97, 102; 7, 29; 9, 3, 9, 21, 27; 10, 3, 6, 7, 10; 11, 1, 7, 30, 40, 41, 42; 12, 2, 16, 17, 21, 26, 27, 95, 98, 114; 13, 12, 13, 31; 14, 11, 12; 15, 17; 16, 10; 17, 5; 18; 19*A*; 22, 9, 41; 42, 26; 53, 3, 4, 27; 59, 18;

 2, 47; 13, 15; 22, 24, 36, 38; 43, 2; 
 12, 85, 88, 105, 114; 62, 25; 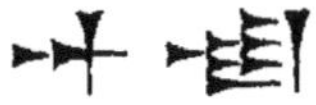
 18, 11, 18; 22, 1, 70; 33, 6.

Muštabarrû-mûtânu (*kakkabu*):  46, 9.

Nabû (*ilu*):  22, 70; 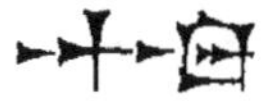 11, 32; 22, 3, 30, 37, 62, 68; 33, 23;  1, 42; ?  22, 28.

NA.GAL.A (*ilu*):  11, 36.

NÍ.DU.[NI?] (*ilu*):  53, 20, 21.

Namraṣit (*ilu*): 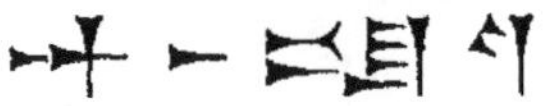 1, 19.

Namtar (*ilu*):  1, 49.

NIN . . . . (*ilu*):  9, 31.

NIN . . . . (*ilu*):  44, 1.

NIN.A . . . . . (*ilu*):  61, 21.

NIN.A.KU.KUD.DU (*ilu*):  42, 23.

Ninib (*ilu*): 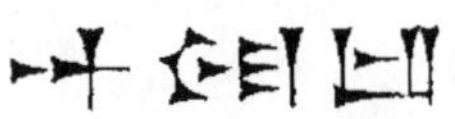 2, 25, 42; 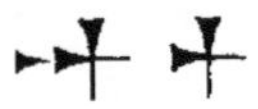 50, 29; 55, 2(?).

NIN.GAL (*ilu*):  1, 31; 5, 13.

NIN.MIN.NA (*ilu*): 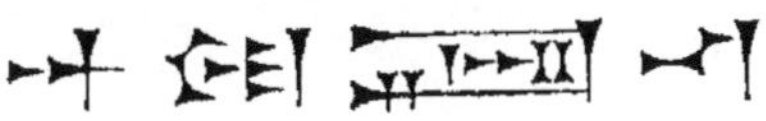 20, 6; 27, 4.

NU(N).NAM.NIR (*ilu*):  27, 1; 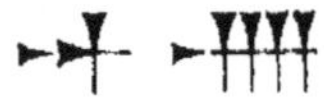
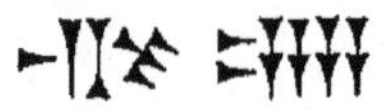 27, 1 *D*.

Nannaru (*ilu*), *cf.* Sin.

Nusku (*ilu*):  6, 18.

Nirgal (*ilu*): 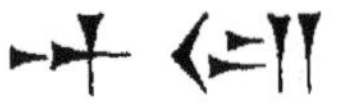 11, 34; 27, 4, 15*A*, 25; 28, 5; 46, 11; 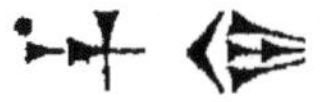 27, 10.

SIB.ZI.AN.NA (*kakkabu*): 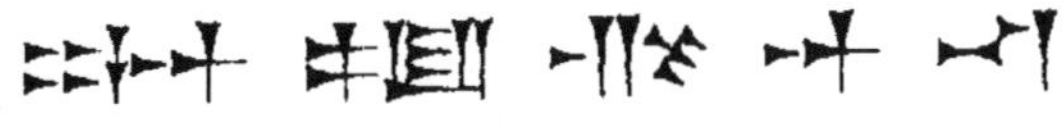 50, 1, 28; 51, 9, 10; 52, 3.

Sin (*ilu*): 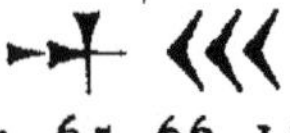 1, 1, 2, 12, 16, 31, 39; 4, 17, 39; 5, 13; 6, 36, 63, 64, 65, 66, 113 *F*; 7, 20, 60; 19, 10; 27, 11 *A*; 23, 8; 24, 5, 6; 27, 8; 31, 11; 50, 14; 53, 24; 54, 2; 55, 3; 56, 9; 57, 4;

58, 6; 59, 12; 61, 16; 62, 16; 𒐏 60, 19; 𒀭𒈪𒀭𒂗 1, 28; 24, 4; 25, 5; 26, 4; 𒀭𒈨𒀭𒂗𒆤 23, 6; 26, 3; 𒀭𒈹𒌋𒂊 1, 1; 6, 70.

Pișû (*kakkabu*): 𒀯 46, 11.

Rammânu (*ilu*): 𒀭𒅎 20, 10, 16; 21, 19, 24, 25, 28, 32, 36; 41, 72, 73, 76, 91; 50, 8; 59, 18.

Šala (*ilu*): 𒀭𒊩 29, 2.

Šamaš (*ilu*): 𒀭𒌓 1, 10, 32; 5, 14; 6, 112, 127; 10, 15, 23, 26, 30; 12, 35; 32, 8; 45, 3; 53, 4, 6, 16, 23; 56, 2; 59, 8, 18; 60, 4, 5; 62, 16; 𒀭𒌓𒁉 53, 19.

Tašmîtu (*ilu*): 𒀭𒁹𒁹𒈨 1, 37, 51, 52; 2, 9, 10; 11, 33; 33, 10, 20, 37, 38.

II.— LIST OF NUMERALS.

I: 𒐕 12, 11, 12ter.

II: 𒐖 22, 31; 35, 9; 51, 9, 10; 61, 11.

III: 𒐗 6, 96; 8, 21; 12, 16, 99, 103, 117; 15, 23; 18, 19A; 25, 7; 30, 27; 32, 4; 40, 13; 52, 4; 61, 4; 62, 25, 29, 30.

VII: 𒐛 11, 37; 25, 8; 31, 9; 40, 7; 61, 11.

VIII: 𒐜 48, 18.

XV: 𒌋𒐛 61, 11.

XIX: 𒌋𒑆 61, 11.

XX: 𒎙 61, 12.

XXX: 𒌍 1, 18; 61, 12.

XXXVI: 𒌍𒌋𒐚 40, 8.

L: 𒐐 35, 15.

CXXXIV: 𒐖𒐏𒐛 30, 31.

III.— PORTIONS OF WORDS AND IDEOGRAPHS OF UNCERTAIN READING.

1, 1 *ú-. . . . .*; 4 *ša-. . . . .*; 24 *ni-. . . . .*; 26 *KAB.MIŠ*; 31 . . . . .*-in-nin-na*; 32 . . . . .*-mat*; 34 *da-. . . . .*; 35 . . . . .*-mu*; *u* . . . . . *-tu dan-. . . . .*; 36 . . . . .*pl*; **2**, 1 . . . . .*-da*; 4 . . . . .*-ki*; 6 . . . . .*-ka*; 45 . . . . . *ḫ-ti*; 48 . . . . .*-šú*; 50 . . . . .*-ra*; **4**, 2 . . . . .*-šu*; 6 . . . . .*-ni*; . . . . .*-šut(?)-. . . . .*; 7 *ši(lim?)-. . . . .*; 13 . . . . .*-mi-at*; 15 . . . . .*-ti*; 16 *šú-ut-lu-. . . . .*; 21 *im-. . . . .*; 28 *dug-gun(?) di-. . . . .*; 33 *aš-. . . . .*; 34 *lut(d)-. . . . .*; 38 *ša-. . . . .*; 47 . . . . .*-zi-zu*; **5**, 1 *ri-i-. . . . .*; 2 *ti-ki-. . . . .*; 4 . . . . .*-bu-ri*; 5 . . . . .*-ur(lik? i. e. [ḫul]-lik)*; 12 . . . . .*-tú*; 13 . . . . .*-in-nin-ni*; 14 . . . . .*-am-ti*; 16 *da-. . . . .*; 17 . . . . .*-mu*; *u* . . . . .; 18 . . . . .*-tum*; 19 . . . . .*-pur(?)-ru-ú*; **6**, 23 *ú-pak-ku-. . . . .*; 25 *IŠ* . . . . .; 26 *uš-ti-. . . . .*; 29 *ri-i-. . . . .*; 29 *A ša-. . . . .*; 30 . . . . .*-kid-. . . . .*; 31 . . . . .*-ya*; . . . . .*-ṭir*; 32 *ilu* . . . . .; 36 *na-. . . . .*; 40 *gi-. . . . .*; 51 . . . . .*-li?-. . . . .*; . . . . .*-ti*; 52 . . . . .*-i-ma*; 53 . . . . .*-nun-šu*; 54 *tuk(išû?)* . . . . .; . . . . .*-nam*; 56 . . . . .*-mu*; . . . . .*-ya*; 57 . . . . .*-sa*; 58 . . . . .*-at*; 59 *ḫu-. . . . .*; . . . . .*-ú*; . . . . .*-ša-nu-nim-ma*; 60 *i-ta-šu-uš-. . . . .-bi*; 61 . . . . .*pl*; 68 *ki-i-. . . . .*; 79 *E* . . . . .*-kid(dan?)-ki*; 83 *da-ta-. . . . .*; 84 *a-ta-. . . . .*; 90 *a-. . . . .*; 91 *pu-. . . . .*; 101 . . . . .*-tú-ki*; 103 . . . . .*-ka*; 104 . . . . .*-bi-ti*; 106 . . . . .*-li*; 108 . . . . .*-na-di-. . . . .*; 109 . . . . .*-ar-ma*; . . . . .*-ta-a*; 110 . . . . .*-lip*; 117 . . . . .*-šú-tú*; 119 *ka-. . . . .*; 121 *lu-. . . . .*; 128 *li-. . . . .*; **7**, 16 . . . . .*-kid?-ki*; 28 *a-. . . . .*; 29 *pu-. . . . .*; 41 *da-. . . . .*; 55 *ú-ši-. . . . .*; 58 *li-. . . . .*; 63 . . . . .*-ša(?)*; **8**, 5 *UZ-ki*; *li-. . . . .*; 22 *mu-. . . . .*; 25 . . . . .*-ki*; *su-. . . . .*; 26 . . . . .*-su-ti*; *MU-ú*; 27 . . . . .*-ḫu*; **9**, 24 *UD.DU-ka*; 28 *ŠA.TAR i-. . . . .*; 30 . . . . .*-tum*; *I* . . . . .; 36 . . . . .*-ma-li-tu*; 42 *UD.DA.GAN*; *sa-an-dak?*; 43 . . . . .*-pal(?)-ki*; 44 . . . . .*-ki*; *ma-. . . . .*; . . . . .*-ut-ki*; 47 . . . . .*-kir*; 49 . . . . .*-bil*; 51 . . . . .*pl*; 55 . . . . .*-ki šuk-. . . . .*: 56 . . . . . *tum(dum?)-. . . . .*; **10**, 3 . . . . .*-ri-šu-nu*; 5 . . . . .*-li-ša(?)*; 11 *ni-. . . . .*; 12 . . . . .*-riš a-tu-. . . . .*; 13 . . . . .*-tu*; 18 . . . . .*-šú-tú*; 19 *ka-. . . . .*; 20 *lu-. . . . .*; 24 *li-. . . . .*; 25 *li-. . . . .*; 28 . . . . .*-ka*; 30 *nap-ti-. . . . .*; 31 . . . . .*-ṭu*; 32 . . . . .*-la*; 33 *RA ZIB.BA MI. . . . .*;

34 . . . . . *A* . . . . .; **11**, 14 *ar-ra-*. . . . .; 16 . . . . .*-ka*; 17 . . . . .*-a*; 19 . . . . .*-ka*; 22 . . . . .*-ni*; **12**, 5 ^{iṣu}[illegible]; *mà-kan-na*(?); 10 *ARA-rad* [? *ištîniš*(*niš*) *RAD*]; 13 *GU.GAD*; 14 *KU*; 17 . . . . .*-ru-bu*; 18 . . . . .*-ú-um*; 19 . . . . .*-šar-šu*; 20 *ṣil-*. . . . .; . . . . .*-lum*; 21 *ša-*. . . . .; . . . . .*-su*; 22 *a-li-*. . . . .; 23 . . . . .*-iz-zu*; 24 . . . . .^{pl}; 26 . . . . .*-ik*; 31 . . . . .*-mí*(?)*-šu-nu*; 34 . . . . .^{pl}; 36 . . . . .*-šir-ši-na*; 37 . . . . .*-tum*; . . . . .*-ri-bu*; 41 . . . . .*-rum*; 44 *ṣi-*. . . . .; 46 *AKA* . . . . .; *ib-*. . . . .; 47 *ú-ma-*. . . . .; 51 *ta-*. . . . .; 52 *ú-šaḫ-*. . . . .; 53 *ku*(?)-. . . . .; 54 *šú-*. . . . .: 57 *BAR.DA* (*maš-da*?); 60 *SAG NA*; 60 *B* . . . . .*-ya*; 63 *B* . . . . .*-ú*; 80 *C KI.RIB MU.NI.NI.SU.U*; 96 *it-tu-ḫu-*. . . . .; . . . . .*-pat-su BI-u*; *KI ŠA NU*; 96 *D* . . . . .*-ú*; 97 . . . . .*-bu-ti-šu*; 102 *ARA* [*ištîniš*(*niš*)?]; 104 *UD.DU* [*muḫur*?]; *ḪUR*; 108 . . . . . *ḪUR*; 109 *lim-*. . . . .; . . . . .*-í*; **13**, 2 *lil-*. . . . .; 3 *í-*. . . . .; 7 *ma-*. . . . .; 11 *li-*. . . . .; 16 . . . . .*-la-at*; 17 . . . . .*-ba šit-ka-*. . . . .; 18 . . . . .*-šap*; 22 *ú-*. . . . .; 30 *ín-*. . . . .; 33 *maḫ-*. . . . .; **14**, 2 . . . . .*-lim*(?)*-man-ni*; 5 . . . . .*-tum*; 13 . . . . .*-lit-su*; 14 . . . . .*-ḫu*; 18 . . . . .^{pl}*-šu*; **15**, 1 . . . . .*-yà*; 2 . . . . .*-tum*; 3 . . . . .*-ku*; 6 . . . . .*-tuk*; 12 . . . . .*-šut-ka*; 13 . . . . .*-mu*; 14 . . . . .*-bu-ka*; 21 . . . . .*-bu-ḳu*; 25 . . . . .*-az*; 26 . . . . .*-ḳu-nu*; **16**, 5 . . . . .*-tú*; 8 . . . . .*-ka*; **17**, 3 *GUR.UD* . . . . .; 4 *lu-*. . . . .; 6 . . . . .*-mi*; *TAR*(*at*); 7 . . . . .*-za*; **18**, 1 *A* . . . . .*-ḳu-*[*ti*?]; 3 *ma-a-*. . . . .; **19**, 2 . . . . .*-šú*; 3 *ma-*. . . . .; 20 . . . . .*-rat-ti-ka*; 23 *PAL-ma*; 27 . . . . .*-ri*; **20**, 1 . . . . .*-ka*; 4 . . . . .*-tim*; 5 . . . . .*-da ši-*. . . . .; 6 *DAGAL* (*ummu*?) *MA SUR* . . . . .; 13 *AN.ZA* . . . . .; 18 . . . . .*-kip*; 19 . . . . .*-ni-bu la'-*. . . . .; 20 . . . . .*-zu šar-*. . . . .; **21**, 1 *bi*(?)-. . . . .; . . . . .*-ru-šu*; 2 *ga-*. . . . .; 3 *tik-*. . . . .; . . . . .*-tim*; 4 *pa-*. . . . .; 5 *šur-*. . . . .; 6 *na-*. . . . .; . . . . .*-ti*; 7 . . . . .*-ti-yà*; *nap-*. . . . .; 9 *mu-*. . . . .; . . . . .*-nu*; 10 *al-*. . . . .; 11 *ša-*. . . . .; 12 ^{ilu}. . . . .; *í-*. . . . .; 13 *da-*. . . . .; 14 *ta-*. . . . .; 15 . . . . .*-ka*; 16 . . . . . *GAR*; . . . . .*-lu*; *ru-*. . . . .; 17 *di-bi-*. . . . .; . . . . .*-an*; 18 . . . . .*-am-ma*; 19 . . . . .*-ka*; 26 *ru-*. . . . .; 27 . . . . .*-iḫ*; . . . . .*-in-na-*. . . . .; 30 . . . . .*-taḫ-ḫa-ma*; 31 *ŠIT* . . . . .; . . . . .*-í-ri-*. . . . .; 32 *ki-*. . . . .; 33 . . . . .*-ni*; 38 . . . . .*-bu-*. . . . .; 39 . . . . .*-a-lá-*. . . . .; 42 . . . . .*-ri aš-ṭu-*. . . . .; 43 . . . . .*-i-di muš-tar-*. . . . .; 44 *ín-ni-*. . . . .; . . . . .*-pal-lu-u šal-*. . . . .; 45 *ší-*. . . . .; *du-*. . . . .; . . . . .*-iz ta-šib-*. . . . .; 46 *ni-*. . . . .; *mí-*. . . . .;

47 [ilu]. . . . .; . . . . .-*ši*(?); 49 *tu*-. . . . .; 51 . . . . .[pl]; *ab*-. . . . .; 53 . . . . .-*tak-ku-ú*; 54 *ta*-. . . . .; 62 *bal*-. . . . .; 69 . . . . .-*yà*; 74 . . . . .-*ta*; 76 . . . . .-*ta-az-nu*; 77 . . . . .-*ḫi*-. . . . .; . . . . .-*ul-ḫu*; 78 . . . . .-*pi-i-ti*; 79 . . . . .-*tu*-. . . . .; 82 . . . . .-*mu-ka*; 83 . . . . .-*du-ú*; 84 . . . . .-*bi-i*; 85 . . . . .-*ḫi it-bu*-. . . . .; 86 . . . . .-*ša-am iz*-. . . . .; . . . . .-*ti-ma*; 87 . . . . . *U.A*; 90 . . . . .-*ka*; **22**, 13 *GUB.BU.DU*; 19 . . . . .-*kiš*; 21 *a-ta*-. . . . .; . . . . .-*ti liš*-. . . . .; 22 [ilu]. . . . .; *ki*-. . . . .; 24 *KAN* . . . . .; *KAN.SIR-ka*(?); 25 [ilu]. . . . .; 26 [ilu]. . . . .; . . . . .-*ka*; 29 *I* . . . . .; 32 *ARA* [? *ištîniš*(*niš*)]; 34 . . . . .-*i*; 35 . . . . .-*ú*; 39 . . . . .-*mar-raš*; 40 . . . . .-*tu-ú*; 43 *ú-tâk-ku* . . . . .; 46 *ki-di*-. . . . .; 47 . . . . .-ʾ-*a-tu*; 48 . . . . .-*na ik-ṣa*-. . . . .; *DI.DI*(*iš*); 49 *UGU-ma*; 50 *kil-lim*-. . . . .; 51 . . . . .-*ka*; 52 *im-mur*-. . . . .; 53 . . . . .-*a-ni*; 54 . . . . .-*ti*; 55 *ka*-. . . . .; . . . . .-*ya*; 56 . . . . .-*šid*; 57 . . . . .-*ka*; 58 . . . . .-*a*; **23**, 4 . . . . .-*da-ar-ti*; 9 . . . . .[pl]; **24**, 1 . . . . .-*id*; 2 . . . . .-*bit ik*-. . . . .; 3 *ra*-. . . . .; **25**, 2 *dir*-. . . . .; 3 *a-ṭi*(*di*?)-*ra*-. . . . .; 4 *lu*-. . . . .; 6 . . . . .-*ki-im*; 7 . . . . .-*ti*; **26**, 2 . . . . .-*bil*; 5 . . . . .-*ši*; . . . . .-*šal-tú*; 8 . . . . .-*an-ma*; 10 . . . . .-*ḫur*; 11 . . . . .-*tim*; **27**, 6 *LA.TI-šu*; 22 . . . . .-*ṣir*; 26 *A* . . . . . *IN.DUL-ki*; **28**, 7 . . . . .-*ú*; **29**, 3 [ilu]. . . . .; **30**, 4 *in-na*-. . . . .; 5 *a-ku*-. . . . .; *ši*-. . . . .; 8 *di*-. . . . .; 9 *ki*-. . . . .; 11 *li*-. . . . .; 12 *MUN.GU*; *da*-. . . . .; 20 *URU TI*; 24 *SID*(*di*); 25 *ARA* [? *ištîniš*(*niš*)]; 26 *MU.ŠAL*; *MI*; 29 *ki*-. . . . .; *tu*-. . . . .; **31**, 7 [ilu]. . . . .; 9 *tar-bi*(?); **32**, 1 . . . . .-*bu*; 6 . . . . .-*na*; 8 . . . . .-*ti-ma*; 12 . . . . .-*ni-ki-ma*; *ba*-. . . . .; 13 . . . . .-*ru-ki*; 15 . . . . .-*ki-ma*; **33**, 1 . . . . .-*zu-zu*; 7 *dan*(?)-. . . . .; . . . . . *IL du-ru*-. . . . .; 13 . . . . .-*i-kiš-ki*; 14 . . . . .-*ri*; . . . . .-*si-na US.LIK*; 16 . . . . .-*at*; 17 . . . . .-*riš-ma*; . . . . .-*nu*; 18 *iš*-. . . . .; 19 . . . . .[pl]; 40 . . . . . *GA*; 44 *TAG-ma*; 45 *lil*(?)-. . . . .; 46 . . . . . *KAM ŠAH*(?); *ú*-. . . . .; **35**, 3 *ši*-. . . . .; 7 *DIM* . . . . .; 11 *ŠAG.GA* . . . . .; 13 . . . . .-*mi-ik-ti*; *id*-. . . . .; 15 . . . . .-*saḫ*(?); *A.BA* (*arkat*?); *DA.RA*; **36**, 1 . . . . .-*ki*; 2 . . . . .-*zi*-. . . . .; 4 *šur*-. . . . .; 6 [ilu]. . . . .; 9 . . . . .-*ma*; 10 *ḫa-si*-. . . . .; **37**, 1 [ilu]. . . . .; 3 . . . . .[pl]; **38**, 1 *di*-. . . . .; **39**, 6 *šar*-. . . . .; 7 . . . . .-*i-ti*; *i*-. . . . .; 11 . . . . .-*bu-u*; 13 . . . . .-*ki*; 14 . . . . .-*ya*; 15 . . . . .-*ni-ma*; 17 . . . . .-*maḫ-ra dan*-. . . . .; **40**, 1 . . . . . *DI*; 3 . . . . .[pl]-*šu*; *IM.IL* [ilu]. . . . .; 4 . . . . .-*at*; 5 . . . . . *KUR.NA TU.UD.TA*; 6 . . . . .-*nis-su*-

un-nu SIR; $^{lubu\check{s}tu}$. . . . .; 7 . . . . .*-rit-ta-šú*; *tu*-. . . . .; 8 *AŠ.A.AN ŠIR* . . . . .; 9 . . . . .*-na*; *ZU.DU*; 10 *SI.IL(ḳa)*; 13 . . . . .*-su*; 14 . . . . .*-šu DIM.ŠID*; 15 . . . . .*-bu-ma*; **42**, 2 *na*-. . . . .; 4 *ú-tag-ga*(?)-. . . . .; 5 . . . . .*-ri*? *ki*-. . . . .; 6 *ta-ta-na-ru*-. . . . .; 7 *ri-i*-. . . . .; 9 *ZIG.GIR-ka*; 11 *DIM.KU*; *ir*-. . . . .; 12 *pi*-. . . . .; 14 *mun-nap(b)*-. . . . .; 16 *UD*. . . . .; 17 *ḳi*-. . . . .; 19 *a-zu*-. . . . .; 21 *ul*-. . . . .; **43**, 1 . . . . .*-bu*-. . . . .; **44**, 3 . . . . .*-tu*; 4 . . . . . KU^{pl}; 5 . . . . .*-nu*; **45**, 1 . . . . .*-ti*; 3 . . . . .*-um*; 4 ^{ilu}. . . . .; 6 . . . . .*-ra-ka*; 8 . . . . .*-na ši-it*-. . . . .; 10 . . . . .*-bil*; **46**, 3 . . . . .*-ka*; 6 . . . . .*-ka*; 7 . . . . .*-ši*; 12 . . . . .*-ti*; 21 . . . . .*-tú*; 22 . . . . .*-ti*; **47**, 1 . . . . .*-i ru*-. . . . .; 4 . . . . .*-na-ku-nu*; **48**, 1 . . . . .*-ni-ti*; 2 . . . . .*-a-ti*; 4 . . . . .*-ša*; 5 . . . . .*-a-ti*; 6 . . . . .*-li-ku*; 7 . . . . . *MIN*; 8 . . . . .*-ri*; 9 . . . . .*-šu*; 10 . . . . .*-yà*; 11 . . . . .*-ziz*; 12 . . . . .*-ší*; 13 . . . . .*-zis*; 15 . . . . .*-ki*; **49**, 2 . . . . .*-ú-ti*; 3 . . . . .*-mar*; 4 . . . . .*-a-ti*; 7 . . . . .*-ai-ti*; 9 . . . . .*-lu*; 10 . . . . .*-pú*(?); 11 . . . . .*-ni*; 12 . . . . .*-ru-sa-a-ti*; 13 . . . . .*-ú*; 14 . . . . .*-ú*; 17 . . . . .*-ma*ʾ*-ú*; 18 . . . . .*-ši-la-ku*; 24 . . . . .*-ru-ti*; 26 . . . . .*-ša-an-nu*; 27 . . . . .^{pl}; **50**, 11 *A* . . . . .*-zi*; 19 *ú-šaḫ*-. . . . .; 23 *B ú-šur*-. . . . .; 27 *B* ^{kakkabu}. . . . .; ^{ilu}*DUMU*. . . . .; . . . . .*-tí*-. . . . .; **51**, 3 . . . . .*-pal*; 5 . . . . .*-ma*; 6 *ú*-. . . . .; 12 . . . . .*-za-za*; 14 . . . . . *ŠI*; $^{i\check{s}u}$*NAM* . . . . .; **53**, 2 . . . . .*-ḫi*; 15 *GUR TAP.PI DU*; . . . . .*-šu*; 17 *SU.A.RU.LA*; 18 ^{kimu}; *ŠA.KASKAL*; 20 f. *[NI]DU GAL* (*mušilû*, or *pitû*, *rabû*?); 22 *nam-ṣa-ki-šu-nu*(?); 27 . . . . .*-kis-su*; 28 . . . . .*-yà*; . . . . .*-pal-šu*; 30 . . . . .^{pl}; **56**, 2 ^{ilu}. . . . .; 4 *ki*-. . . . .; 5 *in*-. . . . .; **57**, 11 *mu*-. . . . .; 17 *šú*-. . . . .; 19 . . . . .*-mi*-. . . . .; **58**, 1 . . . . .^{pl}; 3 . . . . .^{pl}; 9 . . . . .*-an*-. . . . .; 10 . . . . .*-ka*; 11 . . . . .*-na*; 12 . . . . .*ḫu*; 15 . . . . .*-ši-ru*; 16 . . . . .*-mi*; 18 . . . . .*-ki*; **59**, 1 . . . . .^{pl}; 2 . . . . .*-ni*; *DUB* . . . . .; 3 *NUN* . . . . .; 4 *BUR* . . . . .; 8 *nu*-. . . . .; 9 *ir*-. . . . .; 11 . . . . .*-ti-ka*; 15 . . . . .*-yà liš*-. . . . .; 16 . . . . .*-li-na-an-ni ma-ḫi*(?)-. . . . .; 17 *in-an-na*-. . . . .; 19 . . . . .*-tab-ba-la-ka ta*-. . . . .; **60**, 4 *KI*; 12 . . . . .^{pl}*-ka*; 14 *at-ta*-. . . . .; 15 . . . . .*-di-ri-ka*; *sa*-. . . . .; 16 *ŠI.MIŠ*; 17 . . . . .*-mat*; 18 . . . . .*-ri NI.RUŠ*; 22 . . . . .*-us*; **61**, 2 . . . . .*-šat-ki*; 3 . . . . . *IN TI*; *nu*-. . . . .; 10 *ŠA.LA*; 15 *at-ta*-. . . . .; 17 *GU.ZUR-ki u-kul-li*-. . . . .; 18 . . . . .*-pi-ka*; *ḪI-ka*; 19

***an-*. . . . .; 20 . . . . . *-tu-un*; 22 . . . . . *MA GU* . . . . .; 62, 4 . . . . .*pl*; 7 . . . . . *-la-mu*; 9 . . . . . *-bu*; 11 . . . . . *-da-a-ti*; 14 . . . . . *pl*; 18 . . . . . *pl*; *iṣ-ṣal-*. . . . .; 19 . . . . . *pl*; *it-ti-iḫ-*. . . . .; 24 . . . . . *-ak-ki ŠAR*.**

ADDITIONS AND CORRECTIONS.

P. 3, l. 11 *leg.*: "*ug-da-ša-ra*", for "*uḳ-ṭa-ša-ra*". — Pp. 3, ll. 18, 20; 113, l. 31 *leg.*: "*sal*", for "*ṣal*". — Pp. 3, l. 22; 33, l. 18 *leg.*: "*ṣíl*", for "*ṣil*". — P. 3, l. 23 *leg.*: "*muḳ*", for "*muk*". — Pp. 3, l. 25; 12, l. 9 *leg.*: "*riḳ*", for "*rik*". — Pp. 3, ll. 27, 32; 57, l. 16 *leg.*: "*yà*", for "*ya*". — Pp. 3, l. 32; 31, l. 6 *leg.*: "*šir*", for "*šir*". — P. 3, l. 35 *leg.*: "*ḳá*", for "*ḳa*". — Pp. 4, l. 2; 29, l. 33; 104, l. 22 *leg.*: "*di-par*", for "*DI.BAR*". — P. 4, l. 10 *leg.*: "*pulânîtum*", for "*pulânitum*". — Pp. 4, l. 16; 28, l. 36 *leg.*: "*îmid-ki*", for "*imid-ki*". — P. 4, ll. 19, 20 *leg.*: "*zík*", for "*zik*". — *Ibid.*, ll. 21, 24 for "*li-ṭá-kil*" poss. read "*li-ṭa-rid*", *cf.* DELITZSCH, *Handw.* p. 303. — Pp. 4, l. 22; 97, l. 25 *leg.*: "*bil*", for "*bíl*". — Pp. 4, l. 25; 97, l. 37 *leg.*: "*lid-dip-pìr*", for "*lit-lu-ud*". — Pp. 4, l. 25; 97, l. 28 *leg.*: "*li-ni-ʾ*", for "*li-ṣal-ʾ*". — Pp. 4, l. 25; 17, l. 29; 24, l. 29; 44, l. 17; 97, ll. 2, 29; 103, l. 10; 110, l. 15 *leg.*: "*kín*", for "*kin*". — P. 4, l. 37 *leg.*: "*bi-íl-tum*", for "*bi-il-tum*". — Pp. 5, l. 18; 35, l. 34; 60, l. 33 *leg.*: "newly shining", for "unique". — P. 5, l. 24 *leg.*: "is mighty", for "he gathers". — P. 6, l. 7 *del.* "(with) shouts of joy". — *Ibid.*, l. 21 *leg.*: "Torch", for "Lady(?)". — Pp. 7, l. 3; 19, l. 17; 27, l. 33; 35, l. 8; 42, l. 36; 47, l. 5; 99, l. 5 *leg.*: "accept", or "accepteth", for "remove", or "take(th) away". — P. 8, l. 8 f. *leg.*: "incantations", for "incantatious". — P. 10, l. 19 *leg.*: "far", for "for". — P. 11, l. 28 *leg.*: "", for "". — Pp. 13, ll. 14, 15, 23; 25, l. 30; 56, l. 6; 57, l. 22; 68, l. 6; 105, ll. 21, 24 *leg.*: "*niš*", for "*nîš*". — P. 13, l. 27 *leg.*: "*ipuš*", for "*îpuš*". — Pp. 13, l. 28; 16, l. 23; 22, l. 6; 52, l. 26; 105, l. 24 *leg.*: "*minûtu*", for "*mînûtu*". — P. 13, ll. 35 ff. *del.* note to l. 30. — Pp. 15, ll. 7, 31; 44, l. 4 *leg.*: "*dil*" for "*ziz*". — Pp. 16, l. 18; 17, l. 17 *leg.*: "*lìḫ*", for "*liḫ*". — Pp. 16, l. 19; 17, l. 23; 29, l. 21; 31, l. 24; 32, l. 20 *leg.*: "*nar-bi-ki(ka)*", for "*lib-bi-ki(ka)*". — P. 16, l. 21 *leg.*: "*burâši*", for "*burași*". — *Ibid.*, l. 28 *leg.*: "*pu*", for "*bu*". — *Ibid.*, l. 33 *leg.*: "*tuš-ti-šir*", for "*tùš-ti-šir*". — P. 17, l. 11 *leg.*: "*pu*", for "*bu*". — *Ibid.*, l. 26 *leg.*: "*bil*", for "*bil*". — *Ibid.*, l. 34, n. 7 *add.* "The dupls. *B* and *C* I have since "joined", and it is now clear that the reading of *B* for l. 24 is  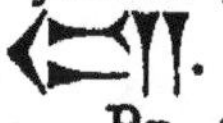. — Pp. 18, l. 5; 19, l. 26; 30, l. 8 *leg.*: "greatness", for "heart". — Pp. 18, l. 33; 27, ll. 23, 26; 35, l. 2; 40, l. 15; 115, l. 19 *leg.*: "judgment", for "judgement". — P. 19, l. 24 *leg.*: "esteem", for "command". — Pp. 20, l. 13; 79, l. 38; 83, l. 30; 90, l. 14; 100, l. 8; 104, ll. 6, 19 *leg.*: "*KIŠDA*", for "*ŠAR*". — P. 22, l. 15 *add.* "but *cf.* LYON, *Sargon*, p. 81". — P. 23, ll. 27, 33 *leg.*: "*bu*", for "*pu*" in *šurbû*. — P. 24, l. 27 poss. read "3. *[rubû] u [šagganakku]* . . . . .". — *Ibid.*, l. 28 *leg.*: "*li-ḳir*", for "*li-piš*". — Pp. 24, l. 33; 25, l. 3; 58, l. 30; 119, l. 11 *leg.*: "*kal*", for "*kâl*". — P. 25, l. 6 *leg.*: "*ṬUR*", for "*TUR*". — *Ibid.*, l. 7 *leg.*: "*[il]-pi-[ši]*", for ". . . . .-*pi*-. . . . .". — *Ibid.*, l. 25 *leg.*: "*lim-[da]*", for "*ši*-. . . . .". — Pp. 25, l. 29; 32, l. 4; 38, l. 6; 75, l. 5; 79, l. 7 *leg.*: "*ib-ša-ki(ku) uznâ^{du}-ai*", for "*ip-ša-ki(ku) uznâ^{du}-ai*", *i. e.* "I have considered thee!". — Pp. 25, l. 32; 32, l. 32 f.; 38, l. 9; 41, ll. 4, 6; 44, l. 34 *leg.*: "*kam*", for "*gâm*". — Pp. 26, l. 6; 32, ll. 2, 10, 16, 21 *leg.*: "*Ba'u*", for "*Bau*". — P. 28, l. 13 *leg.*: "*li'û*", for "*lî'u*". — P. 29, l. 16 *leg.*: "*šú*", for "*šu*". — Pp. 30, l. 22; 31, l. 1; 34, ll. 11, 19 f. *leg.*: "*Nusku*", for "*Nuzku*". — P. 30, l. 22 *leg.*: "*i*", for "*il*". — *Ibid.*, l. 27 *leg.*: *a-bi [ilâni^{pl}]*", for "*a-bi]*-. . . . .". — *Ibid.*, l. 31 *leg.*: "*kil*", for "*kil*". — P. 31, l. 17 *leg.*: "*bu-tuḳ-[tum]*", for "*bu-tuḳ-[ḳu?]*". — Pp. 32, ll. 7, 14; 38, l. 19; 44, l. 23 *leg.*: "*kám*", for "*gâm*". — P. 32, l. 19 *leg.*: "*ili*", for "*ili*". — P. 33, l. 33 *leg.*: K 8605", for "K 3605". — Pp. 33, l. 34; 74, ll. 23, 26; 79, l. 5 *leg.*: "*šîmâti^{pl}*", for "*šimâti^{pl}*". — P. 37, l. 12 *add.*: "but *see ZA* I, p. 56". — P. 39 l 14 *leg.*: "(*si*)", for "(*ši*)". — *Ibid.*, l. 16 *leg.*: "51. *ár-ša-ši-i limnûti(ti) ša*" *etc.* — *Ibid.*, l. 18 *leg.*: "*maruštu*", for "*ša murṣu*". — *Ibid.*, l. 19 *leg.*: "*kalû*", for "*kâlu*". — *Ibid.*, l. 22 *leg.*: "*ár*, for "*up*". — P. 41, l. 16 *leg.*: "*ri-min-ni-ma*", for "*rîmi-nin-ni-ma*". — Pp. 41, l. 25; 82, l. 15 *leg.*: "*dumḳi*", for "*damiḳtu*". — P. 41, l. 32 *leg.*: "*luṭ*", for "*lut*". — P. 43, l. 6 *leg.*: "countenance", for "brightness". — Pp. 43, l. 17; 46, l. 16 *leg.*: "revere", for "behold", *cf.* TALLQVIST, *Maqlû* p. 144. — P. 44, l. 4: K 10354, ll. 2—7, is dupl. of No. 9, ll. 1—5. — *Ibid.*, l. 13: L. 9 is expanded to form 5 ll. in K 10243, which is dupl. of No. 9, ll. 1—13. — *Ibid.*, l. 19 *leg.*: "-*u*", for "*u*". — *Ibid.*, l. 22 *leg.*: "*sal*", for "*šal*"; "-*u*", for "-*u*-". — *Ibid.*, l. 28 *leg.*: "*UD.DU-ka*", for "*urru-ka*". — *Ibid.*, l. 33 *leg.*: "*ti-ru-u*", for "*ti-ru*". — P. 45, l. 5 *leg.*: "*DU*", for "*TUR*". — *Ibid.*, l. 8 *leg.*: "*bul*", for "*búl*". — *Ibid.*, l. 38 *leg.*: "*A*", for "*B*". — P. 46, l. 24 *leg.*: "19. Grant speech, hearing and favour!" — *Ibid.*, l. 29 *leg.*: ". . . . .", for "light". — P. 48, l. 25 *leg.*: "*Ai*", for "*Malik*". — *Ibid.*, l. 26 *leg.*: "-*ram*-", for "-*ram*". — *Ibid.*, l. 30 *leg.*: "-*u*", for "*u*". — Pp. 51, l. 10; 52, ll. 11, 15; 110, l. 19 *leg.*: "*ḳarradu*", for "*ḳarrâdu*". — P. 51, l. 12 *leg.*: "*ban*", for "*pan*". — *Ibid.*, l. 27 *leg.*: "*mûdû-u*", for "*mudû u*". — Pp. 51, l. 31; 88, l. 5 *leg.*: "*bu*", for "*pu*". — P. 51, l. 32 *leg.*: "*mì*", for "*mí*". — *Ibid.*, l. 36 *leg.*: "*mûdû-ú*", for "*mudû-ú*". — P. 53: *del.* l. 8 f. — Pp. 54, l. 10; 87, l. 7; 95, l. 3 *leg.*: "*gušûru*", for "*gušuru*". — P. 54, l. 14 *leg.*: "*gúr*", for "*gùr*". — *Ibid.*, l. 18 *leg.*: "*arki*", for "*arka*". — Pp. 55, l. 2; 58, l. 16; 82, l. 29; 87, l. 8 *leg.*: "*bulul*", for "*tubbal*". — P. 55, l. 4 *leg.*: "*ṣabat-ma*", for "*ṣubut-ma*". — *Ibid.*, l. 18 *leg.*: "*pitû-ú kup-pi*", for "*bîl ú-g(ḳ)up-pi*". — *Ibid.*, l. 26 *leg.*: "*ik*", for "*iḳ*". — Pp. 55, l. 29; 57, ll. 11, 30; 59, l. 4 *leg.*: "*tú*", for "*tu*". — P. 56, l. 11 *leg.*: "-*ša*", for "*ša*". — *Ibid.*, l. 15 *leg.*:

"*-up-pu-*", for "*-ub-bu-*". — *Ibid.*, l. 18 *leg.*: "*tîrtu*", for "*tirtu*"; "*dal-ḫa-ma*", for "*ri-ḫa-ma*". — *Ibid.*, l. 22 *leg.*: "61. *ili-yà* ^{ilu}*ištar amîlûti salima*(*ma*) *liršû-ni*". — *Ibid.*, l. 25 *leg.*: "*iṭiḫû-ni*", for "*iṭiḫu-ni*". — *Ibid.*, l. 29 *leg.*: "*limutti*", for "*limnîti*". — P. 57, l. 2 *leg.*: "*ḳir*", for "*kir*". — *Ibid.*, l. 10 *leg.*: "*úl*", for "*ul*". — *Ibid.*, l. 15 *leg.*: "*ṭâbûti*^{pl}", for "*ṭâbâti*^{pl}". — *Ibid.*, l. 19 *leg.*: "*dumḳu*", for "*damiḳtu*". — *Ibid.*, l. 31 after "reads" *add.* "*ina pi-ka*"; *leg.*: "[cuneiform]", for "[cuneiform]". — *Ibid.*, l. 32 *leg.*: "*til*", for "*dil*". — P. 58, l. 14 *leg.*: "*KU.KU*", for "*DUR.DUR*". — *Ibid.*, l. 18 after "*ḪUL*" *add.* "*LA*". — *Ibid.*, l. 25 *leg.*: "*tú-*", for "*-tú*". — Pp. 58, l. 27; 68, l. 13; 114, l. 19 *leg.*: "*dumḳi*", for "*damḳu*". — P. 58, l. 33 *leg.*: "*lu-u*", for "*lû-u*". — *Ibid.*, l. 35 *leg.*: "*tu-*", for "*-tu*". — P. 59, l. 8 *leg.*: "121. *înuma amîlu ḳaḳḳad-su ikkal-šu lišânu-šu ú-zaḳ-ḳat-su*". — *Ibid.*, l. 36 *leg.*: "far", for "for". — P. 60, l. 17 f. *leg.*: "oil in a vessel of *urkarinnu*-wood", for "the oil of certain woods". — P. 61, l. 2 *leg.*: "illustrious", for "illustrations". — *Ibid.*, l. 9 *leg.*: "29. Who openeth wells and springs, who guideth" *etc.* — *Ibid.*, l. 14 *leg.*: "benefactor", for "director". — *Ibid.*, l. 34 *leg.*: "disturbed", for "bewitched". — P. 62, l. 2 *leg.*: "61. May my god and the goddess of mankind grant me favour!". — *Ibid.*, l. 27 *leg.*: "ointment", for ". . . . .". — P. 65, l. 16 *add.*: "JENSEN, *ZA* IX, p. 128, and TALLQVIST, *Maqlû*, p. 134". — P. 66, l. 6 *leg.*: "transliterated", for "translitarated". — *Ibid.*, l. 27 *add.*: "but *cf.* DELITZSCH, *Grammar*, § 138 (end)". — P. 68, l. 2 *leg.*: "*tas*", for "*taš*". — P. 70, l. 22 *leg.*: "*nam-*", for "*-nam-*". — P. 72, l. 23 *leg.*: ". . . . .", for ". . . . .". — P. 74, l. 21 *leg.*: "4. *bîl bîlî* . . . .". — *Ibid.*, l. 26 *leg.*: "*kalâ-ma*", for "*kala*(?)*ma*". — P. 75, l. 7 *leg.*: "*šú*", for "*šu*". — *Ibid.*, l. 17 *leg.*: "*u*", for "*ú*". — *Ibid.*, l. 29 *leg.*: "4. Lord of lords! . . . . .". — Pp. 76, l. 29; 78, l. 24 *leg.*: "*ú-pi-í*", for "*ú-mì-í*". — P. 77, l. 11 *leg.*: "clouds", for days". — *Ibid.*, l. 13 *leg.*: "unsparing", for "unconquerable". — P. 78, l. 9 *leg.*: "*-ḳăr-*", for "*-piš-*". — Pp. 78, l. 10; 79, l. 15; 116, l. 18 *leg.*: "*dalîli-ka*", for "*dalili-ka*". — P. 78, l. 16 *leg.*: "*GAB*", for "*GAL*". — *Ibid.*, l. 28 *leg.*: "*la-iṭ muḳ-ṭab-lu*", for "*la-id muk-tap-lu*". — *Ibid.*, l. 38 before "*ilu*" *add.*: ". . . . ."; *leg.*: "*šaplu*", for "*šaplû*". — P. 79, l. 4 *leg.*: "^{ilu}*KU.TU.ŠAR*", for "^{ilu}*Marduk tu-šir*". — *Ibid.*, l. 13 *leg.*: "*lîšâ-a*", for "*lišâ-a*". — *Ibid.*, l. 14 *leg.*: "*niḳî*", for "*nikî*". — *Ibid.*, l. 25 *leg.*: "*-i-tí*", for "*-i-ti*". — *Ibid.*, l. 30 *leg.*: "*ú*", for "*u*". — P. 80, l. 33 *leg.*: "the goddess "*KU.TU.ŠAR*", for "the god Marduk". — P. 81, l. 13 *leg.*: "Ruler of", for "who destroyest". — *Ibid.*, l. 23 *leg.*: "90", for "89". — P. 82, l. 7 *leg.*: "*ŠU GIDIM*(*UTUG?*).*MA UḪ*(?)", for "*ḳât utukki-ma imat*". — *Ibid.*, l. 12 *leg.*: "*-u*", for "*u*". — *Ibid.*, l. 33 *leg.*: "*abḳallu*", for "*abkallu*"; "*mûdû-ú*", for "*mudû-u*". — P. 83, l. 3 *leg.*: "*tâmâti*^{pl}", for "*tamâti*^{pl}". — P. 84, l. 10 *leg.*: "Benefactor", for "Director". — *Ibid.*, *del.* l. 22. — P. 85, l. 9 *leg.*: "abundance", for "life". — *Ibid.*, l. 10 *leg.*: "65. Speech and hearing bestow upon me!". — *Ibid.*, l. 20 *leg.*: "*abḳalli*", for "*abgalli*". — P. 86, l. 16

leg.: "K 12922", for "K 13922". — P. 87, l. 24 *leg.*: "*ṭúr*", for "*ṭur*". — *Ibid.*, l. 27 *leg.*: "*ḳid*", for "*ḳid*". — *Ibid.*, l. 28 *add.*: "K 8953 + K 8987, cited as *D*, is dupl. of No. 27, ll. 1—22; the variant readings of *D* are cited in the Vocabulary". — P. 88, l. 37 *leg.*: "*A*", for "*B*". — P. 89, l. 9 *leg.*: "art glorious", for "treadest". — P. 90, l. 11 *leg.*: "*aš*", for "*ḫar*". — *Ibid.*, l. 17 *leg.*: "*ub-*", for "*-ub-*". — *Ibid.*, l. 19 *add.*: "since printing off I have joined No. 28 to K 6639, the dupl. *A* of No. 46, and to K 8953 *etc.*, the dupl. *D* of No. 27". — P. 92, l. 26 *leg.*: "*linnasiḫ*", for "*linasiḫ*"; "*linnisi*", for "*linasi*". — P. 93, l. 14 *leg.*: "*šuʾatu*", for "*šuatu*". — *Ibid.*, ll. 33 ff. *leg.*: "12. May the s. of my b. be removed, may there be torn away the . . . . . of . . . . . 13. May the g. of my h. be loosened". — P. 94, l. 35 *leg.*: "*dannati*", for "*dannâti*". — P. 95, l. 4 *leg.*: "*kurmati*", for "*kurmatî*". — *Ibid.*, l. 18 *leg.*: "Prepare", for "Place". — P. 97, l. 8 *leg.*: "*US.LIK*", for "*azkur(ur)*". — *Ibid.*, l. 15 f. *leg.*: "*pulânîtum*", for "*pulanîtum*". — *Ibid.*, ll. 24, 27 poss. restore "*liṭ-[ṭa-rid]*", for "*lit-[ta-kil]*". — *Ibid.*, l. 26 *leg.*: "*ru*", for "*rn*". — P. 98, l. 4 *leg.*: "*uš-kín-ma*", for "*šuḳḳi?(ḳi)-ma*". — *Ibid.*, l. 5 *leg.*: "*sâlimu*", for "*šâlimu*". — P. 102, l. 19 *leg.*: "*tiṣlîtu*", for "*tiṣlitu*". — P. 103, l. 17 *leg.*: "*parâsi*", for "*parasi*". — P. 105, ll. 25, 27 *leg.*: "*(ár)*", for "*(ar)*". — *Ibid.*, l. 26 *leg.*: "*šuʾati*", for "*šuati*". — P. 110, l. 4 *leg.*: "*líl*", for "*lil*". — *Ibid.*, l. 18 *leg.*: "*ṭab*", for "*tab*". — P. 111, l. 2 *leg.*: "unsparing", for "invincible". — *Ibid.*, l. 9 *leg.*: "13", for "12". — P. 114, l. 25 *leg.*: "K 2808", for "K 2801". — P. 115, l. 30 *leg.*: "besought", for "glorified". — P. 119, l. 13 *leg.*: "*înî*^{pl}*-yà*", for "*îni*^{pl}*-yà*". — *Ibid.*, l. 20 f. *leg.*: "*mîsiru*", for "*misiru*". — Pp. 139, l. 20; 157, l. 7 *leg.*: "38, 4", for "38, 3".

INDEXES.

I

INDEX TO TABLETS AND DUPLICATES.

Number	Page	Plate	Tablet	Duplicates
1	3	1	K 155	K 3332, cited as *A*; Sm. 1382; K 6019 (No. 5), ll. 11—17, cited as *B*; K 3432 + K 8147 (No. 33), ll. 19—38, cited as *C*.
2	16	4	K 2487 + K 2502 + K 2591	K 8122 (No. 3), ll. 10—16, cited as *A*; K 6477, cited as *B*; K 9706, cited as *C*; K 223, cited as *D*; K 11929, cited as *E*.
3	23	6	K 8122	K 2487 *etc.* (No. 2), ll. 11—20, cited as *A*.
4	24	7	K 8105	K 12938, cited as *A*; K 10729, cited as *B*.
5	29	9	K 6019	K 155 (No. 1), ll. 29—35, cited as *A*.
6	30	10	K 2106 + K 2384 + K 3393 + K 6340 + K 8605 + K 8983 + K 9576 + K 9688 + K 11589 + K 12911 + K 13792 + K 13800	K 3285, cited as *A*; K 3330 *etc.* (No. 7), ll. 9—32, cited as *B*; K 9087 (No. 37), ll. 7—13, cited as *C*; K 8815, cited as *D*; Rm. 96, cited as *E*; Sm. 336 + Sm. 1385, cited as *F*; K 5980 *etc.* (No. 10), ll. 7 ff.
7	37	15	K 3330 + Sm. 394 + 81—2—4, 244	K 2106 *etc.* (No. 6), ll. 71—94, cited as *A*; K 9087 (No. 37), ll. 7—13, cited as *C*; K 8815, cited as *D*; Rm. 96, cited as *E*

Number	Page	Plate	Tablet	Duplicates
8	41	18	K 2396 + K 3893	. . . .
9	44	19	K 2558 + K 9152	K 3429 + K 8657, cited as *A*; K 2538 *etc.*, Rev. Col. III, ll. 1—21 (*see* IV R, pl. 21*), cited as *B*; K 10243; K 10354.
10	48	21	K 5980 + K 8746	K 2106 *etc.* (No. 6), ll. 97 ff.
11	51	23	K 235 + K 3334	K 3283, cited as *A*; K 6537, cited as *C*.
12	54	26	K 163 + K 218	K 6733, cited as *A*; K 3151 *b*, cited as *B*; K 2379 + K 3289, cited as *C*; K 10807, cited as *D*; K 7984, cited as *E*.
13	67	32	K 3229	. . . .
14	69	34	K 2793	. . . .
15	69	34	K 2586 + K 7185	. . . .
16	70	35	K 11681	. . . .
17	72	35	K 5668	. . . .
18	72	36	K 8009	K 6804, cited as *A*; K 11326 + K 11975, cited as *B*.
19	74	38	K 34	. . . .
20	76	40	K 10406	. . . .
21	77	41	K 2741 + K 3180 + K 3208 + K 5043 + K 6588 + K 6612 + K 6672 + K 6908 + K 7047 + K 8498 + K 9157 + K 9770 + K 10219 + K 10497 + K 13431 + K 13793	. . . .
22	81	45	K 140 + K 3352 + K 8751 + K 10285	K 6334, cited as *A*; K 6853, cited as *B*; K 8982, cited as *C*.
23	85	48	K 13277	. . . .
24	86	48	K 12922	. . . .
25	86	48	K 13296	. . . .
26	87	48	K 10550	. . . .
27	87	49	K 2371 + K 13791	K 2836 + K 6593, cited as *A*; K 11549, cited as *B*; Sm. 398, cited as *C*; K 8953 + K 8987 *etc.*, cited as *D*.

Number	Page	Plate	Tablet	Duplicates
28	90	50	K 3355 [+ K 6639 + K 8953 + K 8987]	K 2371 *etc.* (No. 27); K 11153 *etc.* (No. 46).
29	92	50	K 13907	
30	92	51	K 3448	
31	94	53	K 7207 + K 9675 + K 13274	
32	95	53	K 3358 + K 9047	
33	96	54	K 3432 + K 8147	K 155 (No. 1), ll. 36—52, cited as *A.*
34	100	56	K 11876	
35	100	56	K 2757	
36	102	57	K 9125	
37	103	57	K 9087	K 2106 *etc.* (No. 6), ll. 71—77. cited as *A*; K 3330 *etc.* (No. 7), ll. 9—15, cited as *B*; K 8815, ll. 3—9, cited as *D*; Rm. 96, ll. 1—7, cited as *E.*
38	104	58	Bu. 91—5—9, 16	
39	104	58	K 8930	
40	105	59	K 2567	
41	106	59	K 7916	
42	106	60	K 3221	
43	107	60	K 13355	
44	107	60	K 14210	
45	108	60	82—3—23, 119	
46	109	61	K 11153 + Rm. 582	K 6639 *etc.*, cited as *A.*
47	111	62	K 8808	
48	112	62	K 8116	
49	113	63	D.T. 65	
50	113	64	K 2808 + K 9490	83—1—18, 500, cited as *A*; K 12937, cited as *B.*
51	116	66	K 8190	
52	117	66	K 6395 + K 10138	
53	119	67	K 3859 + Sm. 383	
54	121	69	Sm. 512	
55	121	69	K 6792	
56	122	69	K 2810	
57	122	70	K 9909	
58	123	70	K 6644	
59	124	71	K 7978	
60	125	72	K 3463	
61	126	73	K 8293	K 3342, cited as *A.*
62	127	74	K 7593	

II

INDEX TO REGISTRATION-NUMBERS.

N.B. The registration-number by which a tablet is cited is printed in black type; when two or more fragments have been "joined", the tablet so formed is cited by the lowest of their registration-numbers. References are placed within parentheses; + = "joined to"; dupl. = "duplicate of".

K 34 (No. 19); **K 140** (No. 22); **K 155** (No. 1); **K 163** (No. 12); K 218 (+ K 163); **K 223** (dupl. No. 2); **K 235** (No. 11); **K 2106** (No. 6); **K 2371** (No. 27); **K 2379** (dupl. No. 12); K 2384 (+ K 2106); **K 2396** (No. 8); **K 2487** (No. 2); K 2502 (+ K 2487); **K 2538** *etc.* (dupl. No. 9); **K 2558** (No. 9); **K 2567** (No. 40); **K 2586** (No. 15); K 2591 (+ K 2487); **K 2741** (No. 21); **K 2757** (No. 35); **K 2793** (No. 14); **K 2808** (No. 50); **K 2810** (No. 56); **K 2836** (dupl. No. 27); **K 3151 b** (dupl. No. 12); K 3180 (+ K 2741); K 3208 (+ K 2741); **K 3221** (No. 42); **K 3229** (No. 13); **K 3283** (dupl. No. 11); **K 3285** (dupl. No. 6); K 3289 (+ K 2379); **K 3330** (No. 7); **K 3332** (dupl. No. 1); K 3334 (+ K 235); **K 3342** (dupl. No. 61); K 3352 (+ K 140); **K 3355** (No. 28); **K 3358** (No. 32); K 3393 (+ K 2106); **K 3429** (dupl. No. 9); **K 3432** (No. 33); **K 3448** (No. 30); **K 3463** (No. 60); **K 3859** (No. 53); K 3893 (+ K 2396); K•5043 (+ K 2741); **K 5668** (No. 17); **K 5980** (No. 10); **K 6019** (No. 5); **K 6334** (dupl. No. 22); K 6340 (+ K 2106); **K 6395** (No. 52); **K 6477** (dupl. No. 2); **K 6537** (dupl. No. 11); K 6588 (+ K 2741); K 6593 (+ K 2836); K 6612 (+ K 2741); K 6639 (+ K 3355); **K 6644** (No. 58); K 6672 (+ K 2741); **K 6733** (dupl. No. 12); **K 6792** (No. 55); **K 6804** (dupl. No. 18); **K 6853** (dupl. No. 22); K 6908 (+ K 2741); K 7047 (+ K 2741); K 7185 (+ K 2586); **K 7207** (No. 31); **K 7593** (No. 62); **K 7916** (No. 41); **K 7978** (No. 59); **K 7984** (dupl. No. 12); **K 8009** (No. 18); **K 8105** (No. 4); **K 8116** (No. 48); **K 8122** (No. 3); K 8147 (+ K 3432); **K 8190** (No. 51); **K 8293** (No. 61); K 8498 (+ K 2741); K 8605 (+ K 2106); K 8657 (+ K 3429); K 8746 (+ K 5980); K 8751 (+ K 140); **K 8808** (No. 47); **K 8815** (dupl. Nos. 6, 7, 37); **K 8930** (No. 39); K 8953 (+ K 3355); **K 8982** (dupl. No. 22); K 8983 (+ K 2106); K 8987 (+ K 3355); K 9047 (+ K 3358); **K 9087** (No. 37); **K 9125** (No. 36);

K 9152 (+ K 2558); K 9157 (+ K 2741); K 9490 (+ K 2808); **K 9576** (+ K 2106); K 9675 (+ K 7207); K 9688 (+ K 2106); K 9706 (+ K 6477); K 9770 (+ K 2741); **K 9909** (No. 57); K 10138 (+ K 6395); K 10219 (+ K 2741); **K 10243** (dupl. No. 9); K 10285 (+ K 140); **K 10354** (dupl. No. 9); **K 10406** (No. 20); K 10497 (+ K 2741); **K 10550** (No. 26); **K 10729** (dupl. No. 4); **K 10807** (dupl. No. 12); **K 11153** (No. 46); **K 11326** (dupl. No. 18); **K 11549** (dupl. No. 27); K 11589 (+ K 2106); **K 11681** (No. 16); **K 11876** (No. 34); **K 11929** (dupl. No. 2); K 11975 (+ K 11326); K 12911 (+ K 2106); **K 12922** (No. 24); **K 12937** (dupl. No. 50); **K 12938** (dupl. No. 4); K 13274 (+ K 7207); **K 13277** (No. 23); **K 13296** (No. 25); **K 13355** (No. 43); K 13431 (+ K 2741); K 13791 (+ K 2371); K 13792 (+ K 2106); K 13793 (+ K 2741); K 13800 (+ K 2106); **K 13907** (No. 29); **K 14210** (No. 44); **Sm. 336** (dupl. No. 6); Sm. 383 (+ K 3859); Sm. 394 (+ K 3330); **Sm. 398** (dupl. No. 27); **Sm. 512** (No. 54); **Sm. 1382** (dupl. No. 1); Sm. 1385 (+ Sm. 336); **D.T. 65** (No. 49); **Rm. 96** (dupl. Nos. 6, 7, 37); Rm. 582 (+ K 11153); 81—2-4, 244 (+ K 3330); **82—3—23, 119** (No. 45); **83—1—18, 500** (dupl. No. 50); **Bu 91—5—9, 16** (No. 38).

Bavarian Academy Press: F. Straub, Munich.

CUNEIFORM TEXTS.

N.B. The numbers which precede the foot-notes refer to the corresponding numbers in the text; when a note refers to one sign only, the number is placed to the right of the sign in the text (*e. g.* . . . . . [1]); when a variant reading is given of more than one sign, the number of the note is placed on each side of the signs referred to (*e. g.* [1]. . . . . [1]); when a note refers to a whole line of the text, the number of the note is placed at the beginning of that line. Duplicates of a text are cited by the capitals *A*, *B*, *C etc.* Restorations are placed within brackets [ ]; dupl. = "duplicate"; l. = "line"; r. = "restored from".

No. 1. OBVERSE.

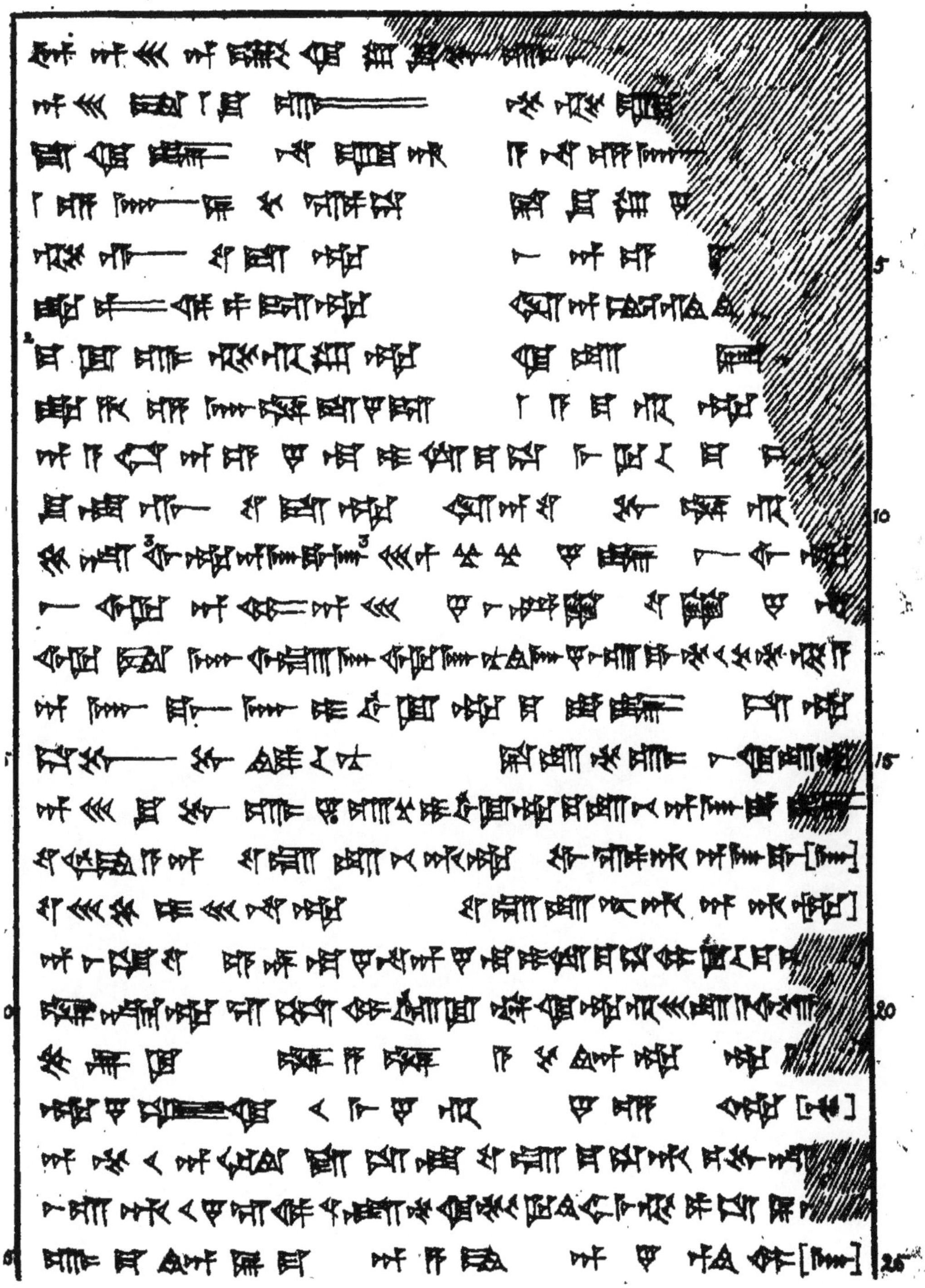

K3332, which I cite as A, is dupl. of ll. 1–10; S 1382 is dupl. of ll. 4–7; K 6019 ll. 11–17, cited as B, is dupl. of ll. 29–35; K 3432 + K 8147 ll. 19–38, cited as C, is dupl. of ll. 36–82.
2. ll. 7 and 8 form one line in A. 3. Written over an erasure.

NO. 1. OBV. (CONT.)

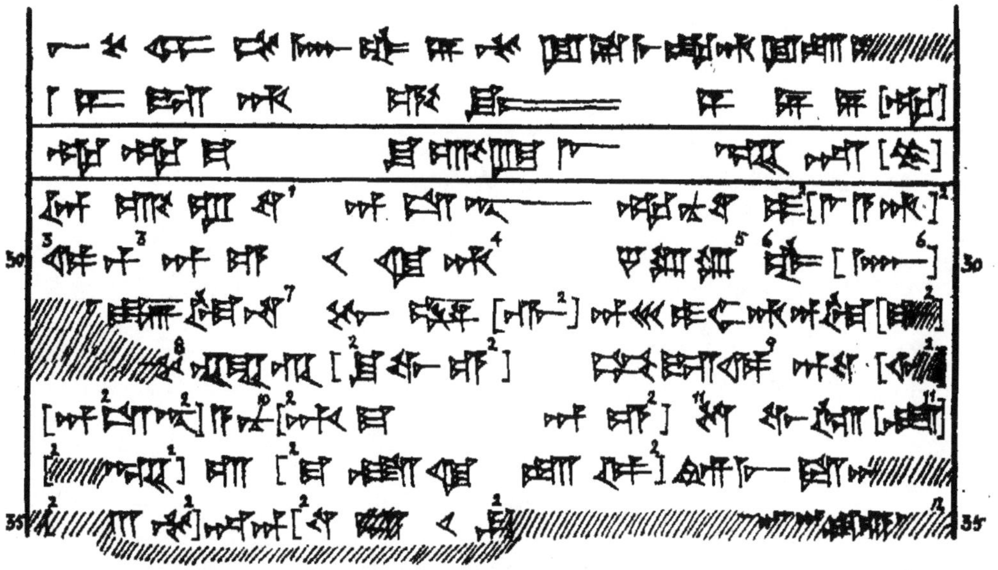

NO. 1. REVERSE.

1. B [cuneiform]. 2. r. B. 3. B [cuneiform]. 4. B [cuneiform]. 5. B [cuneiform]. 6. B [cuneiform]. 7. B [cuneiform]. 8. B [cuneiform]. 9. B [cuneiform]. 10. B [cuneiform]. 11. B [cuneiform]. 12. L. 35 possibly contains ll. 17 and 18 of B. 13. r. C. 14. C [cuneiform]. 15. Ll. 39 and 40 are omitted by C. 16. For l. 41 C reads:- [cuneiform]. 17. Ll. 42, 43 and 45 each form two lines in C. 18. Omitted by C.

NO. 1. REV. (CONT.)

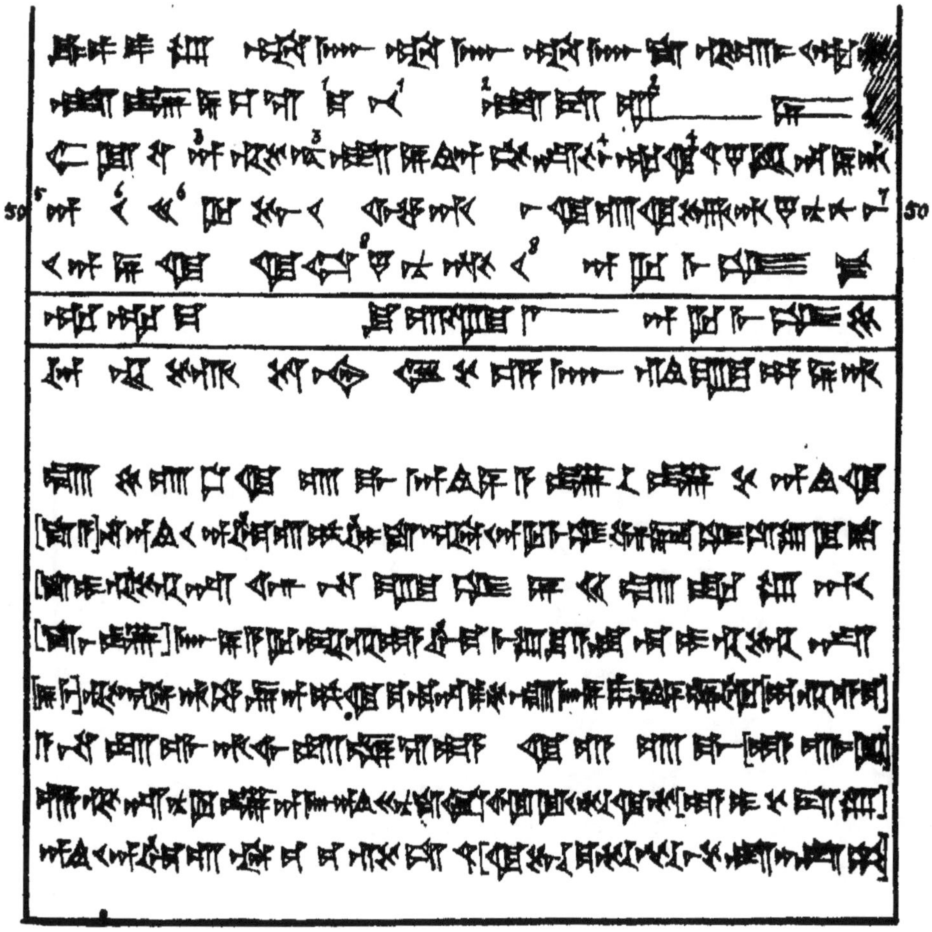

[cuneiform text]

1. C [cuneiform]. 2. C [cuneiform]. 3. C [cuneiform]. 4. For [cuneiform] C apparently substitutes [cuneiform]. 5. ll. 50 and 51 form three lines in C. 6. C [cuneiform]. 7. C [cuneiform]. 8. Apparently omitted by C.

NO. 2. REVERSE.

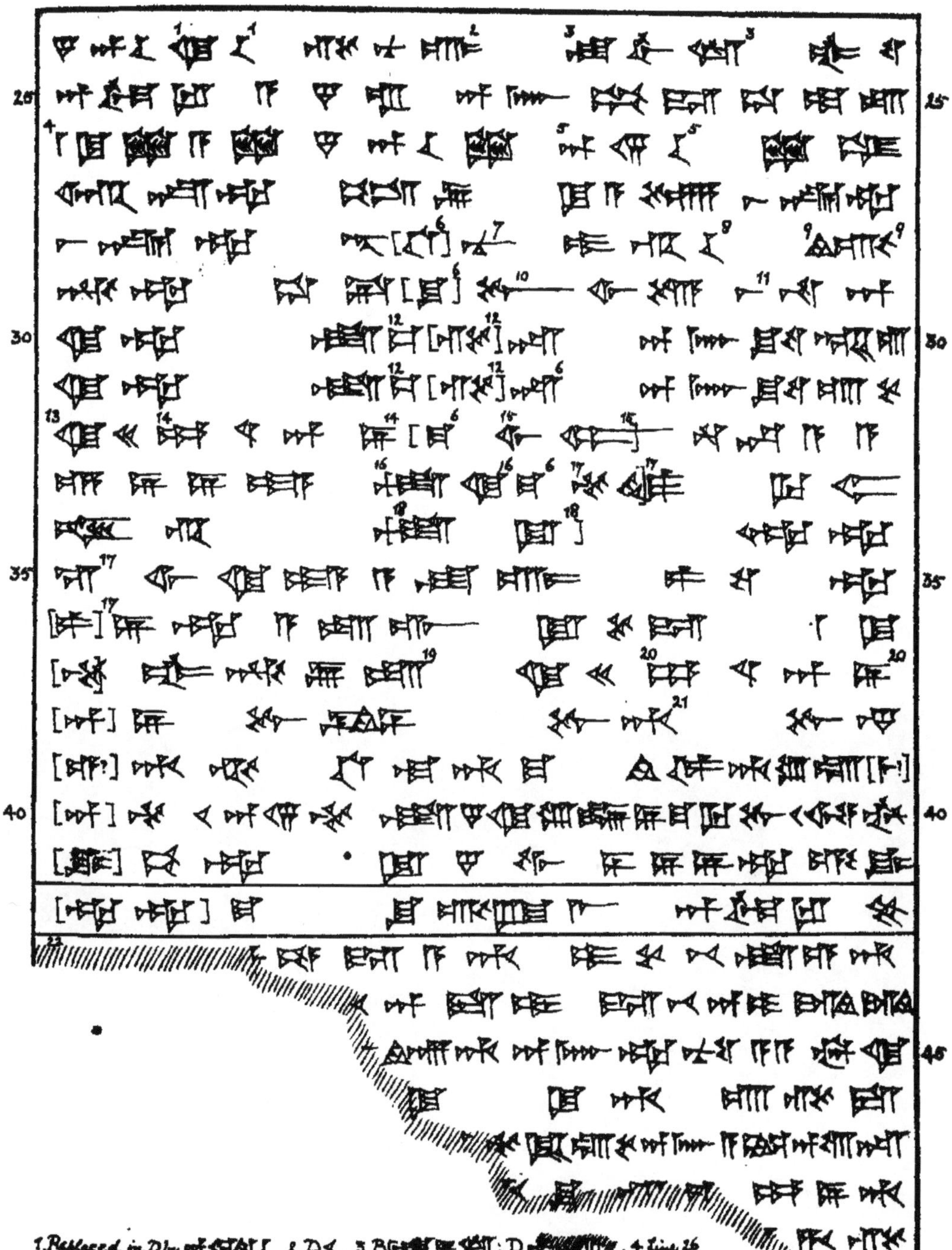

1. Replaced in D by … 2. D … 3. B … ; D … 4. Line 26 forms two lines in D, which read :— … 5. C … 6. v. C D. 7. C D … 8. C D … 9. D … 10. v. C ; D … (possibly for …). 11. D … 12. v. C ; D … 13. D here inserts the formula … etc. in three lines. 14. D … 15. v. D ; E … 16. v. C ; D … 17. v. D. 18. v. D E. 19. D … 20. D … 21. D E … 22. after l. 42 E ceases to be a duplicate and reads :— l. 10, … , and l. 11, … .

NO. 3

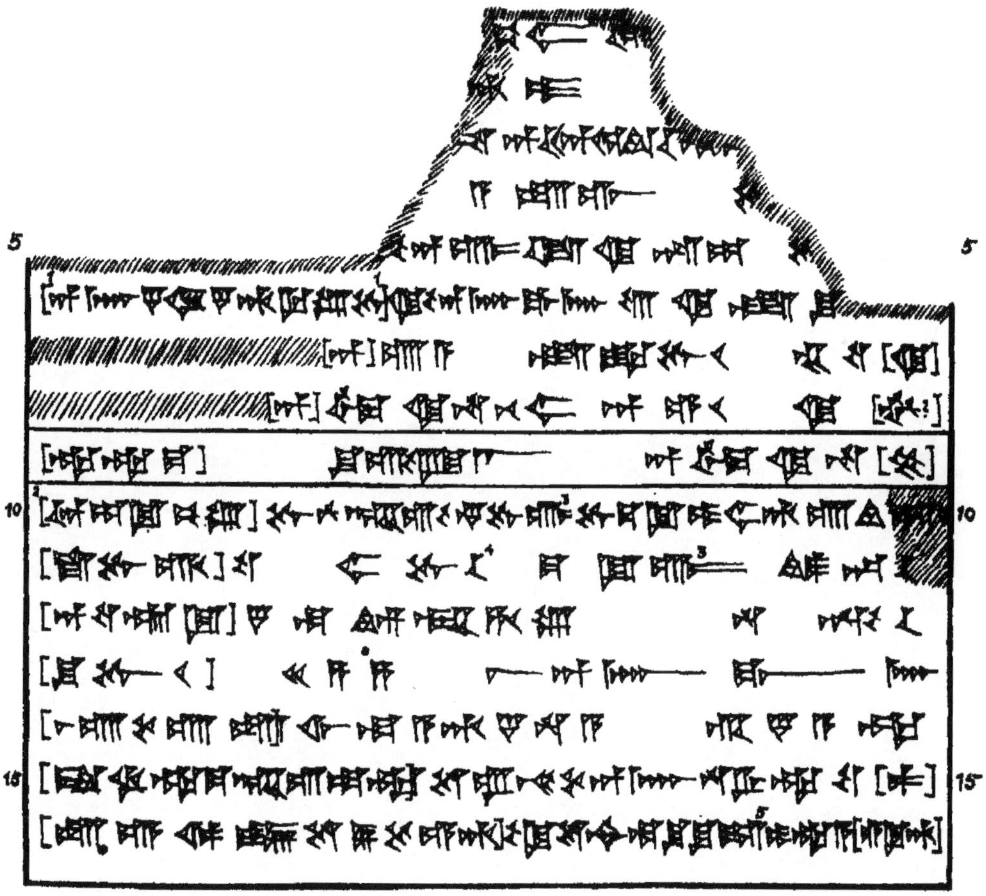

1. v. K 2396 + K 3893, l. 19. 2. Ll. 10–16 have been restored from K 2487 etc. ll. 11–20, which I cite as A; ll. 10, 15 and 16 each form two lines in A. 3. A 𒌋. 4. A [sign]. 5. A [sign].

NO. 4. OBVERSE.

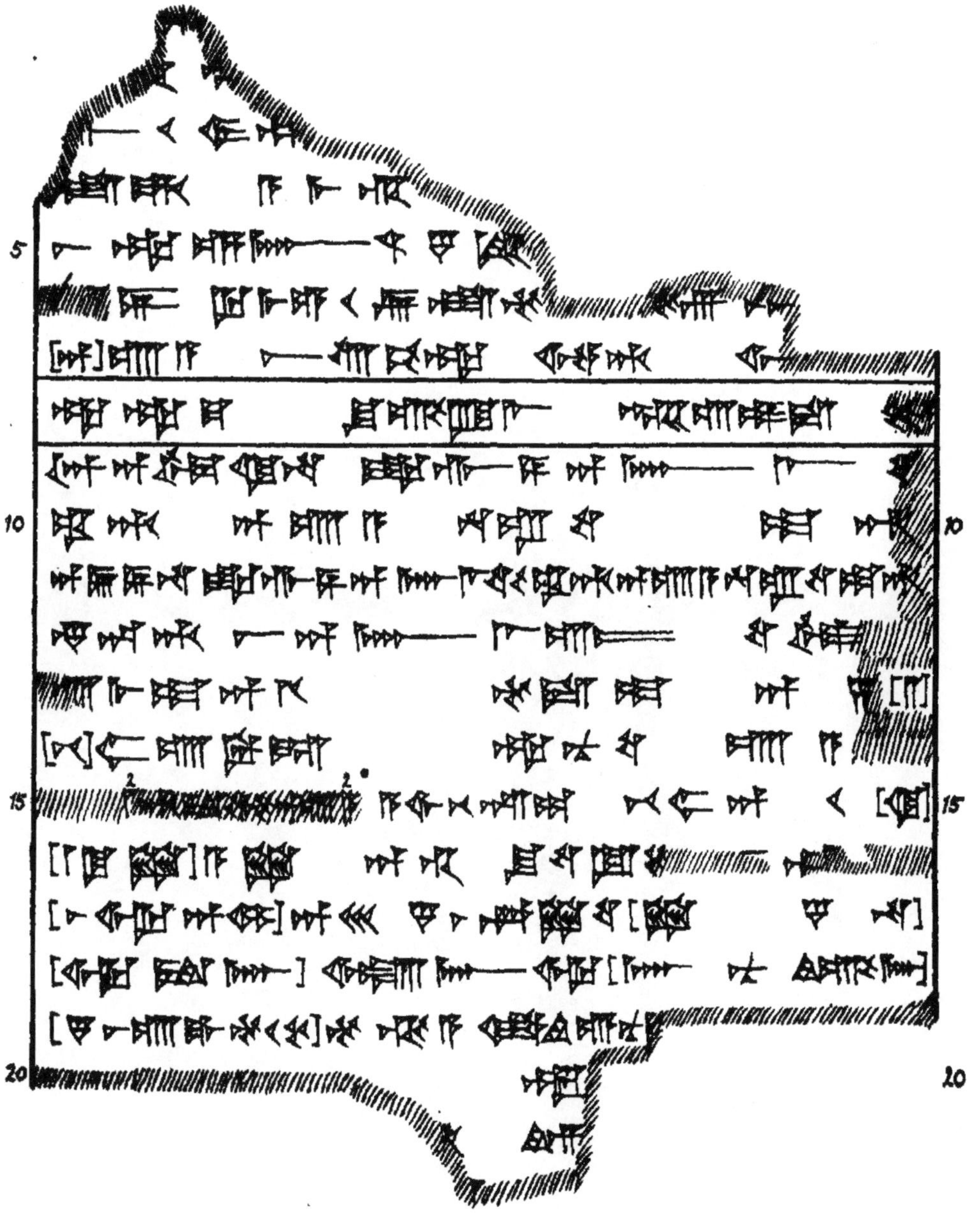

K12938, which I cite as A, is dupl. of ll. 24–29; K 10729, cited as B is dupl. of ll. 32-48.
2. Written over an erasure.

NO. 4. REVERSE.

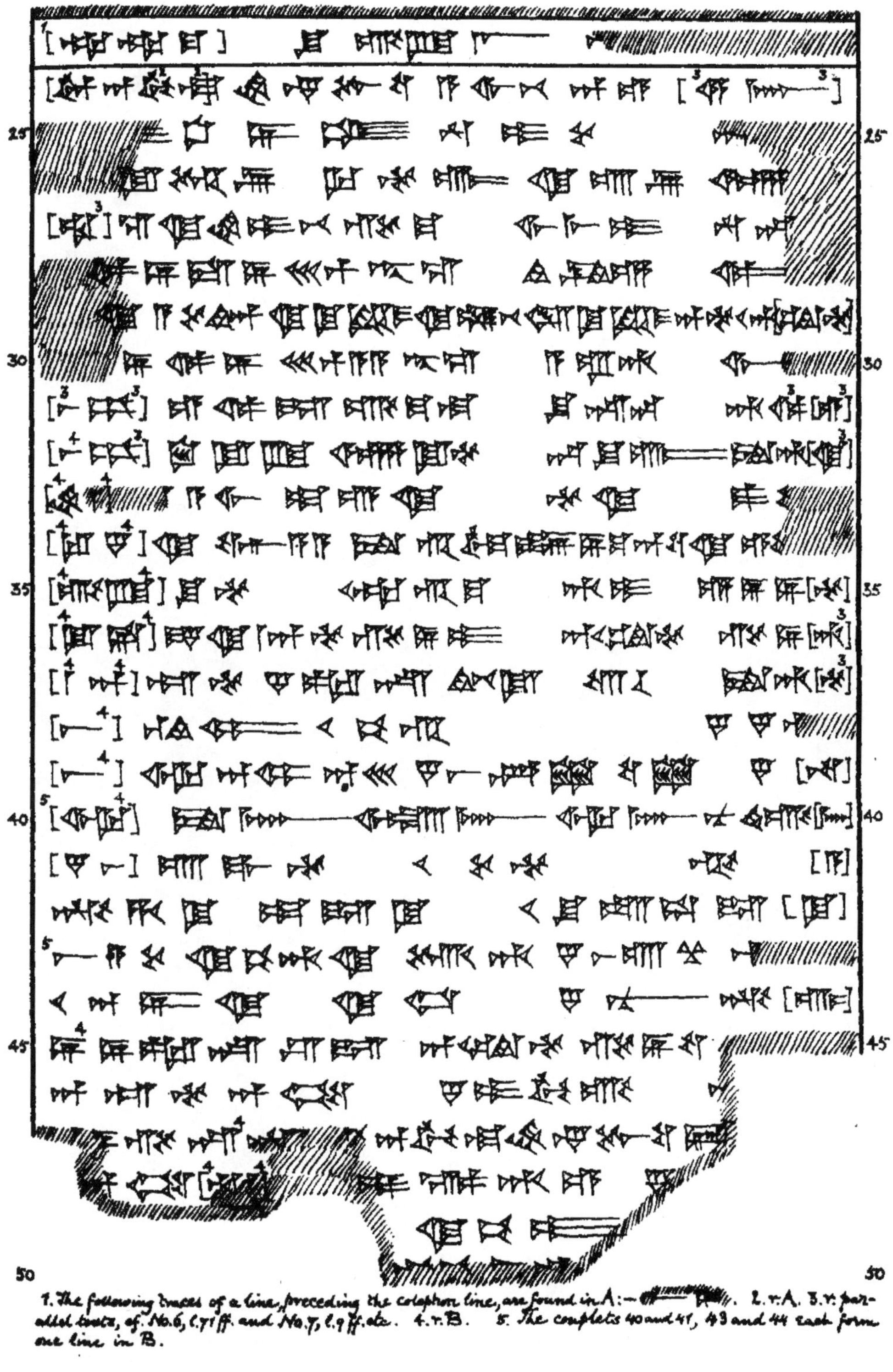

1. The following traces of a line, preceding the colophon line, are found in A:— . 2. v. A. 3. v. parallel texts, cf. No. 6, l. 71 ff. and No. 7, l. 9 ff. etc. 4. v. B. 5. The couplets 40 and 41, 43 and 44 each form one line in B.

NO. 5.

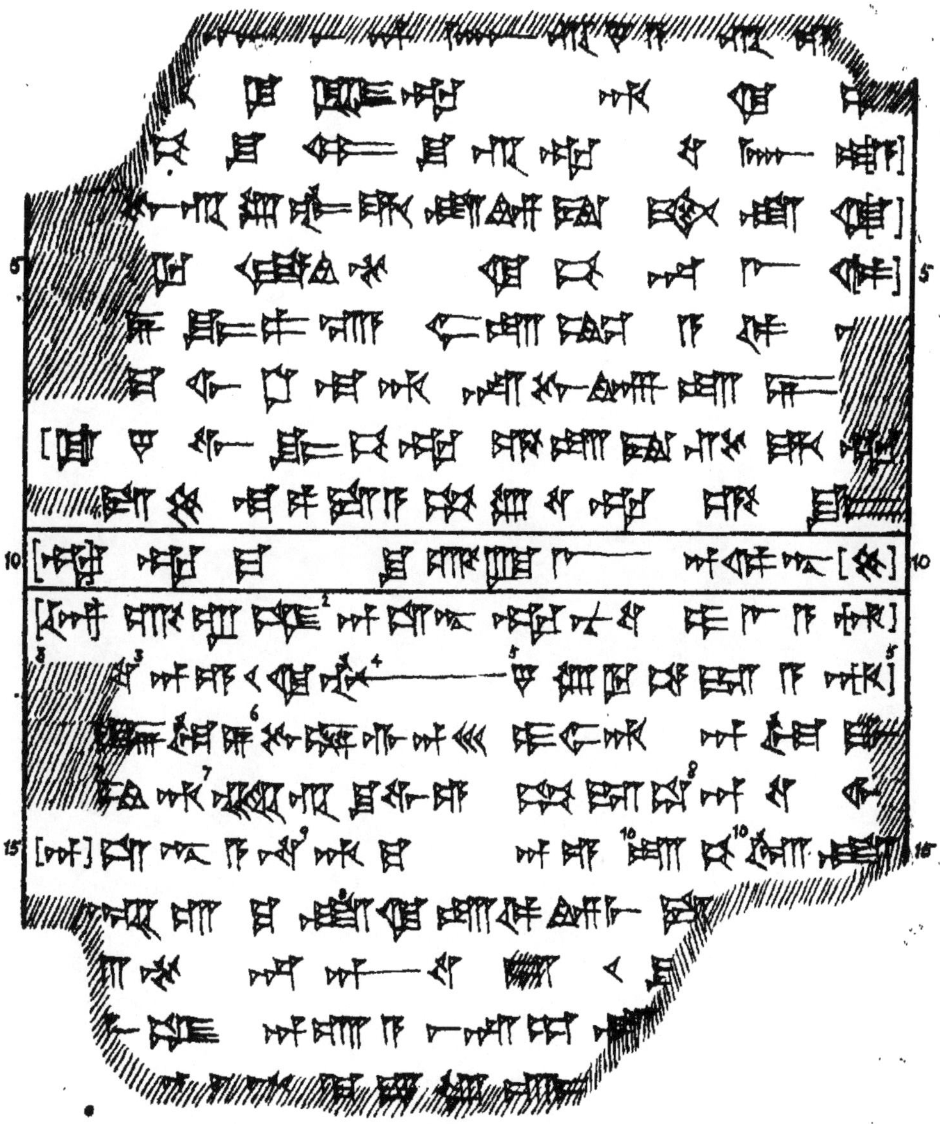

K 155, ll. 29–35, which I cite as A, is dupl. of ll. 11–17. 2. A [cuneiform]. 3. A [cuneiform]. 4. A [cuneiform]. 5. A [cuneiform] [cuneiform] [cuneiform] [[cuneiform]]. 6. A [cuneiform]. 7. A [cuneiform]. 8. A [cuneiform]. 9. A [cuneiform]. 10. A [cuneiform].

NO. 6. OBVERSE.

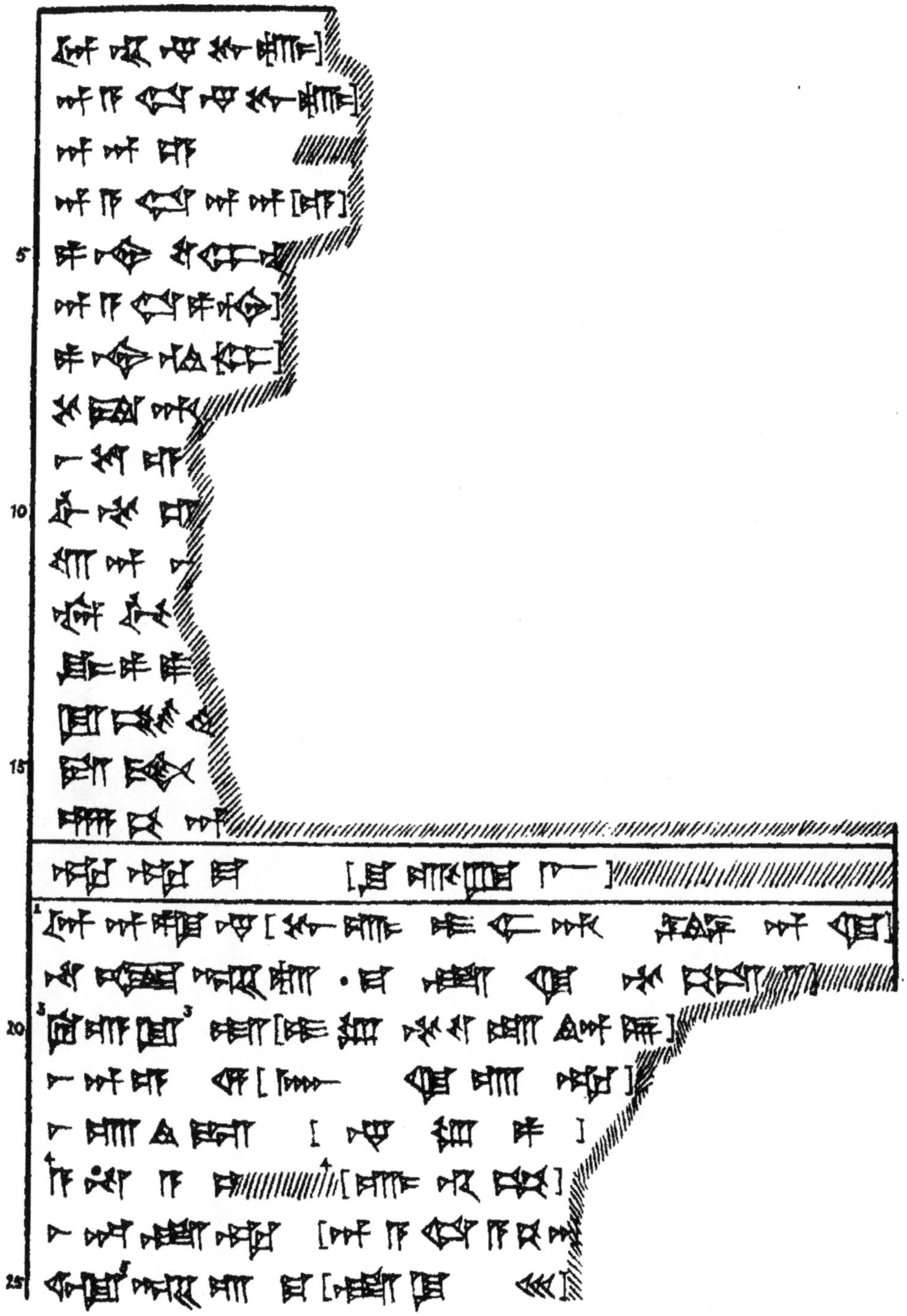

K 3285, which I cite as A, is dupl. of ll. 18–30; K 3330 etc. ll. 9–32, cited as B, is partly dupl. of ll. 71–93; K 9087, ll. 7–13, cited as C, is partly dupl. of 71–77; K 8818, ll. 3–21, cited as D, is partly dupl. of ll. 71–88; Rm 96, ll. 1–16, cited as E, is partly dupl. of ll. 71–81 (E Rev. contains 5 ll. of the common colophon); S 336 + S 1385, cited as F, is dupl of ll. 106–120. 2. The bracketed portions of ll. 18–25 have been restored from A. 3. A [illegible]. 4. A [illegible]. 5. Omitted by A.

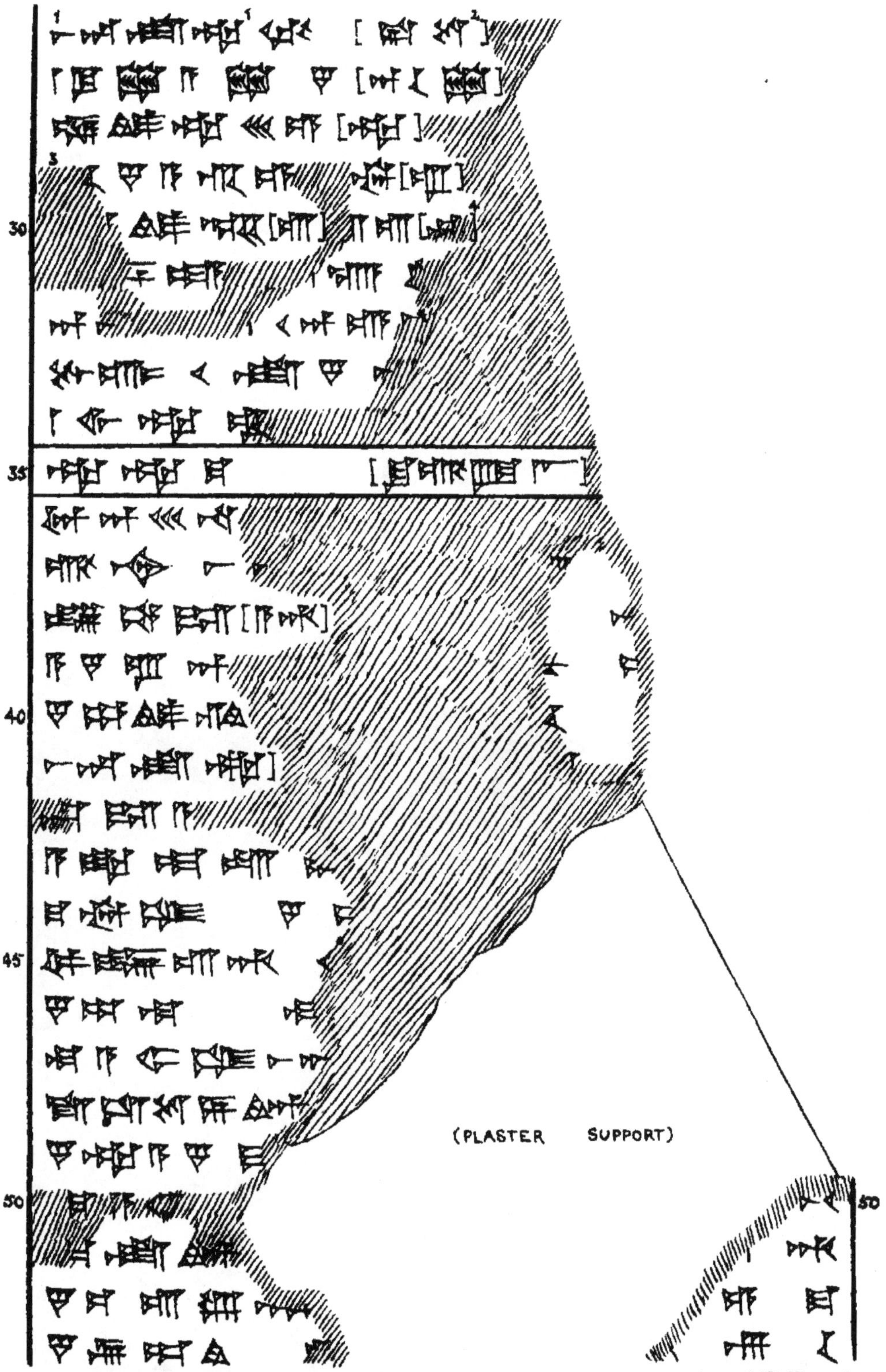

1. A … 2. The bracketed portions of ll. 26–29 have been restored from A. 3. A … 4. r. A.

NO. 6. OBV. (CONT.)

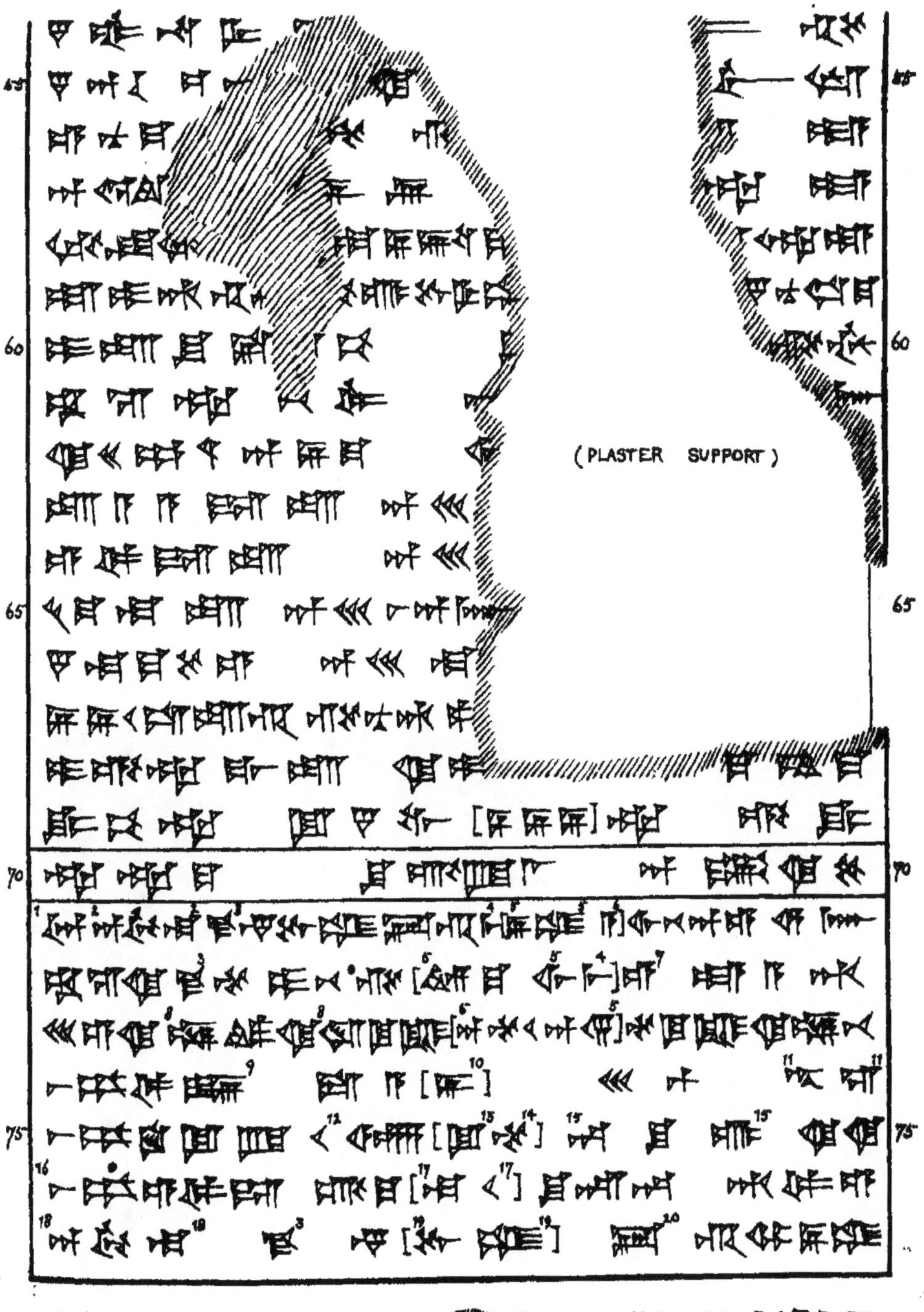

1. Before l. 71 D is not a duplicate but reads:— l. 1, , and l. 2, . 2. BE . 3. BE . 4. CE . 5. r. CE. 6 r. C. 7. CE . 8. B . 9. B . 10. r. BCE. 11. D . 12. Omitted by B. 13. r. BCDE. 14. r. CDE. 15. CE . 16. For l. 76 B (r. EC) reads:— [ ]. 17. r. D. 18. B . 19. r. l. 71; BDE . 20. D .

NO. 6. REVERSE.

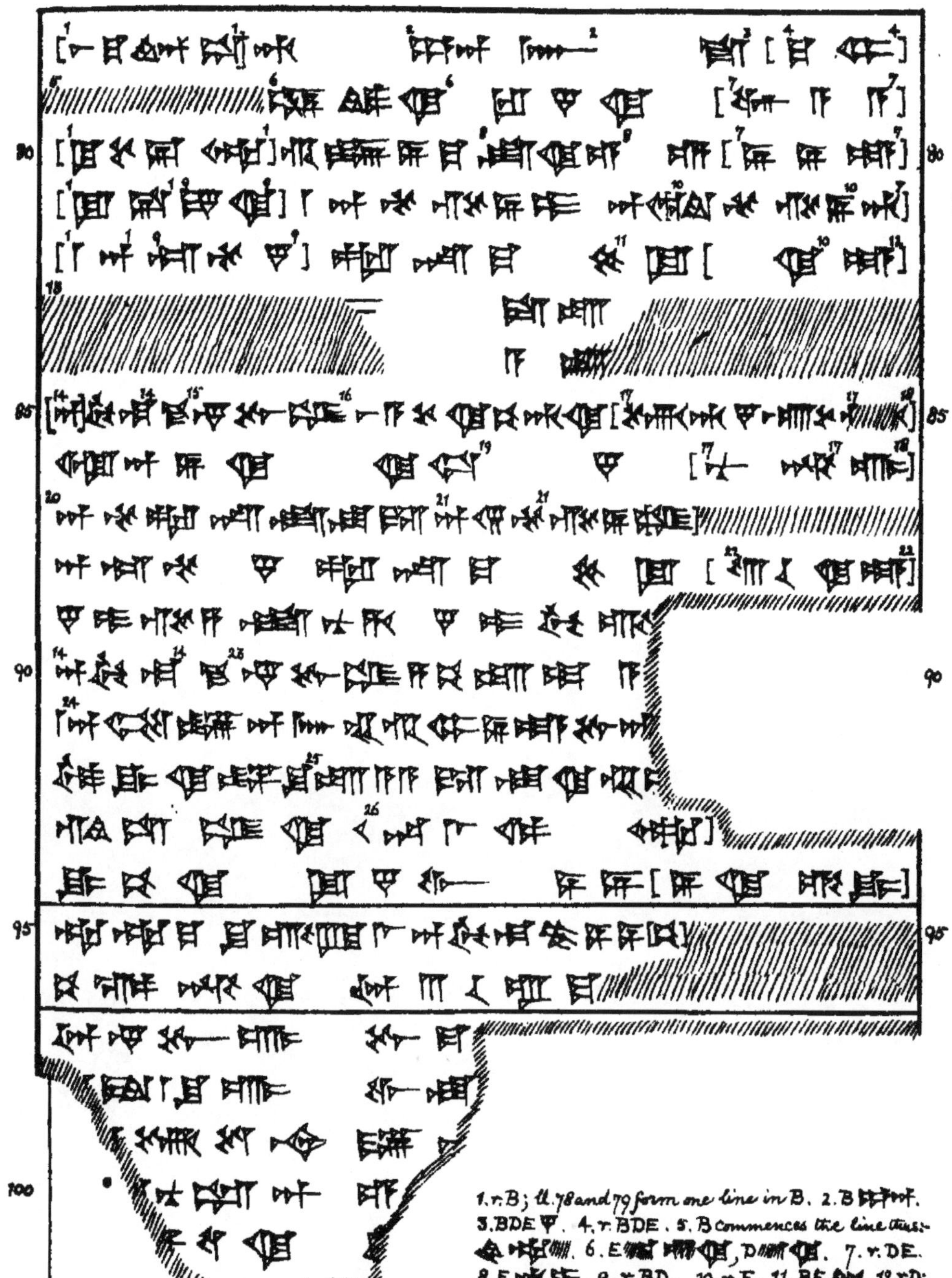

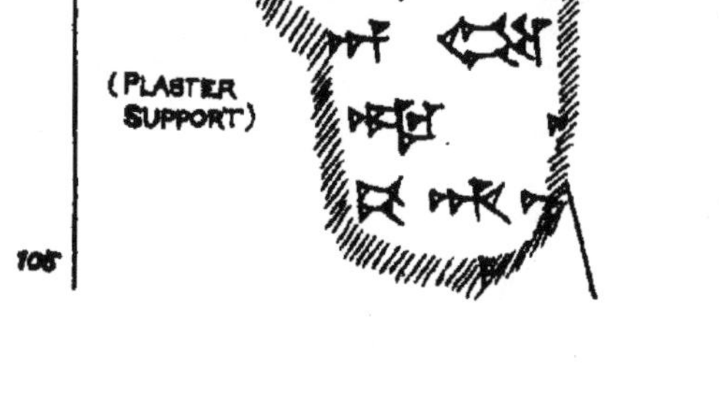

1. r. B; ll. 78 and 79 form one line in B. 2. B . 3. BDE . 4. r. BDE. 5. B commences the line thus:— . 6. E , D . 7. r. DE. 8. E . 9. r. BD. 10. r. E. 11. BE . 12. r. D; E . 13. For ll. 83 and 84 D (r. E) reads:— . Before l. 85 B inserts the formula:— etc. and is supported by E. 14. B . 15 B D . 16 D . 17. r. the parallel text No. 4, ll. 43 and 44. 18. r. D. 19. D . 20. l. 87 forms two lines in D. 21. D . 22. r. No. 4, l. 38. 23 B . 24. B . 25. B . 26. B .

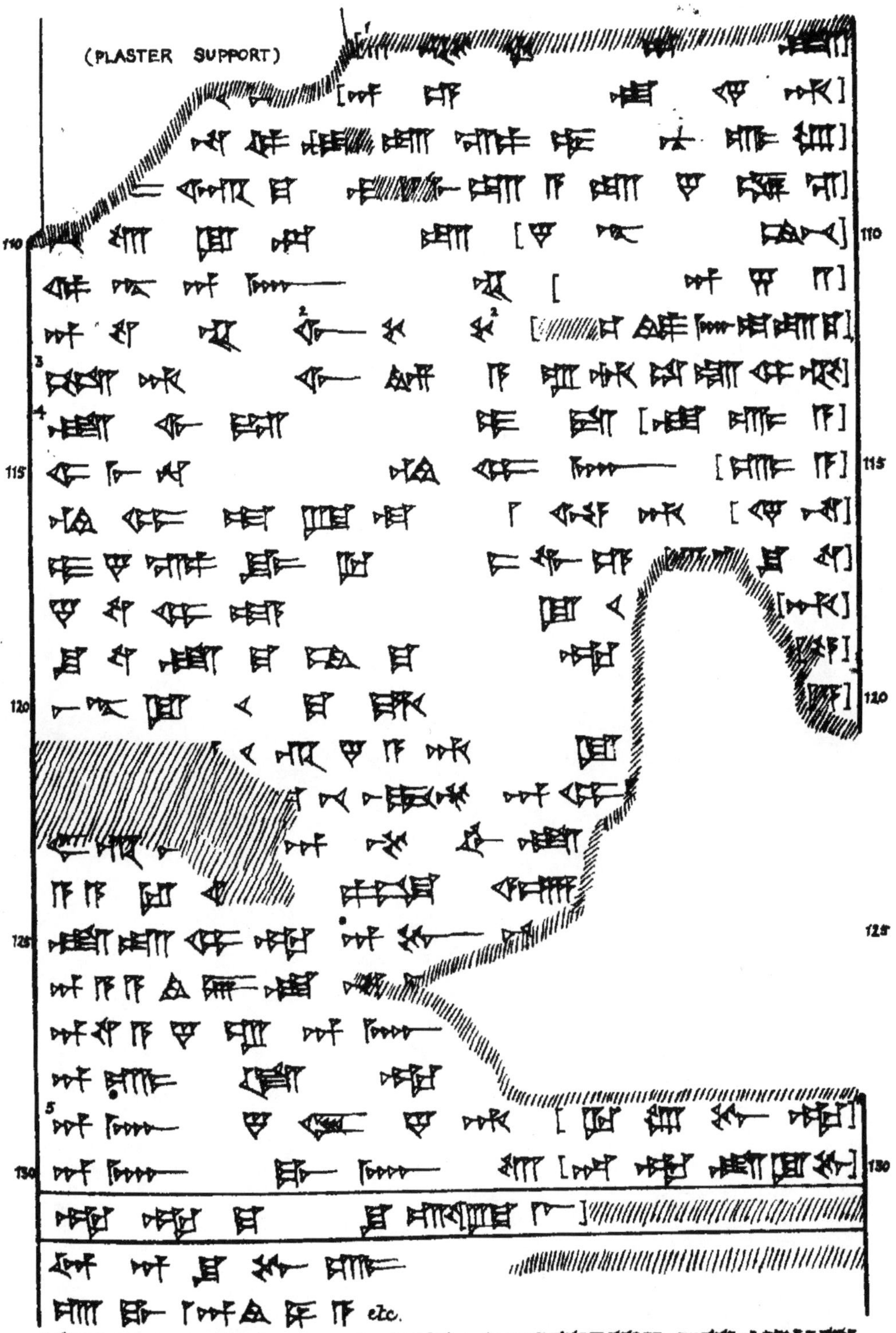

1. Ll. 106–120 v. F. 2. F . 3. After l. 112 F inserts [, which is followed by the formula etc. in three lines. 4. Ll. 114 and 115 form one line in F. 5. Ll. 129–130 v. No. 8, l. 19.

NO. 7. OBVERSE.

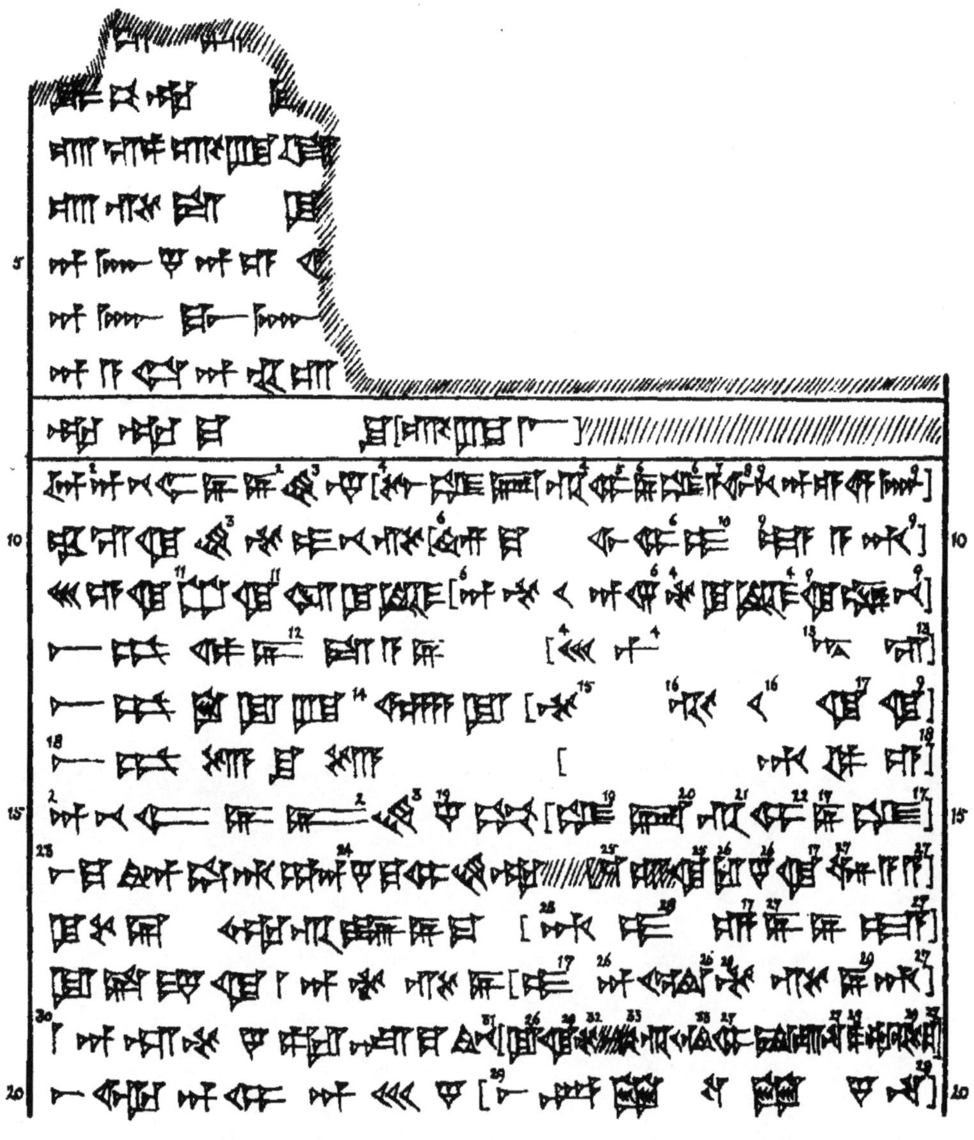

K 2106 etc., ll. 71–93, which I cite as A, is partly dupl. of ll. 9–32; K 9087, ll. 7–13, cited as C, is partly dupl. of ll. 9–15; K 8815, ll. 3–21, cited as D, is partly dupl. of ll. 9–27; Rm. 96, ll. 1–16, cited as E, is partly of ll. 9–21. 2. A . 3 A . 4. r. ACE. 5. r. EC; A . 6. r. CE. 7. r. C. 8. r. A. 9. r. AD. 10. r. CE; A . 11. A . 12. A . 13. r. AE; D . 14. A here inserts . 15. r. CDE. 16. r. CE; AD . 17. r. ADE. 18. r. CE; A (r. D) reads:– . 19. r. CDE; A . 20. r. ACE; D . 21. r. ACDE. 22. r. AE; D . 23. Line 16 forms two lines in ADE. 24. AE . 25. r. E; A . 26. r. AE. 27. r. DE. 28. r. E; AD 29. r. E. 30. Line 19 as far as forms one line in ADE; A omits the latter half of l. 19 and ll. 20–22, reading in their place:– l. 83: , and l. 84: ; D omits ll. 20–22; before l. 20 E inserts . 31. A . 32. r. E; D . 33. r. D.

NO. 7. OBV. (CONT.)

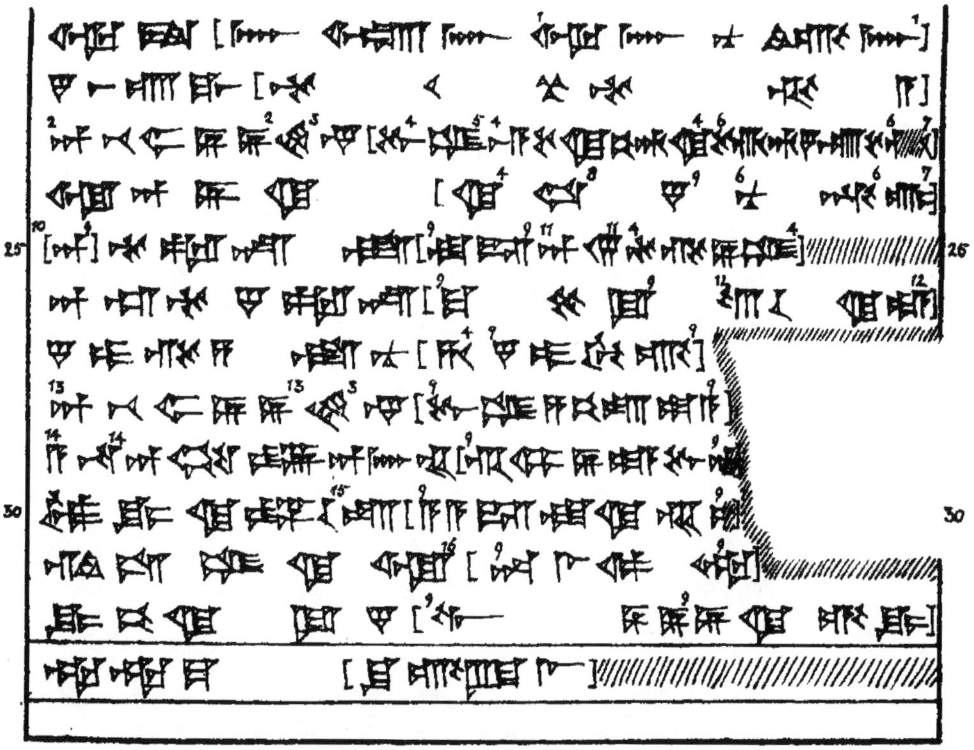

NO. 7. REVERSE.

1. r. E. 2. A D [illegible]. 3. A [illegible]. 4. r. A D. 5. r. A; D [illegible]. 6. r. parallel text No. 4, ll. 44 and 45. 7. r. D. 8. r. A; D [illegible]. 9. r. A. 10. Line 25 forms two lines in D. 11. r. A; D [illegible]. 12. r. No. 4, l. 38. 13. A [illegible]. 14. A [illegible]. 15. A [illegible]. 16. A [illegible].

No. 7. Rev. (cont.)

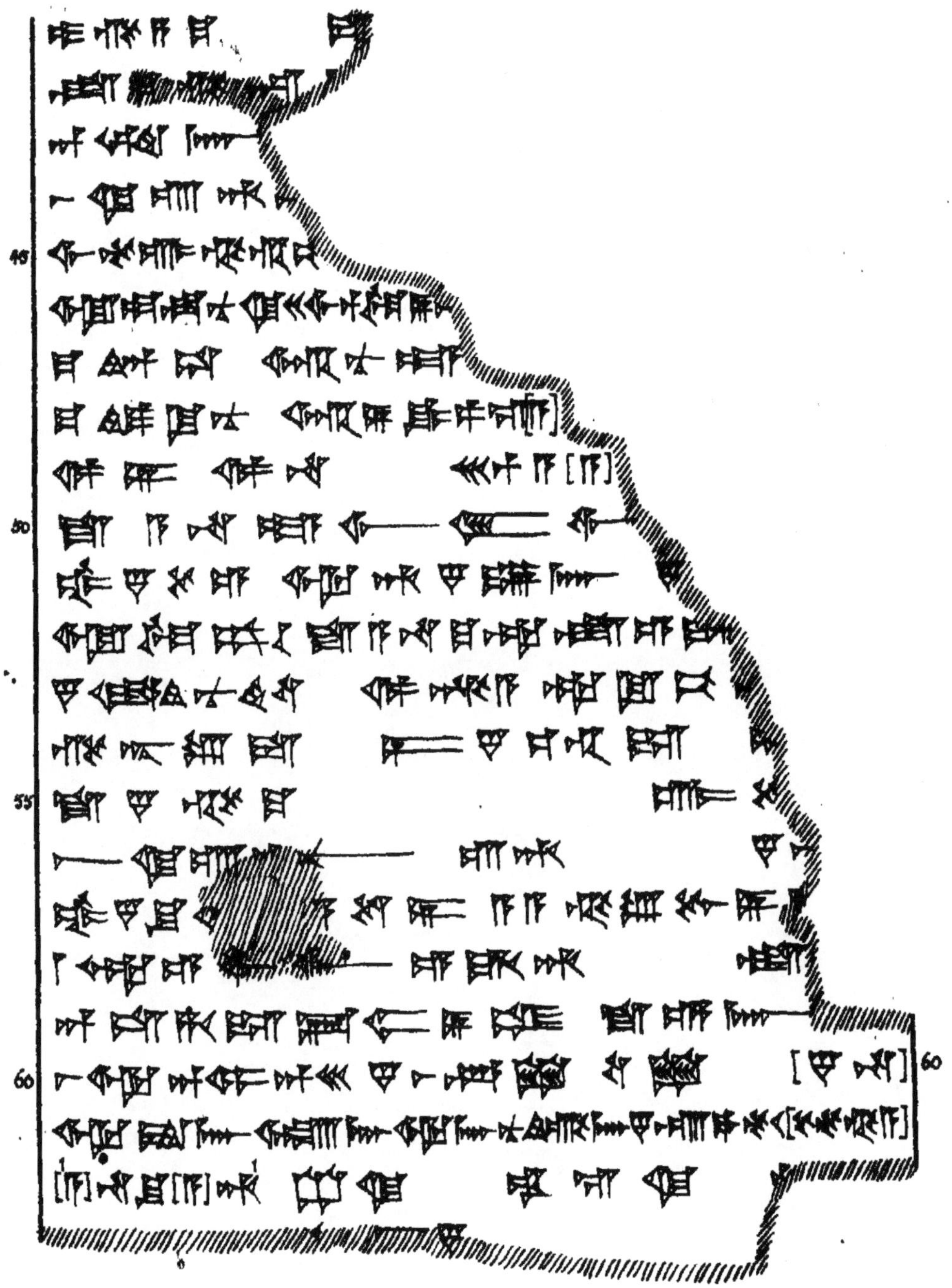

l. r. K9909, l. 7.

NO. 8.

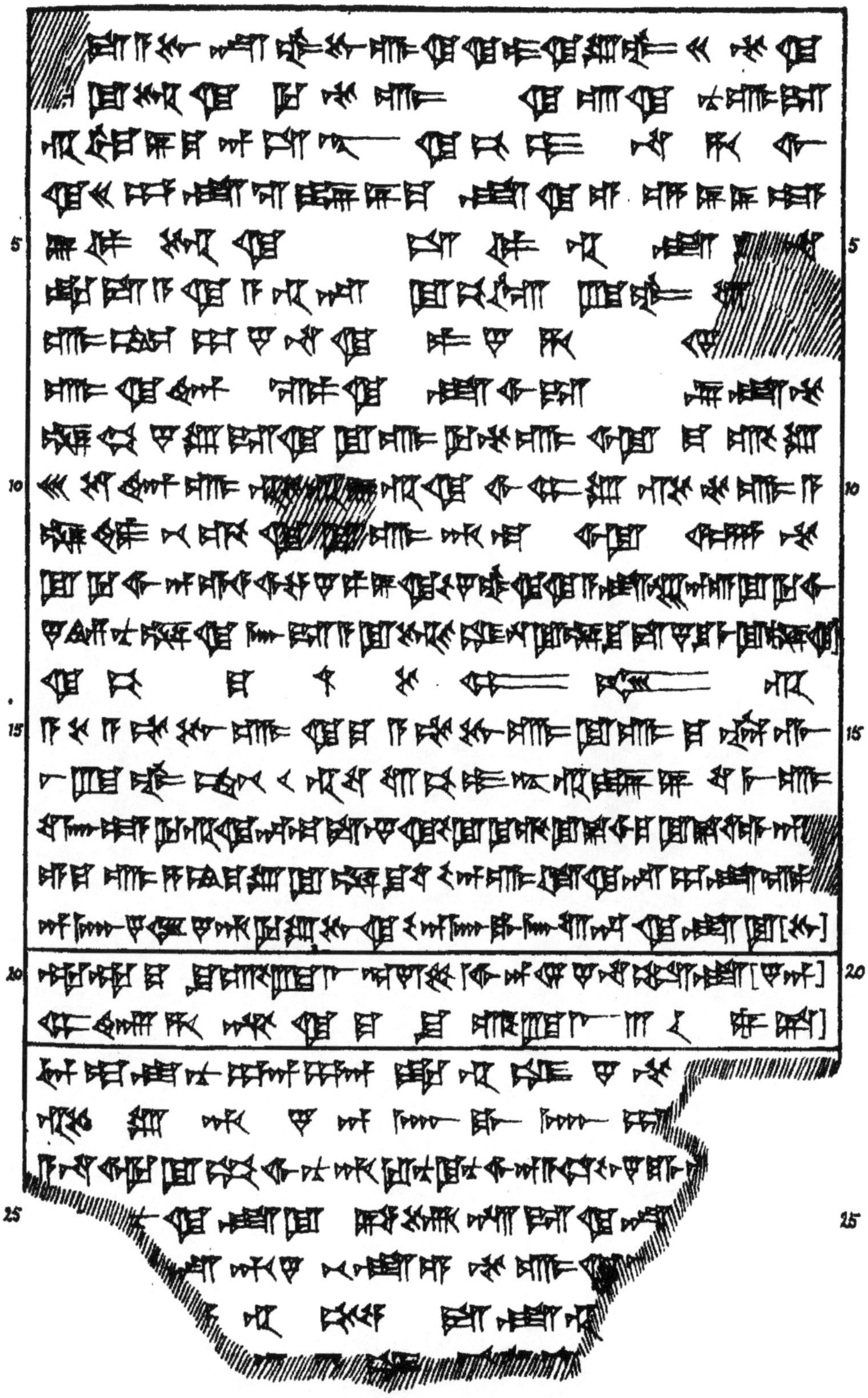

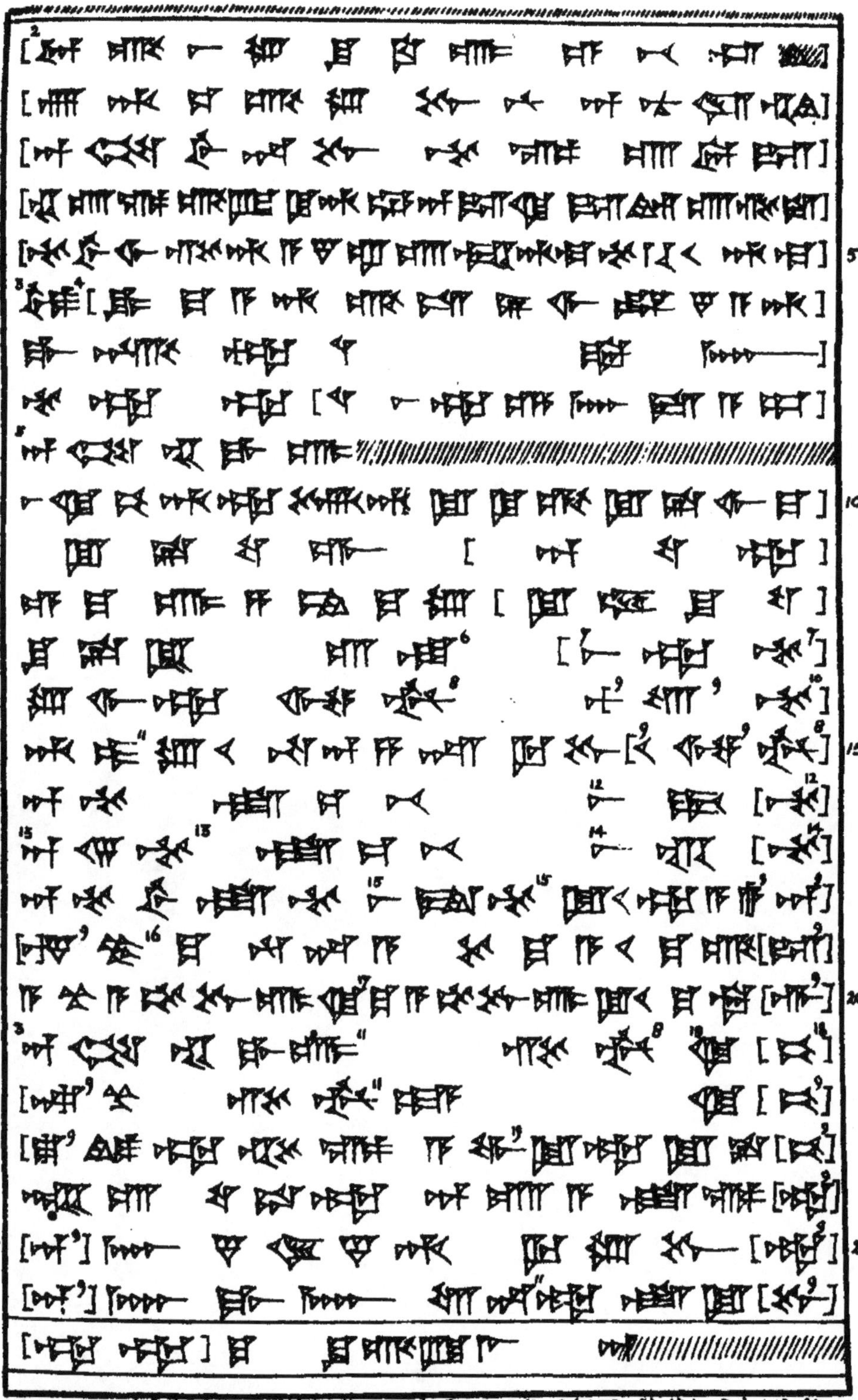

K 3429 + K 3657, wh. I cite as A, is dupl. of ll. 28 ff.; K 2588 etc., Rev., Col. I, ll. 1–21 (cf. IV R, 21*), cited as B, is dupl. of ll. 1–26. 2. ll. 1–12 r. B. 3. In complete copy, 21 + 22 each form one line in B. 4. r. [illegible]; B [illegible]. 5. ll. 9–15 form 4 lines in B, the first line reading: — [illegible]. 6. B [illegible]. 7. B [illegible]. 8. B om. 9. r. B. 10. B [illegible]. 11. Omitted by B. 12. B [illegible]. 13. B [illegible]. 14. B [illegible]. 15. B [illegible]. 16. B [illegible]. 17. B [illegible]. 18. B [illegible]. 19. B [illegible].

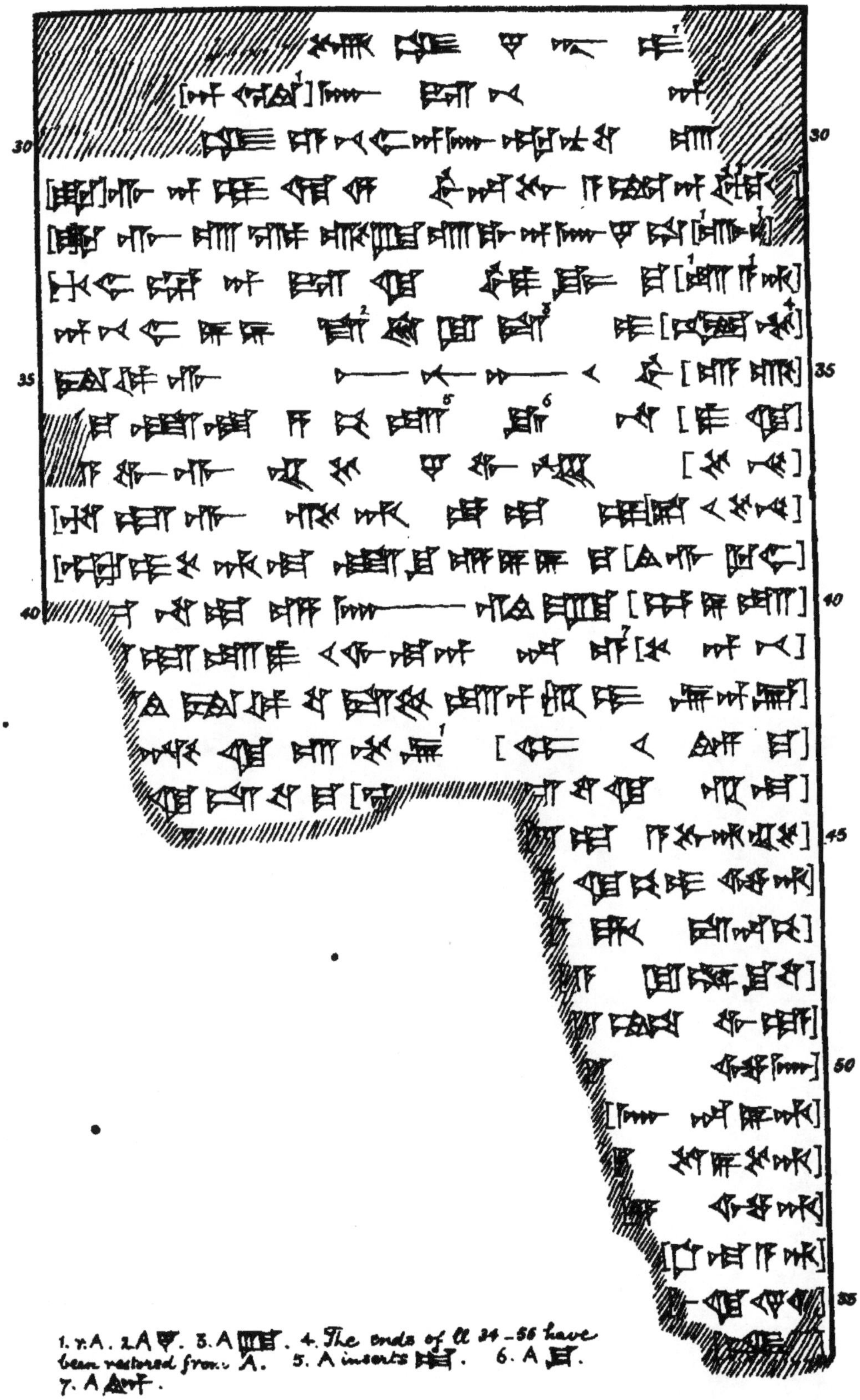

1. v. A. 2. A [sign]. 3. A [sign]. 4. The ends of ll. 34–56 have been restored from A. 5. A inserts [sign]. 6. A [sign]. 7. A [sign].

NO. 10. OBVERSE.

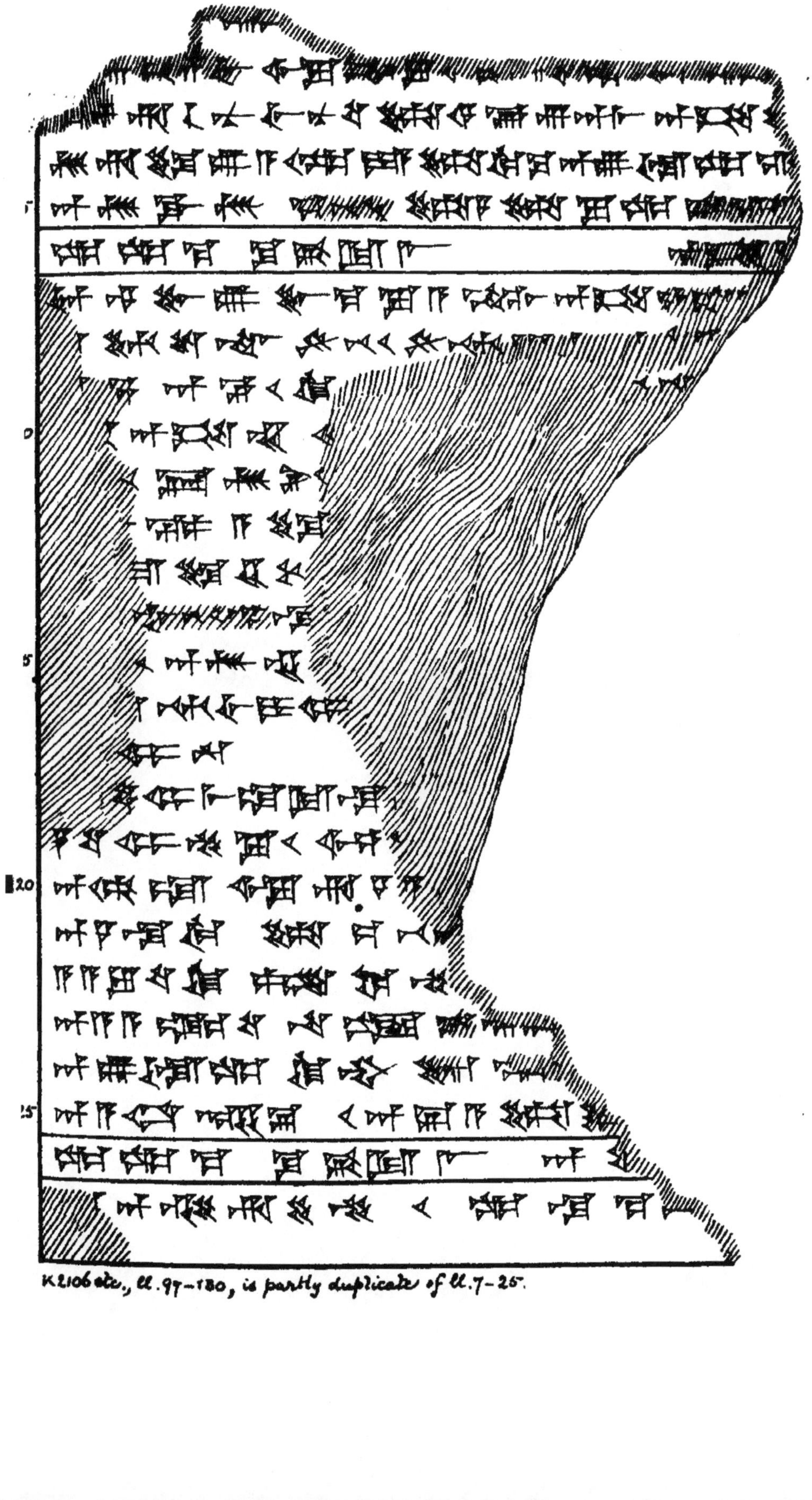

K2106 etc., ll. 97–180, is partly duplicate of ll. 7–25.

NO. 10. REVERSE.

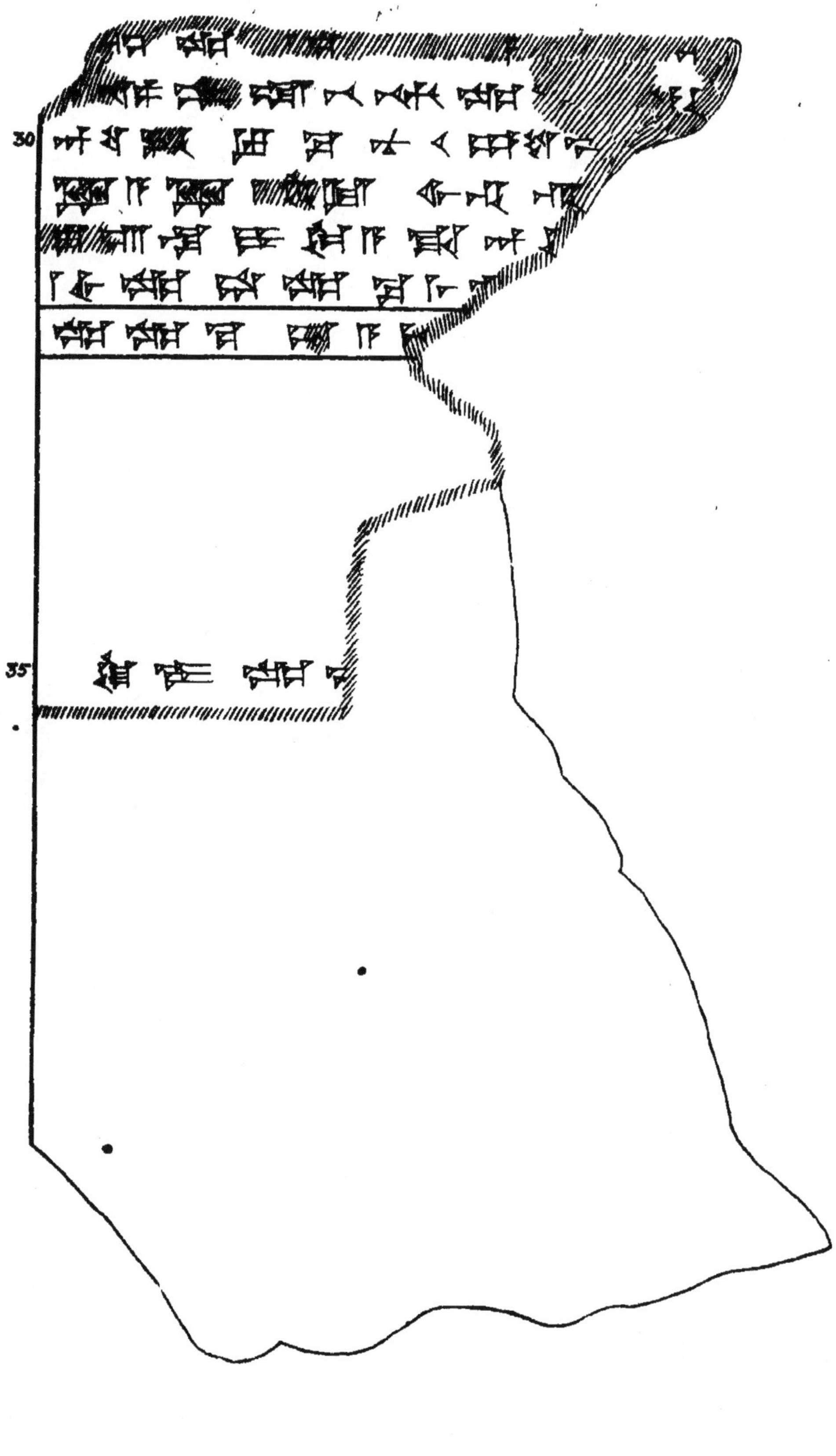

NO. 11. OBVERSE.

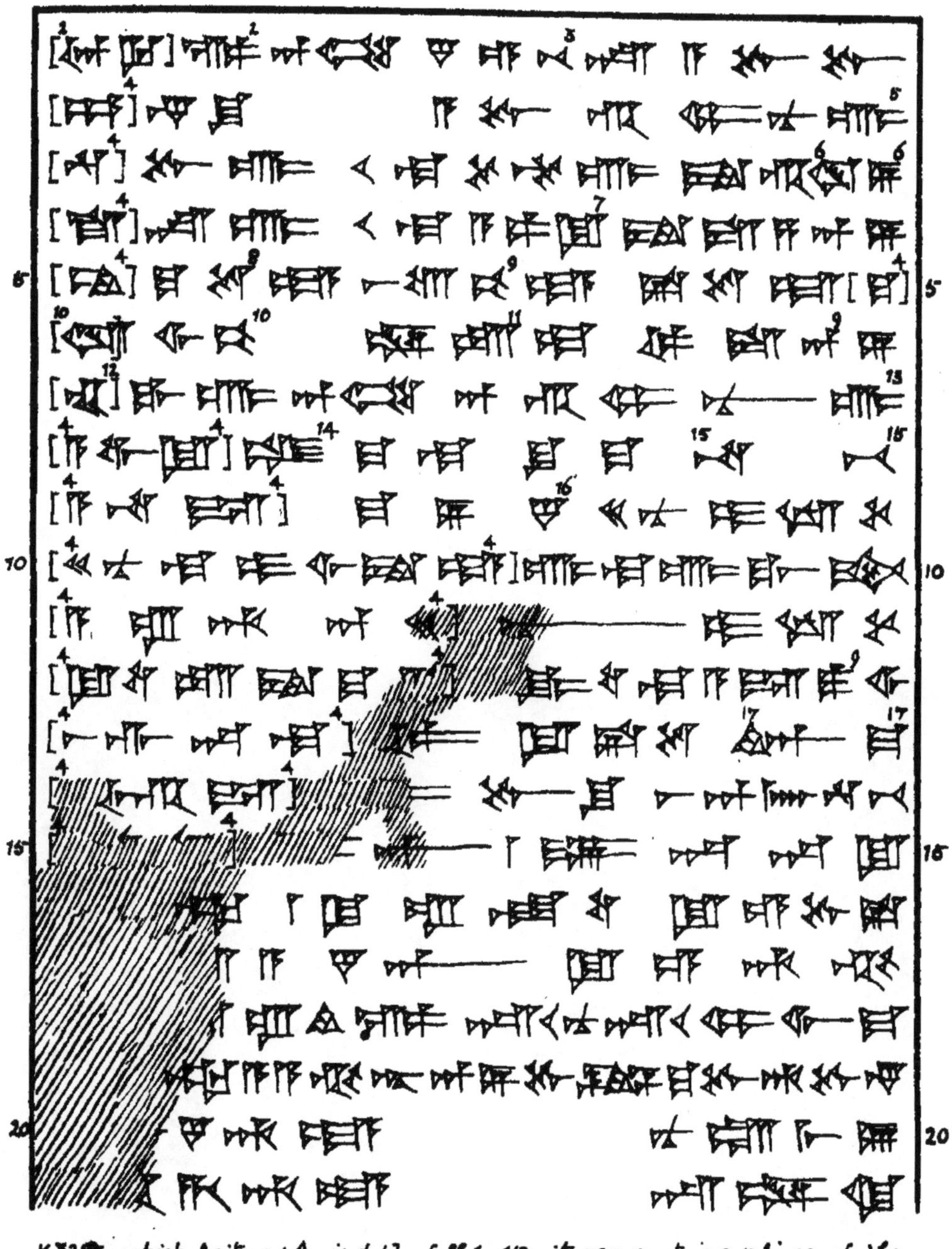

K 3286, which I cite as A, is dupl. of ll. 1–15; its rev. contains 5 lines of the common colophon. 2. A [cuneiform]. 3. A [cuneiform]. 4. ׆ A. 5. A [cuneiform]. 6. A [cuneiform]. 7. A [cuneiform]. 8. A [cuneiform]. 9. Omitted by A. 10. A [cuneiform]. 11. A [cuneiform]. 12. A [cuneiform]. 13. A [cuneiform]. 14. A [cuneiform]. 15. A [cuneiform]. 16. A [cuneiform]. 17. A [cuneiform].

NO. 11. OBV. (CONT.)

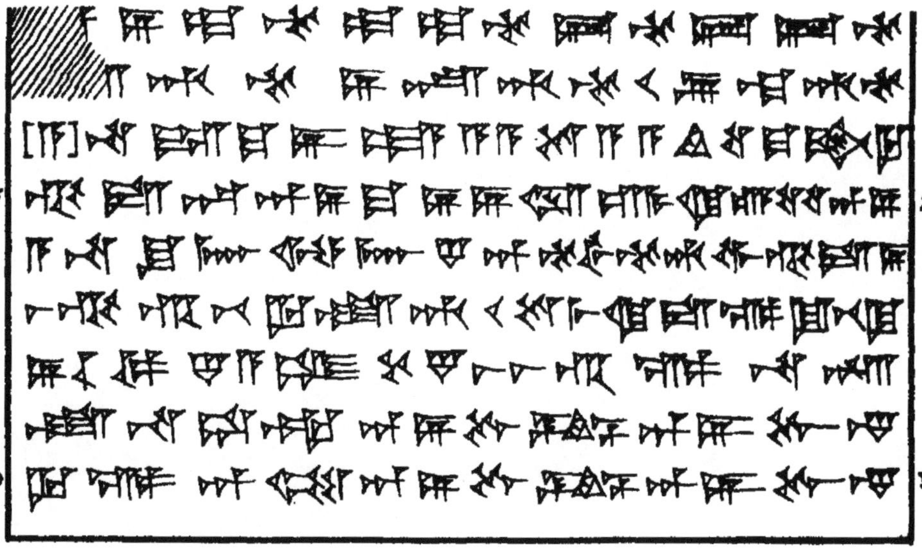

NO. 11. REVERSE.

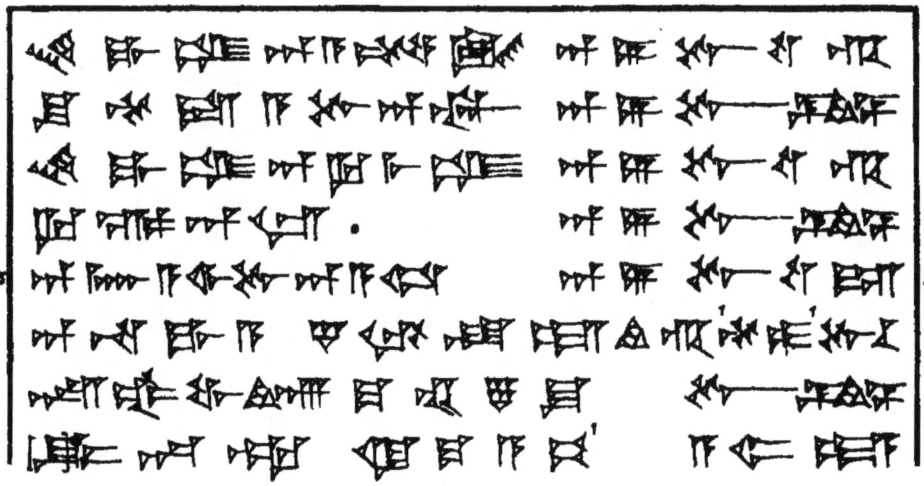

1. Written over an erasure.

NO. 11. REV. (CONT.)

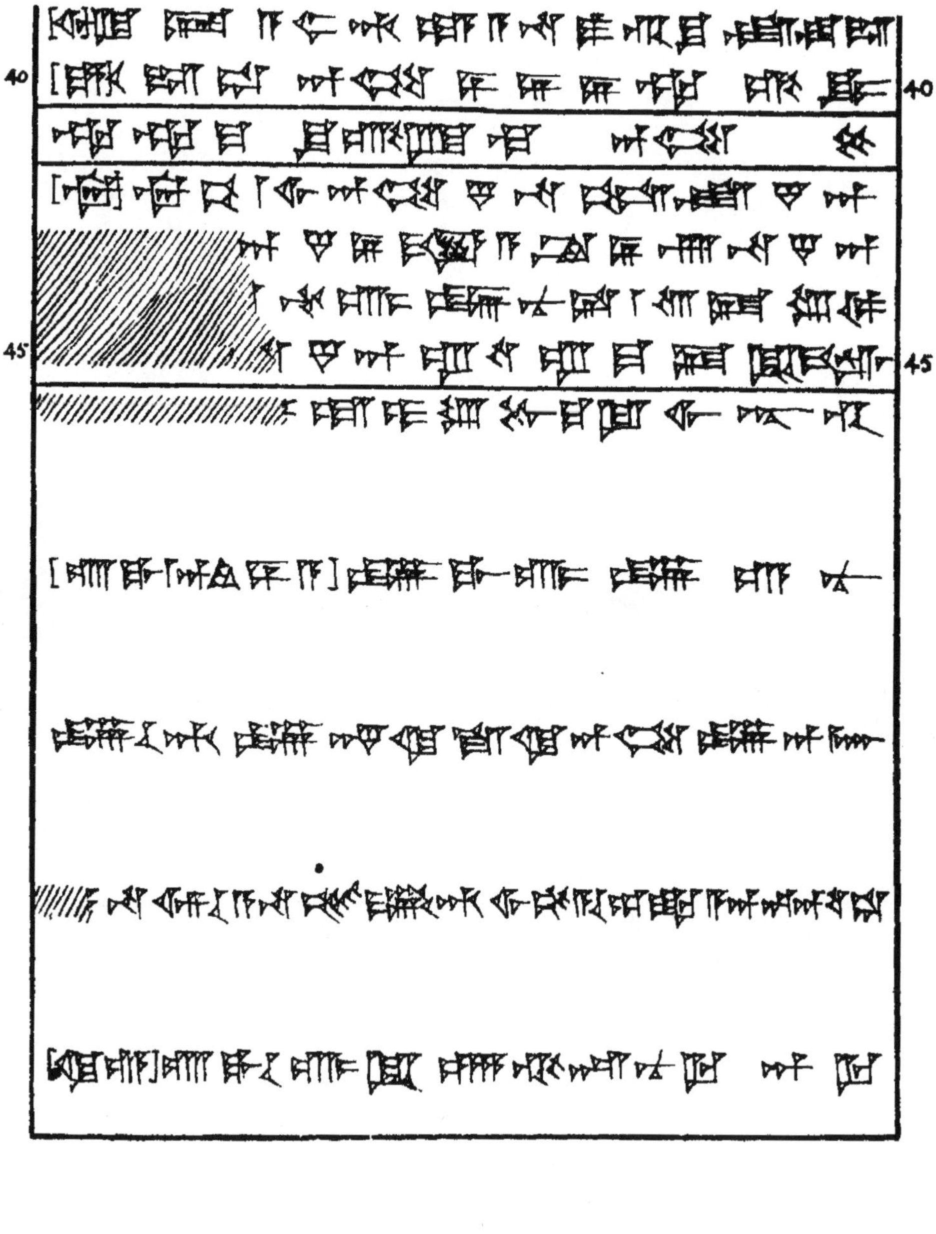

NO. 12. OBVERSE.

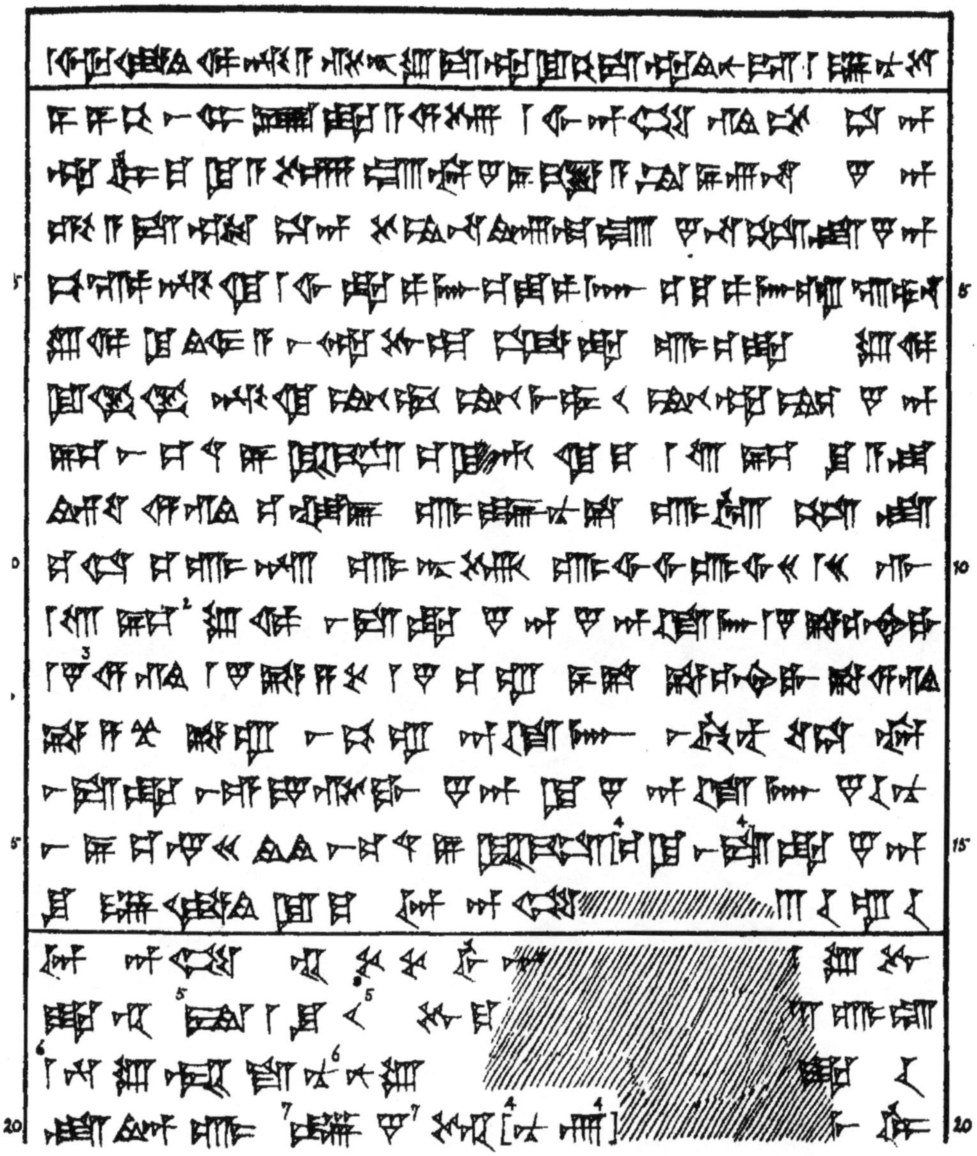

K 6783, which I cite as A, is duplicate of ll. 7–24, the lines however up to l. 16 being differently divided; K 3161, b, cited as B is dupl. of ll. 54–64; K 2379, cited as C, is dupl. of ll. 57–69 and ll. 76–96; K 10807, cited as D, is dupl. of ll. 91–100, and K 7984, cited as E, is dupl. of ll. 104–119. 2. A inserts . 3. A . 4. r. A. 5. A . 6. A . 7. A .

NO. 12. OBV. (CONT.)

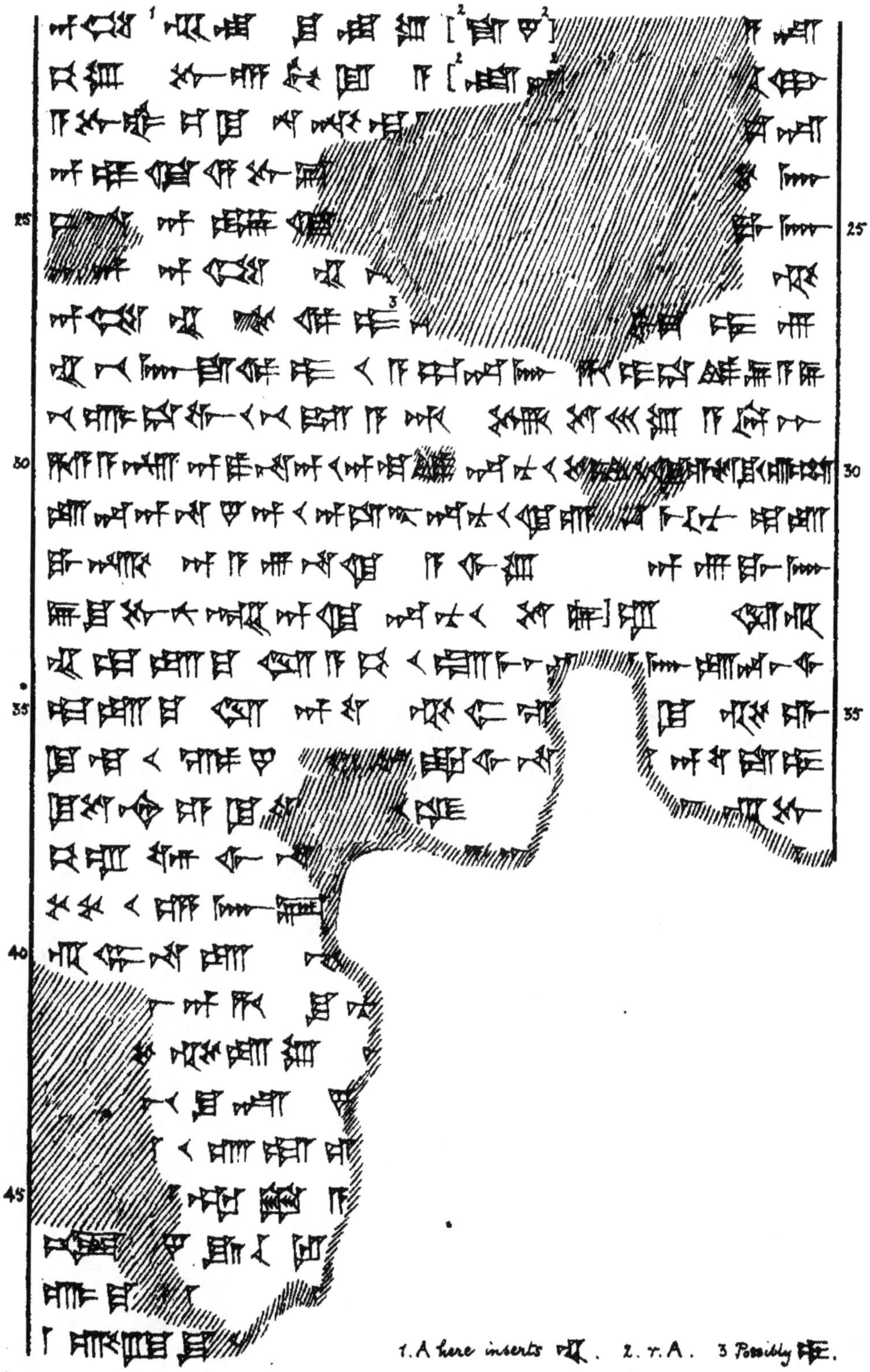

1. A here inserts [cuneiform sign]. 2. r. A. 3 Possibly [cuneiform sign].

NO. 12. OBV (CONT.)

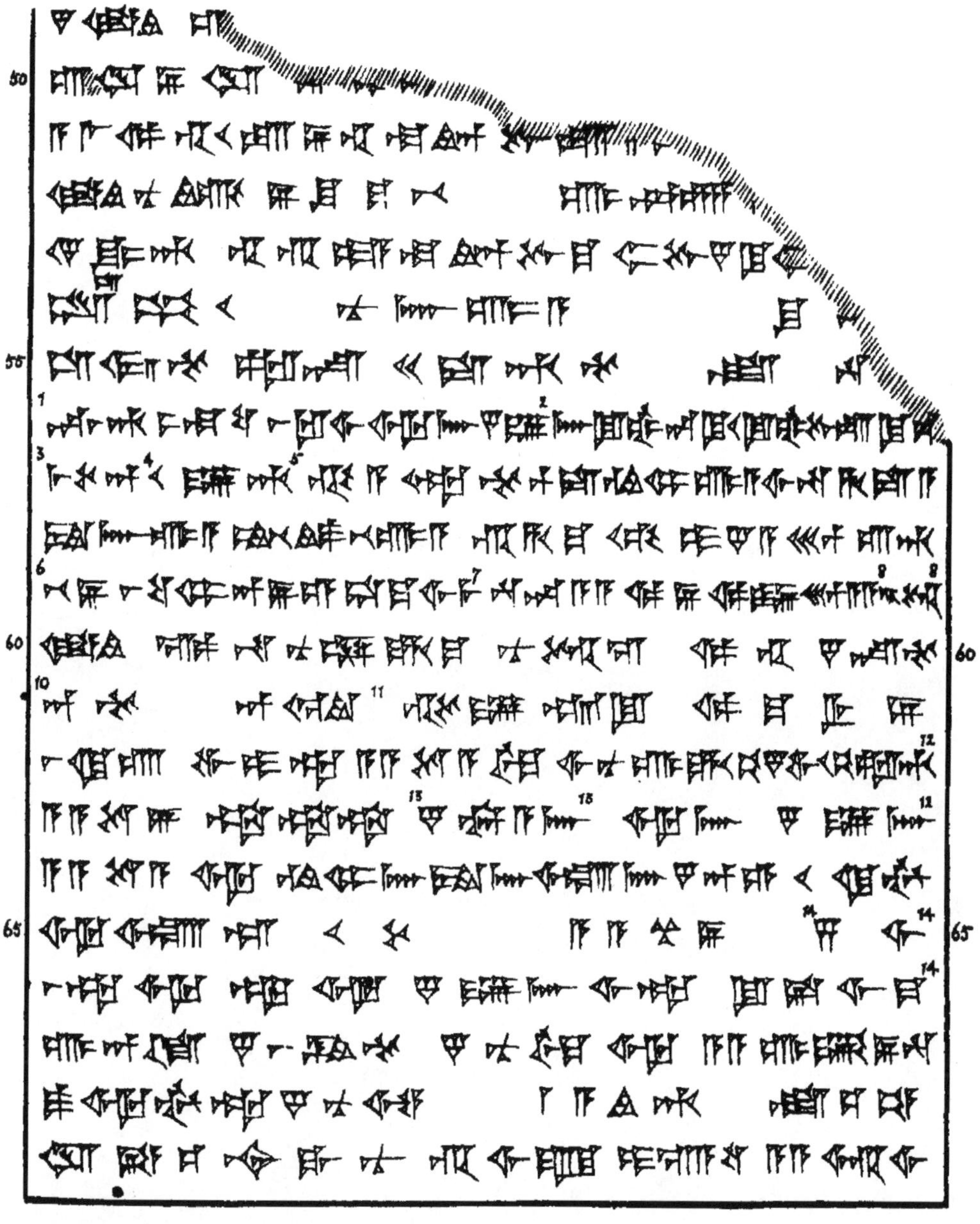

1. Ll. 56, 57 and 58 form 4 lines in B. 2. B . 3. L. 57 forms 2 lines in C. 4. B here inserts . 5. B . 6. L. 59 forms 2 lines in B and C. 7. B . 8. B . 9. L. 60 is expanded in B and forms 2 lines which read:– , and ; C apparently had the same reading. 10. In place of l. 61 B reads:– . 11. Traces of an erased . 12. BC . 13. B . 14. Omitted by C.

NO. 12. REVERSE.

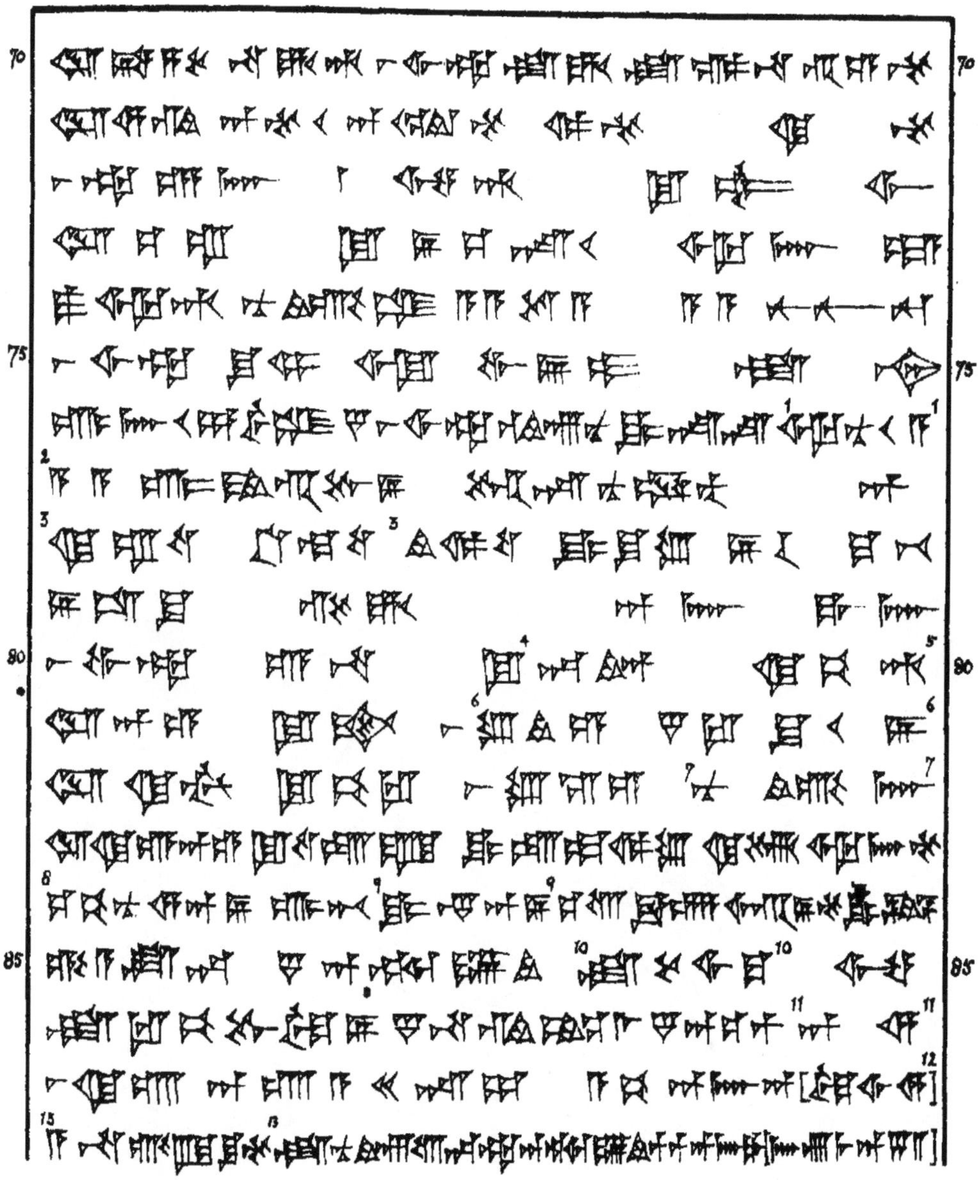

1. C . 2. ll. 77–79 form 2 lines in C. 3. C . 4. C . 5. C . 6. C . 7. C . 8. l. 84 forms 2 lines in C. 9. C . 10. C . 11. C . 12. ll. 87–93 have been restored from C; ll. 87 and 88, though forming 2 lines in C are differently divided. 13. C .

NO. 12. REV. (CONT.)

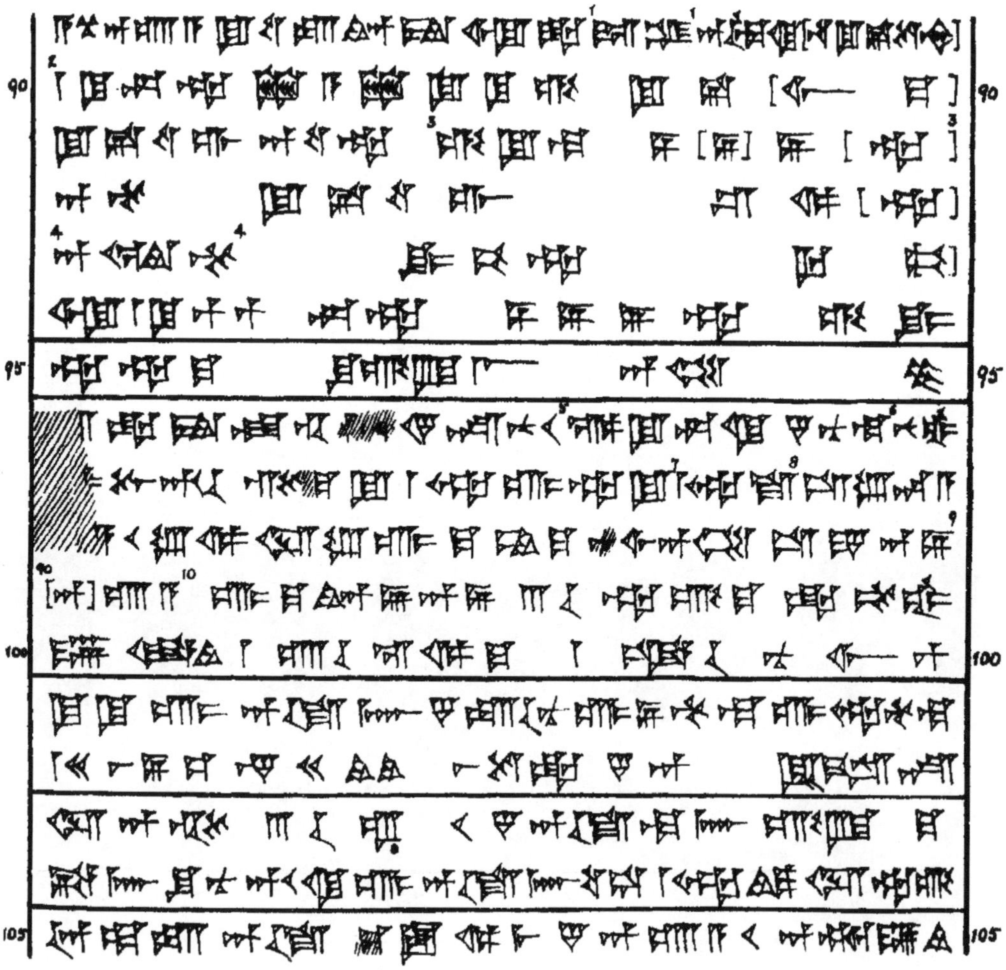

1. C [cuneiform]. 2. Ll. 90 and 91 form one line in C; ll. 92 and 93 form one line in C and D. 3. C [cuneiform]. 4. C [cuneiform]. 5. D [cuneiform]. 6. D [cuneiform]. 7. D here inserts [cuneiform]. 8. D [cuneiform]. 9. Ll. 98–100 form 2 lines in D. 10. [cuneiform] D.

NO. 12. REV. (CONT.)

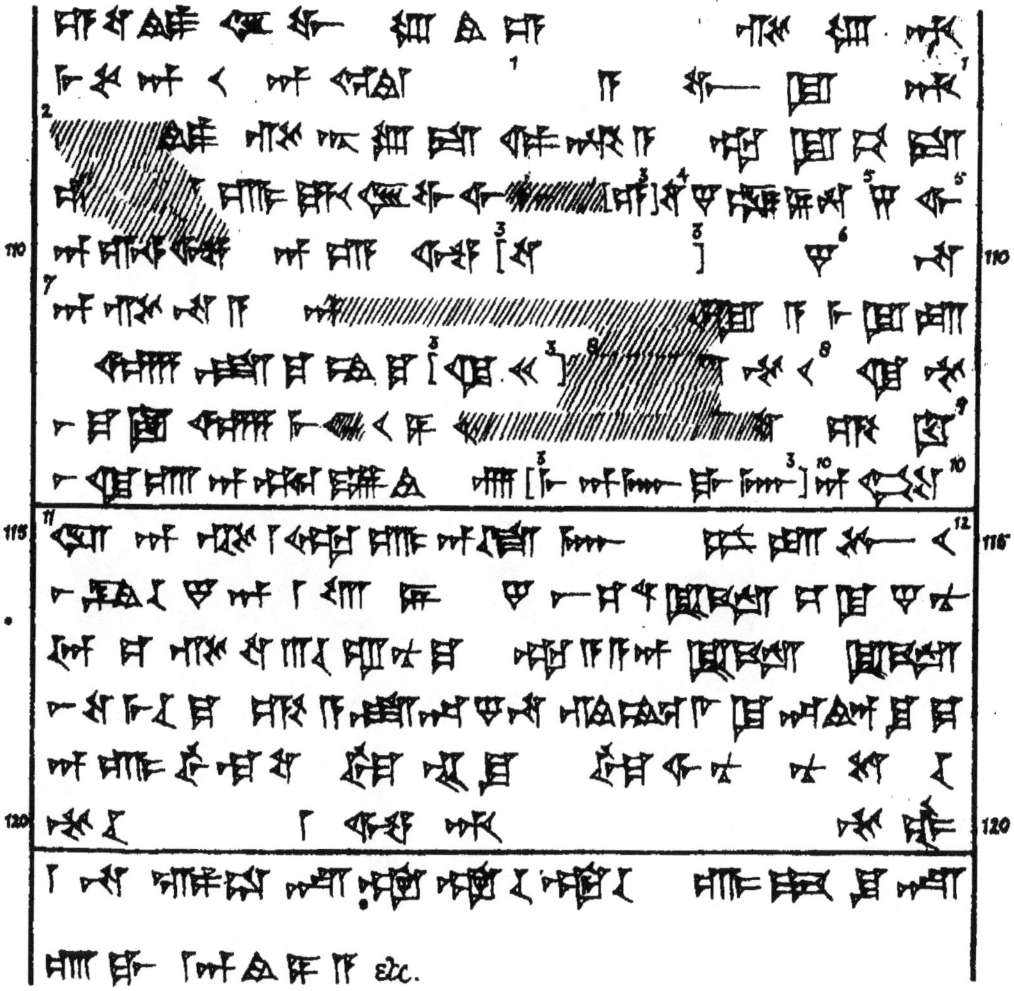

1. E . 2. l. 108 forms 2 lines in E, which read:— , and . 3. r. E. 4. E . 5. E . 6. E . 7. ll. 111 and 112 form one line in E. 8. E . 9. For l. 113 E reads:— . 10. Omitted by E. 11. ll. 115–118 form 3 lines in E. 12. E . 13. E .

NO. 13. OBVERSE.

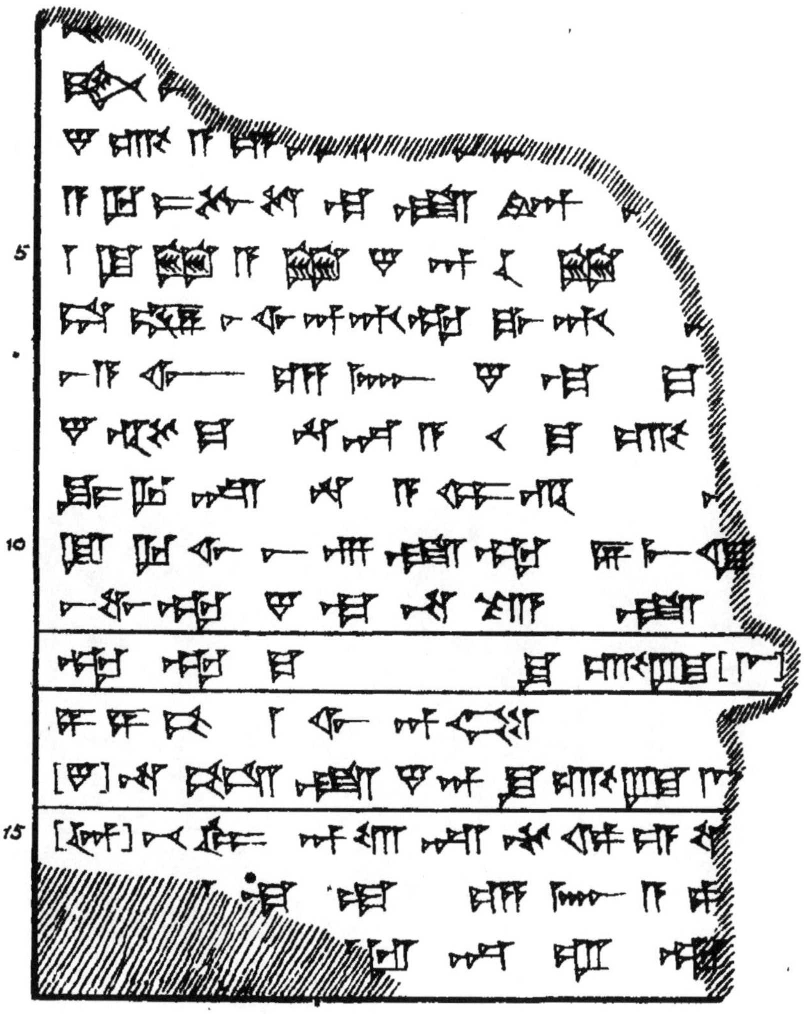

NO. 13. REVERSE.

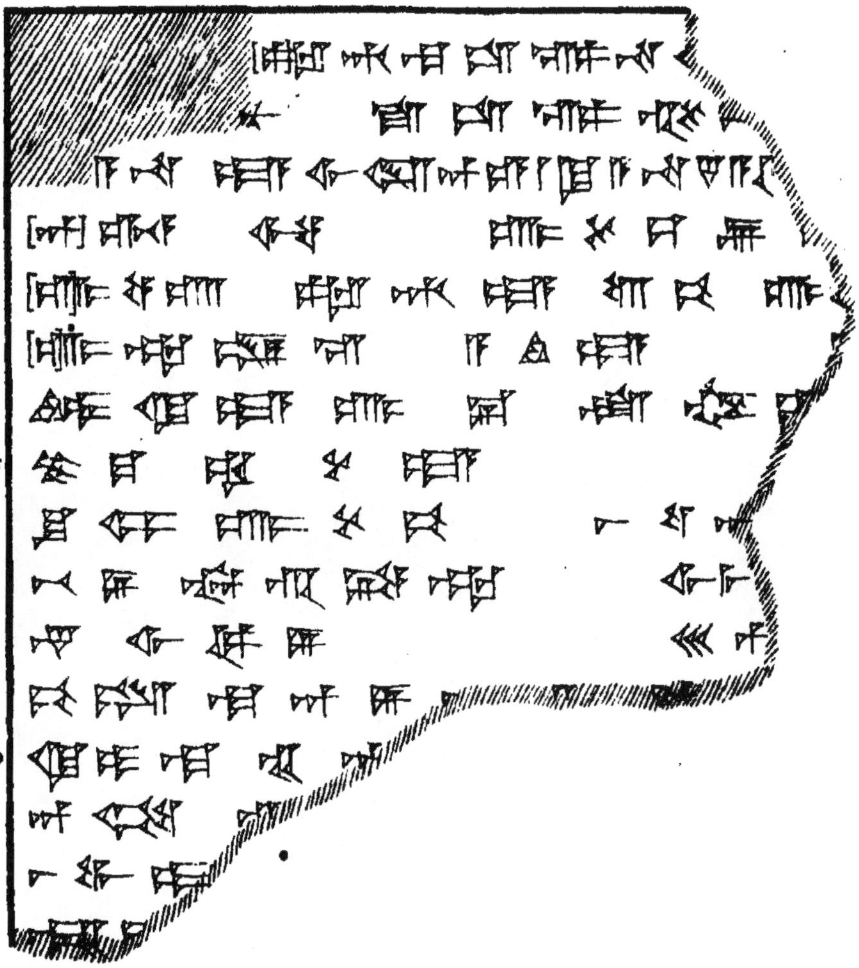

NO. 14.

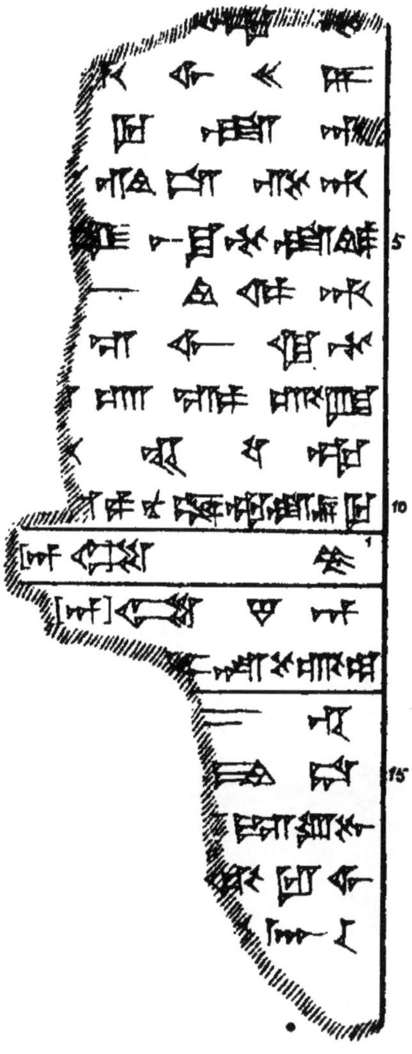

NO. 15.

1. L.11 of NO.14 and l.17 of NO.15 should each be restored:—

NO. 16. OBVERSE.

NO. 16. REVERSE.

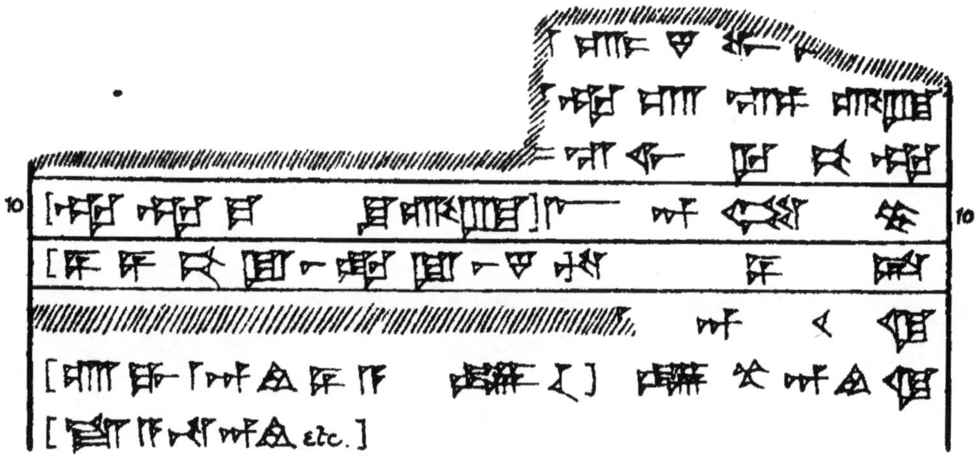

NO. 17.

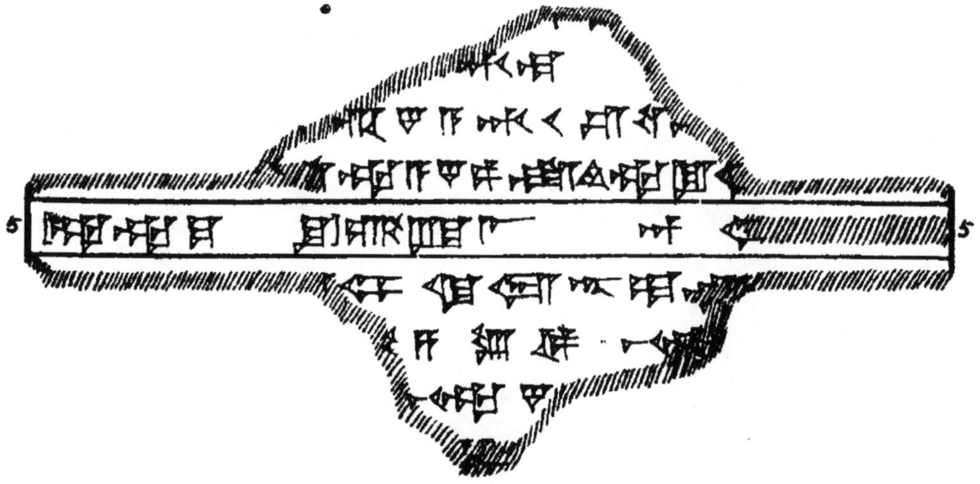

NO. 18. OBVERSE.

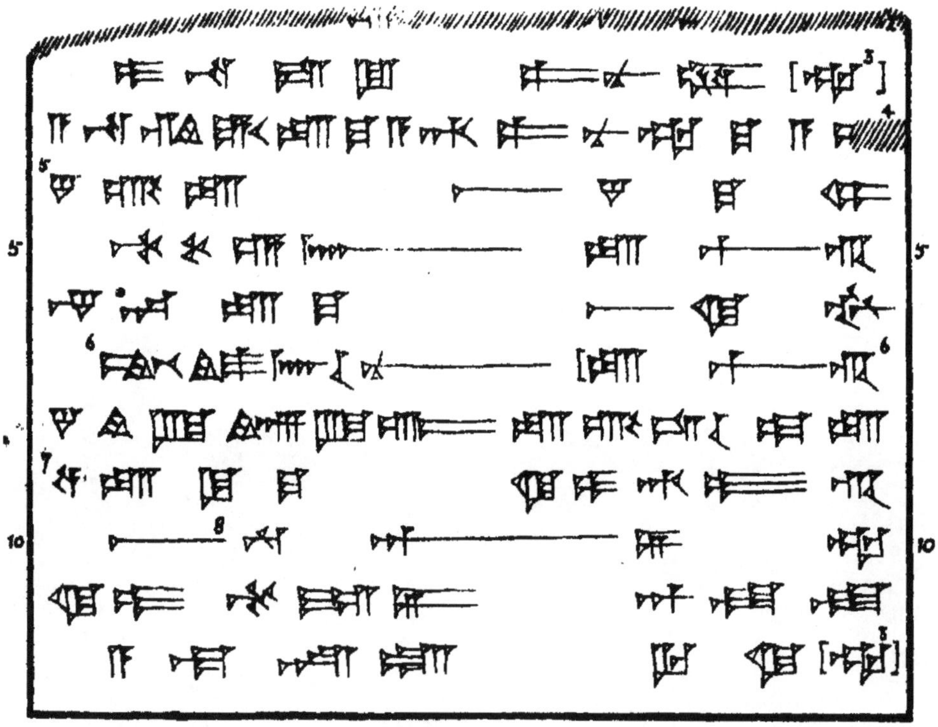

K 6804, ll. 1–18, which I cite as A, is dupl. of ll. 1–18; K 11826 + K 11975, cited as B, is dupl. of ll. 9–19. 2. Ll. 1 and 2 probably formed one line in A, which also gives traces of 2 preceding lines, reading:– l. 1 , and l. 2 . 3. r. A. 4. A . 5. The couplets 4 and 5, 6 and 7, each form one line in A. 6. A . 7. The couplets 9 and 10, 11 and 12, each form one line in A and B. 8. A .

NO. 18. REVERSE.

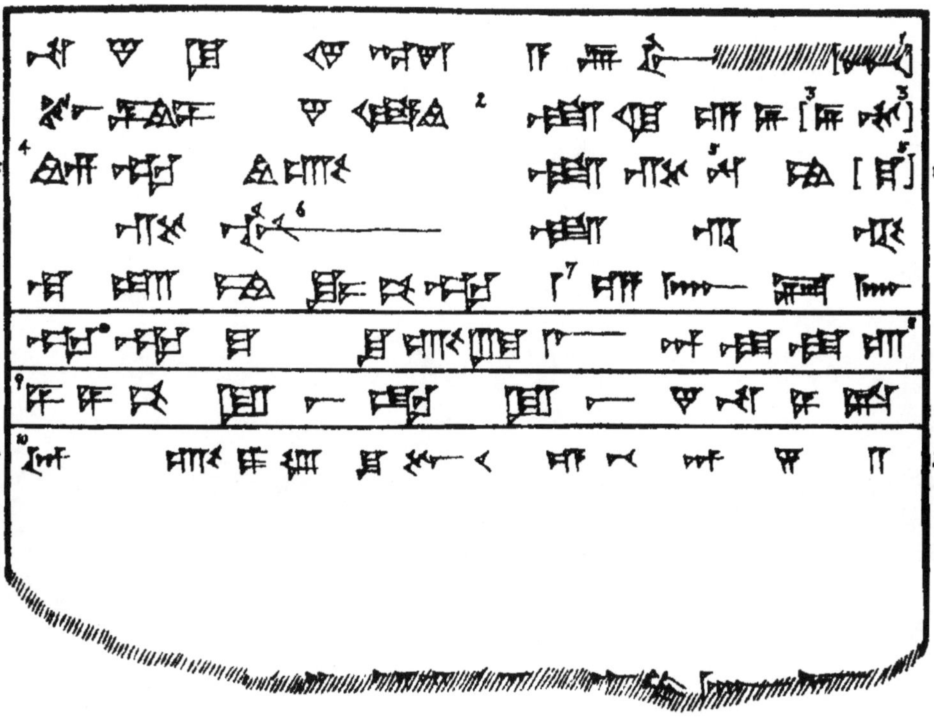

1. r. A   2. B here inserts [cuneiform].   3. r. B; A [cuneiform].   4. ll. 14 and 16 form one line in B.
5. A [cuneiform].   6. B [cuneiform].   7. A [cuneiform].   8. AB [cuneiform].   9. After l. 18 A ceases to be a
duplicate, giving 3 lines of directions for ceremonies :— [cuneiform]
[cuneiform], [cuneiform], and [cuneiform].   10. L. 20 is written in smaller
characters over an erasure; B reads :— [cuneiform].

NO. 19. OBVERSE.

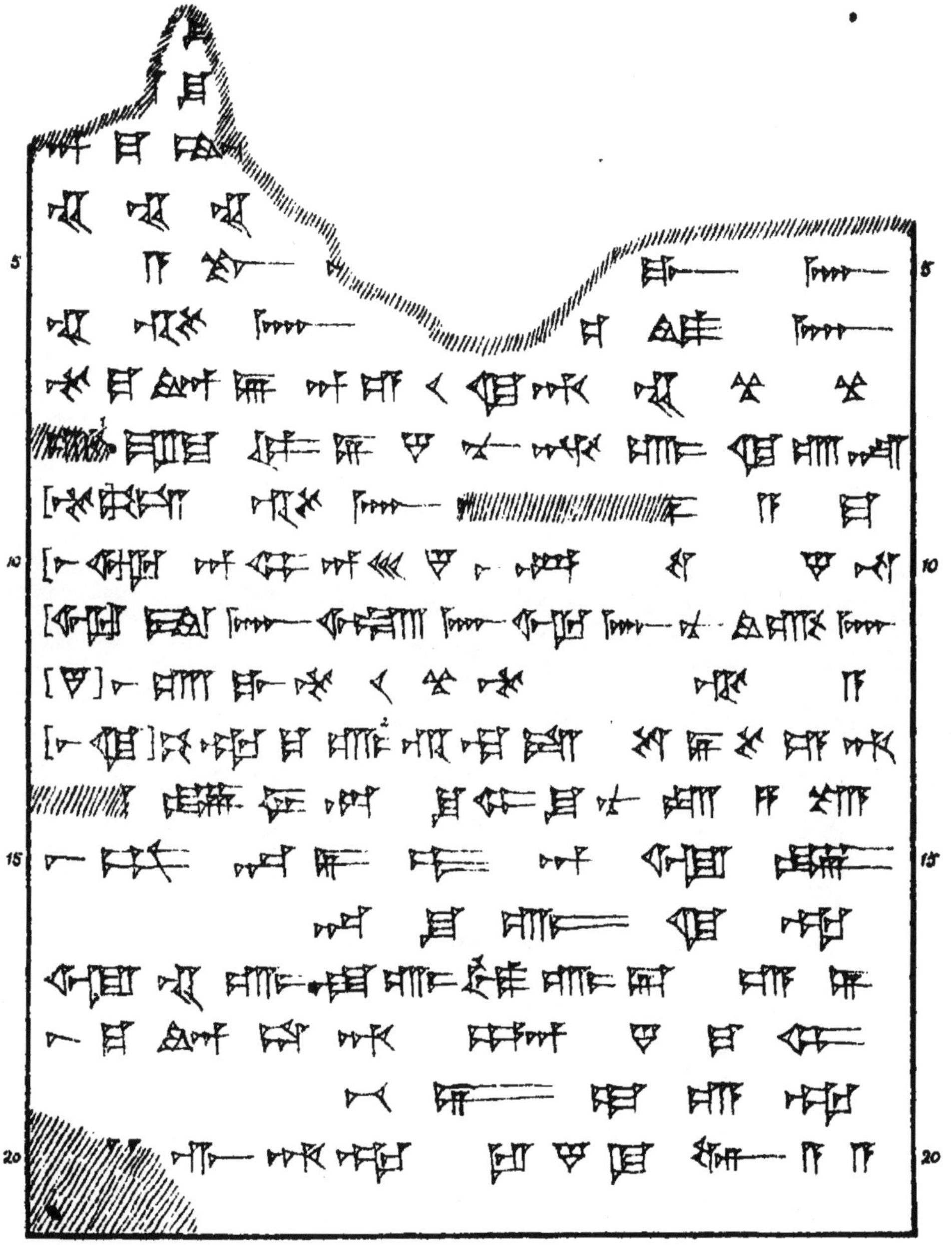

1. Possibly [cuneiform sign]. 2. Written over an erasure.

NO. 19. REVERSE.

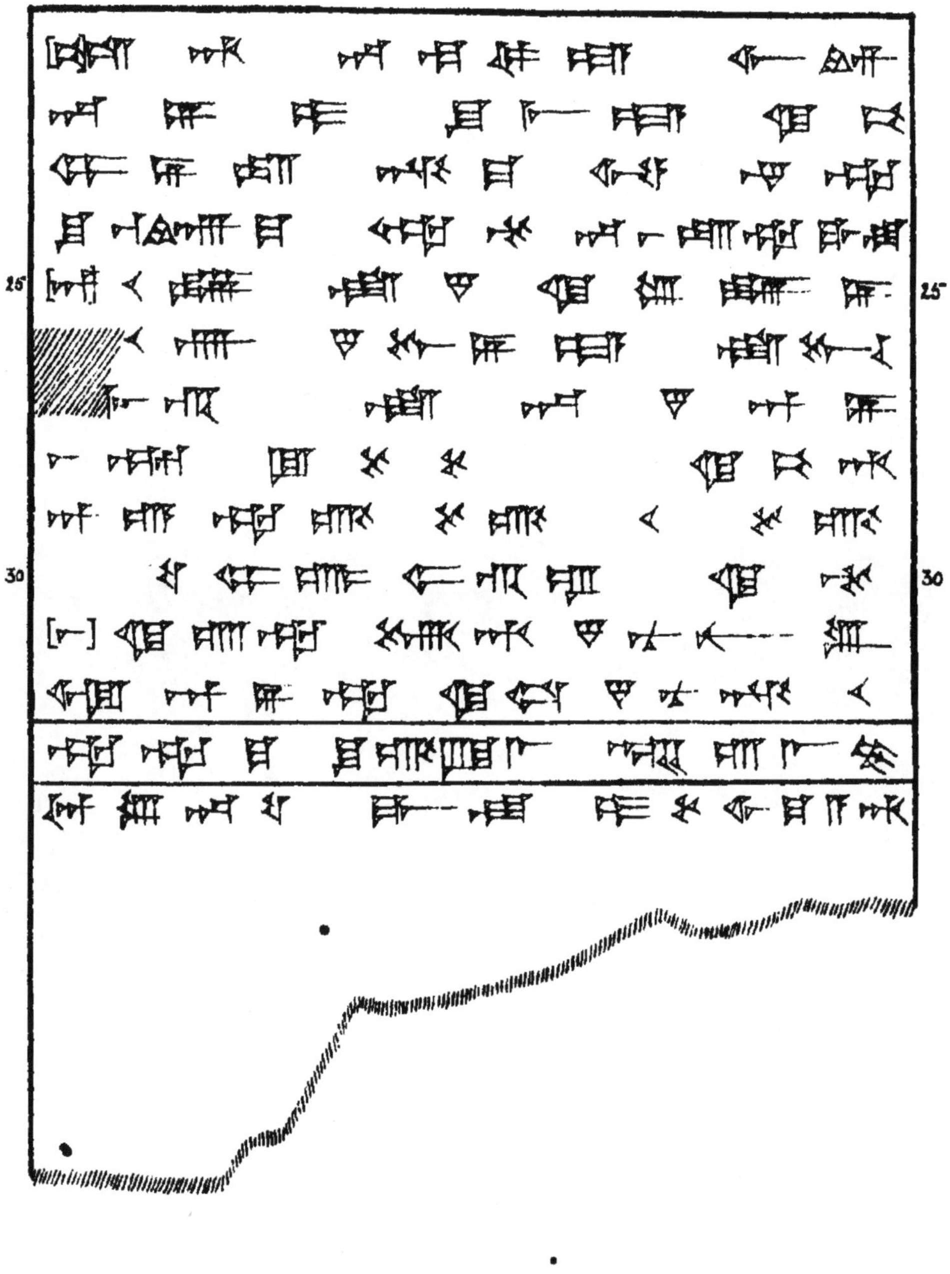

NO. 20. OBVERSE.

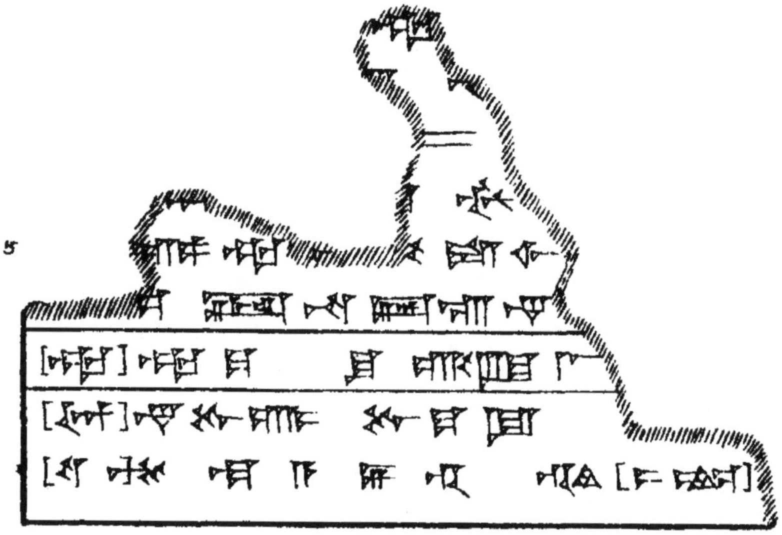

NO. 20. REVERSE.

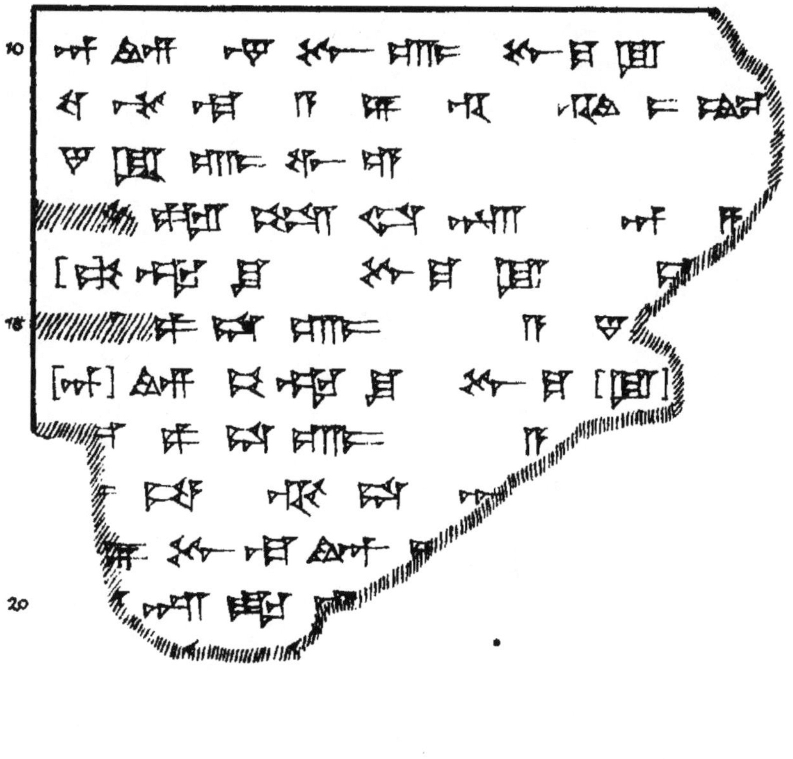

NO. 21. OBVERSE.

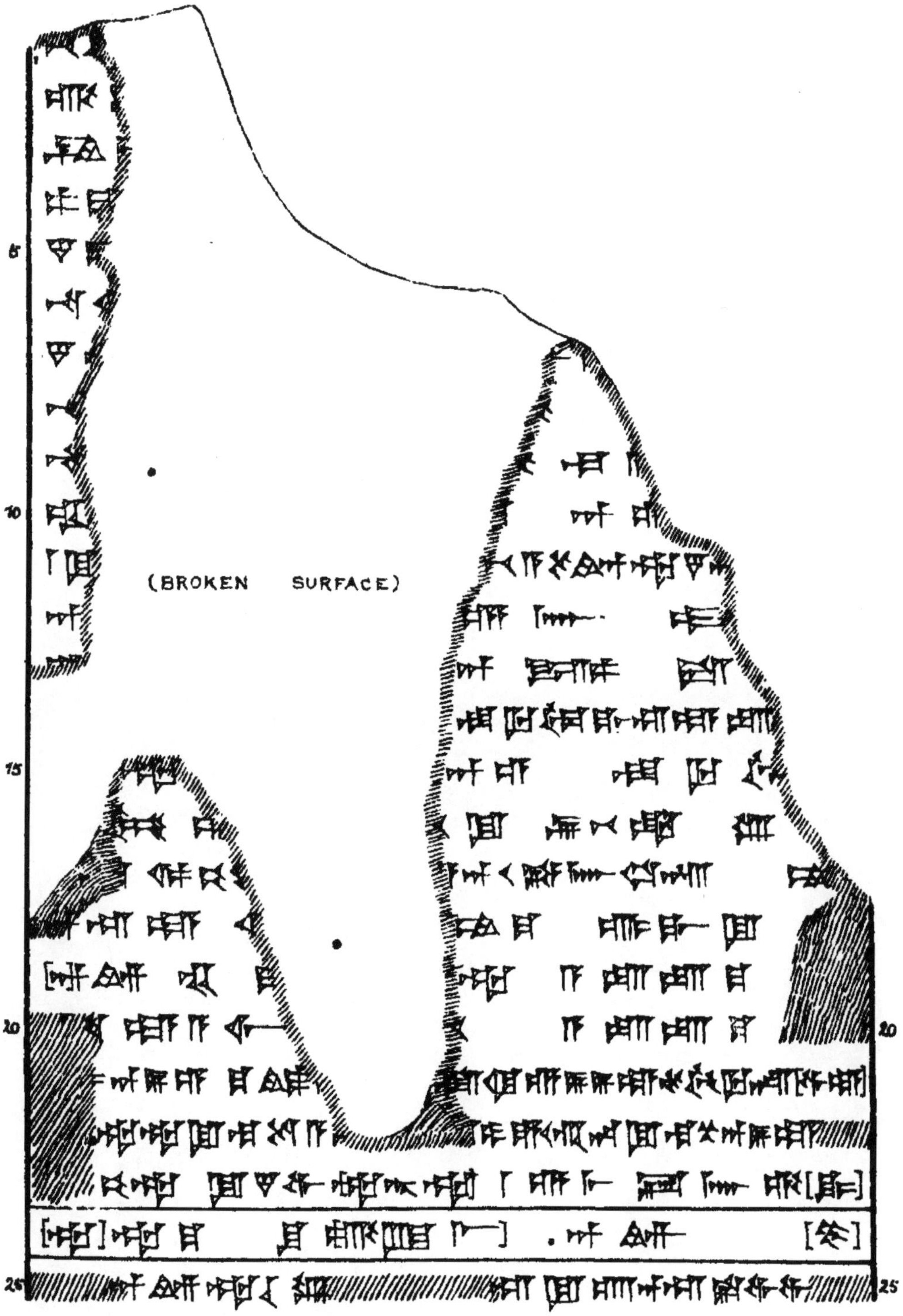

1. About 7 or 8 lines are missing from the beginning of the Obverse.

NO. 21. OBV. (CONT.)

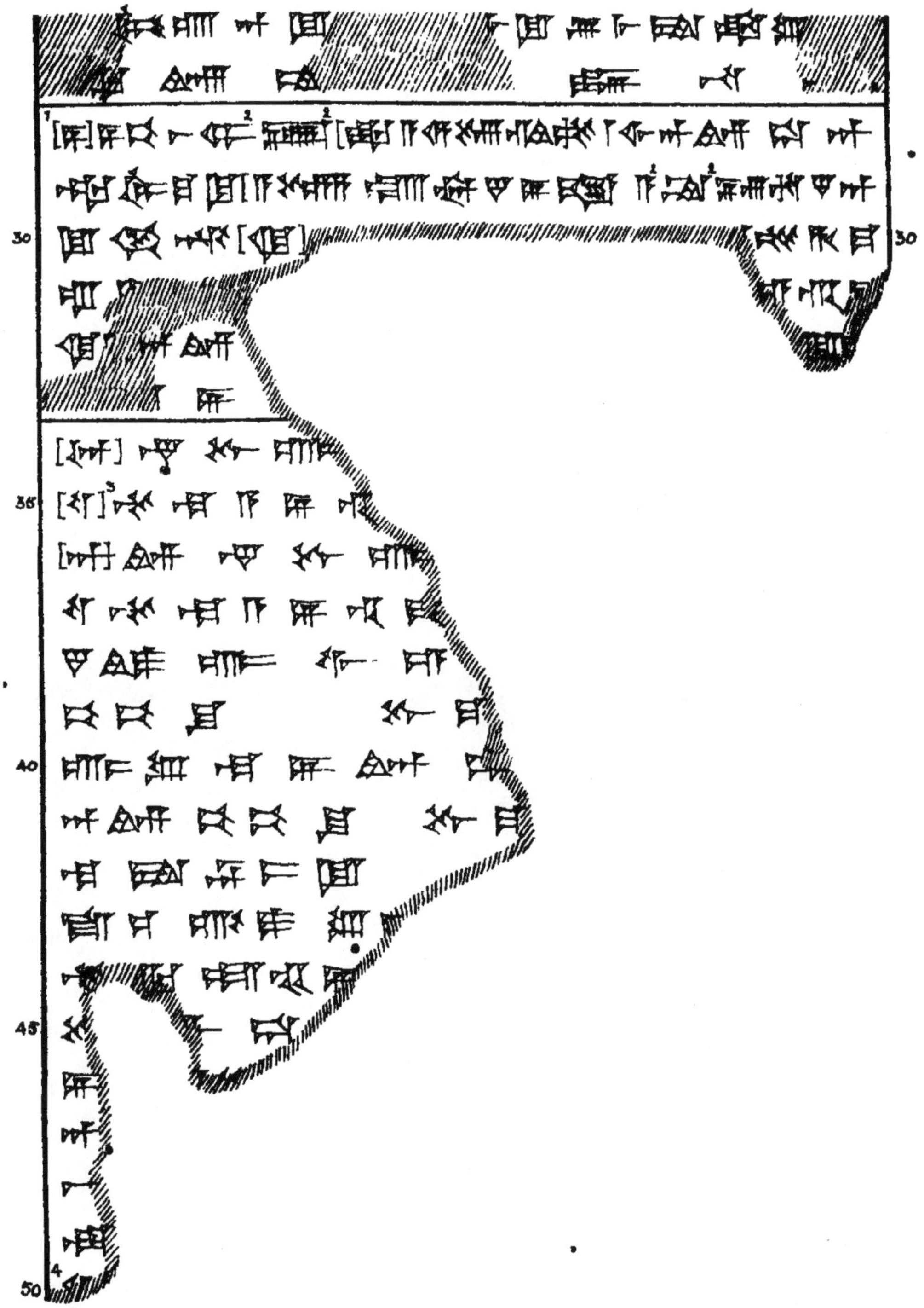

1. ll. 28 and 29 have been restored from NO. 12, ll 2 f. 2. Traces of this character remain.
3. v. l. 37. 4. About 9 lines are missing from the bottom of the Obverse.

NO. 21. REVERSE.

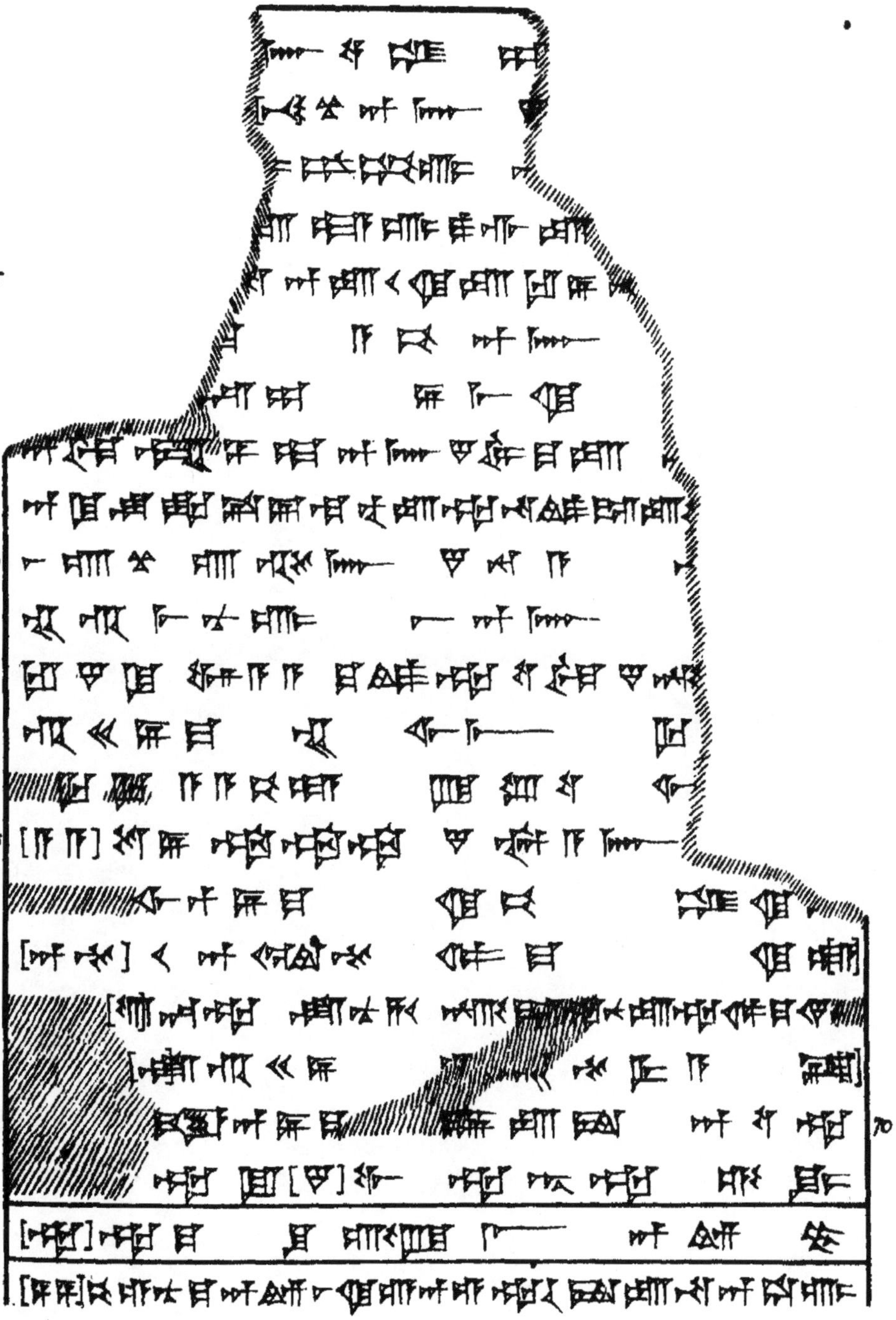

NO. 21. REV. (CONT.)

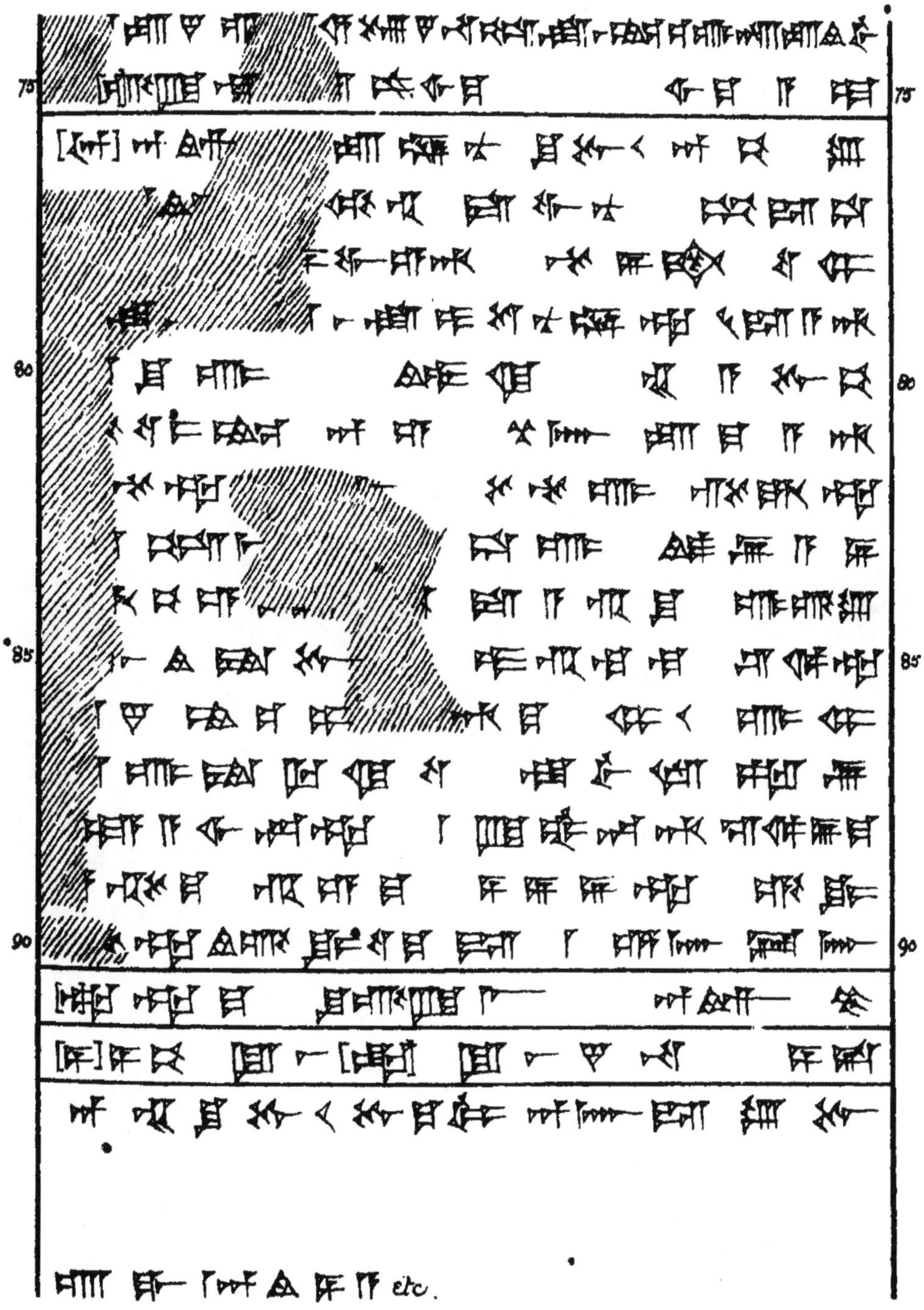

NO. 22. OBVERSE.

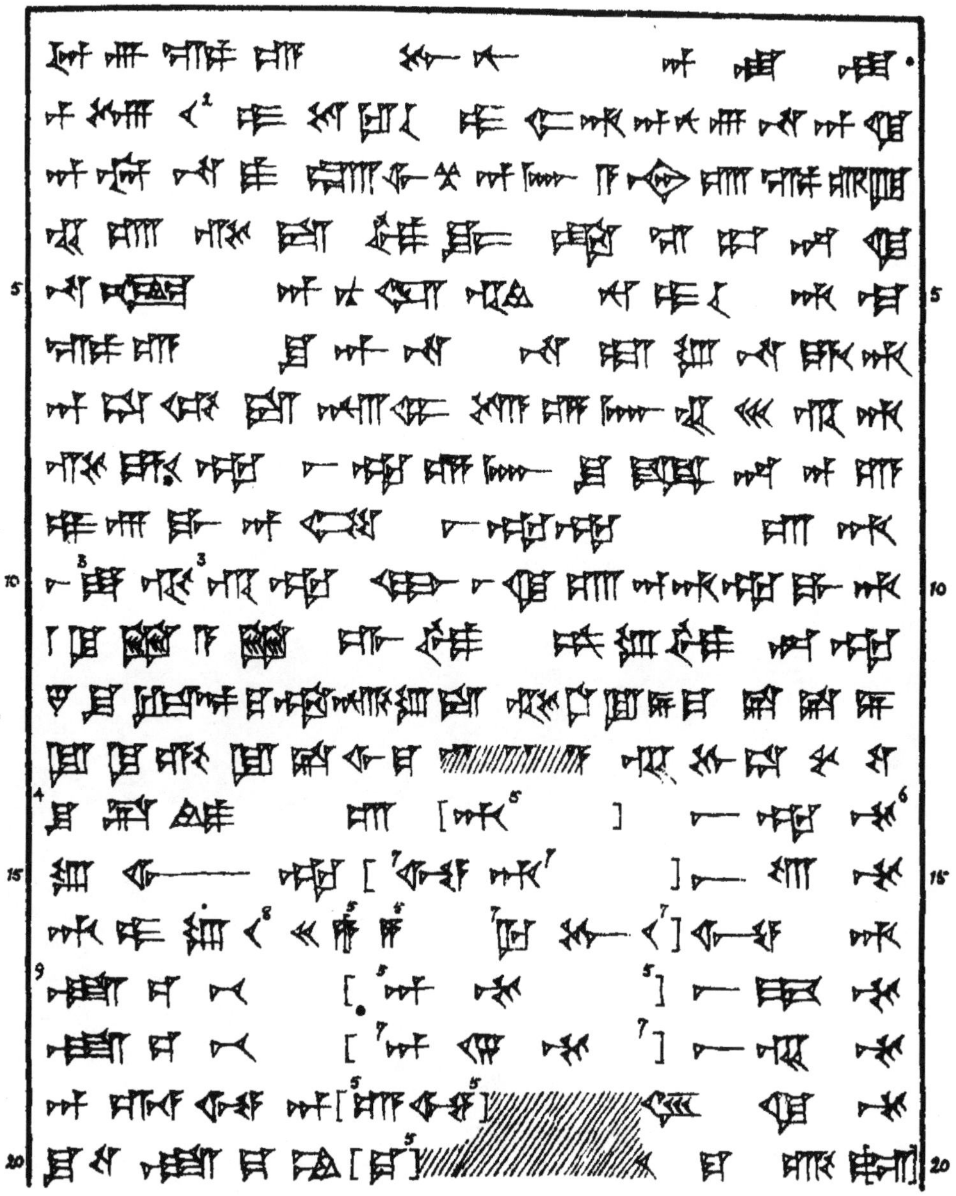

1. K 6334, which I cite as A, is duplicate of ll. 1–9; K 6853, cited as B, is dupl. of ll. 7–24; and K 8982, cited as C, is dupl. of ll. 66–70. 2. A [illegible]. 3. B [illegible]. 4. Ll. 14 and 15 form one line in B. 5. r. B. 6. B [illegible]. 7. attempted restoration from No. 9. 8. Omitted by B. 9. Ll. 17 and 18 form one line in B.

NO. 22. OBV. (CONT.)

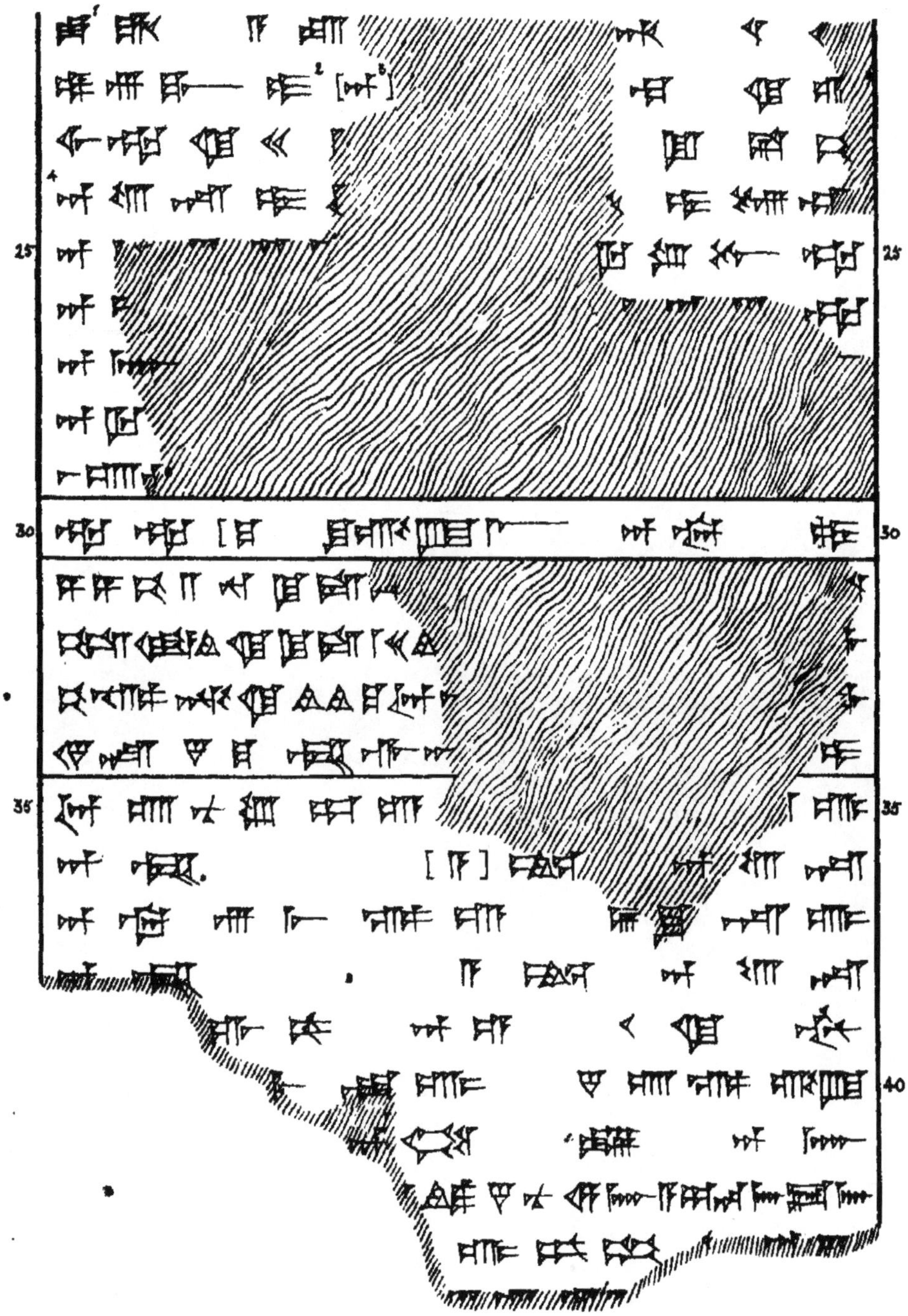

1. B . 2. Omitted by B. 3. r. B. 4. B apparently makes some insertion before .

NO. 22. REVERSE.

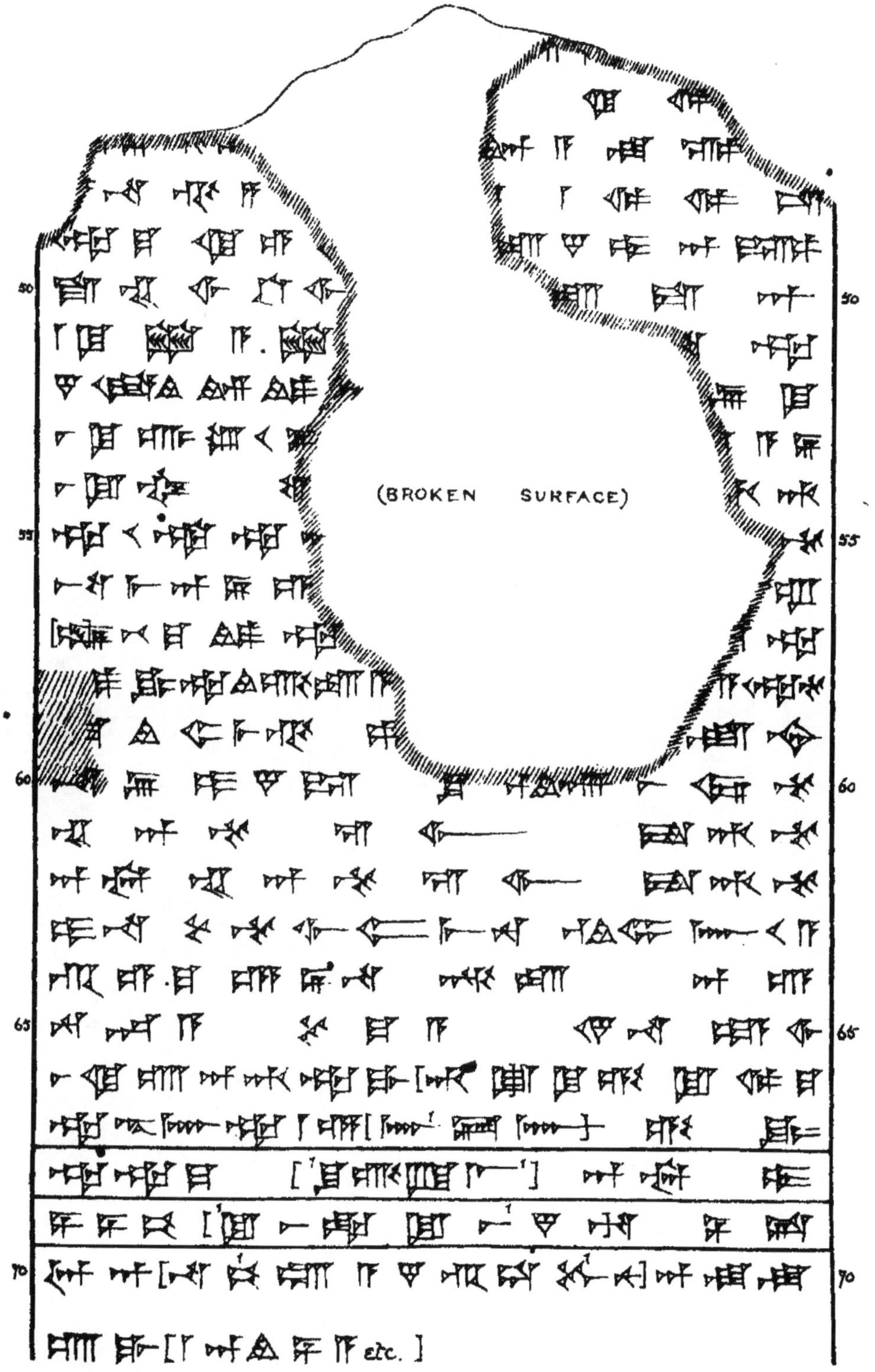

1. Restored from C.

NO. 23.

NO. 24.

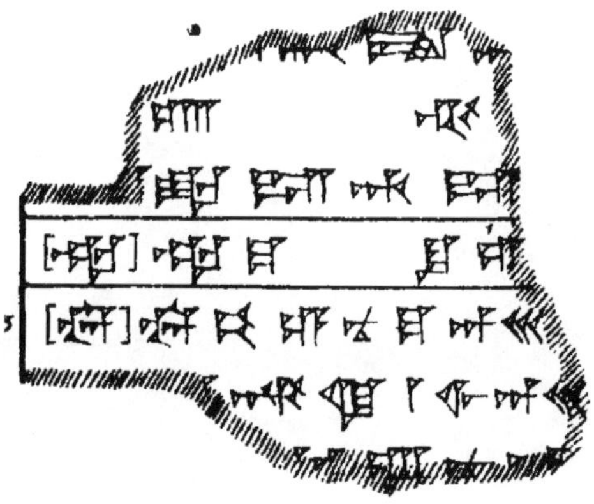

NO. 25.

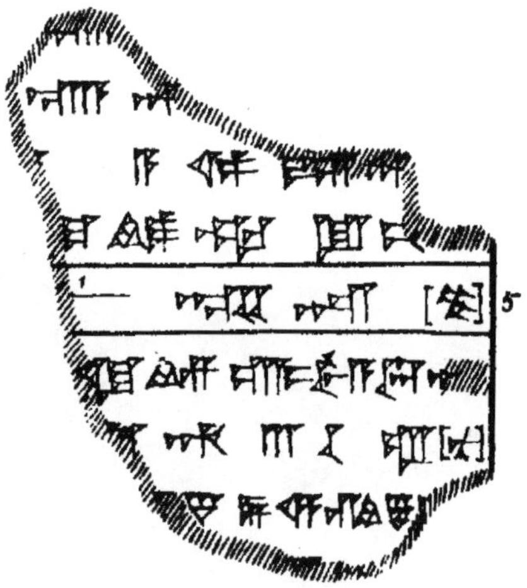

NO. 26 OBVERSE.

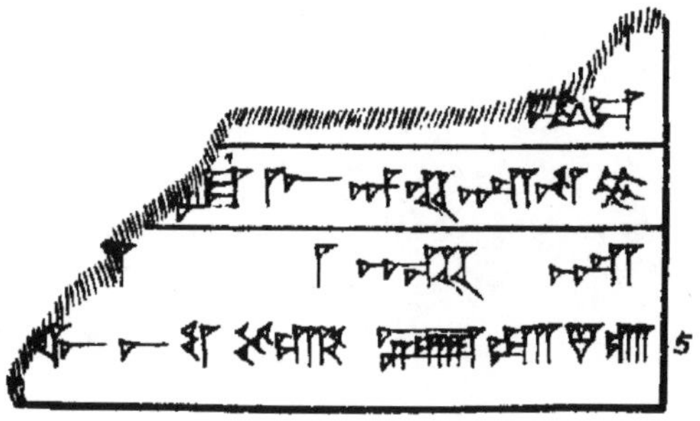

NO. 26. REVERSE.

1. l. 4 of NO. 24, l. 5 of NO. 25 and l. 3 of NO. 26 should each be restored to read :- etc. 2. l. 6 of NO. 23 should probably be restored as l. 3 of NO. 26.

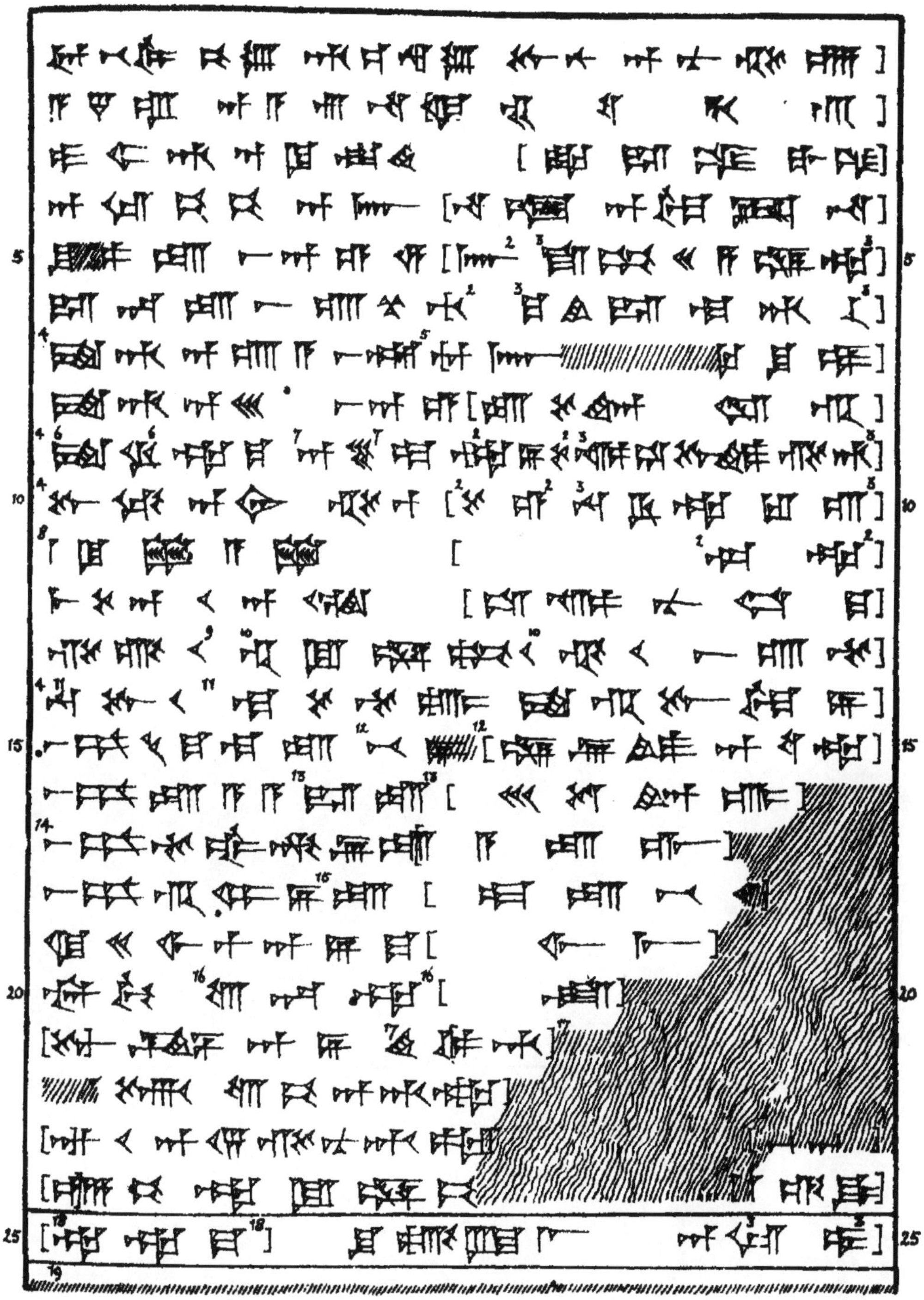

1. K 2836 + K 6593, which I cite as A, is partly dupl. of ll. 1–25; the ends of ll. 1–4, 7 f, 12–20 and 23–25 have been restored from A; K 11549, cited as B, is dupl. of ll. 4–14. 2. r. AB. 3. r. A. 4. Ll. 7, 9, 10 and 14 each form two lines in A. 5. A. 6. A. 7. B. 8. For l. 11 A reads, which is followed by the formula etc. in three lines; ll. 11 and 12 form one line in B. 9. B. 10. A. 11. A; B. 12. A. 13. A. 14. Ll. 17 and 18 are transposed in A. 15. A. 16. A. 17. A. 18. Traces of these characters remain. 19. The text of A concludes with the catch-line.

NO. 28.

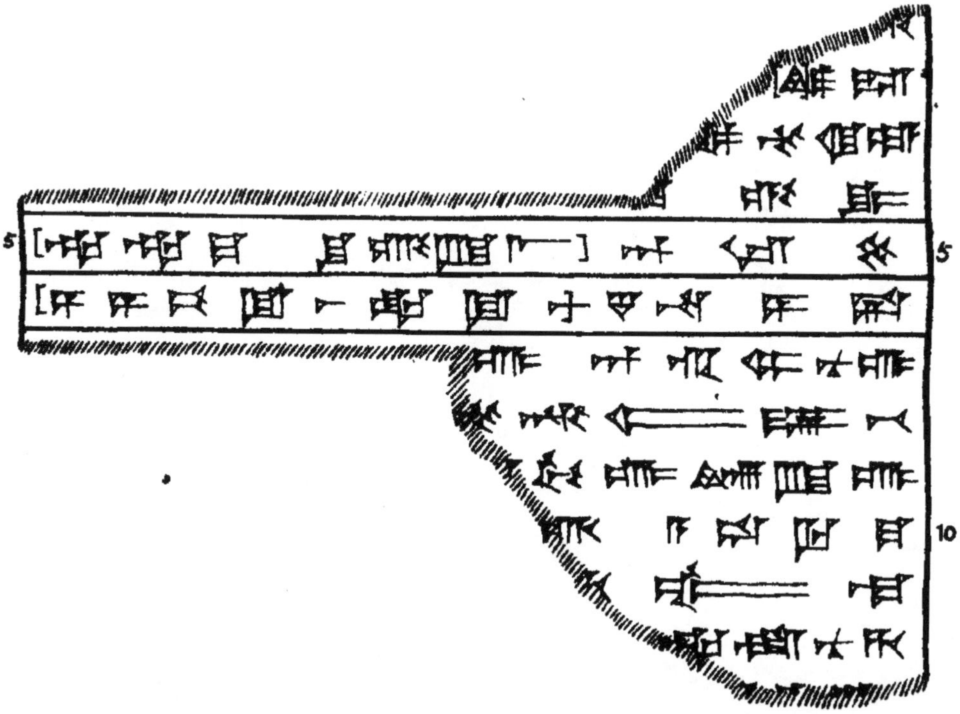

NO. 29.

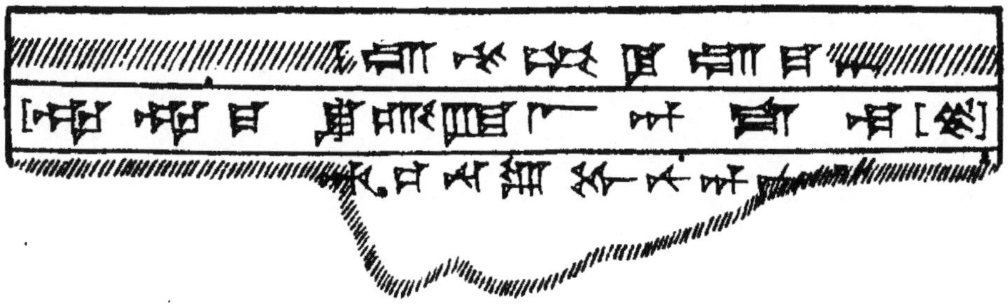

1. Or … *2. This catch-line should possibly be restored from No. 27, l. 1:* […].

NO. 30. OBVERSE.

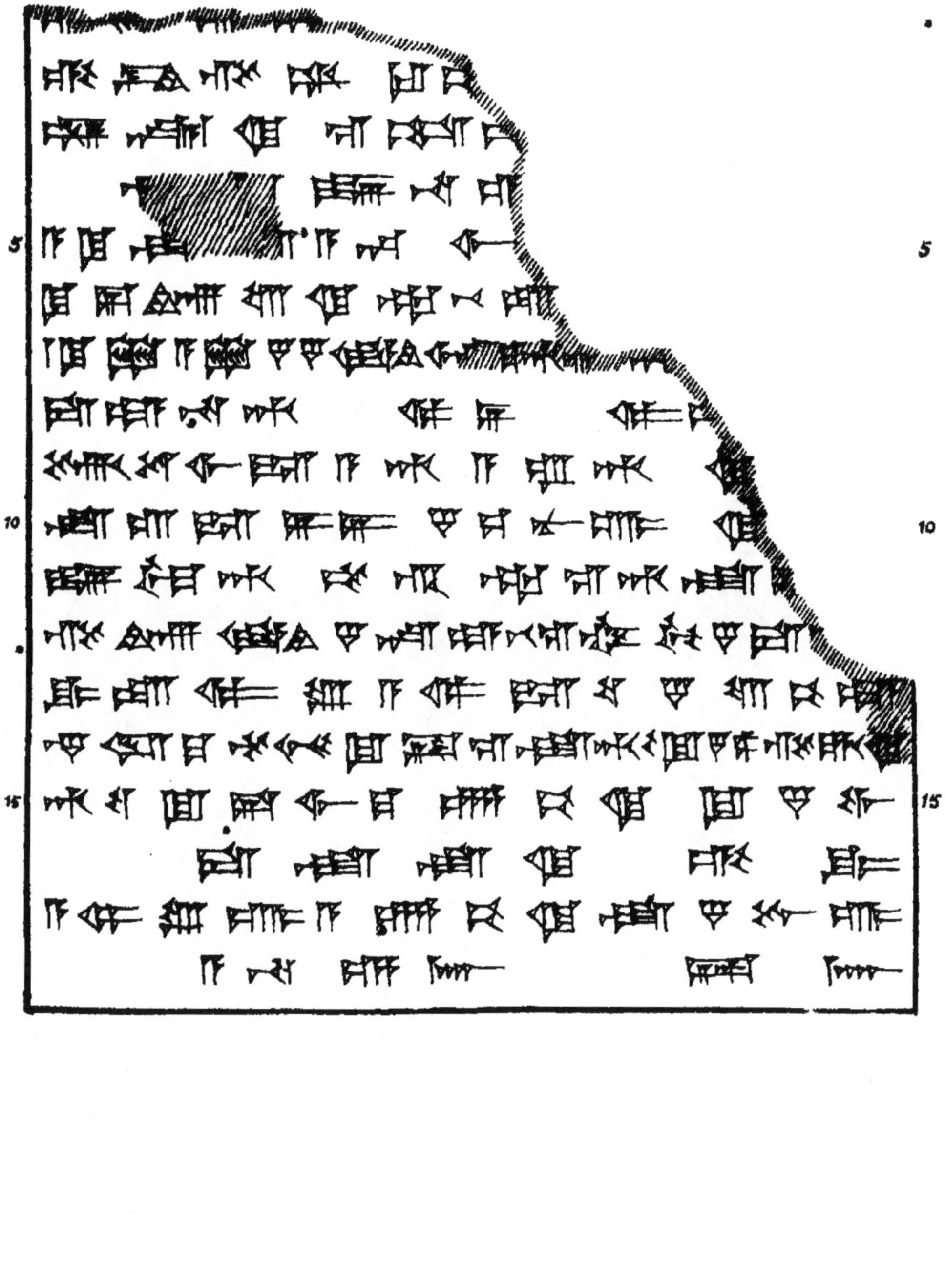

NO. 30. REVERSE.

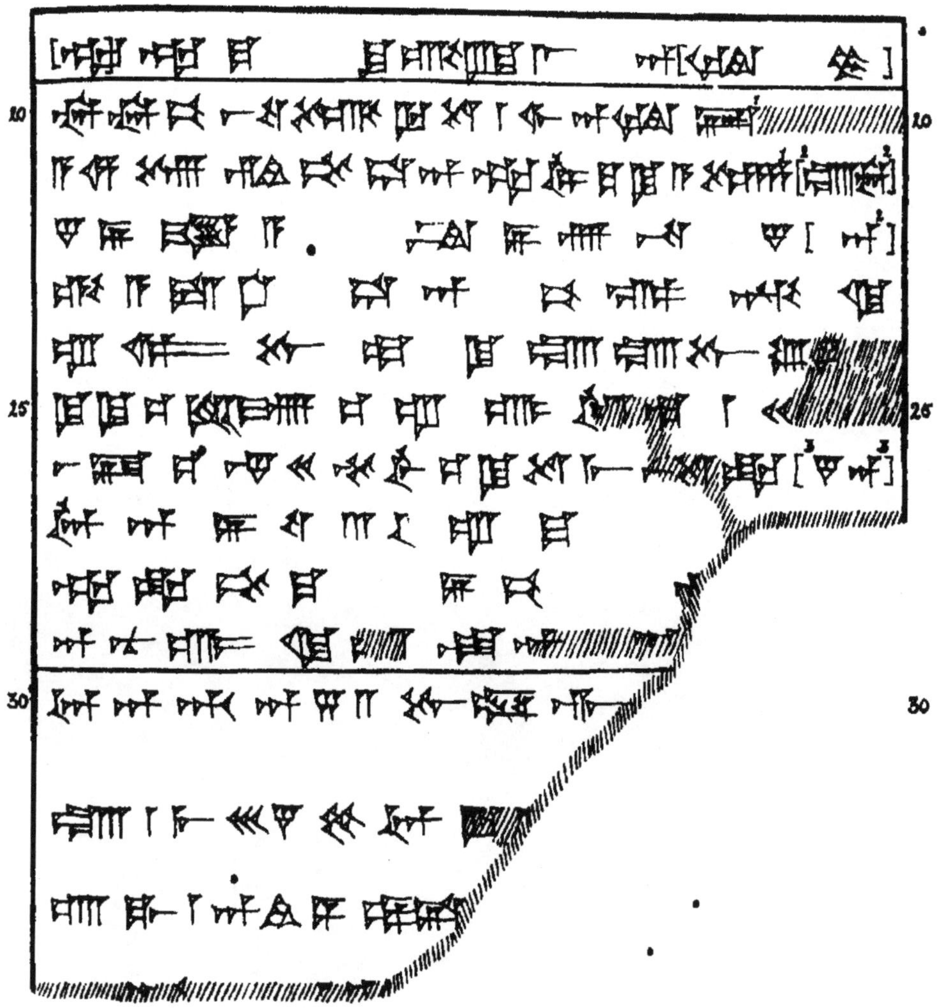

1. Partly obliterated. 2. v. No. 12, l. 8. 3. v. No. 12, l. 102.

NO. 31.

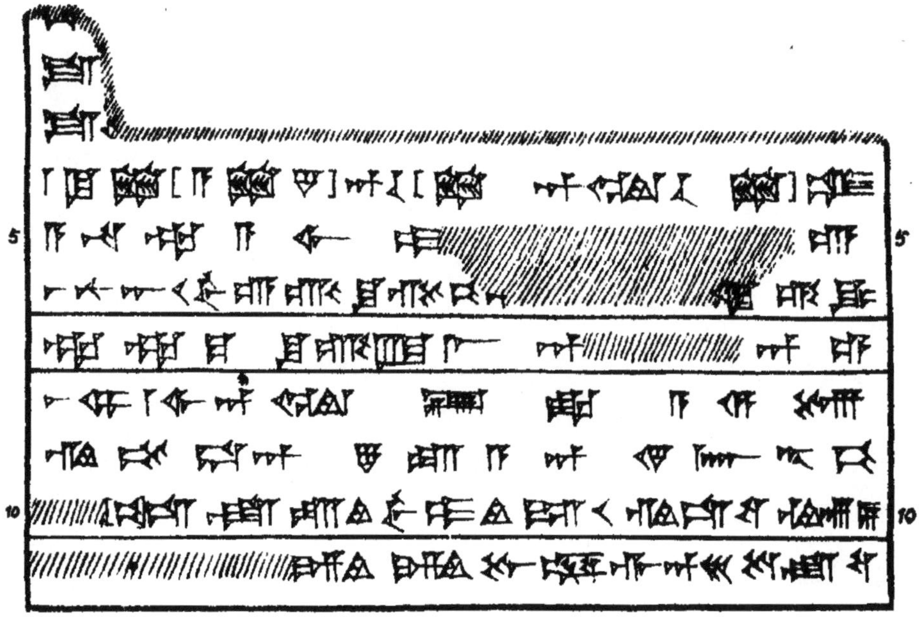

NO. 32.

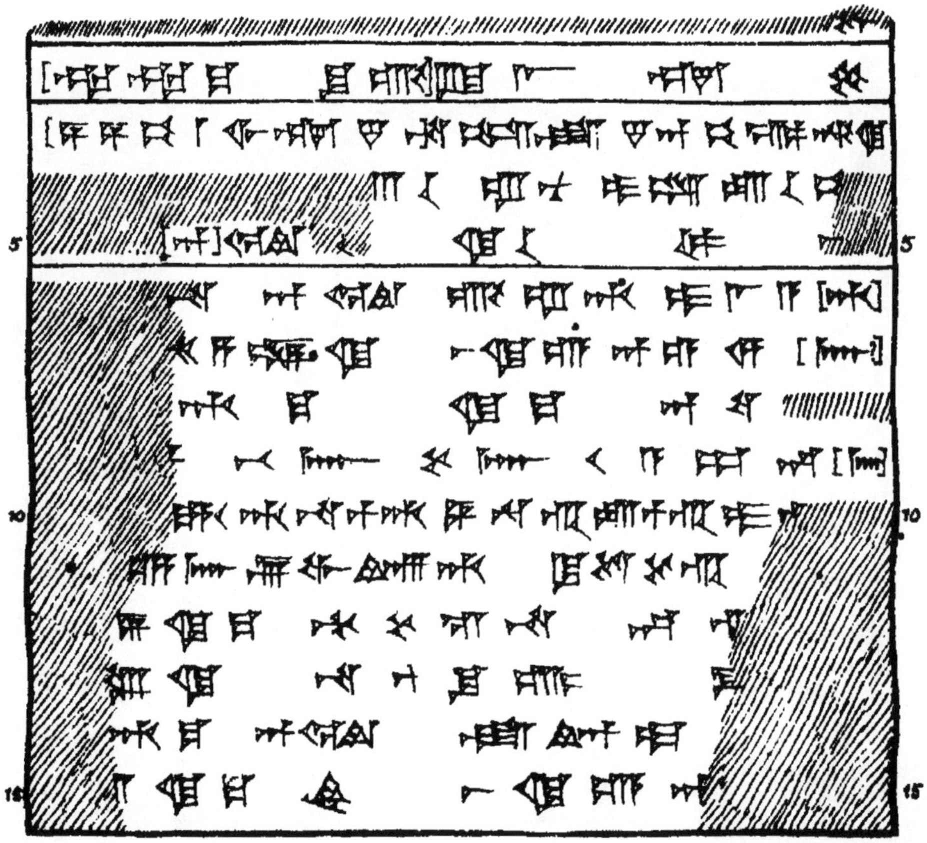

NO. 33. OBVERSE.

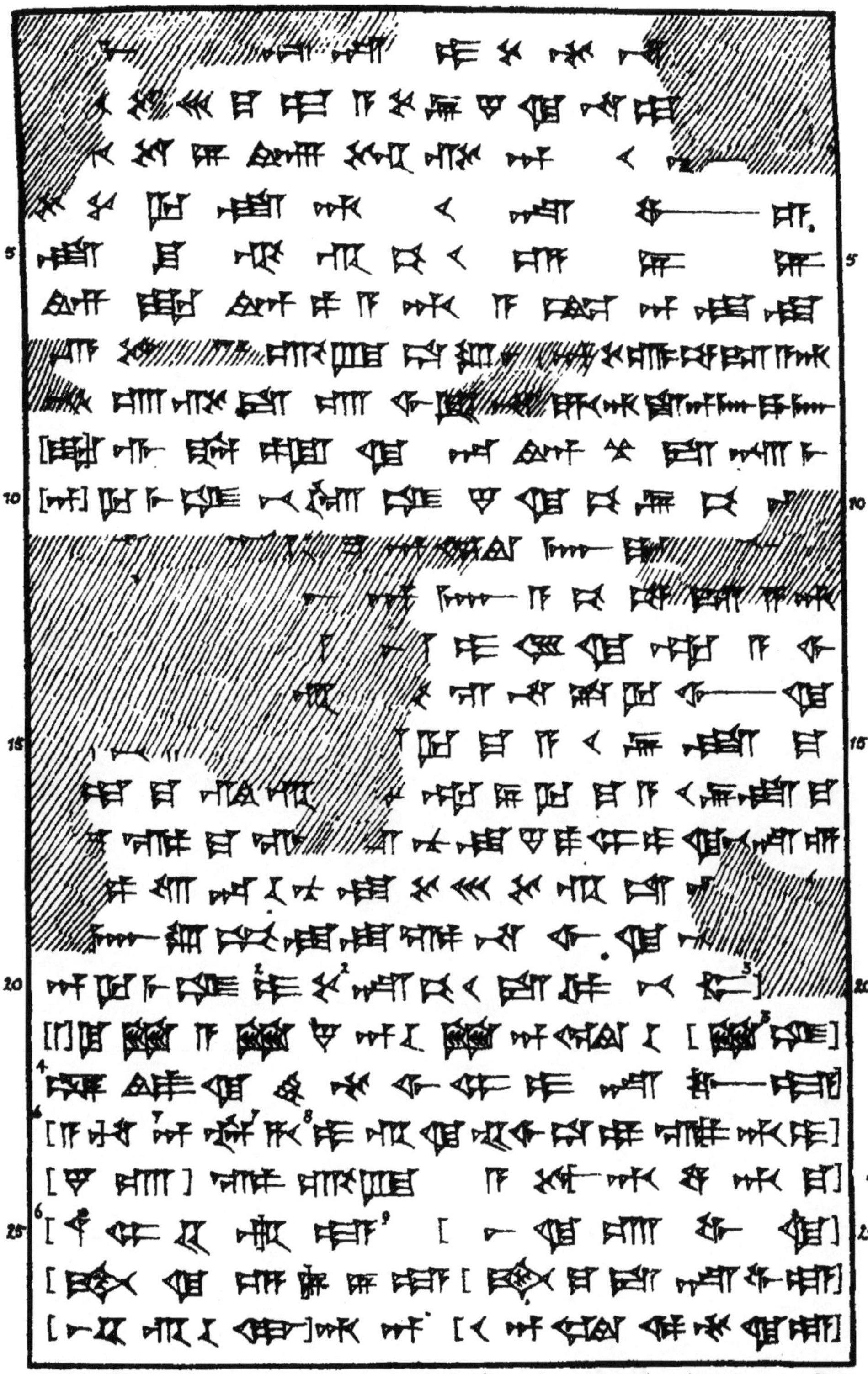

K 108, ll. 36–52, which I cite as A, is dupl. of ll. 19–38. 2. A . 3. r. A. 4. A here inserts the formula etc. in 2 ll., and for l. 22 reads:– . 5. r. A l. 43. 6. Each of the couplets 23 and 24, 25 and 26 forms one line, the latter with division-marks ( ), in A; ll. 23–27 r. A. 7. A . 8. A here inserts . 9. Omitted by A.

NO. 33. REVERSE.

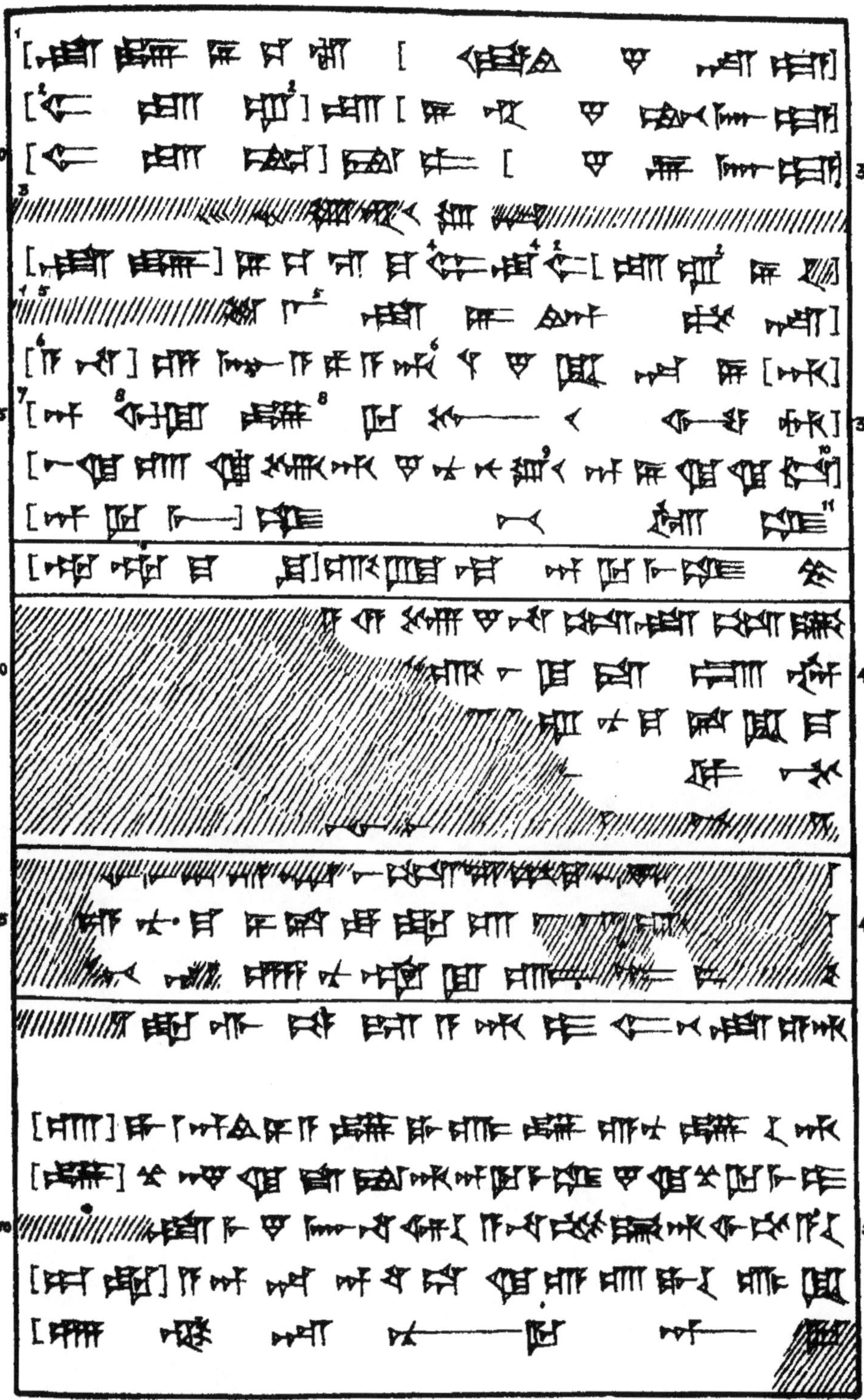

1. Each of the couplets 28 and 29, 33 and 34 forms one line with division-marks in A; ll. 28–38 r. A. 2. A . 3. For l. 31 A reads :– . 4. A . 5. A . 6. . 7. ll. 35–37 form 2 ll. in A. 8. A . 9. A . 10. A inserts . 11. A .

NO. 34.

NO. 35, OBVERSE.

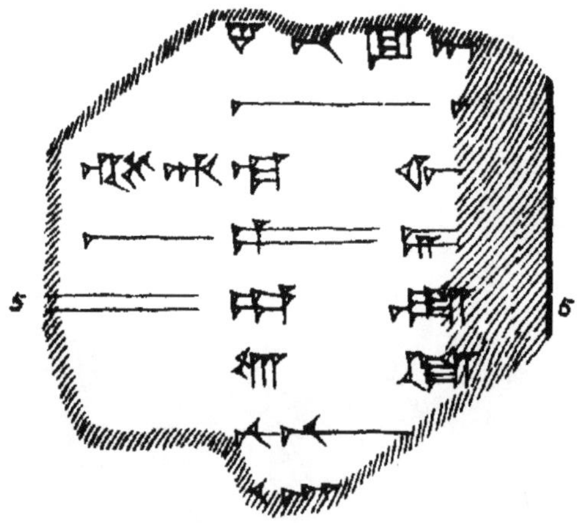

NO. 35 REVERSE.

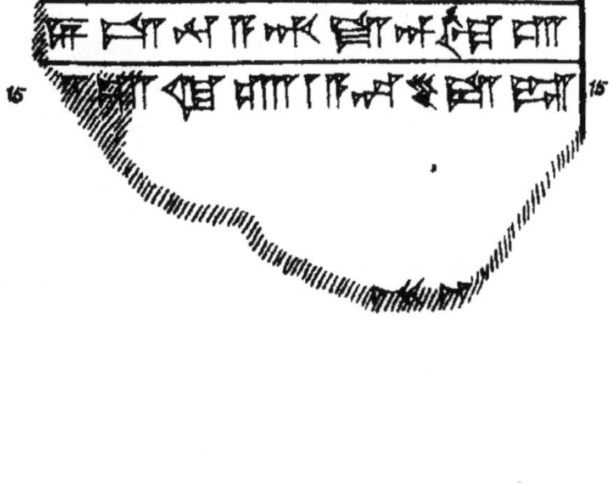

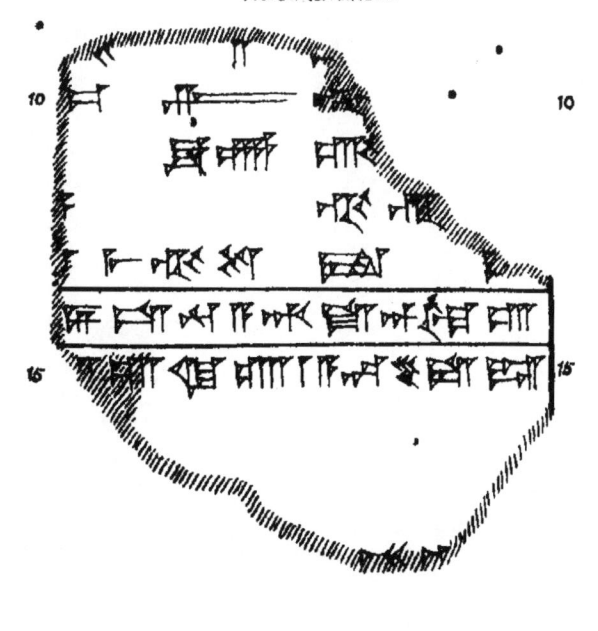

NO. 36.

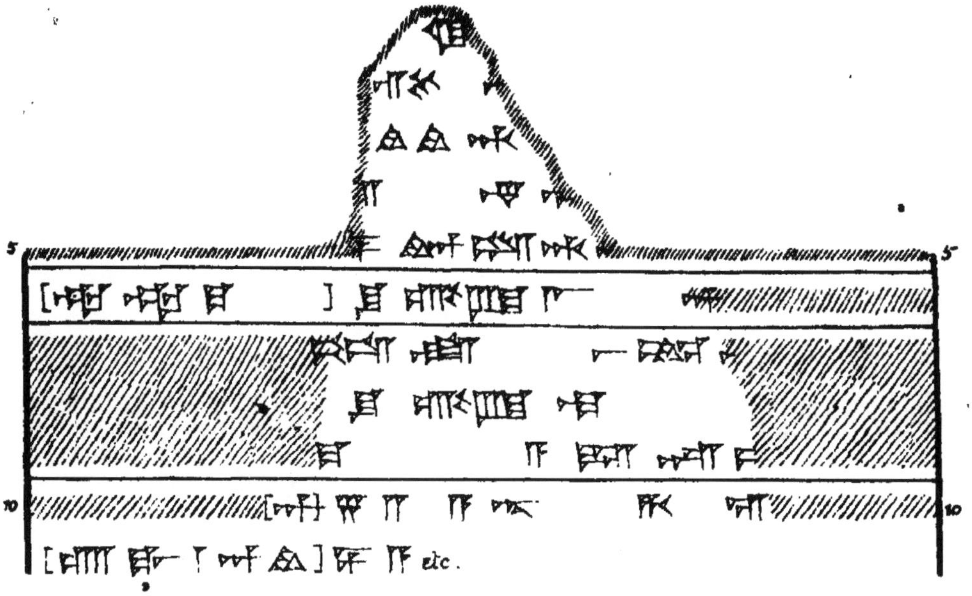

NO. 37.

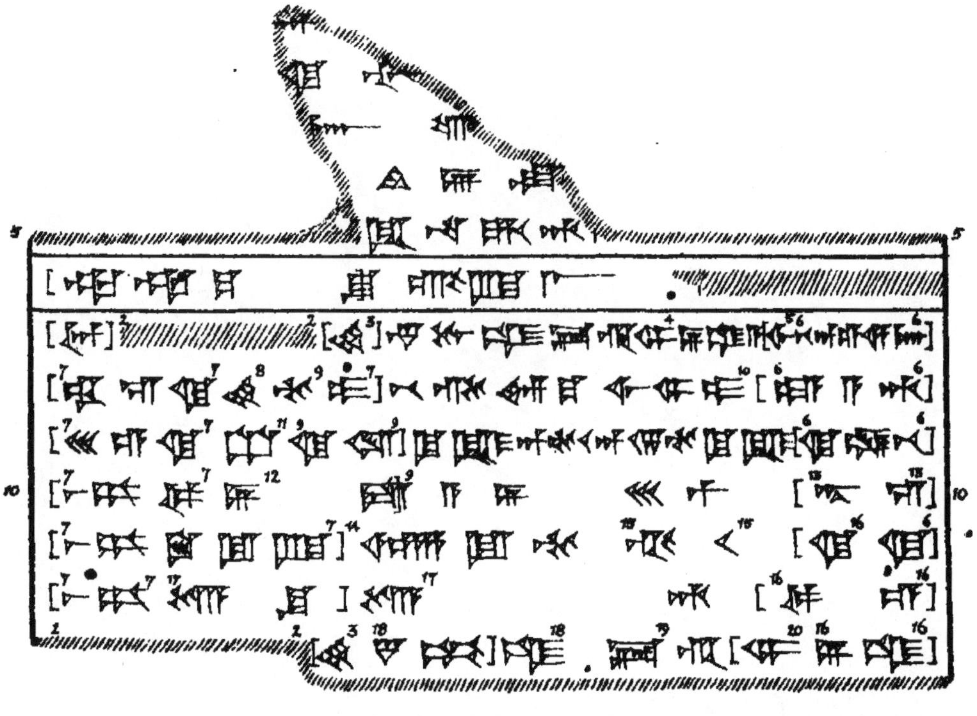

1. K 2106 etc., ll. 71–77, which I cite as A, K 3330 etc., ll. 9–15, cited as B, K 8815, ll. 3–9, cited as D, and Rm. 96, ll. 1–7, cited as E are partly duplicate of ll. 7–13. 2. Possibly to be restored [cuneiform] according to B; A [cuneiform]. 3. r. BE; A [cuneiform]. 4. A [cuneiform]. 5. r. A. 6. r. AD. 7. r. AB. 8. r. B; A [cuneiform]. 9. r. ABE. 10. A [cuneiform]. 11. r. B; A [cuneiform]. 12. r. B; A [cuneiform]. 13. r. AE; D [cuneiform]. 14. A here inserts [cuneiform]. 15. AD [cuneiform]. 16. r. ADE. 17. r. B; A (r. D) [cuneiform]. 18. r. BDE; A [cuneiform]. 19. D [cuneiform]. 20. r. AE; D [cuneiform].

NO. 38.

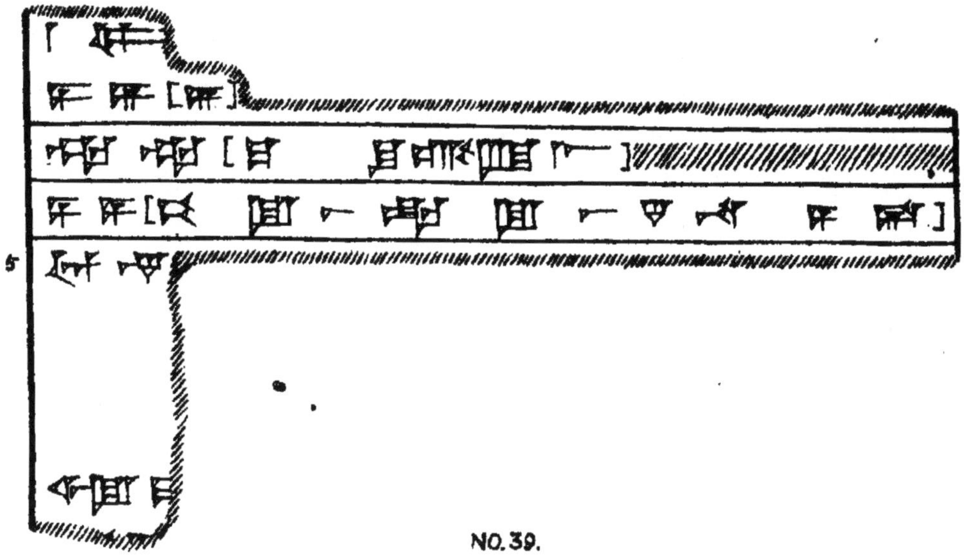

NO. 39.

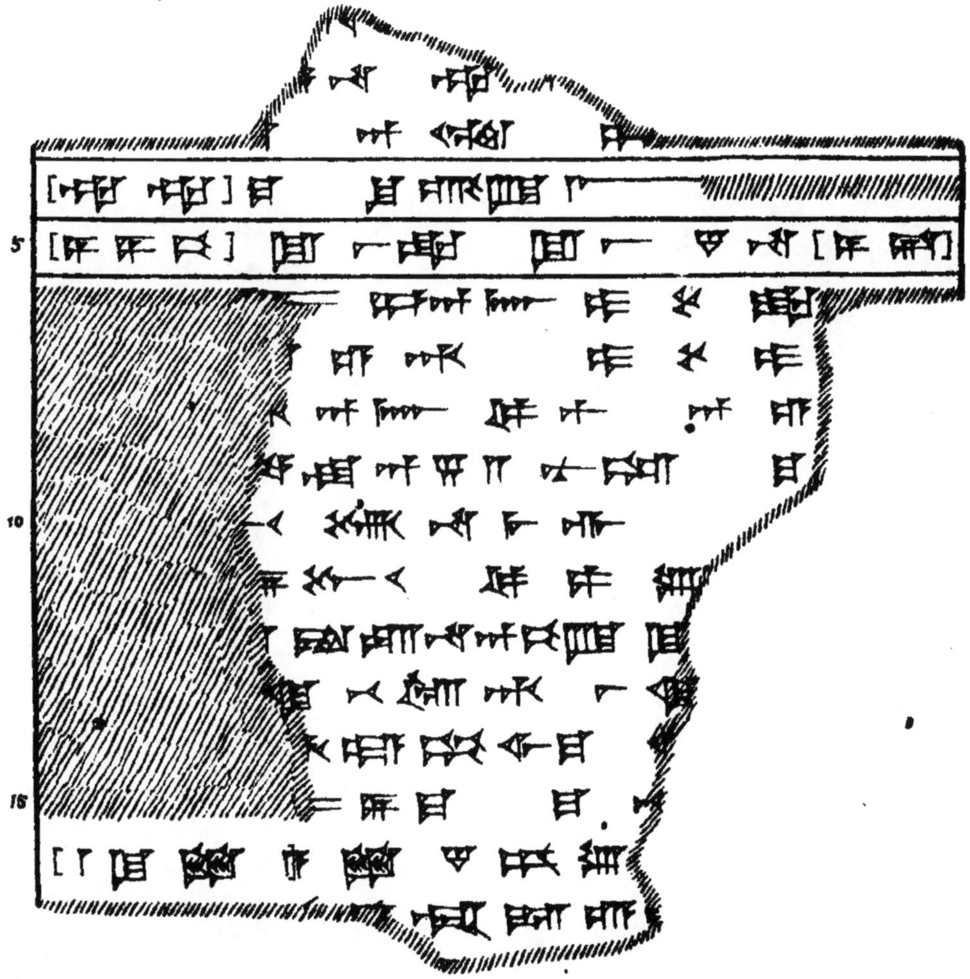

NO. 40.

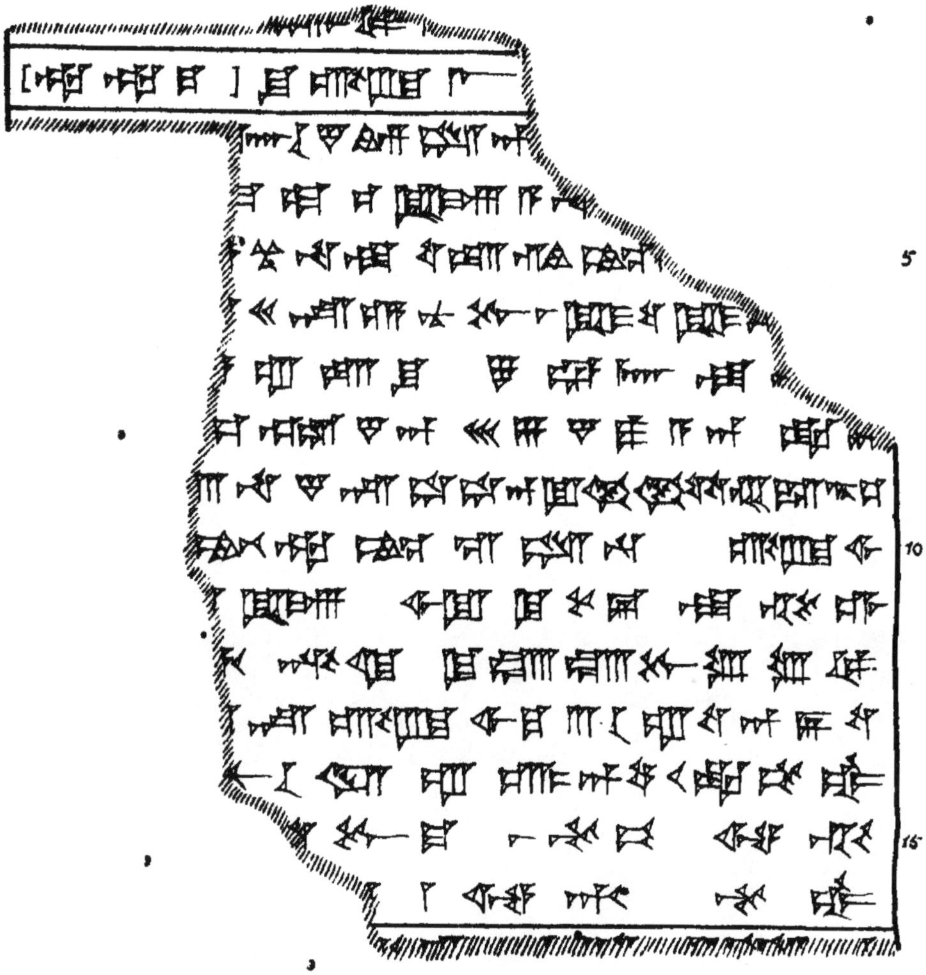

NO. 41.

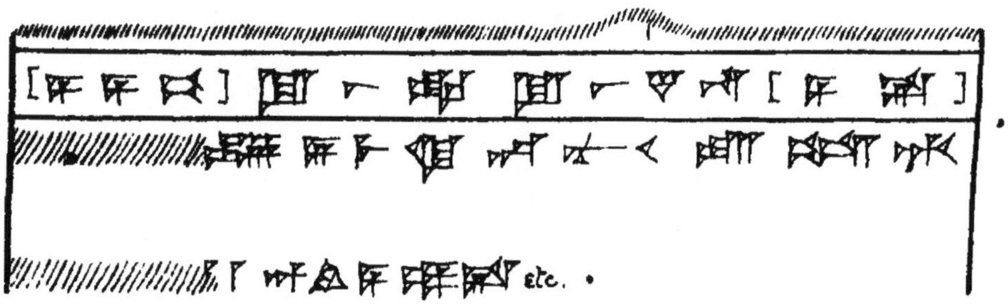

NO. 42. OBVERSE.

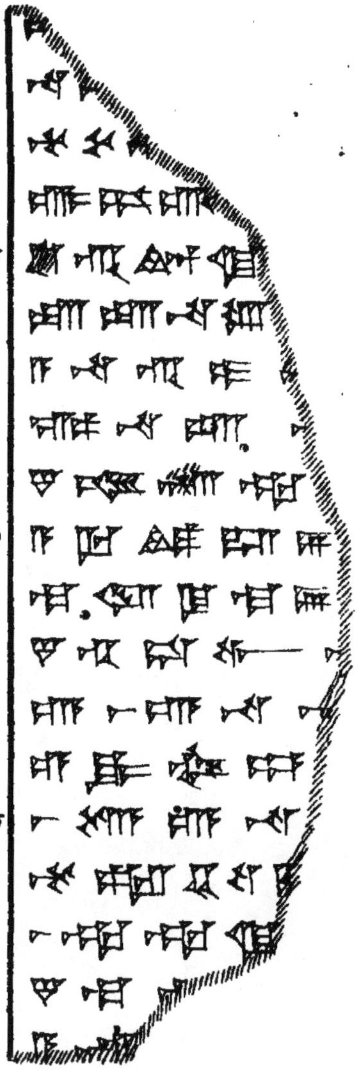

NO. 42. REVERSE.

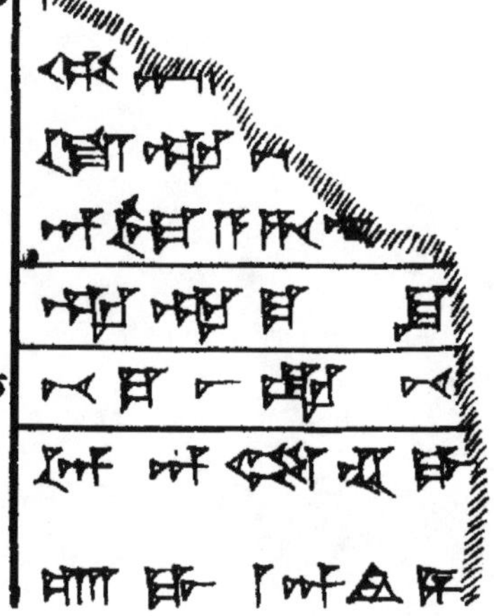

NO. 43.

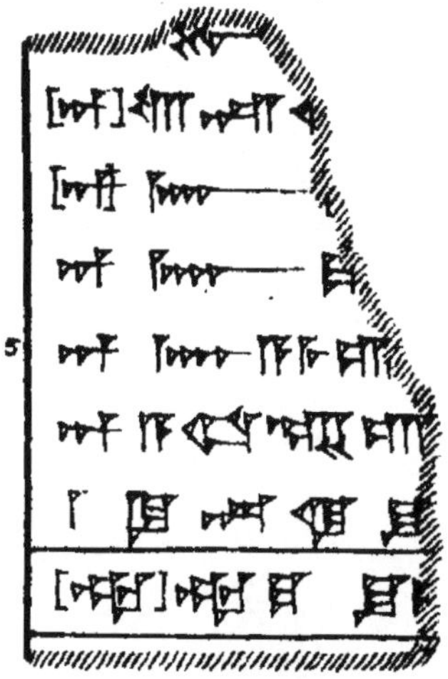

NO. 44.

NO. 45. OBVERSE.

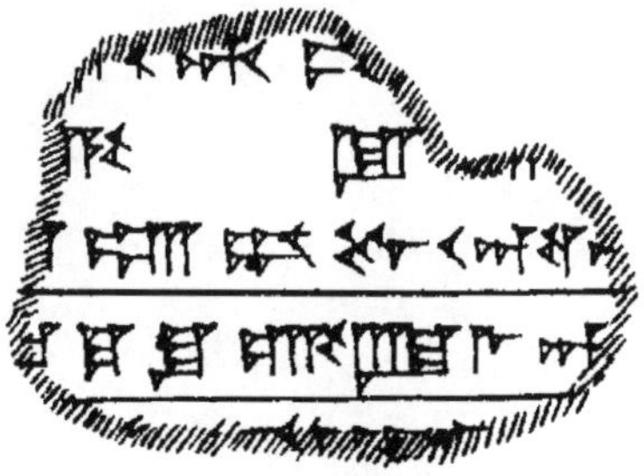

NO. 45. REVERSE.

NO. 46.

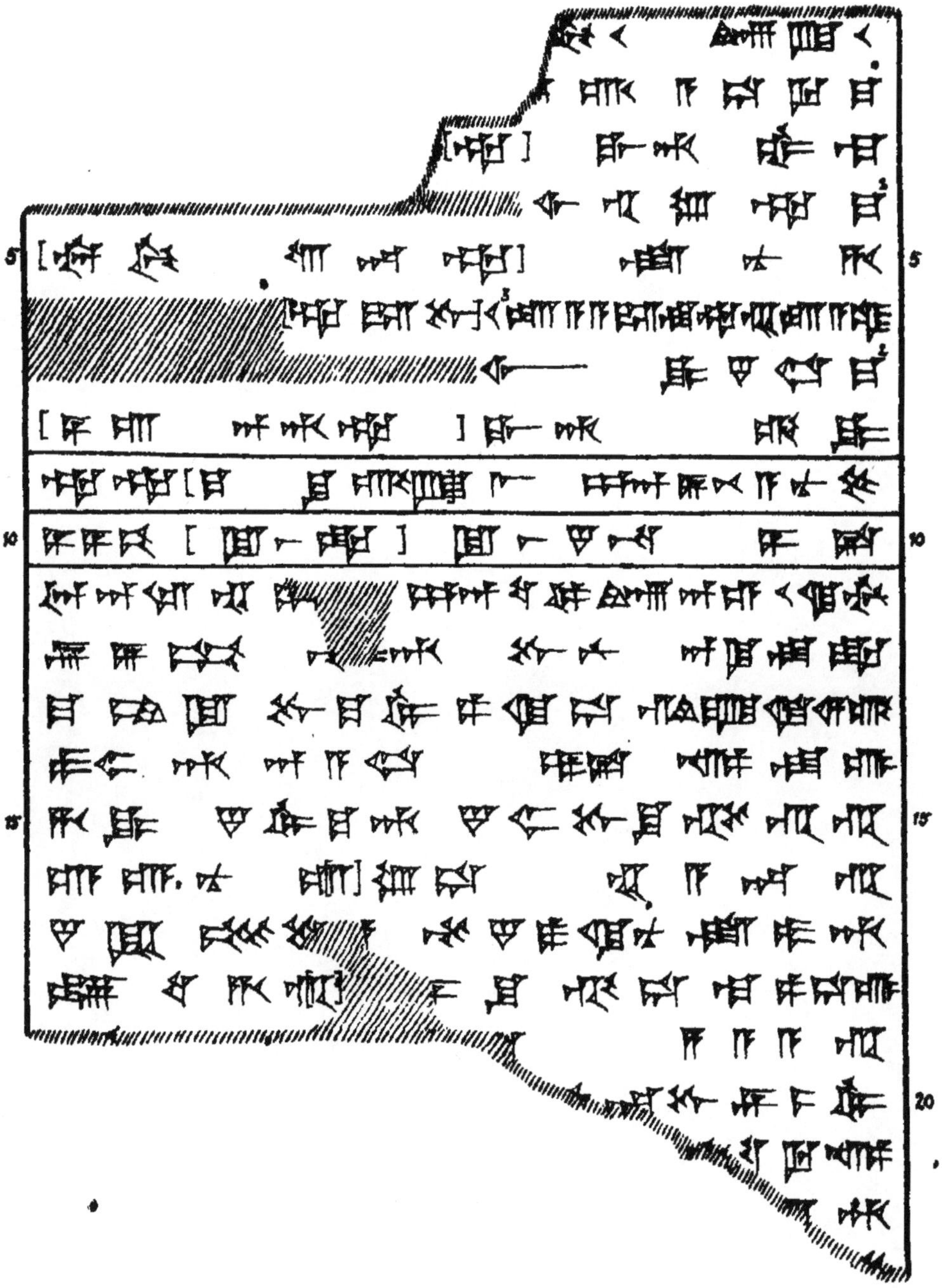

K6689, which I cite as A, is dupl. of ll. 3–12; ll. 3–8 have been restored from A. 2. Each of the couplets 4 and 5, 7 and 8 forms one line in A. 3. A

NO. 47.

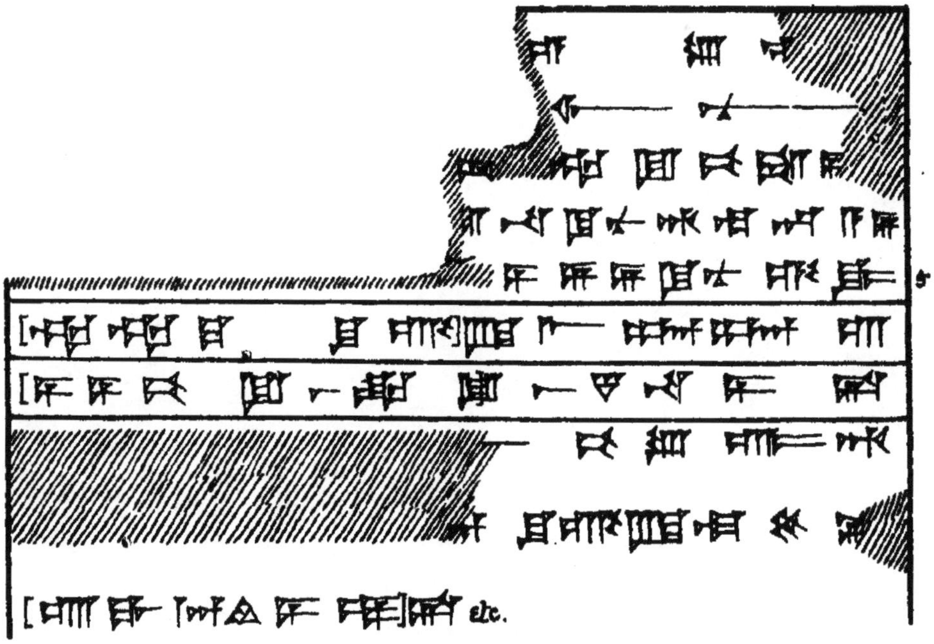

NO. 48. OBVERSE.

NO. 48. REVERSE.

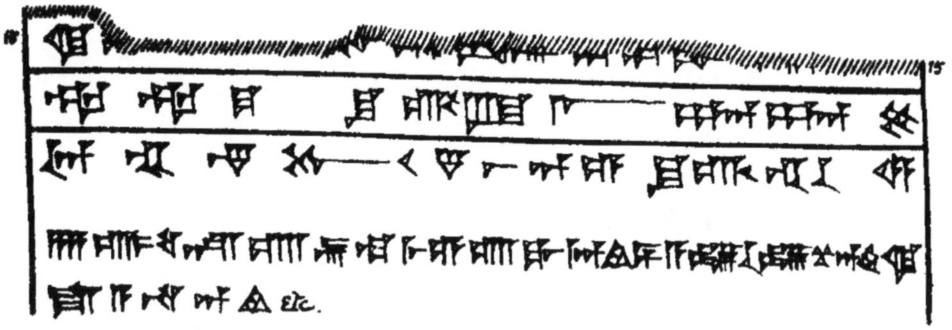

NO. 49. OBVERSE.

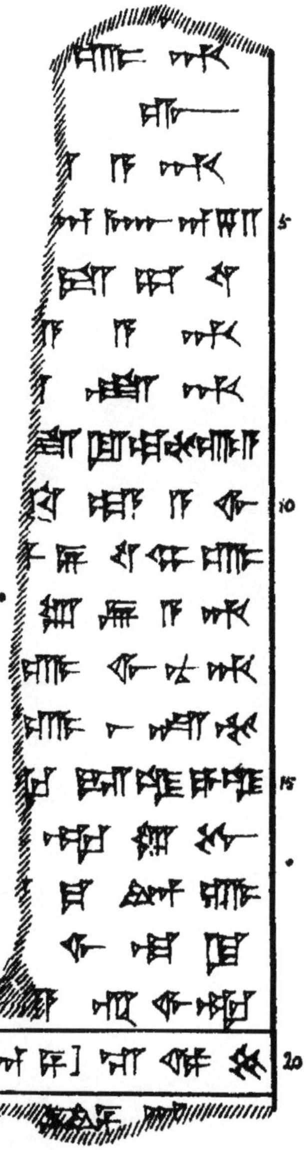

NO. 49. REVERSE.

NO. 50. OBVERSE.

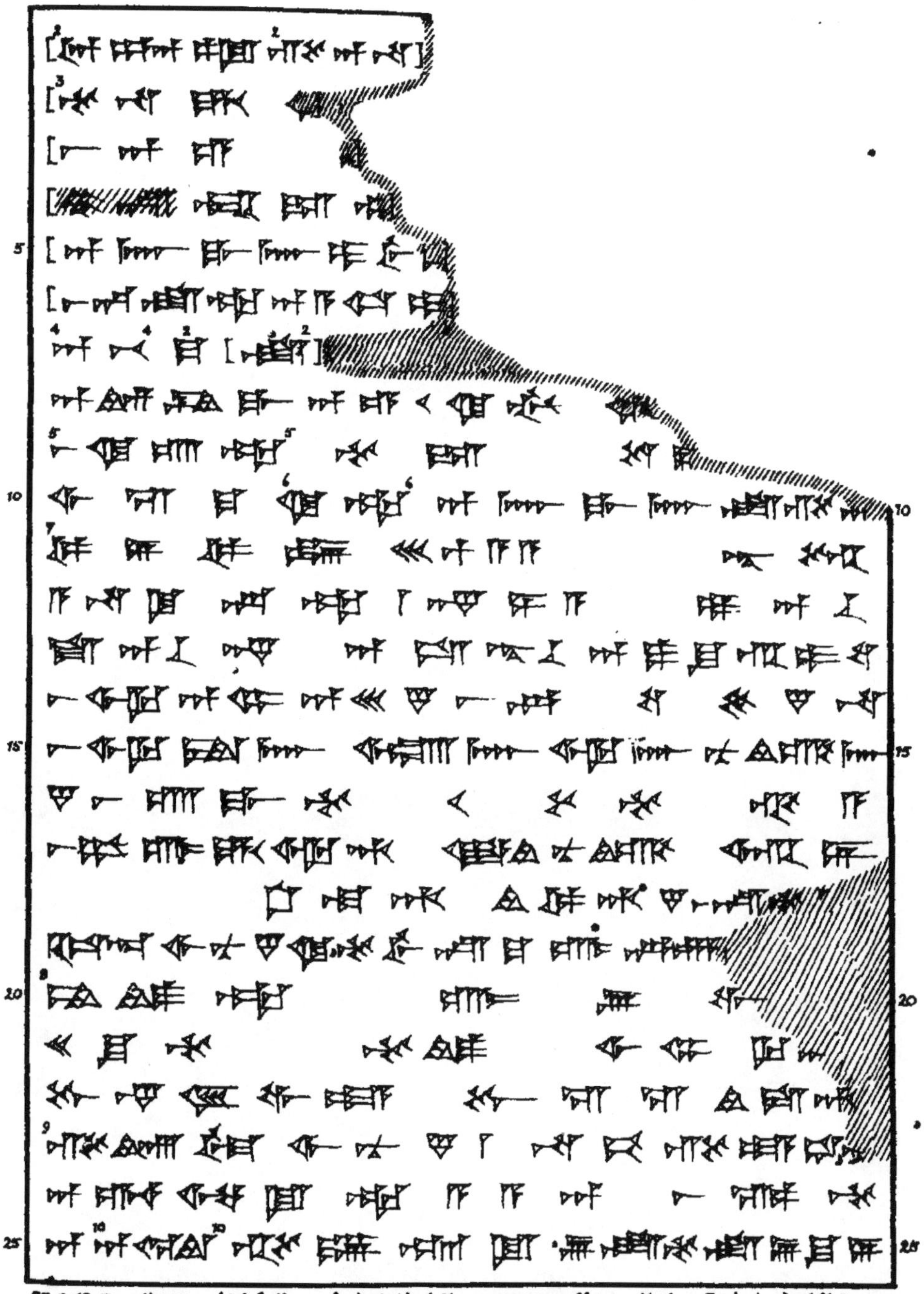

83-1-18, 500, ll. 1-10, which I cite as A, is dupl. of ll. 1-10; K 12937, ll. 1-7, cited as B, is dupl. of ll. 20-27. 2. r. A. 3. ll. 3-6 have been restored from A. 4. A [cuneiform]. 5. A [cuneiform]. 6. A [cuneiform]. 7. For l. 11 A reads: [cuneiform]. 8. ll. 20 and 21 form one line in B. 9. For l. 23 B reads: [cuneiform]. 10. B [cuneiform].

NO. 50. REVERSE.

1. After l. 27 B ceases to be a duplicate and reads: 2. Written over an erased .

NO. 51.

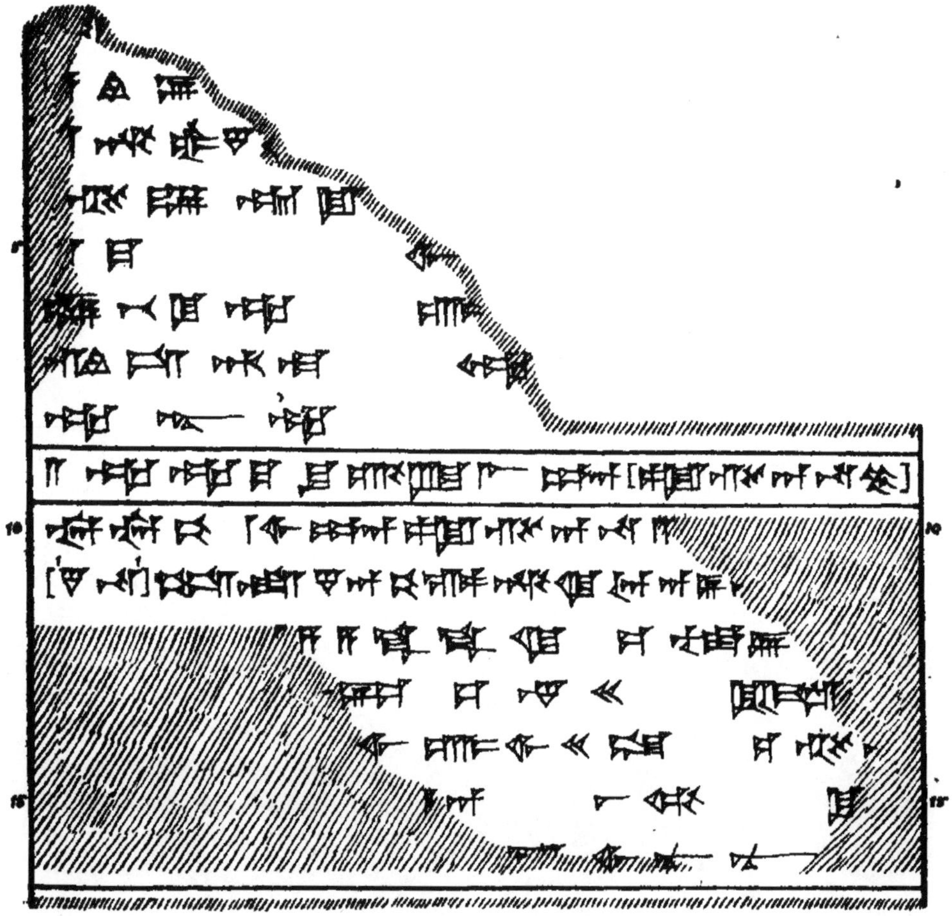

NO. 52.

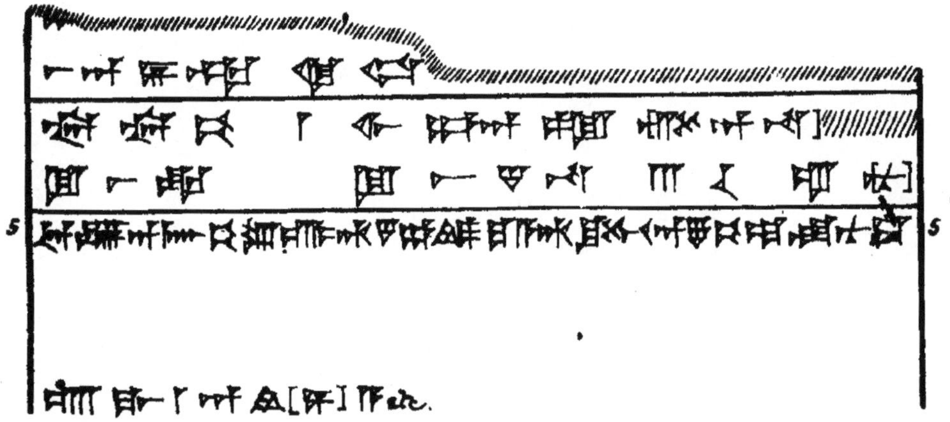

1. Traces of these characters remain.

NO. 53. OBVERSE.

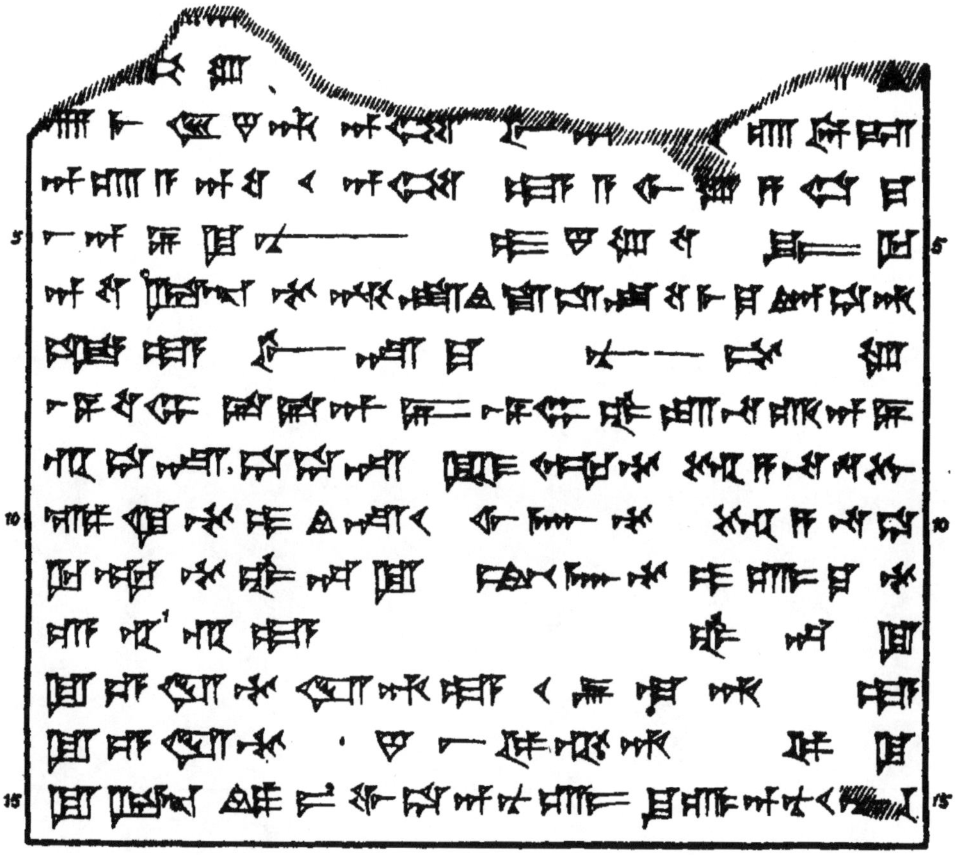

1. Written over an erased .

NO.53. REVERSE.

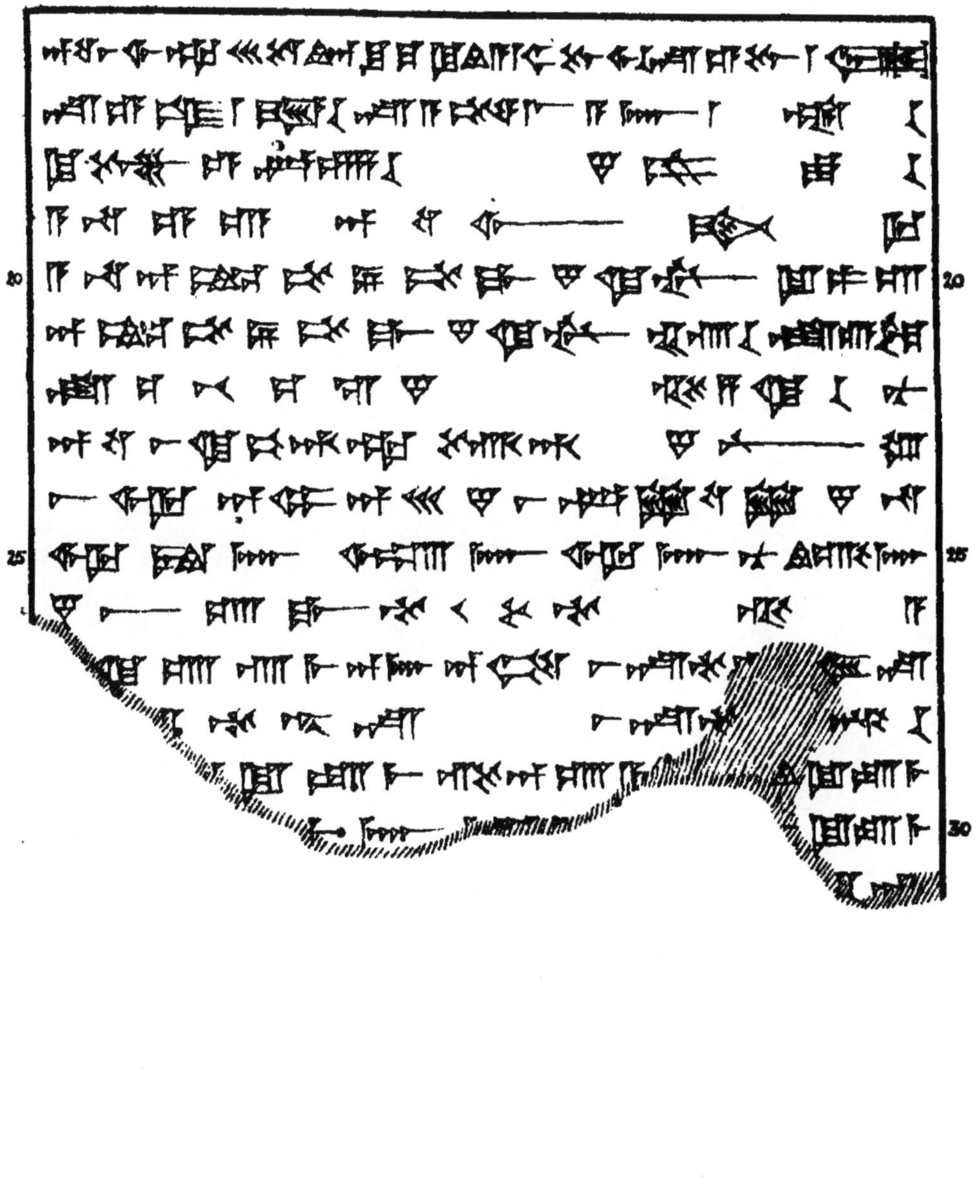

NO. 54.

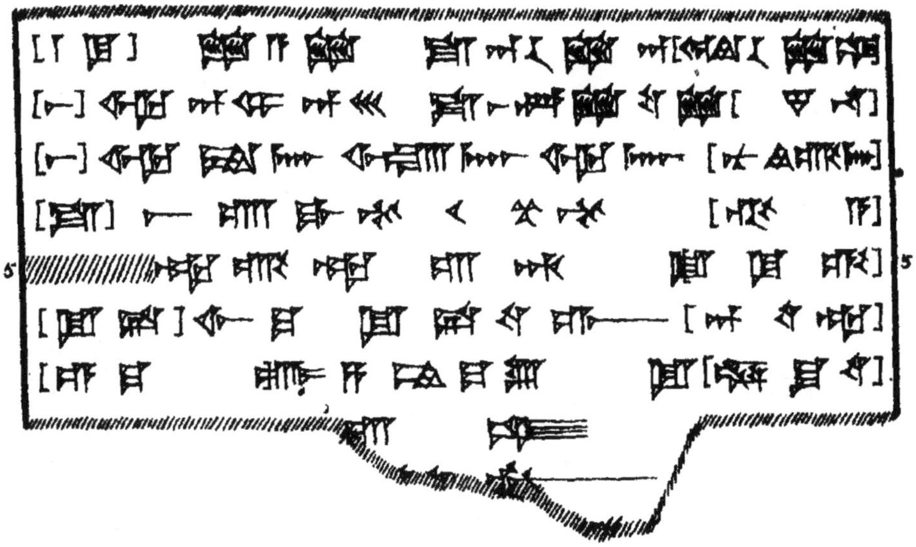

NO. 55

NO. 56.

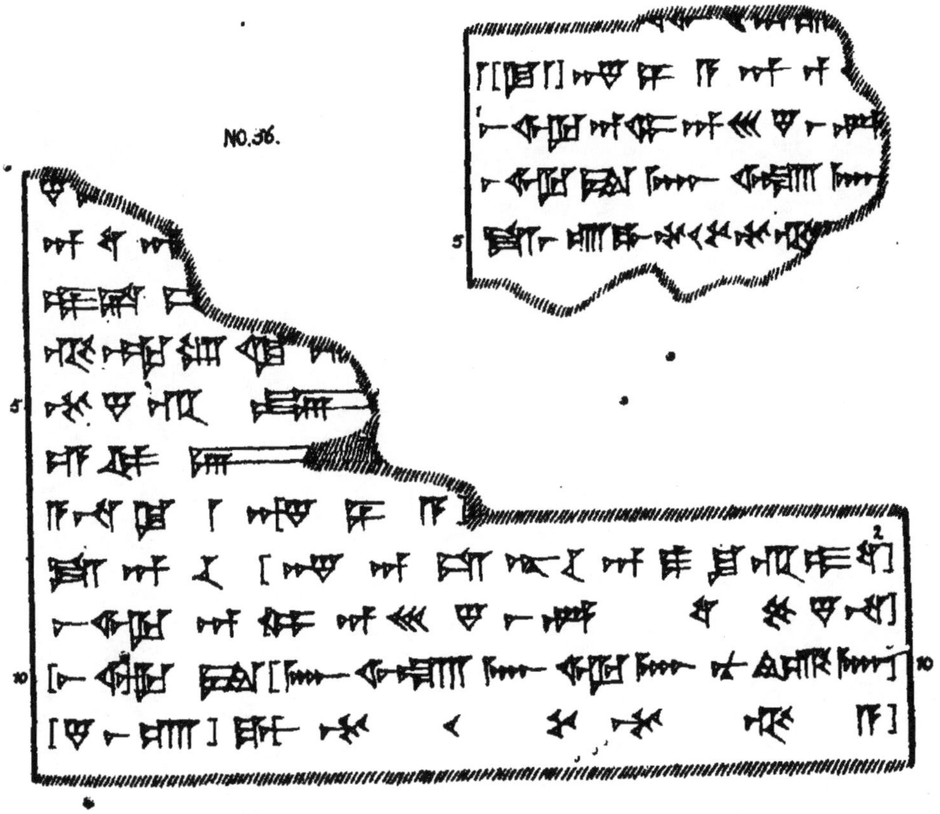

1. Ll. 3f. should prob. be restored according to No. 50, ll. 14f. 2. Ll. 8–11 have been restored from No. 50, ll. 13ff.

NO. 57. OBVERSE.

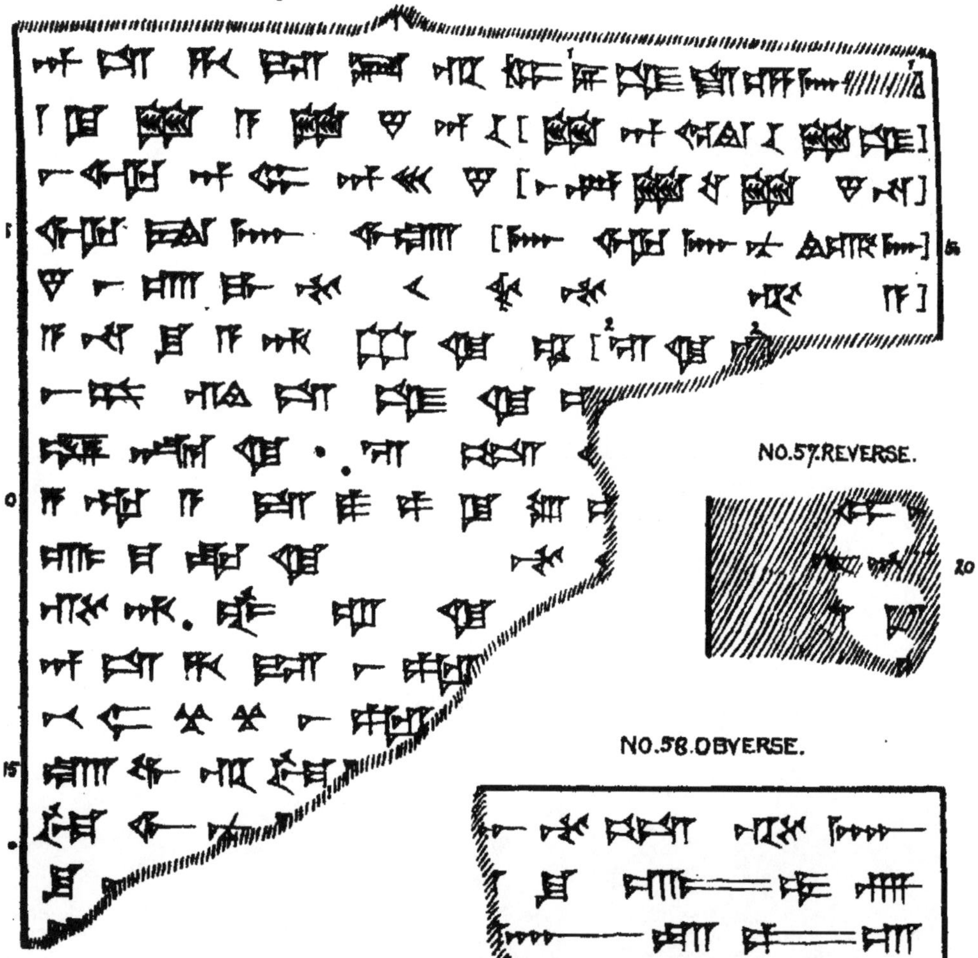

NO. 57. REVERSE.

NO. 58. OBVERSE.

NO. 58 REVERSE.

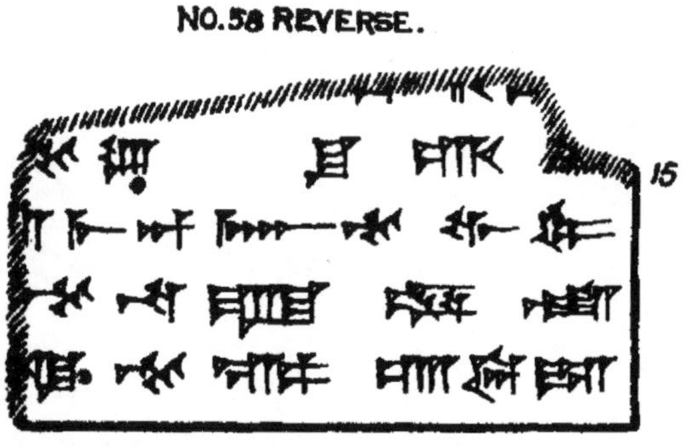

1. v. No. 7, l. 59. 2. v. No. 7, l. 62.

No. 59.

NO. 60. OBVERSE.

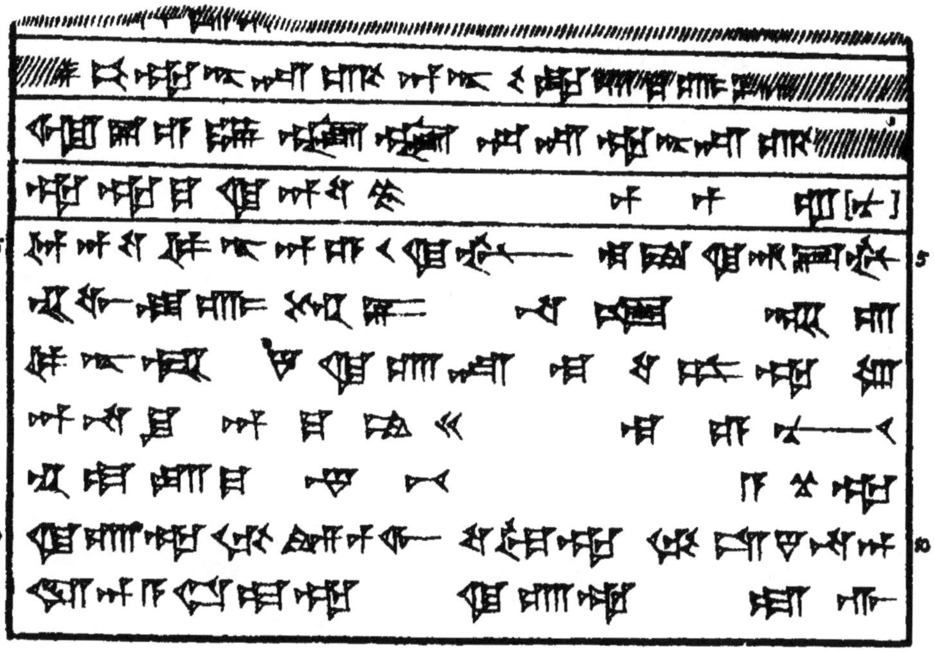

NO. 60. REVERSE.

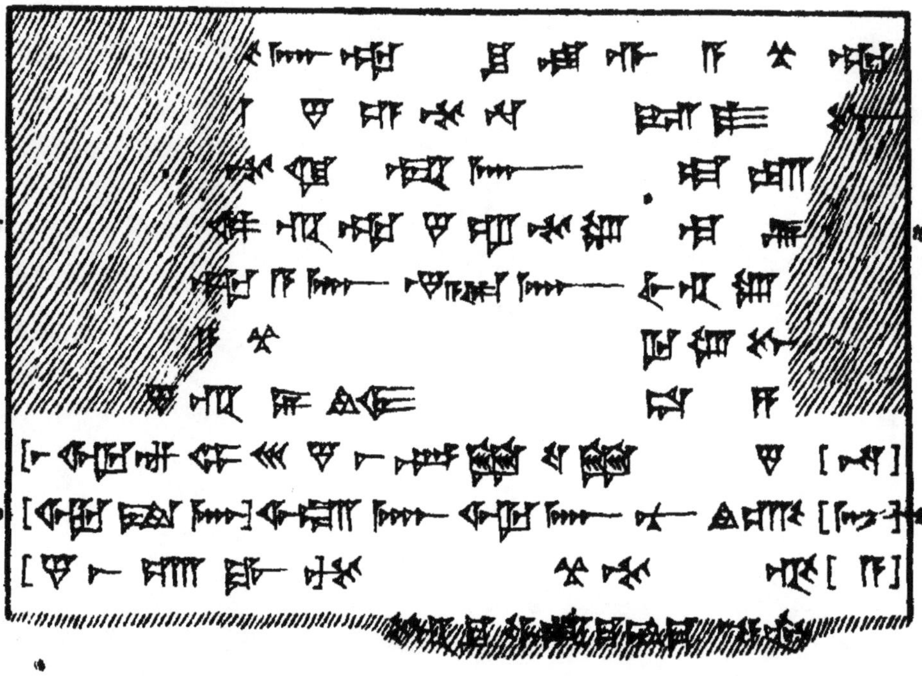

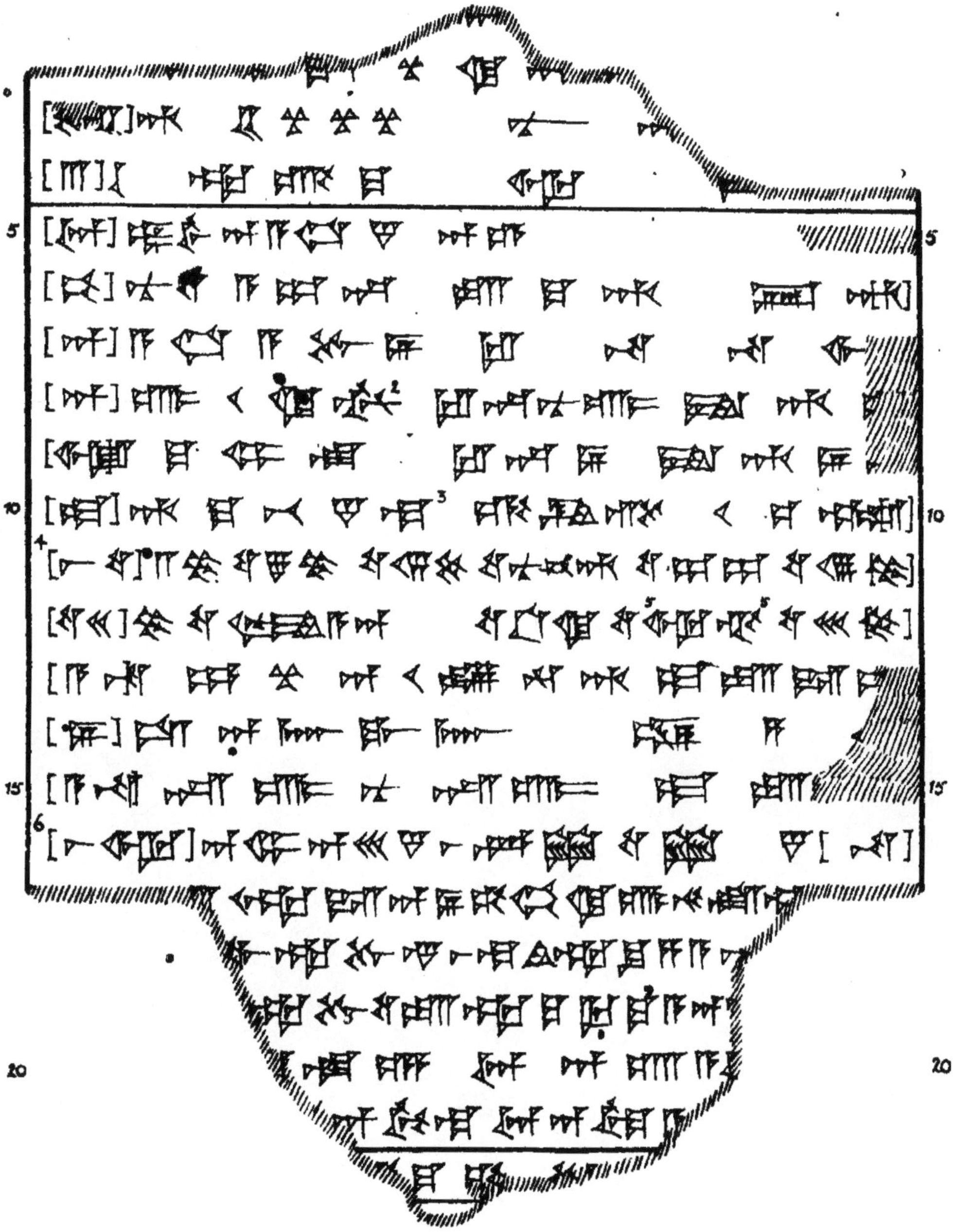

1. K 3342, which I cite as A, is duplicate of ll. 3–18; the beginnings of ll. 5–15 have been restored from A. 2. A . 3. After A reads in smaller characters . 4. ll. 11 and 12 form three lines in A. 5. A . 6. A apparently omits l. 16, and reads: [ ] [ ].

NO. 62. OBVERSE.

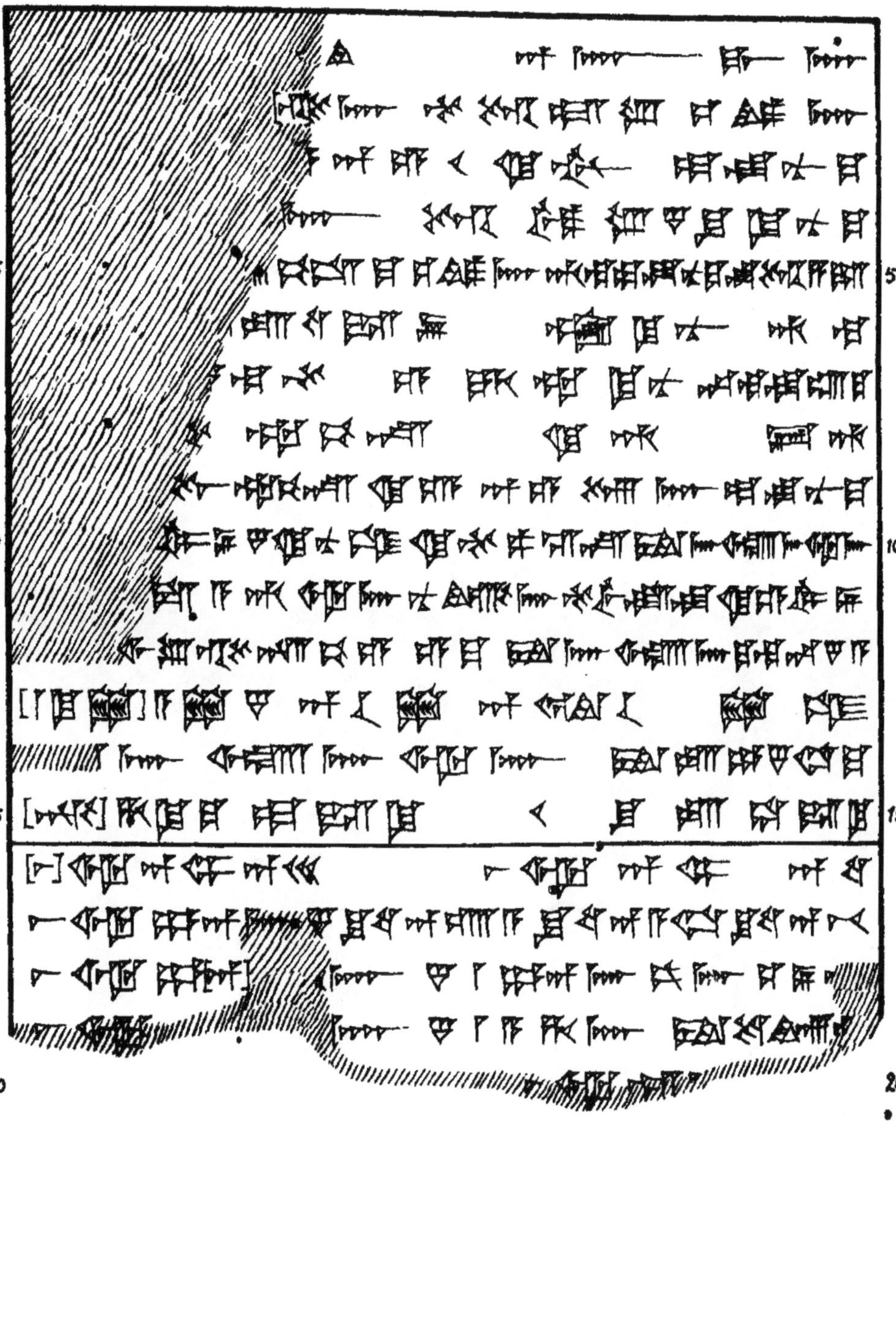

NO. 62. REVERSE.

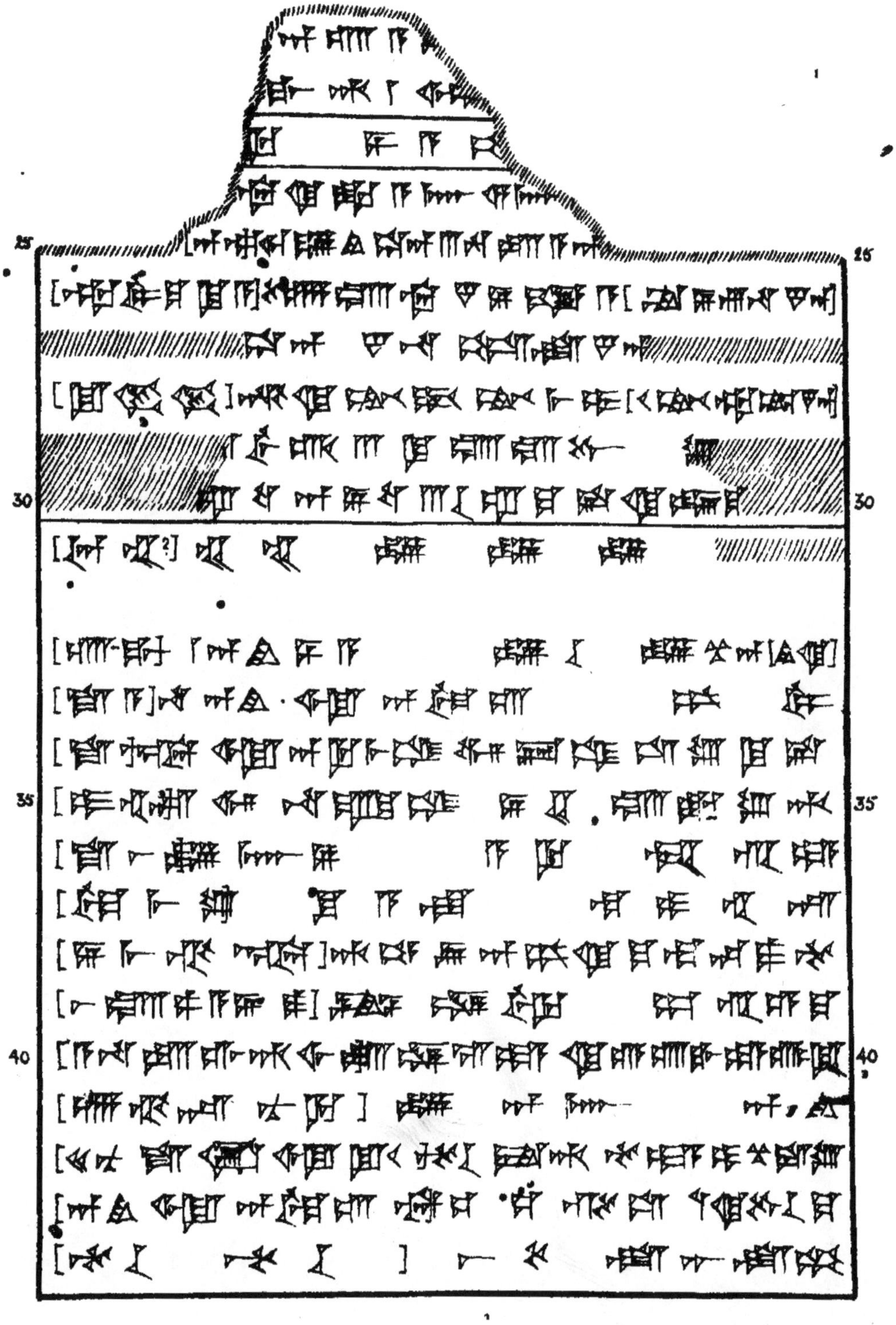

ADDITIONS AND CORRECTIONS.

Plate 2, No. 1, l. 43: after [cuneiform] C inserts [cuneiform].— Plate 3, No. 1, l. 47: C reads [cuneiform]; ibid. l. 81: for [cuneiform] C reads [cuneiform]. Plate 4, No. 2, l. 12: [cuneiform] for [cuneiform] is read by A only.— Plate 12, No. 6, l. 77: D reads [cuneiform] for [cuneiform].— Plate 15, No. 7, l. 16: for [cuneiform] A reads [cuneiform].— Plate 28, No. 12, l. 69: for [cuneiform] C reads [cuneiform].— The text of No. 21, ll. [1]—13 (see Plate 41), increased by the additional fragment K 6612, runs as follows:—

The text of No. 21, ll. 37 ff. (see Plate 42), increased by the additional fragment K 6588, runs as follows:—

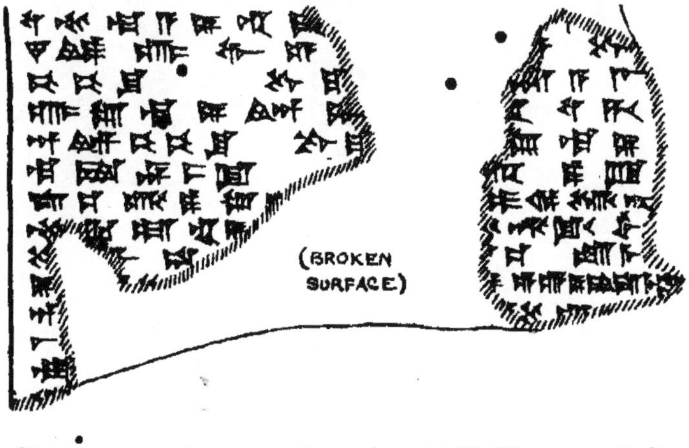

Plate 65, No. 50, Reverse, note 1: before [cuneiform] [[cuneiform]] the sign [cuneiform] should be inserted.

Made in the USA
Columbia, SC
08 June 2025

59094617R00215